Construction Claims
Analysis, Presentation, Defense

Construction Claims
Analysis, Presentation, Defense

Robert A. Rubin
Sammie D. Guy
Alfred C. Maevis
Virginia Fairweather

VAN NOSTRAND REINHOLD COMPANY
NEW YORK CINCINNATI TORONTO LONDON MELBOURNE

Library of Congress Catalog Card Number: 81-23987
ISBN: 0-442-26145-4

Manufactured in the United States of America

Published by Van Nostrand Reinhold Company Inc.
135 West 50th Street, New York, N.Y. 10020

Van Nostrand Reinhold Publishing
1410 Birchmount Road
Scarborough, Ontario M1P 2E7, Canada

Van Nostrand Reinhold
480 Latrobe Street
Melbourne, Victoria 3000, Australia

Van Nostrand Reinhold Company Limited
Molly Millars Lane
Wokingham, Berkshire, England

15 14 13 12 11 10 9 8 7 6 5 4 3 2 1

Library of Congress Cataloging in Publication Data

Rubin, Robert A.
    Construction claims.

    Includes index.
    1. Building—Contracts and specifications—United
States. 2. Construction industry—Law and legislation
—United States. I. Guy, Sammie D. II. Maevis,
Alfred C. III. Title.
KF902.G89   343.73′07869   81-23987
ISBN 0-442-26145-4   347.3037869   AACR2

Foreword

This book grew out of an American Society of Civil Engineers' continuing education course taught by Alfred Maevis, Sam Guy, and Robert A. Rubin. Since 1976, the course "Construction Claims—Analysis; Presentation; Defense" has been presented in cities all across the nation, including Honolulu and Anchorage. Those attending have been a mix of public- and private-sector owners, contractors, and consulting engineers, with a sprinkling of lawyers and claims consultants. During the course discussions, we presided over an exchange of perspectives from a wide range of viewpoints.

We have all participated in the effort to improve contracting practices. Maevis was a member of the National Academy of Sciences', Subcommittee No. 4, U.S. National Committee on Tunneling Technology, which produced the 1974 landmark study entitled "Better Contracting for Underground Construction." Rubin contributed to the 1978 Building Advisory Board, National Research Council, "Study on Responsibility, Liability and Accountability for Risks in Construction," and since 1980 he has been on the Building Research Advisory Board Committee on the Management of Urban Construction Programs. Maevis, Guy and Rubin took active parts in the American Society of Civil Engineers' Construction Risks and Liability Sharing Conference in Scottsdale, Arizona, in January 1980. Rubin, since 1968, and Guy, since 1973, have been members of the ASCE Committee on Contract Administration.

Maevis and Guy, by virtue of their positions in the U.S. Postal Service and the Bureau of Reclamation, have had an opportunity to implement improvements in contracting practices and to observe the consequences. Maevis and Guy have also reviewed and passed judgment on major construction claims filed against their respective agencies. Rubin, who has litigated numerous complex construction disputes, was a law partner of the late Max E. Greenberg, widely recognized as the dean of American construction law.

Hence, this book is the product of our diverse experiences in construction, contract administration, construction claims, and construction disputes resolution—coupled with our involvement with, and commitment to, the improvement of contracting practices.

With that perspective, we approached the task of setting our thoughts to paper. We believe that in most instances a construction claim represents a failure or breakdown in the system. Our primary concern is the avoidance of disputes, from the moment that the contract preparation begins through performance by the contractor and administration by the owner.

But we live in the real world where reasonable people may differ and where some people act unreasonably. We recognize that claims are inevitable. Accepting that premise, we seek objective criteria on how to analyze, present, and defend claims.

Claims are not a game. The object is not for one party to put something over on the other or to get the better of the other party. The contractor should receive what he is entitled to receive. The owner should pay all sums he is legally obligated to pay. We believe that there are objective, engineering and legal criteria and techniques to be applied in dealing with claims. We have presented those principles in this book.

We omit citations to legal precedents for several reasons. Principally, federal law and the law of each state differ. The law in one jurisdiction may not be the law in other jurisdictions. Also, construction law is constantly changing. What may be valid precedent today may no longer be valid on the date of publication. Instead, we refer to the legal rules most commonly followed throughout the United States, pointing out areas that may be changing. We indicate what we believe to be sound rules of law, and which rules we think ought to be changed. For applicable legal precedents, we recommend works published by Federal Publications, Inc., the Practising Law Institute, and the American Bar Association.

The text in all respects represents our consensus. Interestingly, there were relatively few differences among us on what the applicable principles and rules ought to be, despite our disparate experiences and backgrounds.

The book was a collaborative effort. We are very much indebted to Virginia Fairweather, editor of two international construction-related magazines and writer/editor for the American Society of Civil Engineers for ten years. Fairweather helped prepare a first draft of each chapter. She then correlated our comments, additions, and changes. Second, and in many instances, third, drafts of each chapter were prepared until each of us was satisified. She retained her perspective, mediating the differences among our styles and viewpoints, for which we are deeply appreciative.

We have aimed this book at the management level personnel of owners, contractors, and consulting engineers who are learning to deal with construction claims. Students should also find the work helpful. Finally, we think that seasoned construction industry people will find this book a useful resource. We hope all may benefit from our perspectives.

ROBERT A. RUBIN

Contents

Construction Claims
Analysis, Presentation, Defense

Part I: Claims — Understanding and Avoiding Them

1. The Groundwork: the Contract

The scenario for construction claims is invariably written right into the contract documents. Long before men and machines reach the job site, conditions for claims and disputes have often been signed by both parties. This happens, for example, when plans and specifications are incomplete or defective. More commonly, it happens when construction contracts are ambiguous, overly restrictive, or unfairly allocate particularly burdensome risks to one party alone.

RISK MANAGEMENT

The construction industry is notoriously risky. Much of the preparatory paperwork that precedes construction projects can be viewed as the formulation of risk allocation between the owner, the contractor, and the designer.

The Owner.   The owner is taking the risk that his project will not get built on schedule, that it will not get built for what he has budgeted, and that it will not be of the quality he expected. The owner naturally seeks to insure that these three factors will be satisfied, and he often thinks he can accomplish this through the contract language. In some cases, the owner has other risks beyond these for example, building a nuclear power plant or some other project subject to public protest or environmental and regulatory delays. Typically, however, an owner will seek to control whatever risks he can through his contract documents.

The Contractor.   The contractor faces a multitude of risks. Among them are inflation, bad weather, strikes and other labor problems, shortages of materials, accidents, and unforeseen conditions at the construction site. Ultimately, the contractor faces the possibility of losing a great deal of money or of being forced out of the business. Naturally, he too would like the contract wording to be protective of his interests.

The owner usually has the upper hand here. He is the party who generates the contract documents. Contractors, and to a lesser extent designers, merely react to these. One way to react, of course, is not to bid on the job. But that is not the route most contractors take. By and large, contractors tend to be inveterate optimists, believing that either the risk contractually foisted upon them will not materialize or, if it does, that the contract clause by which the risk is being imposed will not be enforced.

In this chapter we hope to convince all parties that allocating or sharing risk fairly can ultimately save time and money for all parties, and get the job done on schedule for the least overall cost. The more enlightened in the industry are convinced that equitable sharing of risks can get the work done for less money and diminish the likelihood of claims and litigation.

3

However, the enlightened seem to be in the minority. Many owners still view the harsh contract as consummate protection. In reality, such contracts often turn out to be bad business, for the following reasons:

1. Harsh contracts discourage responsible bidders. The only way a responsible contractor can protect himself from a high-risk situation is to include a high contingency in his bid. If the risk and the contingency are sufficiently high, his bid will not be competitive, and probably not within the owner's budget.

2. Ambiguous language or exculpatory clauses through which the owner hopes to escape responsibility almost inevitably result in conflict. When the conflict escalates to the courtroom, judges almost always rule against the party who drew up the ambiguous contract—the owner.

3. Such contracts attract those bidders willing to take any kind of chance, or those who expect from the outset to make up their dollars via claims. This is particularly true in the public sector, where, in most cases, by law, the lowest responsive, responsible bidder must be awarded the work.

PUBLIC SECTOR PROBLEMS

As we have just observed, in the public sector the lowest bidder usually gets the job. Public officials are under special pressure; they must answer to the taxpayers. Even if the lowest bidder happens to be a firm that has a reputation for being contentious, it would still be difficult to prove to the public that there is a legitimate reason *not* to award a contract to that firm. Suspected or conjectured irregularities can result in adverse publicity and charges of favoritism or corruption. It is a lot easier to suggest to the public that an official has improperly awarded a contract than it is to show to the public that an award to other than the low bidder was proper.

The result is that many public officials consider the harsh contract their best protection against the contractor, who is often viewed as the enemy. The harsh contract is typically the one that allocates every conceivable risk to the contractor. In reality though, a fair allocation of risk set out in the contract would alleviate most of the problems we've described. The result would be fewer lawsuits and delays and, possibly, better quality work.

TAILOR-MADE CONTRACTS

Were it not for public-bidding requirements, all parties, the engineer, the designer, the owner, and the contractor, might sit down and work out the most equitable terms, with the lowest possible cost and in the most expeditious time-frame.

In the private sector, of course, there is more leeway. Parties may tailor the contract to the job and to the parties' desires. But in both sectors, parties need to be educated. Contractors need to understand contract terms so that they don't assume great risks without clearly realizing the potential consequences. Contracts should be read with care and with skepticism. Owners need to understand that the "toughest" contract is not necessarily the best one.

ANYTHING GOES

Notwithstanding this prefatory warning about inequitable risk allocation, it must be remembered that anything can be written into a contract as long as it is not illegal. For example, an owner could require that workers were yellow socks on the site; if the contractor signs the contract agreeing to the conditions, yellow socks it must be.

In the following pages, we will analyze more commonly used contract terms and give special attention to terms that often cause difficulties and give rise to claims. We will analyze standard contract terms from several perspectives with the caveat that these analyses are conceptual tools, aimed at a better understanding of contracts and of the risks involved. The analyses are perhaps somewhat arbitrary and over-simplified, but each should help shed light on contracts and their inherent risks.

PARTIES TO THE CONTRACTOR/OWNER RELATIONSHIPS

The first analysis is from the point of view of the parties to a contract. The four general types of contractual relationships reflective of current practice are those between an owner and:

1. a general contractor;
2. a turnkey contractor;
3. a construction manager;
4. separate independent contractors.

There are scores of risks inherent in any construction undertaking: availability of labor, materials and equipment, defective design, supplier failure, mistakes, accidents, traffic maintenance, inflation, and differing site conditions, to name just a few.

The allocation of these risks between owner and contractor is central to how people often think of, and define, contractual relationships. But communication is a pivotal problem. If an owner says that he intends to engage a general contractor for project A, whereas he feels a construction manager is better suited to the circumstances of project B, that on project C he wants a turnkey contractor, and that on project D he feels independent prime contractors would be preferable—the owner has his own concepts of each of these relationships and an understanding of how the relationships differ one from another. If a dictionary were consulted—even a construction dictionary—it is likely that the definitions would not satisfactorily differentiate the several types of relationships. Unfortunately, people often use the same terms while each has in mind a different meaning. This leads to confusion and can, in the construction context, lead to claims and disputes when the expectations of one party are not fulfilled by the performance of the other party. Thus, instead of resorting to dictionary definitions of those relationships, one might better define them in terms of how various risks are allocated between contractor and owner in each one. The following is our attempt at such "risk" defintions:

A. General Contractor/Owner Contracts

This is probably the most-widely used type of contractual relationship. The owner engages an independent architect or engineer to prepare detailed plans and specifications for the work to be done. In some cases, the owner has the in-house capability to do this himself. Bids are then solicited from contractors on the basis of those plans and specifications. Here the design responsibility is the owner's; he is deemed to have adopted the design of that engineer or architect as his own. If that design turns out to be inadequate or defective, in so far as the contractor is concerned the owner is stuck. The owner, of course, can turn to the designer for recovery. If the design was generated in-house, the owner naturally bears total responsibility.

The owner can have some of that risk shifted to the contractor in those instances where performance specifications are included. The contract documents may not set forth a particular design but instead simply specify, for example, a sprinkler system that complies with applicable building codes. Performance specifications aside (they will be discussed in another chapter), the design responsibility is the owner's.

Where the contract is for a lump sum price, responsibility for the cost falls on the contractor. He bears all the risk of bringing the job in at the price bid. While there are a number of clauses that can mitigate this risk, it is basically up to the contractor to perform within cost limits and to earn his profit within that limit as well.

The general contractor also assumes liability to subcontractors and typically agrees to indemnify the owner for projected-related damage and liability to third parties.

The contractor is responsible for coordinating the work of the various trades. The owner pays for the project, typically on a monthly basis and according to an agreed upon engineer's estimate of the percentage of the work completed, less the amount agreed upon to be retained until completion of the work.

Usage. This type of contractual relationship is the one most widely used for buildings and for heavy construction—dams, tunnels, sewers, and highways.

B. Turnkey Contractors

In a turnkey operation, the owner gives performance criteria to either a single firm that does both design and construction work or, in some instances, to a co-venture of a designer and a contractor. Thus, the responsibility for the design is shifted from the owner's side to the turnkey contractor side. Liability to subs, cost of work, indemnification for casualties, and the responsibility for coordination of the work are also the turnkey's risks. Financing of the work can also be turned over the turnkey. In such cases, the turnkey is not paid until final completion and acceptance of the work. Financing can also be the owner's responsibility, to pay on a percentage of completion basis.

Usage. Turnkeys are frequently used in the private sector, where an owner may want to turn over all responsibility for a job for various reasons. Complex manufacturing or processing plants are common instances where performance specifications are given. For example, the turnkey is to produce a facility capable of turning so much tonnage of iron ore or refined crude per day into a finished product, i.e., a certain grade of oil or a certain level of ore derivative.

An owner in need of such a facility may have no experience in the field. The turnkey may have an established record in that area. Although this method is frequently used for such projects, it is not limited to highly specialized projects.

C. Construction Management Contracts

An owner may engage a construction manager, or CM, during the preliminary study, the planning phase, the design phase, or in other instances during construction, to provide advice and to effect economies. The CM typically assists the owner in contractual agreements with the subtrades, improving time scheduling, reducing claims, improving plans, and coordinating the work. Those subtrade contracts, however, are generally entered into under the name of the owner or by the CM as agent for the owner. Therefore the subcontractors are entitled to look directly to the owner for payment, unlike the general contractor relationship described above.

The owner may also indemnify the CM from casualities arising from the work. In addition, the owner shoulders the liability for the subcontractors and finances the work. Cost of the project also falls to the owner, in many cases. Sometimes a CM is engaged on the basis of a guaranteed maximum project cost, where the owner and the CM share in savings realized below that figure.

As is the case in each of these relationships, there are various contractual arrangements possible. But the overriding idea is that the CM is to save the owner money through his coordination of the work. The method is less clearly defined than other time-honored approaches. This also means there is not a large body of legal precedent that can serve as a guide when a dispute arises.

Usage. Like the turnkey arrangement, CMs are used where the owner lacks in-house capability, and typically, they are used on large complex projects where an objective coordinator can effect savings in time and money.

D. Separate Prime Contracts

Here the owner bears the responsibility for financing the work, for coordination of the work, and for the design. The separate contractors bear the risk of the cost of the construction under lump-sum contracts, for liability to their subcontractors, and for indemnification for casualties relating to their portions of the work.

Usage. This method can only be used, or should only be used, when the owner has the capability to oversee and coordinate these separate components of the work. For example, an owner with skilled in-house construction management personnel may want to maintain complete control over the project. He may have in-house capabilities for design and for construction management. The separate primes would be in special areas, with the owner managing the project.

SUMMARY

These broad brush-stroke definitions by risk allocation will in each case be altered by the actual contract language. The point is that the name given the relationship means nothing. *The only important thing is how the contract allocates risks as between the owner and the contractor.*

Under the definition given earlier, the owner potentially bears the most risk and responsibility in a construction management arrangement. The CM is essentially immune from contractual responsibility. The contractor bears the most responsibility in the turnkey relationship, as we have defined it. However, with appropriate contract language allocation of responsibility could be completely reversed.

Time is also a factor in the choice of the parties to a contract. The general contractor method takes longer than some other arrangements. This is because all plans and specs must be completed before work can go to bid. However, since they are complete, the final cost should be more predictable. In the CM or turnkey types of arrangements, plans and specs need not be complete before the work is awarded. Fast-tracking, phased construction or other methods of acceleration may be incorporated. If designs do not need to be complete, final cost is also more nebulous. But an owner may be willing to sacrifice a better handle on final cost for swift completion—or at least for the promise of saving time.

The final consideration is the capability of the owner. A large public agency, such as the Army Corps of Engineers, is clearly able to provide design work and to perform construction management functions in-house. However, many public agencies are under some pressure to use private-sector designers for their work, and use outside construction contractors as well. In special assignments such as the air force bases constructed in Israel under an international agreement of the U.S. government, the Corps also contracted out CM work. Thus, there may be special time and "diplomatic" constraints on the contractual relationship, even in the public sector.

In the private sector, many large corporations and utilities have continuing and sizable construction programs, and their choice of contractual arrangement will be dictated by the current capabilities and needs of the organization.

MONEY—THE BIGGEST RISK

Nothing has quite the potential for putting all parties at odds as money and how it is paid. In the first analysis of contracts and the allocation of risk and responsibility commonly assigned, we dwelt on the overall contractual arrangements between the parties. We noted that in many instances, risk of the cost of construction is allocated to the contractor. This risk can be quite finely tuned according to contractual variations that are described in the following pages.

FIXED-PRICE TO COST-REIMBURSABLE CONTRACTS

All contracts fall into a range between a firm fixed-price at one end of the spectrum (where the contractor bears all responsibility for project costs) and actual cost plus fixed-fee, or percentage of cost fee, at the other end of the spectrum (where the contractor seemingly need only present his bill to the owner).

There are variations within this range, and reasons for choosing one type or another. An owner may choose a cost-plus or a fixed-price contract with a general contractor or with a turnkey, or with a CM or with independent primes. The permutations are easy to see. The most common choice is, however, a fixed-price contract with a general contractor. This is in part because the method is the oldest one in use and the one that seems the simplest.

Fixed Price (Hard Money)

The fixed-price contract is most frequently used and is commonly called a "hard money" contract; it can be either a lump-sum or unit-price contract. Whichever is used, it is the type that results in more construction claims than any other type. It does not follow, however, that the widespread use of fixed-price contracts directly relates to the incidence of claims. The likelihood of claims is more related to the high contractor risk in the fixed-price contract.

Before we begin a more detailed analysis, let's look at three variables that govern most jobs and that can be affected by the type of contract. These are time, cost, and quality of the work. Everyone involved wants to get the job done fast. The owner wants to get the highest quality work he can for the money he is willing to pay. The contractor wants to do high quality work out of pride and a desire to maintain his reputation, but is reluctant to risk losing a profit to do so. If the terms of the contract make it unprofitable for him to deliver a high quality job at the time specified and for the contract price, the most likely outcome is a project impeded by claims and costly delays. It's much better to begin with an equitable contract, and one suited to the type of project.

There is no ideal type of contract. Claims can always arise, from circumstances beyond the control of the parties, or from litigious contractors. Owners can make claims against contractors as well. But owners generate the contract, which is the starting point for conflict, or for a mutually profitable relationship.

COST-REIMBURSABLE CONTRACTS

1. **Time and Materials.** At the very end of the spectrum, an owner might engage a contractor to provide men and materials at a rate fixed in the contract. This arrangement is close to rental service.

    Application. An owner might want to use this method when he is in a position to maintain complete control of the work, or in order to complement his own in-house capabilities.

Disadvantages. It is difficult for the owner to control his costs; he bears the entire risk of project cost.

2. **Cost Plus Percentage of Cost.** This type of contract, it should be noted, is prohibited by the federal government. This suggests that there is something wrong with it. There are obvious disadvantages, the principal one being that there is almost a built-in disincentive for the contractor to watch the cost of the project since his fee increases in direct proportion to the cost of the work.

Application. Why then, would an owner want to use a cost plus percentage of cost contract?

One application would be in an emergency such as rehabilitation immediately after an earthquake. In such a case, there would be none but the most rudimentary plans and specs, and work would have to begin at once. Few contractors would undertake work in such conditions without the protection this type of reimbursement affords.

Another application would be where an owner has had a long and harmonious working relationship with a contractor that induces mutual trust. The owner knows that the contractor will not take advantage of him; the contractor knows that the owner is fair.

Disadvantages. The main drawback of this contract type is that the owner cannot control his costs. He doesn't have a good estimate to begin with, and the contractor has no incentive to save money. It is easy to see why these contracts are disallowed in the public sector. Allegations of misuse of funds or of sweetheart deals are easily made and difficult to disprove. The contractor actually stands to make more profit if he spends more of the owner's (translate to taxpayer's) money. That state of affairs can be easily misinterpreted, and of course, abused.

An owner must define allowable costs in the most detailed manner possible to maintain some control over the project. Vagueness here could lead to claims as to which costs are reimbursable and which are not, which are direct costs and which are included in the overhead allowance.

The owner bears most, if not all, of the risk in this arrangement.

3. **Cost Plus a Fixed Fee.** This arrangement is similar to the last, except that the fee is fixed. Thus the risk to the owner is somewhat diminished. Most contracts of this type provide that the fee can be adjusted if there is measurable change in the scope of work to be performed.

Application. This type of contract might be used for similar situations such as those for which a cost plus percentage of cost contract is used, for example, in an emergency or where the parties have had a long working relationship.

Disadvantages. The owner again must define allowable costs carefully. He still doesn't know beforehand exactly how much his project will cost. He does know what his contractor's fee will be, but there could be disputes or claims if the contractor perceives a change in scope when the owner does not. The owner still bears the majority of the risk in this contractual arrangement.

4. **Cost Plus Award Fee.** With this type of cost arrangement, the owner reimburses all allowable costs, agrees to pay a base fee, and sets up criteria on the basis of which the contractor may be paid more.

The criteria for "bonus" pay are set out in the contract documents. There should be no doubt about interpretation. It is also (typically) understood that the owner is the sole judge of the contractor's performance in these areas. The contractor, in signing on, must accept this fact and the idea that there might be a certain subjectivity in these judgments where money is involved. Clearly, parties have to know and trust each other in this arrangement. Early completion in certain areas of the work is an example of an opportunity for an award payment.

Application.   This might be used for projects in which there is some urgency about time of completion and where the owner wants to provide some incentive for the contractor to excel.

The Army Corps of Engineers, the Department of Defense, the Navy, and other branches of the federal government have used such contracts in Vietnam, or elsewhere overseas. The circumstances were deemed special—diplomacy, urgency of completion, or other reasons—so that an award arrangement might be considered a tool to attain swift and proper completion.

Disadvantages.   The method has not been widely used, but where it has been used, the problems have reportedly been minimal. Potential drawbacks are these: a sophisticated organization is needed to administer such a contract and there could be problems in the judging of whether a bonus payment is due. But as stated before, the system does offer incentive for the contractor to work quickly and efficiently.

5. **Cost Plus Incentive Fee.**   This is a more complicated approach to setting monetary incentives for the contractor's performance. A target cost is estimated. A target fee, a minimum fee, and a maximum fee are also set. A fee adjustment formula is set forth. Typically, that formula might provide that the contractor be penalized a percentage of his fee if the final project costs exceed the target estimate. He might be rewarded at a specific percentage if final costs run under that estimate. Incentive is limited to the maximum fee set out; the fee cannot be less than the minimum, however. The maximum fee gives the owner some degree of control over the final cost figure. Ideally, the owner would happily pay the higher contractor fee since by definition that would mean the total project cost is less than estimated.

The advantages of the method are that the contractor has an incentive to save money, and that the owner has parameters on the final cost. The potential seems great for satisfying all parties to the contract.

Application. This method has not been widely used. Obviously, the approach requires a highly sophisticated organization to monitor costs; both the contractor and the owner must be sizable to do this properly or even adequately. This method probably would be used on large complex projects where the parties are amenable to working out these contractual arrangements and can oversee their implementation adequately.

Disadvantages. The incentive for both parties seems great. However, the cost plus incentive-free contract has not been applied in many instances. The greatest drawback would seem to be the difficulty in establishing and documenting cost savings that would result in the higher (or lower) contractor fee, and in determining responsibility for cost overruns that would affect the contractor's fee. Clearly, if the overruns are owner-caused, the contractor will not want to be penalized by a lower fee. Thus, while this arrangement in theory holds great promise, in practice it can become a nightmare.

6. **Fixed-Price Incentive Contracts.** The fixed-price incentive is a fairly innovative attempt at sharing risk and has not been widely used. The fixed-price incentive contract sets a fixed project cost. However, the contractor's risk is mitigated by setting a target cost estimate and a price ceiling. A target profit is also set. A formula is agreed upon for dealing with the amount that the final cost falls below or above the target. The owner is protected by the ceiling price. The contractor has the opportunity to make unlimited profit, i.e., there is no ceiling on his profit—if he lowers cost sufficiently to earn that extra money. His profit diminishes as the final cost approaches the target. If the final cost is above the target estimate, he loses.

This contract resembles the cost plus incentive arrangement described earlier in the cost-reimbursable portion of this chapter. However, in the other version there is a ceiling and a floor on profit and all costs are reimbursable; here there is a ceiling on costs, none on profit.

Application. Use of this contract might be appropriate where the owner has plans and specs sufficient to allow a target cost, yet with enough leeway to allow a contractor to maneuver for that extra profit. Obviously, if plans and specs are complete, the contractor has less opportunity for innovations that might increase his profit.

Disadvantages. As in some of the other contractual arrangements, it takes a fairly sophisticated owner to attempt such a contract. There could be difficulties in setting up the sharing formula and in administering it.

7. **Guaranteed Upset Price.** The guaranteed upset price is a less complicated variation. For example, an "upset" price might be set for an agreed-upon changed condition or a portion of the work. Costs would be carefully audited and a percentage sharing formula set up for the amount above or below that audited cost. In other words, this is a more limited and controlled application of the same idea as the fixed-price incentive arrangement. In the latter, presum-

ably, the contractor would suggest changes in the work to save money and increase his profit.

SUMMARY: COST REIMBURSABLE CONTRACTS

The contract types we have just described are most likely to be used in the private sector. The one overriding advantage of these contractual arrangements is that work can begin before all plans and specifications are complete. The great disadvantage is that the owner cannot have a firm idea of what his final costs will be.

Some of the more promising contract types, in which incentive is provided by the opportunity to earn a larger fee, require sizable organizations to administer them.

For these reasons, there will likely be more use of these contract types by large firms in the private sector: for example, those with in-house construction capabilities and continuing construction programs. In the public sector, such methods might be used in extremely complex projects or "special" cases, such as the Israeli air bases mentioned previously that were part of an international agreement, or in urgent defense programs. The space program or other such special projects where there are many unknowns might be another application.

FIXED-PRICE CONTRACTS

Most construction business in this country is conducted with fixed-price contracts. Anyone involved in the industry should understand this form thoroughly and should be aware of the risks that exist and of clauses that can mitigate those risks.

In a bare-bones, fixed-price arrangement, the project risks fall amost entirely on the contractor. He either brings the work for the bid he proposed, or he takes a loss. This is true whether he is a general contractor, an independent prime, or a turnkey. It can be true with a construction manager as well if the contract is set up that way.

From the owner's point of view, this seems like a protective device. But the simplicity is deceiving. The contractor's bid must be high enough to cover those risks—the unknowns that will surface in the course of construction—and to make a profit as well. It must also be low enough to be competitive. The result of this guesswork is that one side inevitably loses. If the final project cost comes in lower than expected, the contractor makes more money while the owner could have spent less. If the final project cost comes in higher than bid, the contractor will not only lose money, he could go out of business. The owner, whether he wants to or not, can pass off the higher cost to someone else—the consumer, or in the public sector, the taxpayer. The solution could be as damaging in the long run as the contractor's loss is in the short run. An owner could be subjected to harsh criticism or lose sales.

Why Are Fixed-Price Contracts Used So Universally?

- "It's always been done that way." The method has gained respectability with age. Owners, particularly public owners, don't want to take a chance with an "innovative" contractual arrangement. Many managers in large corporations don't want to risk convincing their boss that another way might be better. Finally, most owners don't even think about other possibilities.

- Since the risk in a fixed-price contract sits mainly with the contractor, many owners feel this is the only safe way to go. To a public official, particularly on the local level, the fixed-price contract can be a shield, a way of appearing to avoid favoritism and of saving the taxpayer from venal contractors.

- The owner has the best handle on the final cost, an important consideration in the public sector where projects are funded through bond issues or legislatively limited.

We have noted that the fixed-price contract results in many claims and that they are also the type most often used. One result of this situation has been the development of contract clauses that tend to mitigate the severity of the fixed-price contract. Such clauses shift from the contractor to the owner, some of the major risks over which the contractor has little or no control. The principal clauses in use are escalation clauses, differing site clauses, and variation in quantity provisions. Owners have been slow to accept these, but their use is growing. They can, of course, be incorporated in a cost-reimbursable contract, although the necessity there is marginal. These and other clauses will be dealt with in detail in this chapter.

READING THE CONTRACT

Once the contract type has been chosen, parties often skim over what they consider to be boiler plate and leap into the plans and specifications. This is a major mistake. Much contractual risk is bound into the terms of the general conditions. Since the contractor typically has little voice in the contract choice, it is his responsibility if he wants to stay in business to assess that risk correctly. He may decide, on the basis of that assessment, not to bid at all. More often, if he perceives a high-risk situation, he will bid a higher price. If he gets the job, his awareness of that risk should result in defensive management of the project. He will, or should, take care not to let himself get out on a limb in a risky area of the work. The experienced contractor will measure his risk, too, in terms of the owner's reputation. Some owners are known to stick to the letter of the law, no matter how harsh an interpretation might be.

Owners, as we have pointed out, have a perfectly legitimate concern with self-protection through the contract. Many contracts are formulated by a cut-and-paste procedure, are inadequately reviewed by owners, or are antiquated documents that have achieved sanctity through age. The owner may not have considered the contents for years. This might be especially true in a bureaucratic public owner case.

Most often, however, owners tend to include harsh protective clauses that amount to an ill-advised defense and instead are the breeding ground for claims.

Both sides should, in other words, think about the contract carefully.

RED FLAG CLAUSES

The following are clauses, some of them meant to mitigate risk, that should be scrutinized thoroughly.

1. Time Extension.   Is the contractor entitled to an extension of contract time for acts of God and other causes beyond his control? What, specifically, are the cases in which delay is excused? What about delay caused by problems with the manufacture of materials or equipment? If the contractor is not entitled to time extensions, is he liable for liquidated damages or actual damages for delays? If he falls behind schedule because of a delay that does not entitle him to extra time, is he required to accelerate by working overtime?

To illustrate, two commonly-used contract clauses differ somewhat in setting forth time extension conditions:

The Engineers Joint Contract Documents Committee's (EJCDC, formerly NSPE) Document 1910-8, para. 12.1 says that contract time may only be changed by a change order based on written notice delivered to the owner and the engineer within fifteen days of the event giving rise to the claim. Notice of the extent of the claim with supporting data is due within 45 days. The clause does go on to say that contract time will be extended only in an amount equal to time lost due to delays beyond the control of the contractor.

The American Institute of Architects' (AIA) clause, Document A201, para. 8.30, states that any claim for extension shall be made in writing to the architect not more than 20 days after the commencement of the delay. Otherwise, the claim is waived. The contractor will provide an estimate of the probable effect of the delay on the progress of the work.

These are minor variations in wording, but when the request arises, the correct procedure under the contract must be followed. Also one clause might be more liberally interpreted than the other. The AIA sets out very explicit reasons for delay judged to be beyond the contractor's control. The EJCDC prefaces its list with "shall include, but not be limited to." This leaves the contractual door open a little wider. The AIA version says the architect will decide what a reasonable time extension will be. The EJCDC clause says that the engineer will decide "if the owner and the contractor cannot otherwise agree."

There are also some contracts in which it is stated that the contractor cannot claim any relief other than a time extension. For example, the City of New York's contract documents contain a clause stating that "the contractor agrees to make no claim for damages for delay in the performance of this contract occasioned by any act or omission to act of the City or any of its representatives, and agrees that any such claim shall be fully compensated by an extension of time to complete the work . . . ."

Other municipalities or government bodies or a private owner may include similar clauses, known as "no damage for delay," which certainly put a burden on a contractor (see Chapter on Delays).

In fact—and we stress this fact throughout this book—an owner is free to put any kind of clause he pleases in any kind of contract. We would like the owner to think about the consequences and the contractor to be aware of high-risk contract provisions.

2. Escalation Clauses.   These are clauses that allow reimbursement to the contractor for steep increases in labor or material costs (the latter more rarely) over a long period of time. Sometimes these clauses mention a time period after which the escalation applies; such clauses are most often used in contracts for work that will take at least a year to complete. Inflation, labor agreements, and the like are sometime foreseeable, but the extent, as in the case of inflation, is not. It is reasonable to assume that a contractor cannot account for these in his bid when the project will be of long duration. If he does, he is not likely to get the job.

Neither the AIA nor the EJCDC contract documents include escalation clauses. Lawsuits and defaults are rarely attributed directly to losses from escalation risks. It's easy to see, however, that a contractor who takes a loss because of enormous increases in these areas could default, or in some cases, be looking to make up the money elsewhere, by cutting corners, or through litigation.

Basically, the escalation clause seems fair treatment of the contractor and protects an owner from excessive contingency in bids. One federal agency provides for escalation in contracts that will run for over two years. In part, the provision reads:

"Commencing one year after the date of award of contract, the payments earned thereafter under the contract will be adjusted by the amount of 75% of the difference between the amount of wages actually paid and the amount of such wages if computed at the hourly rates stated (elsewhere in the documents)."

Notice that the clause protects the owner for a year. If the labor rate changes considerably within that time, the owner doesn't pay before the year is out. It is assumed that the contractor might reasonably have foreseen a short-time cost hike.

The shared cost after that time is intended to motivate the contractor to exercise what control he can have over such increases.

Under the Risk section at the end of this chapter, there is a discussion of the results of a survey on construction contract practices. The escalation clause was almost universally endorsed by those responding, who were a mix of owners, contractors, designers, and attorneys.

3. Changed Conditions.   This important provision, sometimes referred to as a "differing site conditions" clause, is now part of the federal government's standard documents, as well as the AIA and EJCDC documents.

Historically, unforeseen subsurface conditions have caused many construction claims and have driven more than a few contractors into default. A changed condition clause allows reimbursement for unforeseen site conditions that affect the cost of work. For example, such unforeseen ground conditions can necessitate the driving of longer piles or the use of more support steel than was first planned. Both operations might disrupt and delay work, throw schedules out of kilter, and cost significantly more than a contractor could reasonably have expected.

However, it has been the almost universal practice for the owner to include contract clauses disclaiming the borings and other data furnished about the site.

When disputes about such unforeseen conditions have reached the courts, the ruling has more often than not been that such clauses are not valid. On the other hand, some judges have upheld the clauses and ruled that contractor's signing of the documents denotes acceptance of the risk.

There are better ways to deal with the risks of subsurface construction, and the changed conditions clause is the principal means used today.

These clauses are included in most standard contract documents. However, there are major cities that refuse to include such terms. Contractors should not take the inclusion of changed conditions clauses for granted. Owners should consider their inclusion as insurance against subsequent lawsuits and against high bids.

The AIA and the EJCDC standard documents include provision for changed conditions in existing structures, as well as for subsurface conditions. The AIA allows for conditions "at variance with," and the EJCDC for conditions that "differ materially from," "conditions indicated by the contract documents." The federal government clause on differing site conditions refers to differing subsurface conditions and also to "conditions at the site of an unusual nature differing materially from those ordinarily encountered and generally recognized as inhering the work of the character provided for in the contract."

The wording in all three cases is open for some interpretation, but inclusion of both subsurface and site conditions is prudent. This is especially true with the increased amount of rehabilitation and restoration work conducted in recent years. Retrofitting for seismic codes or energy-use reduction can result in structural changes for buildings where there are no existing as-built drawings or plans and specs. Nevertheless, the greater majority of unforeseen and differing conditions are found in subsurface work, tunneling and the like. As to wording on notification, the AIA version (A201, para. 12.2.1) says that either party must request a change order within 20 days of observance of the condition. The other two standard clauses, federal form 23A, para. 4 and EJCD 1910-8 para. 4.3, require that the contractor notify the owner "promptly," wording that is open to a range of interpretation.

These clauses shift responsibility for unknown conditions to the owner where it rightfully belongs. No contractor can be expected to have investigated the owner's site exhaustively before bidding (see chapter on changed conditions).

4. Variation in Quantity. Many fixed-price contracts incorporate unit-pricing. This entails the owner's setting forth estimated quantities of materials needed to accomplish the work, or portions of work, into units. For example, the owner might estimate quantities of cubic yards of concrete poured, the quantities being a combination of materials and work. The entire contract could be unit-priced; if the design is complete, the key is the degree to which quantities can be reasonably estimated.

In complex projects, unit-pricing becomes more difficult. The contractor generally takes more of a risk if unit-pricing is used in such cases.

Wrong estimates can result in substantial losses or in windfall profits—for either party. If design changes are made, of course, a change order can allow for the difference in the originally estimated quantities. A different price for those unit-priced items might also be negotiated. But the owner might be hard-nosed and insist on application of the contract unit price.

Where quantities cannot reasonably be estimated, there is a substantial risk that wide variation from estimated to actual quantity will not be adequately compensated by the unit price. Even if the actual quantity is significantly lower than estimated, the contractor may not be able to recover his fixed cost for the work (say, for example, in a grouting operation where there is an expensive equipment setup, regardless of the amount of grout used). In other instances, he may be overly-compensated.

If the actual quantity is significantly higher than estimated, the contractor may have to go to a more costly method. He may have to use a larger piece of construction equipment in an excavation operation, or steel in lieu of timber sheeting for earth support, or he may have a longer haul distance for the disposal of excavated material.

However, the variation in quantity clause is another way to deal with the risk involved in a unit-price element of a contract. This clause distributes some risk by setting a limit on how much that estimated quantity can vary before making some adjustment in the price. For example, on the San Francisco Bay Area Rapid Transit (BART) project, this was the wording (paraphrased) of the variation in quantity clause. If the total price quantity of any contract item that amounts to 5% of the total contract bid price, varies by 25% or less from the engineer's estimate, payment will remain as bid. If the variation is beyond 25%, a change order will be issued.

Under the BART arrangement, it would be possible to credit the District with any reduction in cost or to compensate the contractor for any increase in cost resulting from the changed quantity.

The U.S. Bureau of Reclamation offers a split quantity clause to deal with problems of variation in quantity. According to the agency wording, the provision can be used for contracts where "principal unit prices are susceptible to large variations." In the split-quantity provision, a 65%-35% split is allowed, "unless another percentage is deemed appropriate."

The two ranges are provided so that bidders will include in the unit-price bid for the first 65% of the total estimated quantity for that item "that part of the contractor's cost for construction facilities mobilization and demobilization, plant, fixed overhead, etc." The price for the 65% portion would naturally be higher in most instances since it includes both fixed and variable cost. The 35% portion should only include the variable cost of the operation associated with completing this bid item of work. Therefore, no renegotiation of the unit price is appropriate, regardless of the final quantity, unless a change is made or the final quantity is less than 65% of the estimated quantity. If a change is made that affects the cost of the item of work, then an appropriate adjustment would be made pursuant to the changes clause in the contract. If the 65% threshold is not reached, the contractor is entitled to an adjustment for an unrecovered fixed cost.

The EJCDC and AIA standard forms offer somewhat similar clauses, but are less specifically worded than the BART provision quoted here.

The AIA clause (A201, para. 12.1.5) states that if unit prices are agreed on and if the quantities originally contemplated are so different in a proposed change order, that application of the unit price will cause "substantial inequity" to the owner or the contractor, then the unit price will be equitably adjusted.

This seems to limit the adjustment to change order applications; and in fact, this clause is found in the section on change orders in the AIA document.

The EJCDC clause (1910-8, para. 11.9) states that where the quantity of work with respect to any item covered by a unit price differs materially and significantly from the quantity of such work indicated in the contract documents, an appropriate change order shall be issued, on recommendation of the engineer to adjust the unit price. The EJCDC clause is applicable in a wider range of cases than is the AIA clause.

There is no doubt that variation in quantity clauses, if properly administered, spread construction risks more equitably and protect both parties to a contract. A notable instance illustrates the point. New York City's Third Water Tunnel involved tremendous overruns for unit-priced support steel for which the City had specified a lower-than-cost fixed unit price. There was no changed conditions clause. To oversimplify the events, the contractor sued the City on the grounds that as owner, the City "knew or should have known" that much more steel would be needed. The estimated quantities were vastly off the mark. Work stopped, the City countersued, inflation took its toll, and work remained unfinished for years, during which time taxpayers had substantial maintenance costs to keep the partially driven tunnel from regressing.

A good part of this scenario might have been avoided if a variation in quantity clause had been included in the contract and observed in good faith.

5. Extras and Changes in the Work.   Contracts generally include a clause that gives the owner the right to order extras or changes. For the contractor's protection, these clauses should include the extent of allowable change (for example, not to exceed 5% of the contract price) and a time extension for performing the change. The contractor should also be compensated for the impact of the change on other work, if any. A time limit should be included for payments relating to owner-requested changes. Owners sometimes take inordinate amounts of time to process change orders. This can tie up contractor dollars and erode cash flow. Most contracts do include time provisions for payments to the contractor for base contract work but not for extra work.

It should be apparent that some changes will have a ripple effect, i.e., changes that could bring work into a winter season, call for different equipment, or tie up equipment needed for another portion of the work. That ripple or impact from the change should be compensated for in addition to the direct costs of the changed work.

6. Exculpatory Language.   Contractual disclaimers as to cost responsibility for incomplete plans or specifications, faulty or incomplete site information, or other matters should be viewed with caution. From the owner's point of view, inclusion simply guarantees that most contractors will come in with higher bids as insurance against those risks. When disputes over these clauses have reached the courts, judges have often ruled against the owner, citing "reasonableness." The courts have increasingly taken the position that the owner has the ultimate responsibility for the preparation of a reasonable contract, particularly competitively-bid public contracts. Nevertheless, when such exculpatory language is present in a contract, it can be invoked. Parties cannot be sure how the court will rule.

Inclusion of exculpatory language is often a sign of a lack of professionalism on the part of an owner or designer. It represents an evasion of responsibility, an improper allocation of risk.

7. Disputes.   The omission of a provision for the resolution of disputes can force parties to the courts if negotiation is not successful.

In the public sector, various procedures have been used to provide for the resolution of disputes outside of the courts. The chapter on formal dispute resolution describes boards of contract appeal and other mechanisms that are used at state and local levels to deal with contract disputes.

There are other formalized methods for settling contract disputes short of the courts, and sometimes these are referred to in the disputes clause. Arbitration, mediation, or mediation/arbitration may be alluded to with the proviso that both parties agree to submit to findings of such hearings. These forums are often advocated as being less costly and time-consuming than legal recourse. The advantages and disadvantages of each of these are set forth in the chapter on dispute resolution.

The AIA general conditions (A201, para. 7.9.1) provide for mandatory arbitration of contractual disputes "unless the parties mutually agree otherwise." The AIA provision also prohibits the joinder of the architect in arbitration procedings between the owner and the contractor unless written consent is given by the architect. In the Metropolitan Atlanta Rapid Transit Authority (MARTA) specifications, to give an example of a major project, arbitration was mandated for disputes arising in connection with the contract.

This provision also states that the "arbitrators award and their decision of all questions of law and fact in connection therewith, shall be final and conclusive, and judgment upon their awards may be entered by the U.S. District Court for the Northern District of Georgia . . ."

With the Eisenhower Tunnel, part of a major highway project in Colorado, the contract provided for a preselected panel of industry experts to hear and deal with disputes. This panel considered disputes directly as they arose on the job before the developed into formal adversary proceedings. The method seems to have been successful; however, it requires sophisticated parties who are willing to submit to the judgment of respected individuals in the industry.

8. Plans and Specifications/Other Contract Cautions. There are a number of other portions of the contract documents that may lead to conflicts. To begin with there are detailed specifications and there are performance specifications. In one case, the contractor might be asked to build a roof according to the detailed instructions in those specs. In the other case, he might be asked to build a "watertight" roof.

The contractor and the owner should know the difference. If the roof is built exactly according to detailed specs and still leaks, the contractor's obligation has been satisfied, and the owner will have to pay for repairs. If the contractor is working with a performance spec, the risk is his if the roof leaks. However, he has the opportunity to make more money by deciding himself how to construct that roof.

Other contract items that merit special scrutiny are provisions for the location of utilities, guarantees of right-of-way, and conversely, extension of time if the right-of-way is not available.

Some other provisions are more complex; the difficulty with these rest on whether certain decisions should be made by the designer or the contractor. These might include temporary support for deep excavations, responsibility for the consequences of dewatering, temporary tunnel linings, rock support-steel, use of timber or gunite (for support), the length of foundation piles, and so on. All are potential disaster areas and are often dealt with on a unit-price basis.

Cost is not the only consideration in these areas. The integrity of the structure and the safety of the workers are involved. Claims and delays can be averted by clearly delineating design requirements.

SUMMARY

Throughout this chapter, the owner and the contractor have been repeatedly referred to. Clearly, most of this information is also applicable to designers as to parties to construction contracts. No bias was intended as in this presentation. However, owners generate contracts. In turn designers, that is, architects and engineers, prepare the actual plans, specifications, and contract documents as "independent agents." They are actually part of the owner's team. Contractors are in a position only to react to these documents.

Most claims, not surprisingly, come from contractors. However, all parties need to be educated. Construction contracts should not be cut-and-paste assemblages of clauses picked up from here and there. Nor should they be ancient documents used by city X, or agency Y since time immemorial. Parties should be thinking about the contract documents and their contents; that content should not be taken for granted.

Standard Documents

There are several sets of standard documents we have alluded to; these are reconsidered and revised regularly. These standard contract documents are published by the American Institute of Architects, by the Engineers Joint Contract Documents Committee (composed of the American Society of Civil Engineers, the American Council of Consulting Engineers, and the National Society of Professional Engineers), and by the federal government. These can be adopted and adapted. The important thing, which cannot be stressed too often, is that *all* parties should think about the process and know what is in the contract and which risks are being borne by whom.

Footnote on Risk

Two documents are included in the appendix of this book that show evidence of some change within the industry and that might be used as guidelines in the consideration of risk allocation.

One is the results of a survey conducted by the American Society of Civil Engineers (from the proceedings of a 1979 ASCE Conference on Risk and Liability Sharing). The survey was given at a construction industry conference; respondents were a fair cross-section of industry practitioners: owners, designers, and contractors, with a sprinkling of attorneys, academics, and insurance company representatives.

The results are notable since the great majority of those who responded favored enlightened contract practice, particularly escalation clauses, variation in quantities clauses, and changed conditions clauses, none of which are in standard use today. The respondents also were opposed to exculpatory language in contracts; they also thought that there should be provision for reimbursement for delay, in addition to time extensions.

The group was also polled on risk allocation, as between the owner and the contractor. The results are included in their entirety in the Appendix.

Los Angeles Report

The second item that indicates some changing attitudes is a report to the Board of Public Works of Los Angeles, entitled "Proper Allocation of Construction Risks Between Owners and Contractors as a Cost Saving Concept." The author was at the time the Commissioner of Public Works in that city, and the document contains some unusually enlightened recommendations for sharing risks. The report is included in the appendix; some of the proposals follow.

On the subject of delays, the report suggests that when causes of those delays are out of the control of the contractor, the owner and the contractor share extra costs. An escalation clause for labor is recommended; the owner and the contractor should work out the terms for sharing this increase on a case-by-case basis. The report also suggests that performance bond requirements and retainage be reduced as work progresses in order to reflect the owner's reduced exposure to damage.

The Commissioner concludes by stating that the City could save money by removing some risk from the shoulders of the contractor and that all ambiguous, evasive, catch-all, and exculpatory clauses be eliminated from such contracts.

2. Differing Site Conditions/Changed Conditions

Differing site conditions were briefly discussed in the first chapter. Such conditions are so often the cause of conflict between parties to the construction contract that we feel the subject merits further attention.

The terms "differing site conditions" and "changed conditions" are used interchangeably. In fact, the site does not change. The terms refer to situations in which construction conditions turn out to be different than those represented in the contract documents, or from what the parties to the contract could reasonably have expected from the information available. A common example occurs when true subsurface conditions vary from what typical site investigation borings have revealed.

The federal government added a clause to its standard construction contract, Form 23A, some years ago to deal with such cases. The alternative was, and still is, for a contractor to add a contingency factor to his bid to cover unforeseen situations. If they do occur, that contingency partially reduces the cost impact of those unexpected conditions. If unforeseen conditions don't occur, the contractor profits. There are cases, of course, in which a contractor might assert a claim even though he had included contingency money in his bid. That contingency is more often than not insufficient to cover the cost of unforeseen conditions.

In the first chapter, we discussed theories of risk allocation. The federal government's differing site conditions clause allocates the risk of unforeseen conditions to the owner. The owner doesn't have to pay for the contingency in cases where no changed conditions are discovered, nor does the owner have to risk lengthy and costly lawsuits if changed conditions are encountered. In other words, that risk is mitigated somewhat. The terms of the contract require the contracting officer to pay for the change when justified and substantiated. (It should be noted that the government is in a position to spread its risk over a large number of construction projects.)

Owners other than the federal government have adopted the differing site conditions clause, but it is not universally used. New York State and the Port Authority of New York and New Jersey, for example, do not incorporate such language in all of their contracts. Yet Los Angeles and New York City do. In the private sector, the practice varies. However, changed conditions clauses are gaining favor.

Owners who plan to include a changed conditions clause in their contracts would be advised to use the language in Form 23A of the federal contract. Sufficient cases have been decided by the federal courts and boards of contract appeals to constitute a guide to interpretation and usage. Federal Form 23A, clause 4, and comments follow:

"a. The contractor shall promptly, and before such conditions are disturbed, notify the contracting officer, in writing, of

(1) subsurface or latent physical conditions at the site differing materially from those indicated in the contract,

(2) unknown physical conditions at the site, of an unusual nature, differing materially from those ordinarily encountered and generally recognized as inhering in work of the character provided in this contract."

Comment. The distinction between the two types of differing site conditions allowed in such a clause lie between subparagraphs 1 and 2. The first one deals with misrepresentation of site conditions, intentional or innocent. The second deals with conditions that could not have been reasonably foreseen by either the contractor or the owner.

In general, most rulings have found that the contractor was not required to verify site representations as shown in the contract documentations. This is in spite of the fact that most contracts state that the contractor is "charged with the knowledge" that the owner is not responsible for those representations, and that the contractor shall examine the site prior to bidding and ascertain the prevailing site conditions. This language is exculpatory, and disavows owner responsibility for the boring logs, geological data, and other information furnished with or referred to in the bid documents. As we mentioned in the first chapter, exculpatory language is often disregarded when cases reach the courts or the contract appeals boards. However, this wording also speaks to the first type of changed condition, the one in which misrepresentation is alleged. Site investigations are a sore point in the contractor-owner relationship.

As we have pointed out elsewhere in this book, it would be preferable for the owner to assume this risk. Owners have more time to conduct thorough investigations than do contractors. However, owners often investigate just so far as they need to for design purposes. The contractor may be given the right to make exploratory boring or to conduct other investigations, but in most cases it will not be practical to do so.

For example, if an owner has been designing a tunnel project for several years and performing geotechnical surveys during that period, it does not seem logical to expect each of several contractors to conduct another survey in the six-to-eight week bid preparation period. Imagine the chaos if the bidders preparing a proposal for a tunnel project in New York City were to individually set up drill rigs and make test borings to verify the owner's data!

While the contractor should certainly visit the site and thoroughly examine it, the court rulings have held that he does not have to verify to the extent to which most contract documents require. Even if the owner states in the contract that he does not guarantee all of the representation, the contractor may recover his damages under the changed conditions clause. (However, if the contractor alleges that the owner intentionally misrepresented the facts relating to the site or withheld relevant information, then both parties had better see their attorneys. Intentional misrepresentation constitutes a serious offense; such a claim is not taken lightly and is not easily settled.) At the very least, a changed conditions clause gives parties to the contract the opportunity to adjust time and money if the owner's investigation turns out to be inadequate. The owner is also given an incentive to conduct a more extensive investigation than if the risk of changed conditions were placed on the contractor.

Examples of the second sort of differing site conditions, those that "could not have been reasonably expected," follow. There might be unusual hydrostatic pressure or subterranean water conditions that would require differing and more expensive construction techniques. Another example might be the inability to obtain an adequate water supply where that water is essential to completion of the operation, and where the water would ordinarily be expected to be available. Rehabilitation and restoration of older buildings for which plans are no longer available are also obvious candidates for unexpected conditions that might impact the work.

In most cases, the changed conditions clause would deal with site or subsurface conditions; changes due to unusual weather would not come under a changed conditions clause. However, unexpected soil reaction to such weather may constitute a differing site condition. One such case dealt with unusual capillary action of soils that caused underground ice formations during freezing weather. A subsequent thaw resulted in a collapse.

The standard federal clause also says that the contracting officer shall promptly investigate the conditions. If it is found that such conditions differ materially and cause an increase or decrease in the contractor's cost of, or in the time required for, performance of any part of the work under this contract, "whether or not changed as a result of such conditions," an equitable adjustment shall be made and the contract modified in writing, accordingly. The phrase "any part of the work" in conjunction with "whether or not changed" allows for recovery of ripple or impact costs resulting from the differing site conditions and is a relatively recent addition to the standard clause.

Notice. The federal standard clause also states that the contractor cannot request an equitable adjustment after final payment has been made. Of course, an owner may write his own changed conditions clause and incorporate what he wishes and what a contractor will agree to. That federal clause also states that notice must be given in writing and that this must be done before conditions are disturbed. Failure to comply with these provisions can jeopardize recovery. The Los Angeles version of the changed conditions clause states that failure to give timely notice constitutes a waiver of the claim. The federal government clause states this and also states that the government may extend the time required to report changed conditions. In other words, "promptly" can have different meanings.

The purpose of the time limitation is to permit an owner to make any field investigations necessary to determine whether or not a changed condition does exist. The owner then also has the opportunity to do something about the changed condition: he may devise an alternate construction scheme to overcome difficulties presented by the changed condition. He also has time to keep records of work performance in dealing with the changed condition. Those records will enable him to judge the contractor's claim in a rational manner.

If timely notice is not given and it is possible to reconstruct the nature and extent of the changed condition, the federal government contract appeals boards and the courts have been known to be lenient. In one case, a contractor alleged a sizable change in rock volume, but did not submit his claim until after the site had been backfilled and the structure built. Recovery was allowed, however. The contractor produced the records of an independent survey from which it was possible to to estimate the quantity of rock, and it was established that the owner's representative was on site and knew of the changed condition.

This does not mean that the notice provision can be taken lightly. It is always advisable to follow these provisions to the letter and thus eliminate the need to defend the failure to notify the owner. The lenient example given here is not always the case. It does seem only fair to grant a contractor recovery if there is little doubt that there were indeed changed conditions that impacted the work, assuming that the owner has not been seriously prejudiced by the failure of notice.

If the contractor does not realize that he has a differing site condition until after he has disturbed the site, he is still protected as long as he has given notice immediately on becoming aware of the changed condition.

What happens if the owner declares that there is no changed condition? The contractor must file a protest and state that he expects to be compensated for the change. If he fails to do this, he may waive rights to such compensation on the grounds that he appears to agree with the owner's decision. He must continue with the work. He rarely has the right to stop work, and if he does stop, he makes himself vulnerable under default clauses of the contract.

When the contractor objects to the decision, his next step is to follow the procedures set forth in the contract. There is usually a disputes clause that deals with those procedures (see Chapter 1). In the federal government, there is a provision that once a final decision has been issued by the contracting officer, the contractor has the right to appeal to the agency's board of contract appeals. In all of these cases, the final decision may take some time. It is in the best interest of both parties to attempt some agreement on the claim, rather than to continue through the time-consuming formal routes. Even under the best of circumstances, these all take time and cost money. Chapters 9 and 10 discuss these boards, various resolution methods applicable at other levels of government, the courts, and arbitration.

To sum up, the changed conditions clause can be the best contractual means to deal with changed conditions in the work. Exculpatory language can obscure the intent of these clauses, but is largely useless. The courts more often than not dismiss such language, and properly so.

There are two types of changed conditions: (1) the misrepresentation of the site conditions; and (2) those conditions that could not have been reasonably foreseen (widely known in the industry as type I and type II). Timely notice is called for, and while resolution bodies, including the courts, have been liberal in their interpretation of these claims, it is best to be timely.

The need for changed conditions clauses has been argued for years within the construction industry. Enlightened owners have steadily increased usage of such clauses, but inclusion in contracts is not to be taken for granted. Considering that the federal government incorporated such a provision in its standard construction contract some time ago and that there are many arguments in favor of these clauses, it seems surprising that many owners remain either ignorant or suspicious of these clauses.

However, there are also owners who simply cannot afford a changed conditions clause. For example, a local school board with a strictly limited amount of money would, in most instances, rather use a fixed-price contract, even if it does attract bids with contingency money. At least the school board knows exactly how much the job is going to cost. In other cases, owners are suspicious because they believe that contractors will look for changed conditions where they don't exist and then attempt to allocate costs improperly to those changed conditions.

Even contractors are not in full agreement concerning the use of changed conditions clauses. Some are still gamblers at heart and prefer to take the risks, and along with that risk the potential or a windfall profit. Unfortunately, those risks usually end in a lawsuit when the contractor loses that gamble.

In summary: in the absence of a changed conditions clause, competition may be restricted to the so-called "highrollers," thereby limiting competition. An owner may find this acceptable, or even desirable, but he should be aware of that possibility.

We recommend inclusion of the changed conditions clause to provide an equitable means of paying the contractor for overcoming conditions that neither he nor the owner could have expected from the information available at the time the contract was prepared.

3. Changes

What are changes? For one thing, they are inevitable. The sooner all parties to a contract recognize that fact, the better. Changes can be complicated, but if handled in a cooperative working climate, they should not have to result in disputes, threats to make recourse to the law, threats to shut down the job, or threats to stop payments.

A "change order," according to the Engineers Joint Contract Documents is defined this way:

> "Without invalidating the agreement, the owner may anytime or from time to time, order additions, deletions or revisions in the work. These will be authorized by change orders. Upon receipt of the change order, the contractor shall proceed with the work involved. All such work shall be executed under the applicable conditions of the contract documents. If the change order causes an increase or decrease in the contract price or an extension or shortening of the contract time, an equitable adjustment will be made as provided in . . . (other portions of the document) . . . on the basis of a claim made by either party."

Owners can also require that work be accomplished under conditions provided by the change order as long as these are within the scope of the contract. For example, substitute types of cement can be required for a concrete wall due to a discovery of adverse soils. However, a concrete dam cannot be substituted for an earthfill dam under a change order. Such action would constitute a cardinal change and could invalidate the contract.

CARDINAL CHANGES

There are no hard and fast rules as to what constitutes a cardinal change, other than that such changes are beyond the scope of the contract. One ruling stated that a "cardinal change has been found to exist when the essential identity of the thing contracted for is altered or when the method or manner of anticipated performance is so drastically and unforeseeably changed that essentially a new agreement is created." This is still not very precise, and if a cardinal change is suspected, an attorney familiar with construction law should probably be consulted.

Of course, a contractor may accept the change unless it is barred by applicable law such as a competitive bidding statute for public works. Most public contracts are governed by this sort of statute. In one public-sector example, the contractor accepted a change order to build a tunnel connecting his project to another public building. That portion of the work was later deemed to have required a separate contract competitively bid. The contractor, even though he accepted the change in good faith, risked recovery of his expenses due to the laws governing public contracts.

If an owner requires a contractor to perform changes that are found to be cardinal, he might risk a breach of contract suit. So both owners and contractors should be careful about the extent of any changes—such changes should be within the scope of the contract.

The fact that the definition of a cardinal change is imprecise makes caution all the more important.

CLAIMS

Note that in the change order definition the word "claim" is used to mean a legitimate request for that adjustment in the case of a change. In usage, however, the word often connotes a dispute or a demand. "Claims" should be a neutral term; the expression "a claims-conscious" contractor certainly is not such a term. In this book we attempt to achieve an understanding of claims and changes so that claims need not be a fighting word. A change doesn't necessarily lead to a claim; a claim doesn't have to lead to a lawsuit. In the true sense of the word, a claim is a request for an equitable adjustment due to a change under the contract. However, those requests too often end up in less than neutral situations.

CHANGE ORDERS

Most contracts have a clause stating that a change order must be in writing. Even in cases where there is no such clause, written orders make for better communication on a job. A verbal change order or variation in procedures at the job site, no matter how insignificant at the time or how friendly parties may be at that time, can lead to disputes and claims later on. Recovery for extra costs or time can be difficult if those change orders were not in writing. Even if the owner's representative on the job knows that the changes have been ordered (he may have given the order) and knows that extra time and costs may be involved, some jurisdictions have held that no recovery can be made without that written notice where it is stipulated in the contract terms.

However, some decisions have gone the other way and held that the order need not have been in writing. Those exceptions have been based on prior actions of an owner. For example, if an owner acknowledged other claims related to extra work orders not given in writing, those prior actions might be held against him.

Clearly, it is safest to insist on written change orders. Otherwise, the contractor could have difficulty proving later that a change was ever ordered or that the person who ordered that change had the authority to do so. From the owner's point of view, he should abide by the provisions of the contract or risk surrendering some of the protection afforded by the contract requirement that the changes be ordered in writing.

A Word About Timing. Change orders ought not to be issued between the bidding and the award stages of the proceedings. This has been held illegal on public contracts on the ground that the practice might favor one bidder. In other words, other bidders did not have the opportunity to price the changed or additional work.

Changes also must ordinarily be ordered before final acceptance of the work. If a change is ordered late in the sequence of the work, extra cost allowances might have to be made to the contractor. Most of the labor force may have left the site, or the necessary equipment may be needed elsewhere by the contractor. Compensation for the change would have to take such factors into account. Sometimes parties negotiate a separate contract for last minute changes. However, this can be even more costly. For example, a separate contract let for the last-minute addition of a roof air-conditioning unit could, in effect, nullify the roof warranty. It is preferable, if at all possible, to deal with changes within the original contract.

THE OWNER'S RESPONSIBILITY

The owner sets the tone for claims and changes when he selects the contract type and when he decides, if he does, to put the contract out to competitive bidding. A cost-reimbursable contract arrangement is going to result in fewer disputes over changes, but a lump-sum, competitively bid contract virtually invites such disputes or at least questioning. (See the Chapter 1 for discussion of allocation of risk.) However, the frequency and intensity of disputes can be mitigated by the elimination of exculpatory clauses and by clear contract provisions spelling out allowable costs of changes. A harsh contract with exculpatory language that puts most of the risk on the contractor is clearly going to set the scene for trouble.

Competition based solely on price can also lead to an undesirable job climate. If the job goes to a low bidder who bid too low and intends to improve on that low bid through "equitable adjustments," the job can be beset by claims. Most public bodies are required to accept the lowest responsible bid, so project management must be prepared to deal with the possibility of such a situation.

One might liken the parties in a construction contract to the principals in an arranged marriage. Each puts his best foot forward during negotiations. Once the contract has been signed, the honeymoon period is sometimes brief. We have mentioned the tone set by the contract type selected and the language used. But there are other reasons why that honeymoon period may deteriorate into an adversary scenario. Some of them are described below.

THE ENVIRONMENT FOR CLAIMS AND CHANGES

Here are several situations, often avoidable, that can lead to disputes and claims over changes:

- *Misunderstandings.* There can be perfectly honest failures in communication. The field office may misunderstand or misinterpret what the home office has done, or how they think about a certain aspect of the work. It's important to make sure everyone understands the same version of what has been agreed to. Minutes, memos, and other written records that are circulated can help.

- *Pride.* By this, we particularly mean pride on the part of the architect or engineer who maintains that he has designed the "perfect" project, and who thinks that any requests for changes or claims pertaining to those changes are a threat to his competence.

- *Greedy Owners.*   There are owners who think that "as long as the contractor is here, why can't he do a little extra paving or painting here and there?" More frequently, what the owner might seek to extract from the contractor is to utilize his men, plant, or equipment for longer periods of time at no extra cost. These amount to unacknowledged changes and can only lead to resentment and a job atmosphere ripe for claims.

- *Avaricious Contractors.*   There are contractors who knowingly enter agreements with the idea that they will file claims. No matter how enlightened an owner is, he could be dealing with such a contractor.

- *"Catch-up Profit."*   There are also contractors who realize late in the day that they are losing money on a job, and scurry to see where they can make it up. One way to do this is to put in for claims for changes, even if there is only a shred of justification for doing so. This impulse should be repressed. The time and expense necessary to prepare a claim will not be offset if the likelihood of succeeding with the claim is remote. Few truly unjustified claims are ever settled or recovered in court.

- *Rigid Contract Interpretation.*   Problems with interpretation are likely to occur when contract specifications are not absolutely clear. Sometimes this happens when an unreasonable owner or inspector goes beyond what is normal practice in the industry. The owner sets the tone for an adversary situation in this case.

- *Vindictiveness.*   Once an owner is presented with a claim, he can deal with it on a reasonable basis, or he can retaliate. As we have said, "claims" need not be a dirty word. Some owners adopt an "I'll show him" attitude which can lead to rapid deterioration of the project climate and which is nothing but counter-productive. This attitude can be manifested by tougher inspection, rigid contract interpretations, and other unpleasant actions that only set the scene for more claims.

GROUND RULE MEETING

One way to establish a cooperative working climate is have a meeting early in the project in which the rules for claims and changes are discussed. This serves to clear the air and prevent misunderstandings later on. The idea is to communicate during that honeymoon stage and before construction begins. (The Appendix includes lengthy minutes of a pre-construction conference that show the range of matters addressed and the kinds of agreements reached.)

First of all, the meaning and significance of contract provisions can be clearly presented and questions can be asked. Of course, both parties should always read their contracts before signing, but this doesn't always happen. Thus, the meeting allows the contract administrator to walk through the documents, pointing out salient features that might have been missed or skimmed over. A lot of contract provisions about notice and allowable costs are often regarded as boiler plate until a problem arises. At this kind of meeting, everything that isn't spelled out can be discussed. For example, parties can agree on the mechanics of handling claims, how many copies will be needed, and to whom they should be delivered. Types of costs that will be allowable can also be discussed. Parties might also agree on how these costs will be calculated so that there won't be arguments about methodology later on.

What profit will be acceptable when a change order occurs? What kind of mark-up is going to be acceptable if the change involves subs? There are various manuals that can be helpful in answering these questions, such as that published by the Associated General Contractors of America or the Rental Blue Book, often used to compute costs for heavy equipment. The contract may indicate the use of a certain manual; if it doesn't, parties might discuss this point.

Is the specified date for job completion sacred? If so, parties should talk about it right off. If an amicable relationship is set up, some necessary claims and changes can be handled expeditiously to insure that sacred completion date. Given the myriad construction-related problems that can occur during an ordinary project—weather, strikes, materials, delays, and so forth—the worst thing that can happen is to argue over every change when the job is in danger of being delayed. If parties cooperate, the job can come in on time and possibly within budget, too. That sacred date can, on the other hand, also create an emotionally charged atmosphere in which potential conflicts are escalated into real ones. Pre-construction meetings can prevent such situations.

PRE-CONSTRUCTION DISAGREEMENTS

It is possible that parties can't agree at a pre-construction meeting on the details of how changes will be handled or how costs of changes will be calculated. If this happens, the best the parties can do is to agree to deal with problems on a case-by-case basis. If and when these situations arise later on during the work, things may change. The parties involved may have a better relationship: one side or the other may concede a point in the interest of getting the job done, or other factors may enter the equation. Or, of course, they may have a knock-down-drag-out fight that delays the project further. It's in everyone's best interest to avoid that situation.

TYPES OF CHANGES

There are two basic kinds of changes: (1) those that are directed and acknowledged as changes by owners; and, (2) those that are not. First, the "easy" kind, those that are acknowledged. There are several possibilities for negotiating these:

1. The Ideal Situation. The owner and the contractor both agree that there is a change, and they then agree as to how much money or time need be adjusted because of that change. This is an ideal that can be achieved in a good working climate. If both sides agree on the cost and the time, they need only work out the arithmetic.

2. Unit-Priced Work. If the change involves a portion of the work that has been unit-priced, then simple multiplication of units and costs is all that might be necessary. However, there is an element of a gamble in unit pricing. The contractor may have set a high or a low unit price on one element of the work for other reasons. He may have put a low price on one portion of the job to keep his bid low, hoping that the item would never involve an overrun. In the case of an overrun, of course, he would lose money. He may have put a high unit price on another portion of the work to balance out his risks. In that case, the owner could be forced to spend an inordinate amount of money if a change arises that involved more work in this category. The contractor may also have unbalanced his unit prices to cover the front-end costs of mobilization. By doing so, early items of work would have a higher unit price than strictly necessary to perform that work. Correspondingly, unit prices for work done late might be lower than what the work actually costs the contractor.

Parties should be able to adjust these unit prices in the case of change where one party or the other might suffer. One way for the owner to do this is to go back to the original bids. He can compare unit prices of other bidders for the same portion of the work. Of course, the other bidders may have done the same thing. However, if some prices are substantially lower, this can be a good guide. The owner can also check his own estimate for this portion of the work.

3. Variation In Quantity.   Some contracts include a variation in quantity clause that sets forth a percentage of change after which unit prices will be adjusted. In those cases, the potential for conflict is considerably diminished. For example, a contract could provide for adjustment if unit-priced elements of the work change more than 25%. Some enlightened public owners have incorporated such contract provisions; San Francisco's BART and the Baltimore subway are examples. Chapter 1 discusses this approach. At least one federal agency allows for split quantities, whereby a contractor can place one unit price on a certain percentage of the work in the original bid and another price on the remainder. This would usually be a higher price for the first portion, and a lower for the rest, so the contractor recovers his fixed overhead after performing the first part. All these approaches minimize risk and the potential for disputes.

4. Forward Pricing.   If unit prices are not applicable to the changed work in question, the best approach is to forward price. This means both parties sit down and agree to a firm price for performing the change. This has great advantages to both. The owner knows how much he is going to pay. The contractor can logically integrate the changed work into his schedule. He can still make a profit—both sides agree on how much. And the arrangement retains some element of risk that is congenial to the construction industry. Once the price is set, either side may gain or lose a bit; that is, the work may come in for a little more or a little less than the forward price. But at least the parties have set the parameters of that risk.

How do parties go about setting that forward price? The best way is to have both parties estimate the cost of the change and then negotiate their differences. At least the owner should thoroughly analyze the contractor's estimate. The amount agreed on may either be a lump sum, a unit-price setup or a cost-of-the-work setup with a guaranteed maximum (upset price).

Impact or ripple costs must be considered in forward pricing. These are added costs incurred in performing the other items of the unchanged contract that have been affected by the change. Either the forward price should include impact costs, or the agreement should specifically state that the impact costs of the change are reserved and will be provided for at a later date. The more complex the project or the change, the more difficult it is to assess impact costs. This is a tricky area. Sometimes owners may refuse to allow impact costs on the grounds that the costs are virtually indeterminable. This is one of the areas that should be addressed in a pre-construction meeting when the relationship is cooperative and congenial. At the very least, items of allowable impact cost may be agreed on, such as labor and material escalation, extended job overhead costs, out of sequence work, and so on.

Sometimes, the emergency nature of a change precludes immediate calculations of impact costs. When the walls of a tunnel are caving in, no one is going to sit around estimating impact costs of the repair work. Work done under stress conditions, however, is more likely to have ripple costs; no one has planned for the emergency, schedules are changed, and equipment moved to accommodate such work. If forward pricing *is* attempted, it is possible to estimate impact costs and include them in the price. It is probably preferable, though, to state that these costs will be recoverable when the job is finished and a more accurate tally is possible.

5. Time and Materials. The remaining way to negotiate price changes is on a time and materials basis. When unit prices don't apply and the parties don't wish to forward price, the costs of time and materials are kept, and a profit and overhead figure added in. This is a likely approach in an emergency change. Impact costs can be considered when negotiating an acceptable profit allowance, but it is preferable to keep profit separate and to reserve the right to recover impact costs later when it is easier to judge what they will be.

The time and materials method of assessing the costs of a change is often prescribed by contract and by the regulations of state and federal agencies. First, both parties must agree on what is to be included in the change and must then agree on what kind of records are to be kept to document the costs. Finally, they have to follow up and see that these records are kept.

The ideal situation would be one in which the contractor keeps daily statement-of-work sheets, which are verified by the architect or engineer for the owner. Supplementary records can include time cards, equipment cards, invoices, diaries, and field reports. Any differences encountered between the different sets of records should be settled at once. The resolution should be put in writing and all parties involved should get copies. It is difficult and risky to reconstruct a verbal agreement later on.

RECOMMENDATIONS

It might be useful at this point to refer to the recommendations of the National Academy of Science Committee on Tunneling Technology. That group, as we have mentioned elsewhere, was primarily concerned with contracting practices for underground construction. However, their suggestions have merit for other types of construction.

The Committee report states that "negotiations for contract price adjustments for changes and extra work are unnecessarily protracted under firm-fixed price contracts and needlessly occupy the time of owners, engineers and contractors management personnel that might be spent in completing the work." Some of their recommendations are:

- More contract items should be priced, whether on a lump sum or a unit price basis.
- Provide for lump-sum pricing to cover the costs of mobilization and demobilization and for items not apt to vary greatly in quantity.
- Provide for unit-pricing where item quantity may vary to any substantial extent.
- Provide for adjustment of unit prices where unit costs are affected by substantial increases or decreases (e.g., 15% from the estimated quantities set forth in the bid schedule).
- Provide items, to be unit- or lump-sum priced, to cover work that may become necessary; for example, to overcome problems related to excessive water conditions. (In this case, it might be advisable to provide for unit pricing for successive increments of water that might have to be handled.)
- Provide a percentage amount, or formula, for determining overhead and profit to be paid on changes or provide a bid item for such percentages with a specified basis for bid comparison purposes.
- Provide that interest will be paid by the owner, at a specified percentage, on the money expended by the contractor in the performance of changes and extras ordered or required under the contract, commencing with the date that the owner has verified, or by which he has had a reasonable opportunity to verify, the contractor's proof of costs expended for performance, and then ending with payment.
- Establish a formula or basis for payment to the contractor, covering the use of his own equipment on changes and extras, and which will provide an automatic basis for such payment without room or argument.

IMPACT COSTS

Impact costs merit serious attention. Most owners would like to have the change order release read thus: "This change order is in full compensation for all time and costs arising out of this change, and any additional claims are specifically released . . . " This language absolves the owner of responsibility for unforeseen ripple costs owing to the change.

However, most contractors would prefer this wording: "This change order includes only time and direct costs of the changed work and does not include any allowance for resultant delay or increased cost in performing the unchanged portions of the work, claim for which is specifically reserved." This wording protects the contractor in the event of unforeseen impact on other areas of the work.

Some owners are wary of such clauses, thinking that these give the contractor *carte blanche* to charge anything to impact. However, forward pricing in which ripple costs are provided for may be the best approach for both parties when the cost of the change and its impact can be reasonably estimated ahead of time. Both parties are spared the annoyance and the expense of keeping detailed records of the cost of the changed work and can avoid the potential disputes over items of allowable costs. The owner has a guaranteed price for the work; the contractor can be assured of payment for work as it is performed and will not have to finance the work. He should, of course, be compensated when both parties can agree on the price of the changes, but that might be years later after completion of the job.

NEGOTIATION BREAKDOWNS

Sometimes both parties recognize that there is a change but cannot consummate agreement as to what an equitable adjustment of time or money might be. This can happen when there is a breakdown between the parties after negotiations are completed. Parties can walk away from the negotiating table and change their minds. They can get home and decide that they gave away the farm and back out of that agreement. Sometimes there is an honest misunderstanding. Parties have different perceptions of what went on at the bargaining table, and it is only when the written version is presented that they realize their perceptions were not shared.

Notes and minutes of all meetings should help prevent the latter kind of breakdown. The change of heart or mind is less easy to deal with.

What happens next, in either case? The contractor can accept such a change order with reservations. Those reservations should be down on paper. A good solution is to agree on a draft level change order, if the parties appear to be pretty close to agreement. Both sides can assemble notes and list those items on which there is accord. They can then agree to work out the rest as the work progresses. A fair amount of good faith is assumed here.

In some cases, negotiations break down totally. What often happens is that the contractor stalls to see what his costs are really going to be and how much time the change entails. This means he won't be paid until he is finished and the owner assesses the cost. On the other side, the owner, or his architect or engineer, might find it in his own best interest to wait in order to get a better fix on the contractor's costs. Neither approach is conducive to a least-cost completion because the contractor has no incentive to be efficient without a pre-determined price.

An owner can issue a unilateral change order when parties cannot agree on costs. The contracting officer can say: "Here is my final decision. I will give you X dollars, and X period of time to perform the work connected with this change. Your recourse is through the disputes clause." This will not enhance the morale of the contractor's team. Nevertheless, it does provide for some payment and allows for the next step in an orderly claims process.

If agreement cannot be reached, that draft-level change order is preferred to the unilateral order, of course. However, good faith is not always present.

CONSTRUCTIVE CHANGE

Constructive changes are those caused by an owner that are not acknowledged as such. Up to now, we have discussed ways to deal with changes when both, or all, parties agree that there is a change. In a constructive change, the contractor asserts that an action of the owner or his representative amounts to a change, one that involves an adjustment of the time and money accorded under the contract terms. The owner argues that there is no change.

The term "constructive change" evolved in federal contract usage in a somewhat tortured semantic effort to deal with such disputes under the contract's changes clause. In the private sector, or at other levels of government, the term is less likely to be used. There, ordinarily, a breach of contract would be claimed if an owner refused to concede that a change had been ordered.

Typically, a constructive change situation might arise from differing interpretation of the contract language. Obviously, if an owner orders that the diameter of a tunnel be doubled, we would have an acknowledged change of the nature discussed earlier in this chapter. A constructive change is likely to be a more subtle kind of change. Examples would be unreasonable inspection practices or unduly rigid interpretations of specifications. One party might take the position that these practices effect a change; the other would undoubtedly disagree. "Reasonable customs and standards of the industry" are usually applied when such a dispute arises. The owner might insist, for example, that the concrete work meet a higher standard than the contractor believes he is obligated to meet. That standard may be more rigorous than that customarily accepted, say by the American Concrete Institute or another commonly used concrete standard. Unless the specifications clearly spell out what those special standards are to be, an owner's insistence on this standard would impose on that owner the obligation to pay extra costs arising from that higher standard.

However, a warning: contract language often imposes on the contractor the duty to request clarification when there are patent ambiguities in the specifications. If there is doubt about the concrete work specifications and the contractor didn't inquire about them, it could be held against him.

Another situation that could lead to a constructive change might be improper rejection of work. Suppose a functioning pipe has an inconsequential hairline crack. An order to replace such a pipe would be deemed a constructive change if replacement were unreasonable in terms of normal trade practices, or if such cracks were not proscribed in the specifications. Multiple or differing inspections by an owner's team might also create a constructive change. This would be so if those inspections resulted in inconsistent directives and actual physical hindrance with performance of the work.

Delays in the delivery of owner-furnished equipment could cause a constructive change. The same could be said for owner-furnished equipment that arrives on site in an inoperable condition. If the owner refuses to acknowledge the impact on the work, we have a constructive change situation. Other kinds of interference, such as restricted access to the site, also come under this category. In one such instance, an electrical contractor was working on a job where he was to install conduits and cables in a New York City tunnel, working at night so that traffic interference would be minimal. However, on nights when there was a ball game in the nearby stadium, he was not permitted to work. Thus, he lost several hours of work on such nights. The contractor was entitled to be reimbursed for the costs of the delay caused by the ball-game traffic delays, including the non-productive hours of his employees.

Defective or ambiguous specifications can also lead to what the contractor would contend are constructive change situations if the owner refuses to acknowledge any problem with the specs. While the contractor had the duty to request clarification when specifications are unclear, generally courts have held against the owner when ambiguities can be proved. The reasoning is that the owner made up the specifications and had the opportunity to make them clear. The contractor need only demonstrate that his interpretation is a reasonable one. This rule applies to the contract documents in general, not just to the specifications.

Defective or ambiguous specifications can lead to other kinds of disputes. To take a classic example, suppose the roof of a building leaks. The owner would undoubtedly say that this is due to poor workmanship on the part of the contractor. The contractor would contend, typically, that the specs were defective, that a watertight roof could not have been built following those specs.

A combination of detailed and performance specifications in one set of documents can lead to problems. For example, suppose a contractor is obliged by the specs to meet local building codes and at the same time the specifications detail work which would not meet code requirements. Unless it were an obvious discrepancy, the contractor could not ordinarily be expected to know local code requirements and would be entitled to rely on the designer's expertise.

An example of this would be a case where the plans show the number of fire sprinkler heads, but the building code requires more sprinkler heads per sq ft than provided for in the design. Under such circumstances, it would ordinarily be grossly unfair to compel the contractor to furnish the extra heads without additional compensation. Consequently, the extra work needed to satisfy the local code requirements would constitute a constructive change.

More often than not the two kinds of specifications are mixed in an attempt by the designer to exculpate himself from responsibility wherever he has doubts about the adequacy of the design. Sometimes, though, detailed and performance specifications are mixed for a valid reason. One federal agency, for example, gives a performance specification for the moisture content of an embankment. The agency then specifies how many passes with a certain type of roller should be made over the embankment. The agency has discovered that they need fewer quality control checks as a result of this mix. If performance and detailed specifications are mixed, the reason should be stated and the contractor clearly warned that the detailed spec is only a minimum and that, in any event, the performance must be fulfilled.

Assertions of impossibility or impracticality of performance can also lead to constructive change. An example: an architect specifies a particular decorative finish on a concrete structure exterior. The specification is basically a performance spec; the architect notes that the finish can be accomplished by distressing the formwork. The contractor tries that, and many other methods as well, to achieve the desired result, all in vain. Hand finishing might achieve the architect's vision, but the cost would be inordinate. It would be, in effect, practically impossible to achieve the desired result by the use of formwork, contrary to what the specifications stated. If the owner forces the contractor to proceed with specified performance without any consideration of time and expense, we have a constructive change situation.

Constructive change can also arise from nondisclosure of technical information on the part of the owner. The owner's action could constitute fraud or misrepresentation.

However, it could result from an innocent mistake. For example, certain information may be mislaid, or incorrectly judged to have beeen inconsequential. Therefore, an allegation of withheld technical information is a sensitive area. Allegations of fraud are serious matters. However, if the owner's withholding of technical information has been unintentional, but he still contends that the information in question will not change the work, we can have a constructive change situation. This sort of problem might arise in subsurface construction, where that withheld information, whether or not the witholding was intentional, may be considered to be very important by the contractor's engineers.

ACCELERATION

Acceleration, the speeding up of the job schedule, is obviously a change. A contractor may realize that he is lagging, and be forced to accelerate the work to finish the job on time. This can be quite costly; extra men may have to work overtime and so forth. A contractor may do this and accept those costs because he will have to pay liquidated damages (or the owner's actual damages) on work not completed on schedule. He may have contractual obligations elsewhere that require the same men and equipment and thus find it in his best interest to accelerate. If the contractor is accepting the extra costs, there should be no conflict.

An owner may also direct an acceleration. If he does this, then *he* is shouldering the extra cost. Again, there should be no dispute, except about the actual costs of the acceleration. Good documentation of those costs, as always, is essential.

The next category of acceleration is laden with potential conflict. Suppose an owner makes threats to the contractor about the lateness of the work; that is, he makes reference in thinly-veiled language to terminating the contract because of the failure of the contractor to perform according to agreement. Suppose the contractor believes that any delay on the job is due to the owner's actions and that the owner should pay for any necessary acceleration. Or suppose the owner has refused to grant legitimate time extensions, or has granted them in such untimely fashion that the contractor is forced into acceleration.

All of these situations might drive a contractor into what can be called "constructive acceleration." The acceleration is due to an action of the owner's that he does not acknowledge. In most cases, the contractor is entitled to recover these costs. (Chapter 5 includes a sample calculation of a contractor's claim for acceleration costs.)

In order to avoid such situations, an owner should do several things. One is to accept the fact that if acceleration is necessary, the owner may have to pay. Threatening letters can be held against an owner if the case goes to litigation. The best action for the owner to take if he believes the contractor is lagging is to write as neutral a letter as possible, alluding to the contract agreement and to job schedules without threats; for example, he might say, "I am concerned . . . " The contractor can not claim that he didn't know anything was wrong, but he also cannot say that he was threatened. On the positive side, another thing an owner can do is to be reasonable about granting time extensions when they are justified. These should be processed promptly so that the contractor is not driven into an acceleration situation when time is actually due him. When an owner has a sacred completion date, he should be working with the contractor to meet that date. If acceleration is in order and the owner caused some delay, then he should be willing to pay for that acceleration. This is true whether there is a sacred date or not. Threats to terminate the contract are out of order if the contractor is entitled to time extensions. Deduction of liquidated damages from the contractor's payments when there have been excusable delays on the project will further exacerbate the situation. It should be apparent to all concerned that a lawsuit will cause even more delay.

Chapter 4 deals with this subject in more detail. It should be clear that documentation of the cause and cost of delays are extremely important.

CHANGED SUBSURFACE CONDITIONS

Changed conditions or "differing site conditions" are the changes during work that can most easily lead to litigation. We stated in Chapter 1 and in Chapter 2 that it is best to include such clauses in a contract. Inclusion enables parties to deal with changed conditions on a rational basis and under the terms of the contract.

There are two kinds of changes that come under this heading: those not indicated by pre-bid data but that were "known or should have been known by the owner," and those that could not have reasonably been anticipated. It's easy to see how the first category can lead to disputes and litigation. If the owner knew about the differing conditions, it is possible that he is guilty of fraud or misrepresentation. On the other hand, if he says he didn't, it is difficult to prove otherwise. We are out of the constructive change category here in that we are discussing fairly dramatic change. For example, New York City's Third Water Tunnel is the classic example of a complicated suit that grew out of a dispute over changed conditions. There was no differing site conditions clause in the contract for that tunnel. Rock conditions proved different than what the contractor believed they would be based on pre-bid data furnished by the City. The result was that vastly more support steel was needed, and the contractor sought compensation for that steel. The subsequent legal struggle went on for six years.

A change that could not have been reasonably anticipated by either party is a more benign category. Typically, changed conditions occur in subsurface construction. It is well known that owner-furnished borings can never be absolutely correct, and contractors under ordinary circumstances do not have time within the bidding framework, nor the necessary resources, to perform their own site investigation. So a changed conditions clause sets up a reasonable way to stop and renegotiate time and costs on the basis of such a change.

RELEASE

In all releases, the language should be as tight as possible, and parties should be absolutely sure of what they are agreeing to when they sign off. Recovery of additional costs can be very difficult once a release is signed. In particular, this goes to the point of impact costs. Parties should make certain that a change order either expressly includes consideration of impact costs or expressly reserves the right to claim these later on. Neither the contractor nor the owner should sign a release unless each is certain that he accepts the terms of that release.

On the other hand, in at least one instance, the contract appeals board of a federal agency upheld the contractor's right of recovery for a change after the work was accepted and a release signed. The ruling was based on the fact that the agency officials continued to correspond with the contractor about further costs after the release was signed. Those officials had acted as though the release were not in effect, and the board ruled along those lines.

That ruling may be highly unusual, but it makes a point. An owner should act as though that release is in force once he has the contractor's signature. The contractor, for his part, should not sign a release unless he is certain that he accepts the terms of that release. Further recovery is almost certainly foregone by that signature.

COSTS OF CHANGES

Changes often result in extra costs, though sometimes they can save money. However, when extra costs are incurred, either direct or impact, those costs should be recoverable. (Costs are discussed in Chapters 4, 5, 8, and 9 in this book.)

EXAMPLES OF CHANGE ORDERS

A. A change order that includes allowance of impact costs (see items 2 and 3, page 42–43).

B. A change order with the same parties, in which the contractor reserves the right to claim impact costs at a later date. (See wording on page 45.)

C. A change order in which no provision is made for impact costs, thereby opening up the dispute over a time extension and the impact cost resulting from the change.

Contract No. XXXXX
Specifications No. XXXX

A.

UNITED STATES
DEPARTMENT OF THE INTERIOR
BUREAU OF RECLAMATION

Central Utah Project

Smithtown, Utah, June 22, 1979

ORDER FOR CHANGE NO. 9

Jones, Jones Inc.
PO Box
Farview, Utah 84078

Gentlemen:

Pursuant to clause No. 3 of the General Provisions of Contract No. XXXXX, dated April 14, 1977, for construction and completion of No-name Dam in accordance with Specifications No. XXXXX, the following changes in the specifications and/or drawings as related to the general damsite are hereby ordered:

1. The mass haul diagram available to bidders was not corrected to reflect changes in the construction of the dam access roadway as specified in Supplemental Notice No. 2 dated January 7, 1977. Accordingly, you are directed to distribute materials as required during construction of the dam access roadway in lieu of using the distribution shown on the original mass haul diagram.

2. Perform additional items of extra work, as directed by the contracting officer, incidental to construction of the dam and in support of Government operations in the general damsite. Such items of extra work may include but are not limited to digging test pits for geologic investigations, moving Government-owned drilling rigs, and performing additional excavation to expose parts of the foundation for investigation by Government personnel.

All necessary labor, equipment, and material required for completion of the work covered by this order shall be furnished by the contractor.

Except as modified above, all work shall be performed in accordance with the provisions of Specifications No. XXXX, where these are applicable as determined by the contracting officer or otherwise as directed by the contracting officer.

Adjustment of the amount due under the contract by reason of the changes ordered will be as follows:

a. Distributing materials as required during construction of the dam access roadway in accordance with item 1 above for the lump sum of $125,229

b. Assisting the Government in performing support work in accordance with item 2 above for the lump sum of $14,484

The total net adjustment in the amount due under the contract by reason of the changes ordered herein is an increase of $139,713.

The adjustment in contract price provided for above has been determined to be the equitable adjustment to which you are entitled for increased costs incurred through May 26, 1979, as a result of changes to the general damsite. The adjustment includes allowances for the following:

1. All increased direct costs incurred through May 26, 1979, for performance of the work directed.

2. All impact costs through May 26, 1979, related to the performance of the work directed.

3. All ripple costs to construction of the general damsite through May 26, 1979, resulting from previously directed changes.

4. All indirect costs and profit through May 26, 1979.

No adjustment in the time required for the performance of the contract will be made by reason of the changes and additions ordered herein.

Very truly yours,

_____
Signed
Contracting Officer

Sir:

In accordance with section 1-3.807-3 of the Federal Procurement Regulations, I hereby certify that, to the best of my knowledge and belief, cost or pricing data submitted to the contracting officer or his representatives in support of the cost of the work provided for herein are accurate, complete, and current as of June 22, 1979.

The foregoing Order for Change No. 9 is satisfactory and is hereby accepted. In accepting Order for Change No. 9, the contractor acknowledges that he has no unsatisfied claim against the Government arising out of this change through May 26, 1979, and the contractor hereby releases and discharges the Government from any and all claims or demands whatsoever arising out of this change through May 26, 1979.

Jones, Jones Inc.

By _____ Signed _____

Title _____

Contract No. XXXXX
Specifications No. XXXX

B.

UNITED STATES
DEPARTMENT OF THE INTERIOR
BUREAU OF RECLAMATION

Central Utah Project

Smithtown, Utah, June 22, 1979

ORDER FOR CHANGE NO. 9

Jones, Jones Inc.
PO Box 1228
Farview, Utah 84078

Gentlemen:

Pursuant to clause No. 3 of the General Provisions of Contract No. XXXXXX, dated April 14, 1977, for construction and completion of No-name Dam in accordance with Specifications No. XXXX, the following changes in the specifications and/or drawings as related to the general damsite are hereby ordered:

1. The mass haul diagram available to bidders was not corrected to reflect changes in the construction of the dam access roadway as specified in Supplemental Notice No. 2 dated January 7, 1977. Accordingly, you are directed to distribute materials as required during construction of the dam access roadway in lieu of using the distribution shown on the original mass haul diagram.

2. Perform additional items of extra work, as directed by the contracting officer, incidental to construction of the dam and in support of Government operations in the general damsite. Such items of extra work may include but are not limited to digging test pits for geologic investigations, moving Government-owned drilling rigs, and performing additional excavation to expose parts of the foundation for investigation by Government personnel.

All necessary labor, equipment, and material required for completion of the work covered by this order shall be furnished by the contractor.

Except as modified above, all work shall be performed in accordance with the provisions of Specifications No. XXXX, where these are applicable as determined by the contracting officer or otherwise as directed by the contracting officer.

Adjustment of the amount due under the contract by reason of the changes ordered will be as follows:

a. Distributing materials as required during construction of the dam
access roadway in accordance with item 1 above for the lump sum of $125,229

b. Assisting the Government in performing support work in accordance with
item 2 above for the lump sum of $14,484

The total net adjustment in the amount due under the contract by reason of the changes ordered herein is an increase of $139,713.

~~No adjustment in the time required for the performance of the contract will be made by reason of the changes and additions ordered herein.~~

Very truly yours,

_____
Signed
Contracting Officer

Sir:

In accordance with section 1-3.807-3 of the Federal Procurement Regulations, I hereby certify that, to the best of my knowledge and belief, cost or pricing data submitted to the contracting officer or his representatives in support of the cost of the work provided for herein are accurate, complete, and current as of June 22, 1979.

*~~The foregoing Order for Change No. 9 is satisfactory and is hereby accepted. In accepting Order for Change No. 9, the contractor acknowledges that he has no unsatisfied claim against the Government arising out of this change through May 26, 1979, and the contractor hereby releases and discharges the Government from any and all claims or demands whatsoever arising out of this change through May 26, 1979.~~

Jones, Jones Inc.

By ————————— Signed —————————

Title ——————————————————

*The total net adjustment of $139,713 contained in this Change Order No. 9 is acceptable for the direct cost resulting from the changes described herein. However, the contractor hereby reserves our right to claim impact costs and time resulting from these changes at a later date.

Note: When the contractor received the form from the owner, he crossed out the two paragraphs indicated and added the bottom paragraph to reserve his rights to claim impact costs and time.

Contract No. XXXXXX
Specifications No. XXXX

C.

UNITED STATES
DEPARTMENT OF THE INTERIOR
BUREAU OF RECLAMATION

Central Utah Project

Smithtown, Utah, June 22, 1979

ORDER FOR CHANGE NO. 9

Jones, Jones Inc.
PO Box 1228
Farview, Utah 84078

Gentlemen:

Pursuant to clause No. 3 of the General Provisions of Contract No. XXXXX, dated April 14, 1977, for construction and completion of No-name Dam in accordance with Specifications No. XXXXX, the following changes in the specifications and/or drawings as related to the general damsite are hereby ordered:

1. The mass haul diagram available to bidders was not corrected to reflect changes in the construction of the dam access roadway as specified in Supplemental Notice No. 2 dated January 7, 1977. Accordingly, you are directed to distribute materials as required during construction of the dam access roadway in lieu of using the distribution shown on the original mass haul diagram.

2. Perform additional items of extra work, as directed by the contracting officer, incidental to construction of the dam and in support of Government operations in the general damsite. Such items of extra work may include but are not limited to digging test pits for geologic investigations, moving Government-owned drilling rigs, and performing additional excavation to expose parts of the foundation for investigation by Government personnel.

All necessary labor, equipment, and material required for completion of the work covered by this order shall be furnished by the contractor.

Except as modified above, all work shall be performed in accordance with the provisions of Specifications No. XXXX, where these are applicable as determined by the contracting officer or otherwise as directed by the contracting officer.

Adjustment of the amount due under the contract by reason of the changes ordered will be as follows:

a. Distributing materials as required during construction of the dam
access roadway in accordance with item 1 above for the lump sum of $125,229

b. Assisting the Government in performing support work in accordance with
item 2 above for the lump sum of $14,484

The total net adjustment in the amount due under the contract by reason of the changes ordered herein is an increase of $139,713.
No adjustment in the time required for the performance of the contract will be made by reason of the changes and additions ordered herein.

Very truly yours,

_____
Signed
Contracting Officer

4. Delays

Delays are a way of life in the construction industry. Construction claims dealing with delays are among the most complicated and difficult to analyze. Delays do not occur in a vacuum. Sometimes there are overlapping or concurrent delays. On one project in the course of a few months, there may be a strike, late delivery of critical materials, and a change in design. It often takes considerable skill to analyze these delays and to separate out the numerous factors that contribute to the overall delay in completion of the project. Determining the origin of the delay and the impact on the job, and even more importantly, the responsibility for the delay, can easily lead to conflict.

That potential for conflict is heightened by the fact that some delays are compensable only by time extensions. For others, costs may be recoverable by the contractor. In still other cases, a contractor may have no choice but to accelerate and to pay for acceleration costs, or later to put in a claim for recovery of those costs.

How do we begin to analyze delays on the job in order to avoid conflict? Throughout this book, we have emphasized two precepts: the first is to understand the contract thoroughly; the second is to keep thorough, accurate records, Here, as elsewhere, these two principles apply.

Contract Provisions Relating to Delay

There are a number of contract provisions that speak to delay. It's a good idea to separate these out at the beginning of a project. Two concepts are useful in this analysis: time and money. All contract clauses that deal with time or money relating to delays should be consulted when a delay does arise on the job. We'll begin by discussing the standard clauses. However, there are other portions of the contract that can be relevant to delays.

The AIA general conditions contains this clause:

> "If the contractor is delayed at any time in the progress of the work by any act or neglect of the owner or the architect, or by any employee of either, or by any separate contractor employed by the owner or by changes in the work, or by labor disputes, fire, unusual delay in the transportation, adverse weather conditions not reasonably anticipatable, unavoidable casualties, or any causes beyond the contractor's control, or by delay authorized by the owner pending arbitration, or by any other cause which the architect determines may justify the delay, then the contract time shall be extended by change order for such reasonable time as the architect may determine."

The federal government standard form 23A contains this clause:

"The contractor's right to proceed shall not be so terminated nor the contractor charged with resulting damages if:

(1) The delay in the completion of work arises from unforeseeable causes beyond the control and without the fault or negligence of the contractor, including but not restricted to, acts of God, acts of the public enemy, acts of the government in either its sovereign or contractual capacity, acts of another contractor in the performance of a contract with the government, fires, floods, epidemics, quarantine restrictions, strikes, freight embargoes, unusually severe weather, or delays of subcontractors or suppliers arising from unforeseeable causes beyond the control of and without the fault or negligence of both the contractor and such subcontractors or suppliers:"

The federal clause goes on to define the proper notice limits (ten days) for informing the contracting officer of such delays.

The Engineers Joint Contract Document Committee's standard form (ACEC, ASCE, NSPE) contains a briefer clause relating to delays.

12.2 "The contract time will be extended in an amount of time lost due to delays beyond the control of the contractor if a claim is made therefor as provided in Para. 12.1 (fifteen days). Such delay shall include, but not be limited to, acts or neglect by the owner or others performing additional work as contemplated by Article 7, or to fires, floods, labor disputes, epidemics, abnormal weather conditions, or acts of God."

So we have presented three different versions of standard contract provisions dealing with delay. All three provide that the contractor must give written notice in a certain number of days beginning with the commencement of the delay to the proper party: the architect in the AIA version; the contracting officer in the federal government form 23A; and the engineer in the EJCDC's form. This is the *modus operandi* in all cases. The designated individual examines the facts and determines whether the delay warrants an extension of time. In all cases, however, his determination is subject to appeal.

Even in these standard versions, wording differs slightly and parties should be knowledgeable about what their contract states. Words such as "unforeseeable," and phrases such as "beyond the control of" and "shall include but not be limited to" have some latitude of interpretation. Language concerning subcontractors varies notably. The federal government form 23A specifically limits time extensions for delay caused by subcontractors to the same causes that would be allowable for the general contractor, i.e., those that are "unforeseeable." In other words, if a subcontractor uses poor judgment or undermans the job, in spite of the care and diligence exercised by the contractor and even if the contractor warns the sub about this situation, the delay caused by the sub would not entitle the prime contractor to a time extension.

Other Delay-Related Clauses

Parties to the contract must look further for other clauses relating to time, delay, and to compensation in order to get the total contractual picture. There will be several clauses or phrases in addition to the standard delay clause (or variation thereon). Some examples are as follows: the fixed completion date (or the number of consecutive calendar days or working days assigned for completion of a portion or specified portions of the whole of the work); clauses that authorize the owner to suspend work; and clauses that permit the owner to order that work be accelerated. "Time is of the essence" is a phrase inserted in contracts that gives time clauses the force of law, i.e., that the contractor will assume liability to the owner for delayed completion unless it is excusable.

As to money, all three standard contract documents allow, or at least do not preclude, recovery by either party of damages for inexcusable delay caused by the other party. In other words, under these standard contract forms, compensation to the contractor is not limited to time extensions only; there is the possibility of recovery of monetary damages. Of course, as stated before, any owner may write a contract as he wishes; the standard clauses are guides only.

In the public sector, however, many owners do adhere to language pertaining to equitable compensation in the event of delays out of a sense that it represents a consensus as to good contracting practices. Yet there are many exceptions. New York City, for example, includes a "no damages for delay" clause in its contracts. This inclusion, however, has been rejected by courts in instances of unreasonable owner-caused delay when disputes have reached that level. Courts in some states, though, have strictly enforced such clauses despite their inequity. Parties to contracts should look for exculpatory language such as this. The owner risks that such language will not be honored by the court; the contractor risks that such wording *will* be strictly observed.

"No damages for delay" is not an uncommon clause in public construction contracts. However, other provisions relating to monetary recovery for delay may be in the contract. Payment of liquidated damages by the contractor to the owner if the contractor fails to complete the work by the contract date is one. (See the section on liquidated damages in Chapter 6.) There may be a clause stating that there will be no payment to the contractor for suspension of work (by the owner), or for acceleration. The latter would be an onerous situation for a contractor, but if there are such clauses, he should know about them from the start and plan accordingly. Likewise, he should consult with legal counsel to determine how the courts in his jurisdiction customarily deal with enforcing such clauses.

To sum up, parties to the contract must be aware of the total delay "package." They should have examined all contract clauses relating to time and to money. When a delay does occur, these clauses should be referred to first, in order to deal rationally with remedies.

There are, as we have said, applicable court and contract appeals board precedents as to compensation and time extensions for delay. Once the contract has been consulted, it is advisable to check out these precedents. If in-house staff counsel is not available, it may be wise to seek outside aid before proceeding, depending on the extent of the delay or the money involved.

EXCUSABLE/NONEXCUSABLE DELAYS

Within the framework of the contract wording and the precedents of interpretations, delays may be analyzed as *excusable* and *nonexcusable*, i.e., analyzed on the basis of whether or not the contractor would be entitled to a time extension. If delays are excusable, they can be further broken down into *excusable/compensable*, and *excusable/noncompensable* categories. "Compensable" is understood to mean compensable to the contractor.

It is essential that these distinctions be understood when analyzing delays. It follows that parties cannot negotiate rationally without understanding these differences.

1. **Excusable Delays.** Put as simply as possible, these are all delays not caused by the contractor. In the technical sense, these are all delays for which the contractor is entitled to an extension of time under the contract.

   Examples of excusable delays could be failure of the owner to provide site access, a change in design by the owner, or delays stemming from that list designated as beyond the control of the contractor in the delay clause: unusual weather, strikes, acts of God, and so on.

   In order to be excusable in the technical sense (that is, in order to warrant an extension of contract time or other recovery) the delay must be on the critical path for completion of the project. In other words, the delay must directly affect the ultimate completion of the job. Correspondingly, if the delay, whatever the cause, is not on the critical path, thereby not affecting the ultimate completion date of the work, there will be no compensation. It must be noted here that the critical path may shift. A delay that is not immediately seen as being on the critical path may ultimately affect the completion date. For example, some concrete work may not be on the original critical path; changes in the work and a delay in that concrete work may push other work off schedule. This is a good reason to track the critical path of a job on a regular basis.

   In order to determine whether the completion date will be affected, parties should have progress schedules, bar charts, graphs, or some other visual presentation of the work components so as to document delays. The more complex the job, the more advisable it is to use a CPM chart to track work progress.

2. **Excusable/Compensable.** These delays are due to some act or omission of the owner, for example, lack of site access, or late arrival of owner-furnished material or equipment. In such cases, the contractor would be entitled to damages for extra costs incurred unless there is a valid contract clause barring such recovery.

3. **Excusable/Noncompensable.** These are delays for which neither party is at fault: acts of God, epidemics, etc. as set forth in the delay clause. Time extension is the only remedy for such delays.

4. **Nonexcusable Delays.** These are delays caused by the contractor. These could include failure to coordinate the work, too few men on the job, equipment furnished by the contractor that is late, low productivity, defective work that must be removed and replaced, etc.

Such delays could be compensable to the owner in the form of liquidated or actual damages paid by the contractor for late completion, or could be the basis for contract termination by the owner or for an order to accelerate the work.

CONCURRENT DELAYS

The term concurrent delays is used to describe two or more delays that occur at the same time, each of which if it had occurred alone would have affected the ultimate completion date. These can be difficult to sort out. A critical path method (CPM) chart or other visual representation of job progress is almost essential in order to analyze overlapping delays.

There are three points to bear in mind when looking at concurrent delays. The first is to see if other work could have been accomplished during the delay period. The second is to determine whether both delays impact the critical path. The third is to analyze all delays in the framework just described. Is each delay excusable, nonexcusable, excusable/compensable or excusable/noncompensable?

There are several permutations here. For example, suppose the owner failed to supply certain materials on time. At the same time, the workers who would have installed the material were on strike. The contractor cannot claim damages for work that would not have been accomplished had the owner-caused delay not occurred. He would, however, be entitled to a time extension for the period of the strike unless it can be proved that the strike was due to his own actions. This is an example of concurrent compensable and non-compensable delays. The result is a time extension, but no damages for the contractor.

Another example of a concurrent delay would be if the contractor failed to submit shop drawings on time while the owner failed to provide access to the site; in this case, the owner ought not to penalize the contractor for that late submission. If the workers had been able to gain access to the site, they might have performed other critical path work unrelated to those shop drawings. In other words, site access was on the critical path, but the shop drawings were not. Therefore, in this case the contractor was entitled to both a time extension and delay damages.

Suppose instead that the owner failed to turn the site over in time and also instituted a redesign, both affecting the critical path. Here the contractor has been foiled on two counts by the owner and would be entitled to a time extension and to damages. Both delays were compensable.

If the contractor, on the other hand, caused two simultaneous delays, both affecting the critical path, he would be liable to assume the costs of acceleration, or for payment of liquidated damages to the owner for late completion.

These are simple examples. Concurrent delays often are more complex. If we look at an overlapping delay situation, we can see the difficulties involved. For example, if an owner blocks access to the job site between August 15 and October 1, and the contractor doesn't get his equipment to that site until September 15, is the delay compensable? Ordinarily, the belated site access would be an excusable and a compensable delay. However, the contractor could not have worked anyway for the first four weeks of that delay. Therefore, he is entitled to a time extension, but not to damages for the period of August 15 to September 15, unless he can show that his equipment was available on August 15, and that he held up delivery only due to the fact that the site was not accessible.

The contractor would, however, be entitled to damages and a time extension for the last two weeks of that delay period. The possibility of the work being forced into winter months would also arise, and impact costs for delay might be requested.

Generally speaking, when an excusable and a nonexcusable delay are concurrent, the contractor ought to be entitled to an extension of contract time.

In the case of concurrent compensable and noncompensable delays, the contractor should be entitled to a time extension, but not to damages. In order for the contractor to claim damages, the owner would have had to cause both (or all) compensable delays. As always, the contract may stipulate otherwise. Some contracts state that there will be no damages for delay and that time extensions will be granted for concurrent delays only if both delays are excusable.

COMMON CAUSES FOR DELAY

Two reasons often cited for delay are those caused by subcontractors or vendors and those caused by unusual weather. As usual, the first step in establishing the nature of the delay is to look at the contract. In the case of subcontractor- or vendor-caused delay, the contract clause may have stipulated general contractor responsibility for the subs that he retains. As we pointed out, the federal standard clause indicates that the only delays excusable for a subcontractor would be the same ones that excuse the prime, i.e., those "beyond his control, and including acts of God," etc. Some contracts require the contractor to use a single-source supplier. It might be expected that an owner would be (or should be) more lenient when a delay is due to the actions of a subcontractor dictated by the contract. The better rule is that only if the contractor chose his own subs, should he be held responsible for delays caused by those subcontractors. In a complex job, with many subcontractors, the owner should make certain the contract speaks to such delays. The contractor, as always, should know what is in that contract.

Weather is often cited as an excusable delay that justifies a time extension under the contract. Contract clauses often speak of "abnormal" or "unusually severe" weather, or in some cases weather that is "unforeseeable." The contractor must prove that these descriptive terms apply if he wishes a time extension to be granted. One way to do this is to check meteorological records for past years. These might have to go back five or ten years in order to establish that the weather condition was unusual.

Documenting Weather-Caused Delay

Three basic rules can be used in determining if weather justifies a time extension under clauses stipulating abnormal or unusually severe conditions.

1. There must be identification of the work impacted by the weather as controlling the overall completion of the project; that is, the work affected must be on the critical path.

2. It must be established that the controlling work was delayed by the weather.

3. It must be established that the weather was unforeseeable, i.e., abnormally severe.

The key to time extensions for unusually severe weather is not the cause per se, the weather, but the effect of the unforeseen weather on the work being performed. For example, an exceptionally heavy one-day rain could have a serious adverse effect on a construction site highly subject to erosion. However, the same exceptionally heavy rain would affect exterior painting less than would a lighter rain falling over a longer duration of time.

Another example of an excusable weather-caused delay is that of a light, but dust-laden, wind. Such a wind would preclude painting or the installation of sensitive electronic equipment. Yet another example might be the effect of unusually low temperatures on paving or masonry construction.

OTHER CAUSES OF DELAY

Similarly, not every fire or quarantine or strike would excuse delay. The contract might be one to excavate for a building in an area where a coal mine has been on fire for years, well known to everybody connected with the project, including the contractor, and where a large element of the contract price was attributable to this known difficulty. A quarantine or freight embargo may have been in effect for many years as a permanent policy of the controlling government. A strike may be an old and chronic one whose settlement is not expected. In any such situations where the contractor could have been expected to anticipate these difficulties and provide for them in his bid, no extension is warranted. The same rule could be applied to floods: if normally expected high water in a stream over the course of year is foreseeable, flooding would not justify a time extension.

ACCELERATION

We have referred in Chapter 3 to acceleration as a means of putting lagging work back on schedule. This can mean that the contractor puts extra men on the job, puts his men to work overtime and on weekends, and acquires more and better equipment, or whatever else the contractor thinks he has to do in order to catch up.

The cost of acceleration can be considerable. (See Chapter 5 for a sample claim.) Contractors are not likely to take this step unless it is absolutely necessary. One reason that it might become necessary is that the contract calls for payment of liquidated damages if the completion date is not met. It may be less costly to pay the acceleration expenses than the damages, and the contractor maintains some control over his work. He is, after all, arranging the accelerated work. He can estimate the accelerated costs; he can then accelerate if he thinks this will be cheaper for him. He *knows* what the liquidated damages costs will be; that figure is in the contract.

Other reasons that a contractor might elect to accelerate might be that he stands to lose money on another job if he does not. He might need men and equipment from this job to move to another. He might also choose to accelerate because he risks moving critical portions of the work into winter months.

The owner ordinarily has the right to terminate the contract for unreasonable, nonexcusable delay, and if the contractor fears that this might occur, this would be a most compelling reason for his assuming the costs of acceleration.

In some cases, the owner may direct acceleration even though all delay is excusable. When an owner does this, then he must bear the extra costs. He might do this because he himself has caused the project delays. He would rather pay for acceleration than grant an extension of time. He may have many reasons for preferring that the project stay on schedule, even if it does cost more.

Other owners might order an acceleration no matter which party has been responsible for delays because they truly have a "sacred" completion date. The owner may be building an urgently-needed military facility, or if the facility is in the private sector, profits lost may be so great that acceleration costs diminish by comparison.

Naturally, not many owners would prefer to take this step. Sometimes, owners and contractors agree to share the costs of acceleration rather than argue over who is responsible for the delay. The trade-off might be a waiver of all claims one against the other. (See Chapter 5 for a sample calculations on an acceleration claim.)

CONSTRUCTIVE ACCELERATION

A more problematic situation arises when an owner "requests" his contractor, rather forcefully, to put the job back on schedule, but without actually using the word "accelerate." The contractor may then seek to recover acceleration costs. This situation is known as "constructive acceleration." The term "constructive" is more or less equivalent to *de facto*. In other words, the owner is insisting that the job he completed by the date specified (or a different date) in the contract, but does not produce a written order to accelerate. He may write letters that pointedly refer to the liquidated damages clause and termination clauses and to the job schedule, yet not mention the term "acceleration." In most cases, the contractor has to pay the extra costs himself. He can then invoke the disputes procedures to recover those costs or go to court.

The contractor is most likely to seek restitution if he does accelerate and if he believes delay was caused by the owner. It is human nature, though, for parties to consider that fault is on the other side of the relationship. Here are some points that can help avoid a constructive acceleration situation:

1. The contractor's and the owner's representatives on the job should be in communication throughout the duration of the project, and ample records should be both kept and discussed so the situation doesn't get to the point of constructive acceleration. If the contractor receives a letter that seems threatening, he should ask the contracting officer for clarification. The contracting

officer may then have to come to terms with the situation and recommend that a written order to accelerate be given.

2. An owner can, when writing a letter about a lagging schedule, offer specific instances in which delay was caused by the contractor. That way, the contractor has to stop and think before totally disavowing all responsibility. If indeed the contractor delayed the project, he will recognize that he has to bear the costs of acceleration. If he feels that the information in such a letter is in error, he can again request clarification and discuss the matter with the contracting officer.

3. Sometimes owners let legitimate claims for time extensions get bogged down in paperwork. The result might be that the owner is prodding the contractor to move quickly, even though a time extension is actually due him. If the owner persists and the contractor accelerates, the contractor is most certainly going to seek recovery. The resulting ill-will and possible litigation could have been easily avoided by prompt processing of time-extension requests. Accurate CPMs or other visual representation of the work progress can help avoid such misunderstandings. If these are on display and the causes documented, constructive acceleration situations should not arise.

4. The contractor can help avoid adversary situations by submitting requests for time extensions promptly. He should not wait until the time that he feels the owner is suggesting that he accelerate to go back and decide that he has some time coming. The owner would be justified in refusing to consider the request; it would be "untimely" under the contract language.

   A contractor can also respond to a constructive acceleration situation by complying, with reservations. He can write to the owner and tell him that acceleration is underway and that the contractor will bill the owner for the extra costs. The owner can think things over one more time and accede, or he can refuse and invite a claim by the contractor.

SUSPENSION OF WORK

Suspension of work clauses state that the owner has the right to suspend or delay the work. Such clauses usually provide that the owner allow for adjustment in price or time that is required to complete the work. Thus, under such clauses the owner can, in a sense, acknowledge a delay caused by him and provide compensation by a change order under the terms of the contract, thereby eliminating the need to invoke contract dispute procedures. The length of allowable suspension or delay may be limited by a contract provision.

For example, the Engineers Joint Contract Documents Committee clause states:

"The owner may at any time and without cause suspend the work or any portion thereof for a period of not more than ninety days by notice in writing to the contractor and the engineer that will fix the date for resumption of the work. The contractor will be allowed an increase in the contract price or an extension of the contract time, or both, directly attributable to any suspension if he makes a claim therefor."

The federal government form 23A contains a suspension clause that states:

"The contracting officer may order the contractor in writing to suspend, delay, or interrupt all or any part of the work for such period of time as he may determine to be appropriate for the convenience of the government."

The clause continues:

"If the performance of all or any part of the work is, for an unreasonable period of time, delayed, suspended or interrupted, . . . an adjustment will be made for any increase in the cost of performance of this contract (excluding profit) and the contract will be modified accordingly."

The government form does not define "reasonable," but states that if the owner does not specify a time duration for the suspension, then the adjustment may be considered after that period of time deemed "reasonable." The clause also disallows profit as part of any adjustment made for suspensions ordered by the owner.

The contractor must submit a claim for the costs owing to the suspension "as soon as practicable after the termination of such suspension, delay or interruption, but not later than the date of final payment under the contract."

The EJCDC suspension of working phrasing refers the parties back to Articles 11 and 12, which outline the procedures under which adjustments of cost and time may be made.

If we refer back to categories of delay noted at the beginning of this chapter, a suspension would be an excusable, compensable delay. Under the federal government form 23A wording, adjustment of price or time cannot be made if performance during that period of time (the owner's suspension) would have been "so suspended, delayed or interrupted" through other causes, including fault or negligence of the contractor. In other words, this reasoning is similar to that governing concurrent delays. A contractor cannot ask for adjustment of time or money during a suspension if he causes another delay at the same time that would also prevent work being performed.

All contracts do not include suspension of work clauses. As we have said, the inclusion of such clauses provide an administrative remedy for owner-caused delays and the means by which the contractor can recover by change order rather than by claim. In the absence of such clauses, the contractor would discuss the delay with the contracting officer, and if an agreement is not forthcoming, he would have to pursue recovery through the disputes clause.

RESERVATIONS OF CLAIMS

Many owners in granting time extensions or costs for owner-caused delay or suspension require the contractor to waive any further damages attributable to the items covered in the change order.

Unless impact has been specifically considered and included in the negotiation, the contractor may wish to put a reservation clause in change orders, stating that the orders cover the direct time and costs of the changed work, but do not include any impact or ripple costs, or further extension of time. These are to be "reserved until such time as they can be finally ascertained." It is recommended, though, that parties price out (i.e., forward price) the impact costs as part of the change order wherever possible. (See examples of change orders in Chapter 3.)

FLOAT TIME

Float time often becomes an item of contention when any kind of delay occurs on a project. For example, let us say that two work tasks, A and B, must be completed before task C can begin. Suppose that task A takes two months and that task B takes one month to complete. Generally speaking, the contractor considers that the extra month, defined as "float-time," is his to dispose of. He may begin tasks A and B together and then take workers from task B off to another portion of the project during that month.

Or he may find it convenient to continue work elsewhere and then bring in the necessary workers for task B, one month after task A has begun, assuming they will finish simultaneously and that task C can then commence.

However, suppose the contractor takes the second choice, and during that second month when workers are assigned to task B, there is an unavoidable strike. Task C will not begin on time. If the contractor had begun tasks A and B at the same time, and pursued them both continuously to completion, he would have avoided delay caused by the strike during the second month. (The strike affects only the task B workers; for example, they may be electricians.)

Is the contractor the cause of the delay because he did not prosecute the work diligently? Or is the strike considered an excusable delay warranting a time extension? The latter decision would assume that the contractor is free to schedule float time as he sees fit. Generally speaking, float time should be deemed to "belong" to the contractor, so in the instance described, he would be entitled to a time extension. The reasoning is that the method of running the project is usually up to the contractor, who also defines the critical path. However, some contract clauses specifically state the contrary, i.e., that float time belongs to the owner or that it can be shared.

CHARTING JOB PROGRESS

Up to this point, we have discussed various types of delays. A most important aspect of this subject is record-keeping. The means by which delays are noted and documented depend on the job schedule chart. Such charts may be of several types, and are sometimes specified in the contract documents. They range from simple bar charts to elaborate schedules incorporating computer printouts of job progress.

Here is an example of a contract provision, quoted in part, used for the Fort McHenry Tunnel in Baltimore, Maryland. We are not suggesting that this is unique; it is only an example of provisions governing progress schedules. In practice, such provisions are not always followed or enforced.

"A Progress Schedule

1. General.
a. The contractor shall prepare and maintain a detailed progress schedule. This schedule shall be the contractor's working schedule and shall be used to plan, organize and execute the work; record and report actual performance and progress; and forecast remaining work.

The schedule shall be prepared in the form of an activity-oriented detailed network diagram. The principles and definitions of the terms herein shall be as set forth in the Associated General Contractors of America, Inc. Manual, *CPM in Construction*. In the event of discrepancies, this section shall govern the development and utilization of the progress schedule.
b. The detailed network diagram shall be supported by computer-produced diagnostic reports, a Manpower Requirement Forecast, and a cash inflow projection, as specified herein."

The provision goes on to include precise instruction as to how to construct the diagram:

"The following criteria shall be used to form the basis for the logic: (1) what must be completed before an activity can be started; (2) what can be done concurrently; (3) what must be started immediately following an activity; and (4) what major economic, facility, or manpower restrictions are required for sequencing."

Another item in the provision calls for the diagram to be prepared on "22-inch by 36-inch sheets with a title and revision block in the lower right hand corner." It goes on to say that the diagram

". . . shall clearly distinguish any contractually required and other significant intermediate milestone dates, the contract completion dates, and the predicted status dates for these items. The network shall show a continuous flow from left to right. The current primary and secondary paths of criticality on the network shall be clearly and prominently identified."

The contract also includes dates for submittal of the diagram. It goes on to state that:

"the contractor will participate in a conference with the engineer to appraise and evaluate the proposed schedule at intervals. Any revisions necessary as a result must be inserted within 15 days of the conference. Monthly progress status reports will be submitted to the engineer, in the form of updated computer printouts and narrative reports.

At the request of the engineer, the contractor is to participate in pre-update conferences to verify progress and review modifications to the detailed network schedule prior to the formal monthly submittal.

A revised detailed network diagram and supporting analysis data shall be submitted when one or more of the following conditions occur:

1) when a change or delay significantly affects any special intermediate milestone dates or completion dates or the sequence of activities.

2) when the contractor elects to change any sequence of activities affecting the critical path or to significantly change the previously approved work plan.

3) When, in the opinion of the engineer, the status of the work is such that the detailed network diagram and supporting analysis are no longer representative for planning and evaluating the work."

The Baltimore specifications also provide for changes, delays, and time extensions by stating applicable sections in the general provisions in the following manner:

"a. When proposed changes are initiated or delays are experienced, the contractor shall submit to the engineer a written time-impact analysis illustrating the influence of each change or delay on any specified milestone dates and completion dates. Each time-impact analysis shall demonstrate how the contractor proposes to incorporate the change or delay into the detailed progress schedule. Submission of justification shall be based on revised activity logic and durations in addition to such other supporting evidence as the engineer shall deem necessary. The event times used in the analysis shall be those included in the latest update of the detailed progress schedule or as adjusted by mutual agreement. Each time-impact analysis shall be submitted in five copies and within 30 days after a delay occurs or notice or direction is given to the contractor.

The engineer will, within a reasonable time after receipt of such justification and supporting evidence, review the facts and advise the contractor in writing thereof. Upon agreement by both parties, the influence of changes and delays will be incorporated into the detailed progress schedule at the next monthly update."

The Baltimore provisions also allow for situations in which the contractor and the engineer cannot agree on the duration of time extensions. In such cases, the parties can insert an interim figure, which is not binding on either party, until the engineer has made a final determination of the time extensions duration.

Float time is also mentioned in the Baltimore provisions:

"It is understood and agreed that schedule float time is not for the exclusive use of either (party). Extensions of time for performance under any and all of the provisions of this contract will be granted only to the extent that the equitable time adjustments for the affected activities exceed the total float along the channels involved at the time the delay occurred or notification was issued for the change."

DOCUMENTING DELAYS

To sum up, many contracts will be specific about the type of progress schedule required on the job and the procedures for submittal, updating, and revision. Others, of course, may not. There are several types of charts commonly used for indicating the progress of the work.

Bar Charts. These are the most simple visual presentation of work and time. A bar chart separates the work into categories, with the intended starting date for each activity, the duration, and the intended completion date for each.

CPMs and Network Diagrams. The critical path method (CPM) as the name indicates, shows the interrelationship of the portions of the work. In other words, portion B of the work cannot begin until portion A is completed. Portion Q can't begin until portions M,N,O and P are completed. A delay on any one of these lines impacts the others.

S-Curves. An S-curve represents project progress: slow at the start, a subsequent pickup of momentum, then a tailing off at the end. The actual S-curve can be plotted from the information on the monthly payment requisitions. The horizontal distance between the intended S-curve and the actual S-curve represents how far the job is off schedule at any point in time. The S-curve represents dollars spent to time.

Sometimes a job is so complex that a CPM is a virtual spiderweb. The intended S-curve can be drawn from the information on the bar chart and the trade payment breakdown. The intended S-curve can give some rough idea of progress, it is not as accurate as the CPM, but is more accessible. The case history at the end of this chapter include illustrations of S-curves and other progress schedules. In more sophisticated cases, the S-curve is prepared by a computer from the CPM and the payment input.

SCHEDULE APPROVAL

When delays and subsequent claims occur, parties will look to the schedule for a reference point. It is absolutely imperative that these schedules be understood and used properly. CPMs and other progress charts are like motherhood. More people respect the idea than pay actual attention to the individuals. Here are some points worth remembering about CPMs and other visual representations of project work.

1. Most contracts require that some sort of progress schedule be kept, but are not necessarily clear on the checking-off or approval process. What legal significance does the owner's checkoff of a progress schedule carry? Typically, when a lawsuit occurs, the owner looks at the schedule and says that the contractor could never have built the job in the manner indicated. The contractor's rejoinder is likely to be that the owner "accepted" the schedule.

Both parties should look carefully at the progress charts, and they should understand what the contract says. Some owners "acknowledge" receipt of the schedule without approving it in order to attempt to avoid responsibility for acceptance. There is no hard and fast rule about the legal significance of a schedule. If the owner has the contractual duty to accept the chart, then he has the duty to state his objections if he has them.

If the contractor submits his schedule for approval and the owner does express his objections, then the schedule should be revised and resubmitted before the issue becomes moot over the passage of time.

If the schedule is submitted for approval, parties should not regard that approval as a casual matter.

2. The critical path itself may shift during the course of the work due to change orders, delays, or other variations in the progress of the work. Unless the schedule is updated to reflect the variations, the original schedule will be of little value in the completion of the work.

3. When the critical path changes, the rationale should be recorded. Sometimes when cases reach the courts years after the fact, the CPM shows that the path shifted, but parties no longer recall why.

4. The owner may choose to keep his own CPM or other progress schedule. This might not be shown until a dispute arises, so the contractor should be aware that there may be a progress schedule being checked by the owner.

5. Progress schedules can be mounted defensively. Either side can construct a chart after the fact, purporting to show that its position is correct. Thus, it is advisable to require periodic checkoffs. A "new" schedule can't materialize overnight when both parties are regularly checking off and revising the schedule as a mutual effort.

6. There are scheduling consultants who can be called in to analyze these charts when disputes arise, or to give advice during the course of the work. In very complex projects, it is a good idea to utilize the services of these consultants.

7. Any CPM or network diagram is only as good as the logic used to set up the critical paths. These charts should not be regarded as scripture. They can be changed and revised as the job progresses to give the clearest possible picture of what has happened on the job, and why.

8. When disputes reach the courtroom, a more succinct summary of job progress would probably be in order. It would be unlikely that parties walk through every intricacy of a vast CPM network. This is another good reason to use a scheduling consultant if a courtroom appearance is necessary. That consultant should be able to condense the CPM into an effective summary.

CASE HISTORY

The following hypothetical situation is an extended case history showing how a tangle of overlapping delays can be analyzed. It was originally a chapter that appeared in *Construction Contracts*, published by the Practising Law Institute. It is reprinted here with their permission. While this section is addressed to attorneys, it is not technical, and the analysis and examples are useful to all parties in the construction process.

In this chapter we will deal with how to analyze construction delays. We will consider only the interval of time from the moment the client enters the attorney's office until the claim is prepared for submission to the owner or the complaint is drawn.

The client tells the following story: he had a $700,000, thirteen-month contract to construct a five-story, steel-frame office building. Completion was delayed five months; he lost $250,000 and, to add insult to injury, the owner assessed him $9,000 liquidated damages ($100 per day for three months) plus actual damages of $10,000 representing loss of rentals in the building.

The client lost two months as a result of a change in design from closed-end pipe piles to large diameter step-taper piles. One month was lost due to the architect's delay in approving shop drawings; two months due to a roofing workers' strike and one month as a result of working during the wintertime. The owner ordered the client to accelerate the interior finishing work by working nights and weekends, enabling him to make up one month's delay.

The client wants to know whether he has a case. How much can he collect from the owner and does he have to pay any liquidated damages?

What does the attorney do to answer the client's questions? Several steps should be followed. The first step is to assemble the mass of papers that have survived the construction of the project. (An enumeration of records is omitted; these include, for example, daily reports, payment requisitions, progress schedules, and so forth.)

The second step in analyzing the client's problem is to understand the job thoroughly. The attorney should barrage the client with questions about how the job was actually constructed. He should ask to see the plans, have them explained to him and examine all the available photographs of the job. The attorney should continue to ask the client questions about the job until satisfied that he understands it thoroughly.

The third step in analyzing the client's problems is to read the contract documents, particularly the agreement and general conditions. Usually, a completion date is specified, or a period of completion in consecutive calendar days from the date of a notice-to-proceed from the owner. The contract usually states that time is of the essence. There is often a contract clause that sets forth liquidated damages for each day's delay in completion. There is often a clause setting forth justifiable causes for which the owner will give an extension of contract time. This clause is often coupled with a clause which states that an extension of contract time is the contractor's sole remedy for delay and that in no event will the owner be liable for damages. The legal effect of such a provision will be discussed later.

TYPES OF DELAYS

There are two main categories of delay—nonexcusable delays and excusable delays. Nonexcusable delays are generally specified as those that are the contractor's fault, such as his failure to coordinate his subcontractors, his failure to submit shop drawings on time, the necessity of remedying defective work, and his failure to furnish a sufficient number of workmen.

Excusable delays are generally those that are not the contractor's fault. They fall into two major subcategories: compensable and noncompensable delays.

Compensable delays are those for which the contractor is entitled to claim damages from the owner. These are generally delays caused by fault of the owner, such as his failure to turn over the site on time, suspensions ordered in the performance of the work, defective plans, and the failure to approve shop drawings on time.

Noncompensable delays are generally those which are deemed to be no one's fault, such as strikes, fire, and acts of God.

The two major issues that arise in the excusable delay context are delays caused by weather and delays caused by subcontractors and vendors.

Weather Delays

Some time extension clauses are silent as to weather delays. They merely contain a general category of delays caused through no fault of the contractor. Other time extension clauses limit excusable weather delays to those caused by unusually severe or extraordinary weather delays conditions. These would usually have to be proved by reference to meteorological records that show the weather encountered during a particular interval was more severe than that experienced during the preceding five or ten years. In the absence of such an express limitation, it is an open question whether the contractor should be entitled to an extension of time for ordinary weather delays.

Subcontractor Delays

The second major excusable delay issue is delay caused by subcontractor or vendor default. A contractor will contend that if he exercised good judgment in selecting a reputable supplier or vendor, he should not be charged for delays caused by their default or failure to deliver on time because he had no effective control over them. Many time extension clauses restrict a general contractor's excusable delay on account of subcontractors' delays to those causes which themselves would constitute excusable delay for the general contractor. The contractor's argument for excusability has been advanced more strongly in sole-source-of-supply cases where the owner specifically designated the vendor of a particular item. There, the contractor argues that he had no choice in selecting a vendor, and that by restricting his choice, the owner in effect, warranted and represented that the supplier would deliver on time. The authorities are divided on this point.

Concurrent Delays

Another problem in dealing with time extension clauses involves concurrent delays. Concurrent delays are two delays occurring at the same time, such as, both a strike and a failure to submit shop drawings on time. Where an excusable and a nonexcusable delay are concurrent, the contractor ought to be entitled to an extension of contract time. However, there are contract clauses to the contrary, that state that a time extension will be granted only where both concurrent delays are excusable. In the case of concurrent compensable and noncompensable delays, the contractor ought to be entitled to an extension of contract time but no delay damages.

PREPARING CHARTS AND GRAPHS

The next step in evaluating a client's delay problems is to organize and assemble the facts presented. A most expeditious way is to prepare a number of charts and graphs.

Chart #1—Bar Chart—Intended Schedule

Bar Chart #1 shows the contractor's intended schedule for performing the work. This is known as a bar chart, which divides the work into its major elements or activities.

Chart #1 is greatly simplified. It divides the work into only five major activities: the foundation, structural steel, masonry, roof, and interior work. Adjacent to each activity is a bar representing the intended starting date, the duration, and the intended completion date. Ordinarily, in practice, a bar chart for a project of the scope set forth in the hypothetical example (i.e., a $700,000 five-story, steel-frame office building) would contain anywhere between 20 and 40 separate activities. The problem or weakness with a simple bar chart is that it does not show the interrelationship of the various activities nor the logic behind the contractor's intended performance nor the percentage of completion at any given time.

Chart #2—CPM Progress Schedule—Intended Schedule

From such a simple bar chart one is not able to ascertain which activities are independent of others and which activities are dependent for their start or completion upon the start or completion of other items. This information can best be represented on another type of progress chart, known as a CPM (Critical Path Method) schedule. Chart #2 shows the same construction activities as Chart #1, but laid out in somewhat different manner. Each activity has the same duration; however, the interdependence of the activities is shown. For example, the structural steel is shown to start only upon the completion of the foundation work. Then the chart splits into two segments. The masonry work can be performed at the same time as the roofing work. However, the masonry work takes three months to perform whereas the roofing work takes only two months. It is then shown that the interior finishing work cannot proceed until

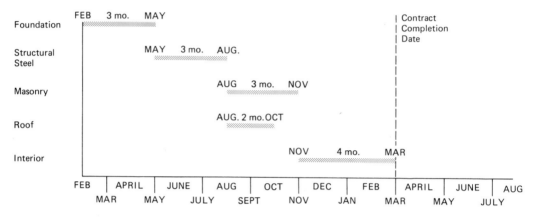

5 STORY STEEL OFFICE BUILDING
$700,000 – 13 mo. contract

Bar Chart – Progress Schedule
Intended Progress

Chart #1.

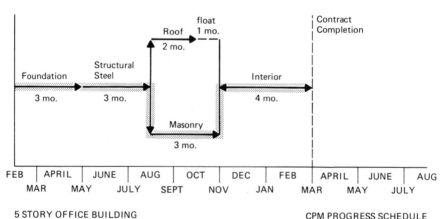

5 STORY OFFICE BUILDING
$700,000 – 13 mo. contract

CPM PROGRESS SCHEDULE
Intended Progress

Chart #2.

the completion of both the roof and the masonry work. The one month excess time on the path of the roofing work is known as "float time." This means that although the roofing work is shown to start at the same time as the masonry work, in fact, the roofing work could start one month later without and delay in the completion of the entire project.

The ▧▧▧▶ line represents the critical path through the project which, by definition, means that the prolongation of any single activity along the critical path will prolong the completion of the entire project. The roofing work is not on the critical path because of the one month of "float time."

Chart #3—Bar Chart—Actual Progress

The following chart requires a meeting with the client and use of his records. Chart #3 is prepared and superimposed upon Chart #1 indicating the periods when the various construction activities were actually performed. This information is often obtainable from the contractor's progress payment requisitions, which indicate the percentage of work completed for each such activity during each month of the job. Information regarding the dates of actual performance can also be obtained from the foreman's time card, the superintendent's daily reports, the correspondence, the job meeting minutes, and the photographs.

An explanation is then requested from the client for each delay, prolongation of work, or change in sequence of the work. For example, we see on Chart #3, that although the foundation work was scheduled to begin February 1, it did not commence until March 1. The client then recalls that there was a strike at the outset of the job which prevented the start of foundation work for one month. Then we see that the foundation work proceeded for one month during March and then was suspended for one month in April. The client says that this suspension was ordered by the owner after it became apparent that the specified closed-end pipe piles were being driven much deeper than anticipated. The architect took one month to conduct these tests to redesign the work. We then see that the work was resumed in May and proceeded three months until completion in August. This indicates that the aggregate time for performance of the foundation work was four months rather than the three months intended. Your client explains that the driving of the large diameter step-taper piles proceeded more slowly than the closed-end pipe piles as a result of the different pile driving equipment required to be used.

We then see that the structural steel work did not begin until September, one month after the completion of the foundation work, although it was originally scheduled to have begun immediately upon completion of the foundation work. The client explains that while he submitted structural steel shop drawings at the time required, the owner's architect unreasonably delayed approving them, thereby preventing the start of the structural steel work until September. We see that the structural steel work was performed in a duration of three months, as it was originally scheduled to be performed.

We next see that upon completion of the structural steel work, the masonry work commenced immediately, but had a duration of four months rather than the three months originally scheduled. Your client explains that the additional month of performance time was caused by the work being pushed into the winter months. Originally, the masonry work was to be performed from August to November, during good weather. However, it actually had to be performed in the middle of the winter which resulted in one month's lost time. We next see that the roofing work, while originally scheduled to begin at the same time as the masonry work, did not begin until one month later. Your client explains that, as originally scheduled, there was one month of float time, which he decided to take advantage of because he knew that the masonry work would be prolonged during the winter. However, after proceeding for a month, the roofing work was suspended for two months during February and March. Your client explains that there was an industry-wide roofers' strike, which prevented the performance of any work during this period. Thereafter, we see that the roofing work took two months to complete from April to June, a total performance time of three months, whereas only two months was originally scheduled. Your client explains that defects were found in the roofing work by the architect which took your client approximately one month to repair.

You then see that the interior work started in May and was completed in a duration of three months rather than the four months scheduled. Your client explains that in May the owner demanded that your client accelerate performance by working evenings and weekends in order to complete the project as quickly as possible and that one month's time was made up by performing the work in this manner.

Chart #4—CPM Progress Schedule—Actual Progress

Your next step in analyzing your client's claim requires you to insist that he prove each and every delay to you from the available records rather than rely upon his memory. Some clients have a tendency to accentuate the positive and eliminate the negative. Time dulls memories, especially unpleasant memories. As noted previously, it is apparent that your client has forgotten or neglected to tell you several relevant facts regarding the case, such as the initial one-month delay caused by the strike. Now you must use the records in order to test the validity of each of his contentions.

This is best done with the aid of another form of CPM progress schedule. Actual progress is laid out in a ▨▨▨▨ line, in much the same format as was the original CPM schedule. The original critical path and critical path activity duration, is indicated by the ▭▭▭ line. The ▬▬▬ line represents the actual critical path through the job. It is significant to note that whereas, as originally scheduled, the critical path went through the masonry work, now the critical path shifts and goes through the path of the roofing work. It is also noted that the critical path is not through the entire roofing work, but only a portion of it. The ▭▭▭ line and the ▨▨▨▨ line represents delays. A ▭▭▭ line represents a total suspension of work. A ▨▨▨ line represents a delay that occurs over an interval of time. For example, the one-month prolongation of the masonry work occurred during the four-month interval from December to April.

Using Records to Verify Delays

In reviewing your client's records you find that the one-month intial strike is substantiated. You next find that, in fact, the architect did order a one-month suspension in the foundation work and that the foundation work did, in fact, take one month longer to perform using the different equipment required for the step-tapered piles. This is ascertained by comparing the production records of the closed-end pipe piles for the month of March, prior to the suspension, with the pile driving records from May through August.

You then find that the one-month steel shop drawings delay is not properly attributable to the owner, but, rather, was your client's fault, albeit unbeknownst to him. You find that your client's steel erection subcontractor did, in fact, submit shop drawings on time. These were promptly reviewed by the architect and returned to the subcontractor for correction because they contained substantial errors. The subcontractor then delayed in correcting the errors and the architect finally approved the revised shop drawings promptly after resubmission to him. This information is ascertained both from an examination of the shop drawing log maintained by your client and a close examination of the shop drawings themselves.

Frequently, architects use the vehicle of shop drawings to effect substantial design changes. It is therefore necessary to examine carefully each comment and correction made by the architect on the shop drawings to determine whether he is merely correcting errors made by the contractor or whether he is, in effect, redesigning the work.

You then see that the one-month delay in starting the roofing work was simply a matter of your client's exercise of choice not to commence the roofing work until that time. However, he did not know that there would be a roofers' strike which, in fact, delayed the roofing work for two months. Thereafter it took two months to complete the roofing work, of which, one month was due to repairs required by the architect because of defects in the workmanship—the fault of the client. However, it is noted that the repair of the defects did not prevent the interior finishing work from commencing, i.e., the repairs did not fall on the critical path.

Your client's records indicate that in fact he did work overtime and weekends and that the one month shortening of the intended four-month interval for interior work was directly attributable to that overtime work.

Deciding on Excusability and Compensability

Consider whether each of the delays was excusable or nonexcusable and, if excusable, whether it was compensable or noncompensable. The one-month initial strike is excusable but noncompensable. The one-month suspension due to a redesign of the foundation is both excusable and compensable. The one-

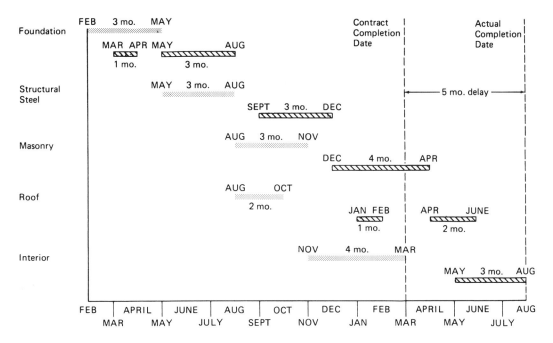

5 STORY STEEL OFFICE BUILDING
$700,000 − 13 mo. contract

Bar Chart − Progress Schedule
Intended vs. Actual Progress

Chart #3.

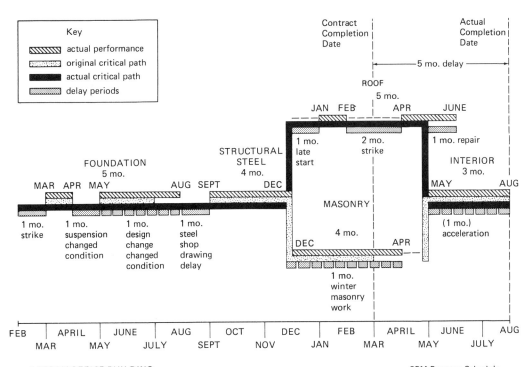

5 STORY OFFICE BUILDING
$700,000 − 13 mo. contract

CPM Progress Schedule
Intended vs. Actual Progress

Chart #4.

month prolongation of the foundation work directly attributable to the change in design would also be both excusable and compensable.

Change Orders

Here, however, it is important to note that your client's records must be examined carefully to find out whether he waived any further rights to compensation on account of the change in design. Frequently, in granting change orders, an owner requires the contractor to waive any further costs attributable to the work encompassed by the change order and specifies a total extension of time that will be allowed for the change. Since the ultimate effect on final completion of the entire job often cannot be determined at the time the changed work is being performed, it is advisable for contractors to execute change orders with a reservation clause. This clause should state that the change order is for the direct cost of the changed work, and, and does not include any impact costs or extension of contract time, which are specifically reserved until such time as they can be finally ascertained.

The one-month steel shop drawing delay is nonexcusable.

Analyzing Concurrent Delay Effects

Now you come to the split paths of masonry/roofing work. These include concurrent delays and the analysis is a rather complicated one.

Start with the masonry path. The one-month prolongation of the masonry work as a result of the necessity of performance in the winter would ordinarily be inexcusable, since, in our case, the winter was an ordinary one, not an unusually severe one. However, in our case, there were three preceding months of excusable delay. If your client had started masonry work three months earlier, in September, it would have been completed prior to the onset of winter. Therefore, the masonry delay, considered alone, ought to be excusable. There were, however, only two months of precedent compensable delay. (See the earlier discussion concerning when delay is excusable, compensable, nonexcusable or noncompensable.) If he had started the masonry work two months earlier, in October, the work would have been performed in two months of good weather and one month, December, of winter weather. In such event the masonry would undoubtedly have been prolonged for a period less than the one month it was actually prolonged. Therefore, considered alone, before analysis of the concurrent roof delays, there would be somewhat less than one month of compensable delay for the masonry work, even though the entire one month delay is excusable.

Next, we consider the delays in the roofing work. The initial one-month late start of the roofing work by your client's choice raises the issue: Who owns the float time? While this has not been raised in many cases, the prevailing view is that the contractor owns the float time. The two-month delay in the roofing work, therefore, ought to be excusable. However, if there was precedent inexcusable delay attributable to your client, pushing him into the strike, the strike ought then to be inexcusable. In the same way, if there was precedent compensable delay which pushed the contractor into the roofing strike period, the time of duration of the roofing strike ought to be both excusable and compensable. Here we find that there were three months of precedent excusable delay. Had the roofing work been started three months earlier, the strike would have been avoided. Here, also, we find that there were two months of precedent compensable delay. Had the roofing work been started two months earlier, it would have been completed before the roofing strike. Therefore the roofing strike delay should be both excusable and compensable, when considered in the absence of the concurrent masonry delay.

In considering the masonry path and the roofing path, we find that there was an aggregate delay of two months along these paths. There were two months of excusable delay in the roofing path and one month of excusable delay in the masonry path, with the remaining month in the masonry path being float time. The net result should thus be two months of excusable delay.

In the masonry path, there was somewhat less than one month of compensable delay and there were two months of compensable delay in the roofing path. Therefore, the aggregate of these concurrent delays would be something less than one month of compensable delay. (See above discussion of concurrent delays.)

DETERMINING RESPONSIBILITY FOR DELAY DAMAGES

Now you are in a position to answer the questions posed by your client. Was the order to accelerate a valid one? Yes. As of May, when the order was given, there was a six-month delay, only five of which were excusable. Therefore, the owner was entitled to demand that your client make up the one-month of nonexcusable delay by accelerating performance.

If the order were not a proper one, the owner would be liable in damages for the overtime wages paid your client's employees plus the loss of productivity attributable to the increased number of hours per day and the increased number of days per week that the employees worked. Studies have shown that men working under these conditions are less productive than when working a normal week.

May Contractor Recover Damages From Owner?

Is your client entitled to recover any damages from the owner? In spite of the contract clause stating that the contractor's sole remedy is an extension of contract time, it has been held in New York and elsewhere that such a clause is not enforceable and that an owner will be liable in damages for the unreasonable delays he causes. The delay resulting from the change in foundation design aggregated something less than four months—two months while the foundation work was being performed and then some period less than two months during the concurrent performance of the masonry and roofing work. Your client is entitled to recover mobilization and demobilization costs and equipment standby rental values attributable to the one-month suspension while the architect redesigned the work. He is entitled to labor and material escalation costs attributable to the prolongation of the work.

He is entitled to recover the loss of productivity, aggregating something less than one month's delay, during the masonry work. This is best computed by comparing actual records of masonry work performed in early December, before the winter conditions set in, with the work performed during the winter conditions. If this is not possible, other methods which may be used include a comparison of the actual cost of the masonry work with the reasonably estimated cost of the work, or the application of productivity reduction factors from studies that have been conducted in the industry. The client is also entitled to recover any additional costs of winter protection of the masonry work.

The client is entitled to be compensated for the extended period costs of something less than four months. This would include extended superintendence and supervision, trucking, vehicles and equipment, insurance, miscellaneous field expenses such as telephone, light, shanty, and an allocable proportion of central office overhead for the extended period.

Assessing Liquidated Damages

The next question is whether the owner was entitled to assess liquidated damages for three months. No liquidated damages were properly assessable because the aggregated delay was five months and there were five months of excusable delay.

In the absence of excusable delay, liquidated damages will generally be enforced, as the owner's sole remedy, if they are found to be "reasonable and not a penalty." The sum specified as liquidated damages must be found to be reasonably related to the damages the owner might expect to incur as of the date that he entered into the contract. In the event that the liquidated damages are deemed to be a penalty, the owner may only collect the actual damages he can prove.

The owner is not entitled, in most jurisdictions, to collect both liquidated damages and actual damages. Therefore, if the nature of the project is such that the owner's damage could be easily computed, it would probably be better for an owner not to include a liquidated damages clause. Excluding the clause would permit the owner to collect all of his actual damage in the event of inexcusable delay in completion. If, however, delay damage is not easily computable, such as damage that would occur to a school district from delayed completion of a school, or damage that would accrue to a congregation from delay in completion of a church, it would be advisable to insert reasonable liquidated damages into a construction contract.

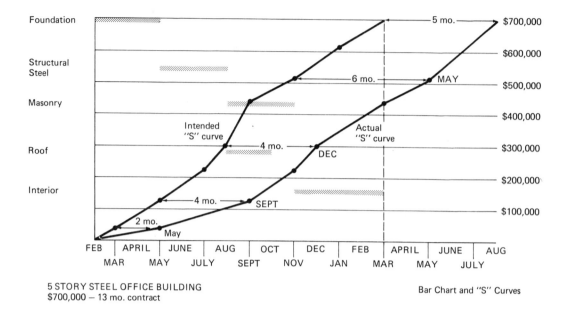

5 STORY STEEL OFFICE BUILDING
$700,000 – 13 mo. contract

Bar Chart and "S" Curves

Chart #5.

Chart #5—Bar Chart With "S" Curve

As you can see, even with the use of an oversimplified example, the CPM method of analysis can get quite complicated. In the example chosen, the analysis of the concurrent roof and masonry delay, in light of precedent delays, was exceptionally complicated. One can imagine that if some 50 different activities had to be charted, rather than five, each with different periods and causes of delay, a CPM analysis could become impracticable. Therefore, another method of analysis is often used. This is represented by Chart #5 and includes the super-imposition of an "S" curve over the contractor's intended bar-chart schedule, Chart #1. It should be noted that on the right-hand side of Chart #5 the contract price is plotted in intervals of $100,000. It is possible to compute the amount of money that would be earned per month if the job had proceeded on schedule (from the intended bar chart and the trade payment breakdown). This is represented by the line at the left hand side of Chart #5 labeled Intended "S" Curve. One might think that this ought to be a straight line. However, experience has proven that construction projects often begin somewhat slowly, pick up their rate of progress during the middle of the job, and then tail off towards the end. Thus, the resulting curve is in the shape of an "S." The actual payments made to the contractor each month can be plotted against this curve. Care should be taken however, to exclude change order work from the payments, so that the comparison is valid. Then, at any point along the actual "S" curve, the horizontal distance between the actual curve and the intended curve will indicate the duration that the job is behind schedule at that date.

Chart #5 indicates that, as of May, the job was behind schedule two months: in May, at the time of the owner's order to accelerate the work, the job was six months behind schedule, confirming our prior CPM analysis. "S" curves are helpful in ascertaining whether the job is behind schedule for purposes of termination of contract and orders to accelerate the work. They are also helpful to explain delays in a simplified manner when a CPM analysis is not practicable.

CONCLUSION

There are several conclusions that can be drawn from our discussion. First, the importance of using actual records to analyze delays cannot be overemphasized.

Second, the validity of a CPM analysis is entirely depedent upon the validity of the assumptions made. It is like a deck of cards. If one assumption is proved incorrect, then the entire analysis may collapse. For example, in our hypothetical case, if, in fact, the interior work could be started independent of the completion of the roofing work, the entire analysis and result would be changed. It is important, therefore, in most substantial cases, to retain an outside expert consultant to evaluate the assumptions of the critical path logic to ascertain whether or not they are correct.

5. Contractor's Costs of Delays

Once the contractor decides that he has a legitimate claim for costs due to owner-caused delays, he must next quantify these. The owner, for his part, should be knowledgeable about costs for which he might be liable and about the amounts that are justifiable. If parties disagree about these amounts, they may have to defend their positions in a formal disputes resolution proceeding. Therefore it is important for both to have accurate records and accurate calculations.

Costs can be approached in two ways: (1) actual costs; and (2) estimated costs. With actual costs the contractor keeps records as the work progresses. Depending on the complexity of the situation and the level of communication between the parties, an agreement may be reached as these costs accrue on the job. There is, however, a basic flaw in this approach. The contractor frequently has no reason to be efficient during such an operation, and thus the costs may be greater than they might otherwise have been.

However, estimated costs are subject to question, too. The logic on which the estimates are based may be in error. There are many ways to estimate the costs; none may be actually incorrect, but disputes can arise over which is the most accurate or acceptable.

There are some areas in which it is common practice to accept a formula-based cost calculation. The Eichleay formula, which will be discussed in more detail later in this chapter, is widely used to allocate overhead costs. The AGC manuals and other similar books are used to calculate the cost of contractor-owned equipment on the site. Sometimes contracts contain clauses that specify how costs attributable to delay are to be computed.

TYPICAL DELAY-CAUSED COSTS

Costs that may increase due to a delay on the project may be many. They can include direct labor costs and costs related to labor, such as social security, unemployment taxes, union benefits, compensation, and other insurances. Other costs could include materials, tools and supplies, equipment, fuel and repairs on equipment, subcontracting costs, bonds, the cost of capital, and the main office, district and job-site office overhead.

The following are examples of how some of these costs can increase: standby costs; extended job supervision; extended field expenses; extended equipment costs; increased labor costs due to moving into a period of higher labor rates; and increased costs of labor and materials owing to moving the work into winter months.

The list above includes items that are usually recoverable. Among the items that are almost never recoverable are attorney's fees. There are a very few states that allow recovery for those fees; otherwise, they are rarely recoverable. The federal government has recently changed position on this issue, but it only allows attorney's fees in very limited circumstances. However, as always, there may be a contract clause that specifically allows recovery.

Reduced ability to take on other profitable work is another item that is rarely ground for recoverable damages. The contractor would have to prove that he was offered other work that was precluded because of the delay on the project in question, and what is more, he would have to prove that the other work would have been profitable. Such claims are generally considered too speculative to be valid.

Contractors sometimes request compensation for the cost of the claim preparation. This, too, is frequently not granted. Those preparing the claim do not typically keep time records, for one thing. In cases in which recovery was granted for the cost of claim preparation, the argument has been that the cost was due to the contract requirement regarding the submission of claims. In other words, the cost was a result of the contract wording. Finally, there have been claims based on the devaluation of money during an inflationary period. Any recovery in current dollars is worth less than the dollars the contractor originally laid out, the argument goes, and therefore should be increased to reflect inflation. As far as we know, there has not been a decision favoring such reasoning, although at current inflation rates, it certainly is a real damage.

ALLOWABLE COSTS

The following list are costs that are commonly allowed. The amount and the method of estimating that amount may be questioned, however. Here are some points to bear in mind when calculating these costs:

1. Main Office Overhead.   This includes every cost involved in operating an office: building rent; depreciation (if owned); depreciation on equipment such as a computer; lights; heat; telephone; stationery; and payroll costs with their add-ons such as taxes, insurance, and benefits. Most contractors keep such office overhead records for tax purposes, and these can be used to allocate costs due to the delay. If we are talking about a major project, particularly if it is a joint-venture, there will be a full staff at the job site that handles the project with little input from the main office for daily overseeing of the project. In such cases, the main office overhead of each partner may come out of the job profit, or the joint-venturers will have previously agreed on a lump-sum payment to each main office on a monthly basis or a project basis.

In other cases, where the project receives sizable input and supervision from the main office, including payment of invoices, cost accounting, and payroll, a main office cost will be assigned to the project as either a fixed sum or a percentage of the work performed.

For claims purposes, the Eichleay Formula is commonly used to apportion overhead costs to a particular project. This formula was used in a 1960 Armed Services Board of Contract Appeals decision, Eichleay Corp. 60-2 BCA ¶2688, and has been widely accepted. Overall central office overhead is allocated on the basis of the ratio of the dollar amount of the contract in dispute to all other contracts billed during the same period of time. Therefore, an "extra," any additional work, should carry the same percentage markup for home office overhead as the original contract carries. The rationale is that central office overhead is a necessary expense of doing business. To put it another way, the contractor's office is a "benefit conferred" on the owner. For instance, estimators, purchasing departments, data processing equipment, and the like are all part of job expenses.

Like many formulas, the Eichleay Formula is an oversimplification and cannot be applied indiscriminately. Another theory for allocating home office overhead is this: only an increase in home office overhead *directly traceable to the change* should be allowed. That is, if a contractor can demonstrate that his home office overhead escalated as a result of the change, then the increase is an allowable expense of the change. The following variables illustrate how difficult a task it is to determine what home office overhead would or would not have been without the change: variations in dollar volume or work; variations in complexity of work, in type of work, and in form of contracts and risks related thereto, variation in location of the work, in the management capability, and in escalation, and state-of-the-art.

When the contractor has the burden of proof, which is usually the case, he uses historical records adjusted for the factors listed above, and any other factors applicable, to attempt to measure the amount of the increased office overhead. The Eichleay Formula and similar formulas have won wide acceptance because of the problems of quantifying the actual increased office overhead costs and of proving that they were attributable to the change.

A determination must be made as to the involvement of the main office in the project and whether the main office is used strictly for bidding new work and/or maintaining corporate headquarters. In some cases, one job that is actually a small part of the contractor's total billed work may be the cause of disproportionate overhead costs. These costs might be due to more secretaries typing letters, more accounting, etc. because of delays and disputes on that one job. In such a case, the Eichleay formula would not reflect true overhead costs for delays on that one job.

It should be noted that formulas akin to the Eichleay Formula have been rejected in some courts, and accepted in others. For example, a 1978 New York decision held that the Eichleay Formula could not be applied, and that in order to use any formula, proof would have to be given that the chosen formula was a reasonable measure of the actual damage sustained by the contractor. Calculating "actual" damage is not easy. One approach would be to carefully analyze the effect of the underlying impact problems caused by the delays. The contractor may have had to write more letters, hold more meetings, prepare more shop drawings, etc. It should be clear that allocating the time spent by the contractor's employees and proving that some of that time was directly attributable to the delay can be a formidable and costly effort.

So while most jurisdictions will accept the Eichleay or other similar formulas as fair assessments of central office overhead, a contractor should check to make sure that this is the case. Any such formula should be applied with some common sense. Excessive claims for office expenses are sure to be questioned. On the owner's side, he should recognize that central office overhead is itself a legitimate expense. The amount claimed and the method by which a figure is derived may be questioned, however.

2. Intermediate Office Overhead. Some contractors might claim intermediate or field office overhead expenses owing to the delay. These can be valid if the contractor is large enough to maintain regional offices, for example, those that oversee several projects. Similarly, overhead expenses may accrue at the job site, or field office. Supervisory and other overhead staff including the project manager, office manager, accountants, time-keepers, the master mechanics, and drivers of pick-up trucks and other vehicles not directly connected with a work item may be considered as overhead. Also the cost of site buildings, light, heat, telephone, water, sewage disposal, office supplies, watchmen, maintenance of haul roads, and other such facilities and items can be charged to job overhead.

Obviously, the Eichleay or other such formulas would not apply unless the intermediate office is used for more than one project. If the office is overseeing only one project, then the contractor has to show that his office overhead was increased as a result of the delay. As we have shown, it is difficult to show how the extra work did or did not increase overhead. It is common practice to allow job overhead on the same percentage basis as historical records show for other contract work.

3. Labor costs. The actual labor costs can generally be computed by using payroll records to show what was paid during the period of time in question. However, when a delay is involved, the problem consists of showing the increased cost of performing the work due to the delay. This is more complex. The contractor must prove the actual cost and also prove what the work would have cost if there had been no delay. Escalation of labor costs may be relatively easy to prove; for example, a new union contract may have been signed as the result of a strike settlement.

4. Loss of productivity. Loss of efficiency or productivity (the two terms are used interchangeably) can be more difficult to document. Either term can be used to apply to numerous situations where the work takes longer to perform or must be performed in a different manner. These can be situations where work is forced into adverse weather, or where there is a change in the sequence of work, or where the work is repeatedly stopped and started.

Additional costs from such situations can arise as a result of the loss of actual worker productivity, such as that due to fatigue from working overtime. Losses due to shift changes, time lost in getting one crew in and another one out, and time lost in explaining the work and training new personnel are all possible items under the heading of loss of productivity. Time lost in explaining and training is often referred to as impact on the "learning curve."

Excessive numbers of workers in an area can contribute to lowered productivity. So can the performance of more than one operation in the same area. These situations can arise as a result of delay, or from acceleration, or from a change of sequence in the work owing to delay, or from numerous changes to the work.

A contractor can prepare charts to demonstrate what the job would have cost in man-hours had there not been a delay. These can be compared to a chart that shows what the actual costs of the delay were. Such a comparison can be convincing and is sometimes accepted as proof of loss of efficiency. Recovery for inefficiency as a percentage of actual costs has been obtained in the wide range of between 5% and 50% of the actual labor costs paid to the contractor during the delay period.

There are also published figures based on industry statistics that are used for loss of productivity. These should be used with caution. One should attempt to be certain that the conditions under which these data were assembled are similar to those in one's claim.

Expert witnesses can be used to prove the contractor's argument as to increased costs arising from the loss of efficiency. There are also cost consultants who specialize in analyzing cost data. Sometimes a large owner has the in-house staff to make judgments of losses due to inefficiency on a percentage basis. The actual increased costs, however, often cannot be tracked with any real accuracy.

A problem with the percentage calculations is that there are plausible arguments against their use. One is that the contractor could have estimated this job incorrectly. Another is that the conditions on the job in question differed from the assumed conditions on which the statistics were based.

So, to sum up, in most jurisdictions, recovery is allowable for loss of productivity or efficiency due to owner-caused delays, interferences, and acceleration. Determining the proper amount of recovery, however, can be difficult.

5. Insurance and Bonding.   Fringe benefits and payroll-associated insurance costs are relatively simple once the labor costs have been agreed on. These costs are based on the billings to the contractor from the insurance carrier and are easily proven by audit.

Property insurance, insurance for theft, fire, flood, etc., is time-linked. If the job is delayed through compensable delay, the contractor can ask the owner to pick up the premium after the contract time has expired. Liability insurance is also part of the increased costs; such insurance is based on the labor force on the job.

If the claim results in an increase to the amount payable to the contractor, there will be an additional bond payable. Again, proof is readily available in the bond agreement between the contractor and the bonding company. While the percentage will undoubtedly be small, in the range of 1% to 1 ½%, it is a legitimate part of the claim for extra costs to the contractor. There may also be specialized insurance necessary and the additional costs for these may be part of the claim. For example, water-borne equipment may be involved for the portion of the work affected by the delay and thus marine insurance may have to be extended.

6. Materials.   A delay can affect the cost of materials. The most obvious effect would be escalation of prices due to the delay. The price may also be increased due to shortages that would not have been encountered were it not for the delay or because additional materials were needed owing to the delay.

In the case of acceleration, costs of materials could be higher because of a delivery earlier than that originally required, or from a different supplier. This idea can also apply to a delay that stems from a change in the sequence of the work. Some materials that might have been used later in one sequence, might need to be used earlier in the changed order of work. There can be a premium for buying and/or delivering materials in smaller quantities than those originally planned. For example, a contractor may purchase water pumps to dewater a site. Because of a delay, he must buy new pumps because the original pumps wear out before the original work can be completed. The smaller number of new pumps cost more than the larger number of the original purchase (per pump).

Unusual transportation costs owing to the changed sequence of work can be included in the claim, too. Tight scheduling of deliveries may add to transportation delivery costs.

7. Equipment.   If the equipment used on the job has been rented from an independent source, records of bills paid will ordinarily suffice as proof of the cost of such equipment. Difficulties could arise if the renter had committed the equipment elsewhere at the completion of the agreed-on rental period. Other equipment might have to be located for the delayed portion of the work at an increased rental cost. However, in either case, paid invoices should suffice as proof, provided the arrangement is with an outside rental company as opposed to a wholly contractor-owned equipment subsidiary.

It is rare in rental equipment disputes for expert witnesses to be retained. Paid invoices or the industry standard rental publications rates are usually accepted (See Appendix for examples of commonly used and accepted equipment value guides).Federal agencies sometimes have their own rates stated in the contract. Occasionally, when a contractor and owner cannot agree on the value of equipment in order to calculate a daily expense rate, an expert might be called in.

If the contractor owns the equipment, the situation is quite a bit more complicated. Some jurisdictions will accept a rental value as set forth in standard trade books such as the so-called "green book" or "blue book" rates, or a percentage of such rates. Sometimes, the contract includes a specific rate for equipment rental and mentions one of those manuals by name. Rates should be specified if the project requires the use of specialized or unusual equipment. (See Appendix, items 4a and b.)

Other jurisdictions will allow recovery on a computed ownership expense basis, such as the Associated General Contractors method, which takes into account factors such as age, initial cost, useful life, operating hours, and maintenance and repair costs for each piece of equipment. Still other jurisdictions limit recovery to added operating expense, unless the contractor can prove that the equipment could have been used elsewhere if the delay had not occurred.

In some cases, the contractor owns a separate equipment owning/leasing company and uses this company to bill the job for the leasing of equipment. Generally, this equipment will be considered as being owned directly by the contractor.

Another complication that can arise from a dispute over contractor-owned equipment involves the theory of "benefit conferred." The contractor confers certain benefits on the owner by making the equipment available to the owner for an extended period of time. The equipment represents a sizable capital investment by the contractor.

Suppose, for example, a fully-depreciated, specialized, and costly piece of equipment owned by a contractor sat on a job six months longer than anticipated and that this was due to an owner-caused delay and that the owner wished to reimburse the contractor for out-of-pocket expenses only. The contractor would claim that he was entitled to a fair and reasonable rental for the period. The equipment was there for the owner's benefit, whether he used it or not.

Suppose the contractor had no other use for the specialized equipment during those six months, and it could not have been rented to others. The contractor could still seek to assert a claim on the ground that he was providing something of great value to the owner. The fact that the owner did not actually use the equipment and that the contractor could not have gained other income from the equipment ought not to make a difference. The owner had the benefit of the equipment; the fact that he could not take advantage of it was due to his own delay.

Establishing the actual value of equipment related to delay is difficult, and reimbursement of the out-of-pocket direct expenses may not be fair compensation for the contractor. Thus, the benefit conferred theory of compensating for these costs is preferred. Another example is apt. An owner, operating under the damages, or actual expenses theory might seek to diminish the amount of recovery because the equipment had been paid off. It had been completely depreciated, and therefore, in the eyes of the owner, the contractor should be entitled to less compensation. What the owner ignores in such situations is that despite the fact that the equipment was completely depreciated, it has value and is usable by the contractor for the benefit of the owner.

A final note on equipment costs as related to delays: this category need not be limited to major and costly equipment. Lesser items such as tools would also be recoverable if their use is related to the delay.

8. Interest Expenses. Interest on claims is recoverable depending on local statutes and on the contract language. In jurisdictions where interest expenses are allowable, the rate is usually well below the market rate. The date after which such interest accrues is often well after the date the added expense was first incurred. For example, in the state of Pennsylvania, no interest on a delay claim is recoverable prior to judgment, and thereafter only at a rate of 6%. In claims against the City of New York, interest starts to run when the increased costs are incurred, but only at the rate of 3%.

The federal government under the Contract Disputes Act of 1978, allows recovery based on the interest rate that is set every six months by the Secretary of the Treasury, starting from the date when the claim was formally presented to the contracting officer and certified by the contractor as to its validity. That rate varies, but has always been below market rates. In some cases, as we have noted, such low interest rates act as a disincentive for an owner to settle expeditiously. If an owner had to pay 20% interest on any money due a contractor, he would undoubtedly be more anxious than when the rate is 3–6%. However, the point here is that interest can be allowable. Parties should check the contract and the local applicable statutes or other relevant law to see what the rate and starting date (for the interest to begin running) should be.

Sometimes a contractor has to borrow money to finance added costs imposed on him by the owner's delay. If he can prove that he had to borrow this money, some courts have allowed recovery of the added actual interest expense. Proving that the contractor was actually forced to borrow that money for a special claim item can take considerable effort, which may provide unavailing in the end.

9. Profit on the Amount Claimed. Profit on delays may be difficult to recover depending on whether the delay is considered to be pursuant to the changes clause or a suspension of work clause. In Federal Form 23A, profit is specifically excluded on a suspension of work. However, if the contractor is not clearly suspended by the owner, it can be argued persuasively by the contractor that profit is allowable because the delay is really a change pursuant to the changes clause, wherein profit is rightfully a part of the equitable adjustment. Common practice varies widely depending on the form of contract, the owner, and the forum of litigation.

Finally, if a project is large and complex, it would be wise to retain a cost consultant to help prepare and document a claim for delays. The contractor should be familiar with the applicable law before setting his staff or computer to work to calculate his damages and costs. There may be several ways to calculate different items. Different jurisdictions may allow some items and not others.

The law as to recoverable damages changes constantly. It makes sense for a contractor and his staff to include all reasonable, legitimate and provable items of damage in a claim. The law or a decision in a similar case may change during the litigation period. Unreasonable or extraordinary claims are never recommended. They tend to discredit the validity of the entire claim, and may result in an onerous decision.

What follows here are two sample cost calculations for a claim, which should help illustrate many of the points made in this chapter. The first involves changed conditions; the second is a claim for costs due to acceleration.

SAMPLE CLAIM AND CALCULATIONS/CHANGED CONDITIONS

Rock Differing Site Conditions, Reach Two

During the early days of an excavation, it was found that the location and amount of rock within the limits of the trench cut were not as predicted based upon the geological data available. The contractor gave notice that the unexpected rock was considered to be a differing site condition for which additional time and money was due by serial letter #72, dated May 22, 1979.

During the bidding process, the geologic data were quantified into cost of excavation for Reach Two. To enable quantification, certain assumptive extrapolations from the exploration logs had to be made. These assumptions were based on the contractor's understanding of the geology of the area as described in the specifications.

The geologic descriptions state that some of the bucket auger holes encountered caliche and/or limestone layers which they could not penetrate.

The overall picture of the materials to be excavated was that they would be generally unconsolidated, soft and granular, with occasional caliche layers which would be hard and difficult to penetrate with an auger. This meant that most of the material would be easy to excavate and that the only excavation difficulties would be with the layers of caliche and limestone which would classify as rock. Estimating effort was therefore concentrated on predicting how much of such rock would be encountered. This meant that the contractor would have to use "site specific" exploration data and extrapolate from there.

The main source of information for determining the expected amounts and locations of rock at bid time was the logs of augered holes taken in the vicinity of the pipe line. In total, there were 70 explorations made along Reach Two, 28 of which were made with a 24″ bucket auger, 40 with a 6″ flight auger and two which were core drilled. The bucket augered holes, in most cases, would not penetrate the rock layers; therefore, their most significant contribution in regard to information pertaining to the rock was to indicate the depth at which it could be expected. The 6″ flight augered holes usually penetrated the rock layers, and therefore the thickness of the rock layers was known. The combination of the two sources provided what the contractor believed to be a reasonable basis from which to estimate the thickness at points of auger refusal.

The horizontal extent of the layers of rock was extrapolated from the boring data provided in the vicinity. In some instances, the layers could be predicted to extend from borehole to borehole. In other instances, it was obvious that the rock layer terminated between auger holes. In these cases, the horizontal extent was estimated, based upon the thickness of the layer, the distance to other auger holes, and the breadth of other similar layers whose extent was more accurately determinable. Based upon these extrapolations, it was estimated that 25,000 cy of rock would be found in the trench.

The contractor's extrapolation of the horizontal extent of the rock layers at bid time was we believe, reasonable and logical, considering the origin of the sediments. As indicated by the specifications, the sediments were very lenticular and discontinuous, with localized lenses of caliche and limestone. This fits with the fact that the sediments were laid down by braided streams flowing from the higher areas down into the valley basin. Their routes of flow were wandering and rates of flow were highly variable. This produced channels of more pervious sediments heterogeneously interlayered and irregular in trend, and each channel became buried by some later deposition. The more previous lenses produced in this manner tended to hold mineral saturated groundwater for long periods of time and more frequently than the surrounding, less pervious sediments. This produced the carbonates and sulfates which subsequently precipitated and formed the concentrated cementing agent that created caliche lenses. The limestone layers were the product of localized ponding and precipitation of carbonates in quiet water ponds and lakes. All of this resulted in rock lenses of variable length and direction.

The location of the material in the trench had a significant bearing upon the excavation production. When there was one layer of rock in the trench above invert, it could usually be excavated with the Cat 245 backhoe without severely slowing the production. However, when the layer was a thick one, greater than two feet, the productivity was greatly reduced because it usually required the use of the pumpkin ball to break up the rock so that the backhoe could remove it from the trench. When the rock layer was in the invert of the trench, it was extremely hard to excavate because it could no longer be undercut to allow easy breakage with the pumpkin ball. Therefore, the rock had to be worn down to grade by backhoe, pumpkin ball, tractor and dozer, hoe-ram, drilling and blasting, pavement breakers, or a combination of the above. Other combinations of the above conditions had combined effects on the productivity.

In the actual case, there were two major differences encountered relative to the rock. The first case was in the quantity, where a total of 85,000 cy was actually encountered. This represents about three and a half times the quantity which could have been reasonably anticipated. This excessive overrun in quantity demonstrated that the conditions encountered differed materially from that expected. The second major difference was the location of the material within the limits of the trench excavation. There were two instances where the rock layers were indicated to be above the invert and were found to be in the invert. Similarly, an area where one layer of rock was indicated sometimes contained two or more layers. However, in some cases the condition actually improved from that which was expected.

The production rates for the actual conditions encountered contained the usual every-day occurrences such as utility interferences, setting trench jacks, and so on. However, for those occasions when unusual or prolonged delays occurred, such as broken water line, floods, relocating past tunnels, crossing intersection, and major repairs, the data had been excluded from the production rate development so as not to distort or overlap costs charged elsewhere, and to be able to exclude noncompensable costs, as well.

An excavation production analysis showing the historical production rates achieved for the various conditions encountered is included for review and use in evaluating this proposal. Application of the data included in this analysis yields a performance time of 3565 hours for the expected conditions and 4507 hours for the actual conditions for a net extra of 942 crew-hours. For the two-crew setup employed, this represents 471 job-hours, 59 workdays and 83 calendar days.

A summary of the increased costs resulting from the extended performance period and some typical examples of calculations of these costs are included in the following sections.

COST SUMMARY

	LABOR	EQUIPMENT	SUPPLIES	TOTAL
Extended Operations	$534,071	$350,340	$118,744	$1,003,155
Cost Escalation	57,005		42,770	99,775
Consultants' Expense			11,101	11,101
Subcontractor Costs			79,455	79,455
Backfill Costs			132,408	132,408
SUBTOTAL	$591,076	$350,340	$384,478	$1,325,894
Overhead @ 61.3% of Labor				362,330
SUBTOTAL				$1,688,224
Profit @ 10%				168,822
SUBTOTAL				$1,857,046
Home Office Expense @ 5.16%				95,824
SUBTOTAL				$1,952,870
Additional Bond @ $5.09/1000				9,940
SUBTOTAL				$1,962,810
Less Reimbursed Labor Escalation*				(102,523)
TOTAL				$1,860,287

*Contract provides for escalation on labor including changes. Therefore, previous payments are a credit to the change order.

EXTENDED OPERATIONS

	LABOR	EQUIPMENT	SUPPLIES	TOTAL
Steel Pipe Crew				
Nov. 9, 1979 to June 30, 1980				
Labor $596.40 × 380 Hrs.	$226,632			
Equipment $386.92 × 380 Hrs.		$147,030		
Supplies $132.86 × 380 Hrs.			$ 50,487	
July 1, 1980 to Sept. 4, 1980				
Labor $645.31 × 76 Hrs.	$ 49,044			
Equipment $386.92 × 76 Hrs.		$ 29,406		
Supplies $146.07 × 76 Hrs.			$ 11,101	
Second Shift Crew				
May 14, 1980 to June 30, 1980				
Labor $252.88 × 46 Hrs.	$ 11,632			
Equipment $264.25 × 46 Hrs.		$ 12,156		
Supplies $50.21 × 46 Hrs.			$ 2,310	
July 1, 1980 to August 13, 1980				
Labor $272.13 × 9 Hrs.	$ 2,449			
Equipment $264.25 × 9 Hrs.		$ 2,378		
Supplies $55.41 × 9 Hrs.			$ 499	
RCP Crew				
January, 1979 to June 30, 1979				
Labor $530.44 × 69 Hrs.	$ 36,600			
Equipment $363.86 × 69 Hrs.		$ 25,106		
Supplies $116.70 × 69 Hrs.			$ 8,052	
July 1, 1979 to Sept. 25, 1979				
Labor $562.91 × 72 Hrs.	$ 40,530			
Equipment $363.86 × 72 Hrs.		$ 26,198		
Supplies $125.46 × 72 Hrs.			$ 9,033	
Sept. 26, 1979 to Mar. 27, 1980				
Labor $562.91 × 297 Hrs.	$167,184			
Equipment $363.86 × 297 Hrs.		$108,066		
Supplies $125.46 × 297 Hrs.			$ 37,262	
TOTAL	$534,071	$350,340	$118,744	$1,003,155

CREW HOURS
SUMMARY

	CREW HOURS RQ'D W/O EXCESSIVE ROCK	CREW HOURS RQ'D WITH CHANGED CONDITION (ROCK)	ADDITIONAL CREW HOURS
Steel Pipe			
Nov. 9, 1979 to June 30, 1980	1,420	1,840	420
July 1, 1980 to Sept. 4, 1980	939	1,023	84
SUBTOTAL STEEL	2,359	2,863	504
January, 1979 to June 30, 1979	179	248	69
July 1, 1979 to Sept. 25, 1979	328	400	72
Sept. 26, 1979 to Mar. 27, 1980	699	996	297
SUBTOTAL RCP	1,206	1,644	438
PROJECT TOTAL	3,565	4,507	942

CALCULATION OF SECOND SHIFT EXCAVATION CREW HOURS

A second shift excavation crew was worked between May 14 and August 13, 1980. A total of 63 second shifts were worked during this period with a production of approximately 20,600 cy of excavation for the steel pipe. This excavation quantity represents 9.6% of the total steel pipe excavation.

The additional steel pipe crew hours shown above are therefore adjusted as follows:

	CREW HOURS	FACTOR	2ND SHIFT WORK HOURS	2ND SHIFT PAY HOURS	FULL CREW HOURS
11-9-79 to 6-30-80	420	9.6%	$40 \times 8/7$	$= 46$	380
6-1-80 to 9-04-80	84	9.6%	$8 \times 8/7$	$= 9$	76
TOTAL	504	9.6%	$48 \times 8/7$	$= 55$	456

SUMMARY
EXCAVATION PRODUCTION

CLASS CODE	DESCRIPTION	WORK DAYS	HOURS	QUANTITY CY	PRODUCTION CYH
1	Wet Ground/Sheet Pile Area			9,680	N/A
2	Misc. Disruptions			48,569	N/A
3	Common Exc.	52	416	47,589	114
4	Caliche in Invert	92	736	39,623	54
5	Caliche in Trench < 2'	69	552	54,256	98
6	Caliche in Trench > 2'	131	1,048	90,564	86
7	Caliche Inv. & 1 Layer < 2'	40	320	15,072	47
8	Caliche Inv. & 1 Layer > 2'	59	472	21,686	46
9	Caliche 2 or more Layers in Trench	55	440	38,598	88
	TOTAL	N/A	N/A	365,637	N/A

N/A → Not available

PRODUCTION SUMMARY
EAST HEADING

SHEET NO.	CASE 1 WD	CASE 1 CY	CASE 2 WD	CASE 2 CY	CASE 3 WD	CASE 3 CY	CASE 4 WD	CASE 4 CY	CASE 5 WD	CASE 5 CY	CASE 6 WD	CASE 6 CY	CASE 7 WD	CASE 7 CY	CASE 8 WD	CASE 8 CY	CASE 9 WD	CASE 9 CY
1	7	1,258																
2	22	4,433																
3	21	278																
4	19	1,607																
5	23	782																
6	20	1,322																
7	3	0	17	8,360	3	3,238												
8	5	0	17	8,112														
9			9	5,317	11	9,586	3	1,489										
10			2	506	5	4,334			7	6,113	5	3,975						
11			5	2,211														
12			6	4,165			3	978			9	2,159	1	546				
13					3	2,413			3	2,194	10	6,236					3	1,552
14					2	1,553	1	330	3	2,312	9	5,913					8	5,344
15			3	797							8	6,445			7	3,266	3	2,120
16			1	394	1	1,077	1	518	3	2,325	6	3,912			4	2,157	7	4,044
17			2	946														
18					1	1,443	7	3,621			7	3,879	3	1,463	5	1,920	2	1,209
19							8+2	3,652			5+2	3,944	7+7	5,094			1	1,009
20							1	552	6	5,536	11	9,066					2	1,290
21			1	-0-	5	4,744	6	4,441	1	1,135	3	3,436	3	912				
22									12	7,465	18	12,019	1	742	7	352		
23							2	962			5	3,648					7	4,497
EAST TOTAL	120	9,680	63	30,808	31	28,388	34	16,543	35	27,080	98	64,632	22	8,757	23	7,695	33	21,065

PRODUCTION SUMMARY
WEST HEADING

SHEET NO.	CASE 1 WD	CASE 1 CY	CASE 2 WD	CASE 2 CY	CASE 3 WD	CASE 3 CY	CASE 4 WD	CASE 4 CY	CASE 5 WD	CASE 5 CY	CASE 6 WD	CASE 6 CY	CASE 7 WD	CASE 7 CY	CASE 8 WD	CASE 8 CY	CASE 9 WD	CASE 9 CY
1			2	532														
2			4	0			3	1,102					5	796	8	851		
3			1	0			3	1,342	1	1,050			12	5,463	4	1,117		
4			3	0			13	6,272	2	1,344	4	1,987						
5			5	1,126	1	1,065	13	5,892			4	1,674						
6			16	2,200	3	2,725	2	1,163										
7			10	4,903	5	4,668	2	1,748	3	1,828								
8			5	4,156	6	5,474	1	762	7	6,647	2	1,814			2	1,231		
9			4	0			15	3,513										
10							6	1,286	2	1,637	2	1,757			5	578	8	6,657
11					1	935					1	599	1	56	13	7,408	3	2,423
12					1	1,067			1	857	14	12,743			3	2,806		
13			6	1,682					5	5,200	4	3,531					8	6,556
14			11	2,653	4	3,267			3	2,339							3	1,897
15			7	509					10	6,274	2	1,827						
WEST TOTAL	—	—	74	17,761	21	19,201	58	23,080	34	27,176	33	25,932	18	6,315	35	13,991	22	17,533
EAST TOTAL	120	9,680	63	30,808	31	28,388	34	16,543	35	27,080	98	64,632	22	8,757	23	7,695	33	21,065
JOB TOTAL	120	9,680	137	48,569	52	47,589	92	39,623	69	54,256	131	90,564	40	15,072	58	21,686	55	38,598

85

STEEL PIPE CREW HOURS WITHOUT EXCESSIVE ROCK
What Should Have Been (typical reach)

BEGINNING STA	END STA	LENGTH	AVG WIDTH	AVG CUT	CY	CLASS NO	CY/HR	CREW HOURS BY CLASS							
								3	4	5	6	7	8	9	TOTAL
9-25-79 To 6-30-80															
1008+24	1009+70	146	11.6	20.3	1,273	3	114	11							
1009+70	1010+70	100	11.8	22.2	970	5	98			9					
1010+70	1020+75	1,005	11.9	21.6	9,125	3	114	85							
1020+75	1022+75	200	11.9	21.5	1,895	4	54		35						
1022+75	1033+00	1,025	11.7	21.8	9,683	3	114	85							
1033+00	1036+50	350	11.5	18.1	2,698	6	86				31				
1036+50	1048+50	1,200	11.7	14.2	7,394	3	114	65							
1048+50	1051+50	300	11.6	17.5	2,256	6	86				26				
1051+50	1061+50	1,000	11.9	16.1	7,096	3	114	62							
1061+50	1064+50	300	12.0	16.9	3,004	6	86								
1064+50	1075+00	1,050	12.4	16.0	7,716	3	114	68							
1075+00	1078+00	300	12.3	14.8	2,023	6	86				24				
1078+00	1094+00	1,600	12.4	16.5	12,124	3	114	106							
1094+00	1095+10	110	14.4	21.3	1,250	6	86				15				

	Station	Length			Volume								
Tunnel													
1096+14	1118+00	2,186	17.7	18.9	19,433	9	88						221
1118+00	1122+88	488	11.8	19.6	4,180	6	86					49	
1164+10	1171+00	690	12.0	15.2	4,661	3	114	41					
1171+00	1173+00	200	12.1	16.3	1,464	9	88						17
1173+00	1175+50	250	11.9	16.8	1,851	3	114	16					
1175+50	1177+00	150	11.8	17.0	1,114	9	88						
1177+00	1181+00	400	11.6	16.4	2,818	3	114	25					13
1181+00	1183+00	200	11.5	15.7	1,337	5	98			14			
1183+00	1194+00	1,100	11.7	19.0	9,057	3	114	79					
1194+00	1197+00	300	11.4	15.9	2,014	5	98			21			
1197+00	1202+22	522	11.5	16.8	3,735	4	54		69				
Tunnel													
1204+14	1211+00	686	12.0	15.0	4,573	4	54		85				
1211+00	1224+90	1,390	11.0	17.5	9,910	6	86					115	
Tunnel													
1228+58	1228+20	38	11.5	21.8	353	3	114	3					
TOTAL								646	189	44	260	251	1,420

STEEL PIPE CREW HOURS REQUIRED WITH CHANGED CONDITION (ROCK)
Actual (typical reach)

NOVEMBER, 1979 TO JUNE 30, 1980

BEGINNING STA	END STA	LENGTH	AVG WIDTH	AVG CUT	CY	CLASS NO	CY/HR	CREW HOURS BY CLASS							TOTAL
								3	4	5	6	7	8	9	
915+50	1008+24	CCN #17 Area													
1008+24	1008+85	61	11.5	19.7	512	4	54		9						
1008+85	1009+45	60	11.7	21.0	546	7	47					12			
1009+45	1009+95	50	11.7	21.5	466	4	54		9						
1009+95	1012+10	215	11.9	22.8	2,159	6	86				25				
1012+10	1012+65	55	12.0	22.8	557	9	88							6	
1012+65	1013+45	80	12.0	22.4	796	5	98			8					
1013+45	1014+50	105	12.0	21.3	995	9	88							11	
1014+50	1016+15	165	11.7	20.0	1,429	6	86				17				
1016+15	1016+94	79	11.8	20.3	701	3	114	6							
1016+94	1017+75	81	12.0	20.6	742	5	98			8					
1017+75	1019+15	140	11.8	20.9	1,281	6	86				15				
1019+15	1020+05	90	12.0	21.2	848	3	114	7							

1020+05	1020+90	85	12.0	21.6	816	6	86			9	
1020+90	1021+80	90	12.0	21.6	864	3	114	8		32	
1021+80	1024+60	280	11.7	22.5	2,710	6	86				24
1024+60	1027+10	250	11.7	22.9	2,483	5	98		25		
1027+10	1029+35	225	11.7	22.0	2,136	9	88			20	
1029+35	1031+30	195	11.5	20.6	1,713	6	86				
1031+30	1033+10	180	11.6	20.1	1,553	3	114	14			8
1033+10	1034+00	90	11.7	18.9	737	9	88				
1034+00	1035+45	145	11.6	17.4	1,083	5	98		11		
1035+45	1037+65	220	12.0	15.9	1,557	9	88				18
1037+65	1039+45	180	11.8	14.7	1,157	6	86			13	
1039+45	1040+00	55	11.5	14.1	330	4	54		6		
1040+00	1040+95	95	11.5	14.1	571	6	86			7	
1042+40	1043+36	96	11.6	13.7	565	9	88				6
1043+36	1055+20	1,184	11.6	15.9	8,105	6	86			94	
1055+20	1055+95	75	11.5	16.2	518	4	54	10			
1055+95	1058+80	285	11.7	15.3	1,895	8	46				41
1058+80	1059+95	115	11.7	16.3	812	6	86			9	

COST ESCALATION DUE TO EXTENDED OPERATIONS
Summary

	LABOR	EQUIPMENT	SUPPLIES	TOTAL
Line Crews	$40,898			
Miscellaneous Crews	16,107			
Supplies			$32,350	
Backfill Material			10,420	
TOTAL	$57,005		$42,770	$99,775

ESCALATION DUE TO EXTENDED OPERATIONS

Line Crews

As a result of the delays described herein, the work force was moved into periods of wage escalation to a greater degree than originally anticipated. The extra costs resulting from this shift are as detailed below:

Hourly Cost	7/1/78 RATE	7/1/79 RATE	INCREASE	7/1/80 RATE	INCREASE
Steel Pipe Crew	$459.57	$492.08	$32.51	$540.99	$48.91
Second Shift Crew		185.96		205.21	19.25
RCP Crew	432.21	464.68	32.47		

Escalation Calculation

	HOURS	RATE	AMOUNT
Steel Pipe Crew			
7/1/78 to 7/1/79	35	$32.51	$ 1,138
7/1/79 to 7/1/80	749	48.91	36,634
Second Shift Crew	46	19.25	886
RCP Crew			
7/1/78 to 7/1/79	69	32.47	2,240
TOTAL			$40,898

MISCELLANEOUS CREWS WAGE ESCALATION

	7/1/78 HOURLY RATE	7/1/79 HOURLY RATE	7/1/80 HOURLY RATE
Laborers 4 Each	$ 56.36	$ 61.40	$ 65.96
Case 580 B/H Operator @ 1/3	6.21	6.50	7.31
Motor Grader Operator	18.75	19.65	22.06
Mechanics 4 Each	75.04	78.60	88.48
Service Truck Operator	18.23	19.13	21.53
Carpenter	17.02	19.84	20.04
Teamster @ 1/2	6.77	7.49	8.07
CREW TOTAL	$198.38	$212.61	$233.45
Hourly Rate Increase	N/A	$ 14.23	$ 20.84

Wage Escalation Calculation

	HOURS	RATE	AMOUNT
7/1/78 to 7/1/79 Rate	35	$14.23	$ 498
7/1/79 to 7/1/80 Rate	749	20.84	15,609
TOTAL			$ 16,107

SUPPLY ESCALATION

Supply Cost — One Year Period Ending March 31, 1979	$352,949
Annual Escalation Rate — 22%	
Annual Escalation Amount	$ 77,649
Delay Period — 5 months	
Delay Escalation	
$77,649 ÷ 12 months = $6,470/month × 5 months =	$ 32,350

Subcontractor Costs

As a result of the extra rock encountered on this project during construction of the steel pipeline, Ajax Welding incurred extra cost for which we request reimbursement. Excavation was slowed by the extra rock quantity which in turn slowed Ajax Welding crew and caused an inefficient operation in the field.

Based on the extent of the rock changed condition defined by a comparison of actual conditions with anticipated conditions, we have calculated a crew delay of 11 weeks. The cost of this delay, slowed production, and inefficiency is as follows:

11 weeks × 40 hours per week = 440 hours	
440 crew hours × $142.75 per hour	$62,810
Overhead, 15%	9,422
Subtotal	72,232
Profit 10%	7,223
TOTAL	$79,455

The following is a tabulation of the hourly crew cost:

GENERAL WELDING CREW COST

Labor

1 — Foreman	$ 24.72/hr.
1 — Welder (D)	23.83/hr.
1 — Welder (S)	23.83/hr.
TOTAL HOURLY LABOR COST	$ 72.38/hr.

Equipment

1 — Pickup	$ 7.20/hr.
1 — Pickup, 1 T	8.73/hr.
1 — Welding Tr., 1 T	14.25/hr.
2 — Fans @ $5.48/hr.	10.96/hr.
3 — Welders 200 A G @ $5.36/hr.	16.08/hr.
1 — Welder 250 A D @ $4.58/hr. × ½	2.29/hr.
TOTAL HOURLY EQUIPMENT COST	$ 59.51/hr.
S T & S @ 15% Labor	10.86/hr.
TOTAL HOURLY LABOR COST	72.38/hr.
TOTAL HOURLY CREW COST	$142.75/hr.

EQUIPMENT RATES

AJAX WELDING

1. Pickup, 1/2 Ton
    (AGC p. 45) $7,500

$$\begin{aligned} \text{Depr.} &= 30\% \\ \text{Tax \& Ins.} &= \underline{\ 3\%} \\ \text{Annual Ownership} &\ \overline{36\%} \end{aligned}$$

    Hourly Ownership = 33% ÷ 1800 =   .0183%
    Hourly Repair & Maintenance Expense = .0310%
    Subtotal   .0493%

    Acquisition Cost = $7,500

    Hourly Ownership, Repair and Maintenance = $3.70/Hr.

    Estimated Operating Expense

Fuel	1.50
Oil and Grease	0.10
Parts and Supplies	0.90
Service Labor	0.75
Tires	0.25

    TOTAL HOURLY COST = $7.20/Hr.

2. Pickup, 1 Ton $9,500

$$\begin{aligned} \text{Depr.} &= 22.5\% \\ \text{Taxes \& Ins.} &= \underline{\ 3\ \%} \end{aligned}$$

    Hourly Ownership + 25.5% ÷ 1250   = 0.0204%
    Hourly Repair & Maintenance Expense = 0.0310%
    Total Ownership, Repair and Maintenance = 0.0514%

    Hourly O R & M = $9,500 Acquisition × .0514% = $4.88/Hr.

    Estimated Operating Expense

Fuel	1.50
Oil and Grease	0.10
Parts and Supplies	1.00
Service Labor	0.75
Tires	0.50

    TOTAL HOURLY COST = $8.73/Hr.

3. Welding Truck $18,000

    Hourly O, R, and M (same as Item 2) = 18,000 × .0514% = $9.25/Hr.

    Estimated Operating Expense

Fuel	2.00
Oil and Grease	0.20
Parts and Supplies	1.20
Service Labor	1.00
Tires	0.60

    TOTAL HOURLY COST = $14.25/Hr.

4. Blower $6,000
   (AGC p. 51)

   Depr.   = 20%
   Taxes & Ins. = 3%
   Total   23%

   Hourly Ownership = 23% ÷ 2000 = 0.0115%
   Hourly Repair & Maintenance   = 0.0081%
   Total   0.0196%

   Hourly O, R & M Cost = 6,000 × .0196% = $1.18/Hr.

   Estimated Operating Expense

Fuel	2.50
Oil and Grease	0.10
Parts and Supplies	0.90
Service Labor	0.75
Tires	0.05

   TOTAL HOURLY COST = $5.48/Hr.

5. Welders, 200 Amp Gas $3,000
   (AGC p. 52)

   Depr.   = 18%
   Taxes & Ins. = 3%
   Total   21%

   Hourly Ownership = 21% ÷ 1400 = 0.0150%
   Hourly Repair & Maintenance   = 0.0588%
   Total O, R & M Rate   0.0738%

   Hourly O, R & M = 3,000 × .0738% = $2.21/Hr.

   Estimated Operating Expense

Fuel	1.80
Oil and Grease	0.10
Parts and Supplies	0.50
Service Labor	0.75

   TOTAL HOURLY RATE = $5.36/Hr.

6. Welder 250 Amp Diesel $4,200
   (AGC p. 52)

   Hourly Ownership   = 0.0150%
   Hourly Repair & Maintenance = 0.0261%
   Total O, R & M Rate   0.0411%

   Hourly O, R & M Rate = $1.73/Hr.

   Estimated Operating Expense

Fuel	1.50
Oil and Grease	0.10
Parts and Supplies	0.50
Service Labor	0.75

   TOTAL HOURLY RATE = $4.58/Hr.

LABOR RATES

AJAX WELDING	FOREMAN	WELDER
Base	$15.96	$15.21
Vacation	1.00	1.00
Health & Welfare	1.18	1.18
Pension	1.25	1.25
Apprenticeship Fund	0.04	0.04
FICA 6.13%	0.98	0.93
SUI 4.8%	0.77	0.73
FUI 0.7%	0.11	0.11
Subsist $19/Day	2.38	2.38
W/C 6.58%	1.05	1.00
TOTAL RATE	$24.72/Hr.	$23.83/Hr.

REIMBURSED LABOR ESCALATION

CREW	HOURS	REIMBURSED HOURLY RATE	REIMBURSED AMOUNT
1) *Steel Pipe Crew*			
Nov. 9 to June 30, 1980	380	$60.76	$ 23,089
July 1 to Sept. 4, 1980	76	$92.58	$ 7,036
2) *Second Shift Crew*			
May 14 to June 30, 1980	46	$26.90	$ 1,237
July 1 to August 13, 1980	9	$39.28	$ 354
3) *RCP Crew*			
Sept. 26, 1979 to Mar. 27, 1980	297	$58.66	$ 17,422
4) *Escalation Section*			
a) Line Crew			
Steel Pipe Crew	749	$36.68	$ 27,473
Second Shift Crew	46	$14.44	$ 664
b) Miscellaneous Crew			
Sept. 26, 1979 to June 30, 1980	69	$17.58	$ 1,213
July 1, 1980 to Nov. 20, 1980	749	$32.09	$ 24,035
TOTAL			$102,523*

*This number is on summary page of cost.

STEEL PIPE CREW (typical)
Reimbursed Labor Escalation
July 1, 1980 through September 4, 1980

DESCRIPTION	#EACH	HOURLY RATE	HOURLY ESCALATION AMOUNT	HOURLY R & S LABOR AMOUNT
Laborers Group 3	13	$3.20	$ 41.60	
Operators	10.3	4.07	41.92	
Operators—HDR	2	4.12	8.24	
Teamsters	3.5	2.79	9.77	
R & S Labor				$104.32
TOTALS			$101.53	$104.32

Field Labor Escalation

$101.53 × 75% Reimbursement $ 76.15

R & S Labor

$104.32 × 21% = $21.91 × 75% Reimbursement $ 16.43

    TOTAL Reimbursed Escalation Per Hour $ 92.58

STEEL PIPE CREW COSTS (typical)
Rates Effective 7/1/78

	LABOR	EQUIPMENT	SUPPLIES	TOTAL
Labor:				
Labor Foreman	$ 14.55			
Laborers 12 @ $14.09	169.08			
Operator Foreman	19.54			
245 Backhoe Operator	18.62			
580 B/H Operator 1/3 @ $18.62	6.21			
Loader Operator 2 @ 18.62	37.24			
Crane Operator	18.76			
Travel-Lift Operator	18.62			
Roller Operator	18.62			
Dozer/Roller Operator	18.62			
Oiler 2 @ 17.40	34.80			
Mechanic 2 @ 18.76	37.52			
Teamsters 3½ @ 13.54	47.39			
SUBTOTAL	$459.57			
Supplies:				
Misc. Supplies @ 27% of Labor			$124.08	

STEEL PIPE CREW COSTS (continued)

	LABOR	EQUIPMENT	SUPPLIES	TOTAL
Equipment:				
Water Truck @ 1/2	$ 2.92	$ 5.51		
Mechanic Truck	1.21	6.43		
Compressor 175 cfm	1.70	6.48		
245 Backhoe	18.25	68.35		
580 Backhoe @ 1/3	2.84	5.18		
966 Loader—2 ea.	12.18	46.12		
LS-98 Crane	7.30	27.05		
Travel-Lift	4.39	31.78		
Roller, Single Drum	10.95	40.83		
Roller, Double Drum	7.30	29.28		
Dozer, D-3	6.09	18.75		
Dump Truck, 3 ea.	29.19	101.16		
TOTAL	$563.89	$386.92	$124.08	$1,074.89

This is a typical breakdown of a crew cost.

SAMPLE CLAIM AND CALCULATIONS/ACCELERATION

Example of Method of Computing Contractor's Claim

Description of Facility. Commercial, light processing plant with some office and retail space. Site and full set of plans and specifications were provided by the owner. The contract was based on Standard Form 23A of the federal government.

The contract provided for a lump-sum bid including grading, parking areas, landscaping, and a structure to be ready for manufacturing and occupancy on completion of the project.

Completion time of construction was set in the contract at 18 months (547 calendar days) from receipt of the owner's notice to proceed.

Actual completion date was 740 days after notice to proceed.

Within 30 days of start of work, the contractor submitted a changed condition request concerning a foundation problem. Within a short period, another such request was submitted for another changed condition. In both cases, the owner agreed to a "direct cost plus overhead" arrangement for the changes but gave no extension of time. As the project progressed, there were a total of 65 change orders issued for such items as:

- differing site conditions
- owners changes
- plan errors and omissions
- delayed review of shop drawings

Of the 65 change orders (COs), it was finally determined that 50 involved extensions of time and that most of the situations giving rise to these COs occurred during the first six months of the project.

Of the 50 COs involving time extensions, only four were issued before the original contract completion date. Another two were issued before the actual completion date.

The remaining 44 were issued after the project was accepted and beneficially occupied by the owner. The actual days of extension granted by the owner were as follows: 35 days were granted during the original contract completion period; five days were granted during the 193 days of time overrun; and 330 days were granted after the job was complete and accepted. Total was 370 days.

The owner, at the end of the first six months of work on the project, issued a letter to the contractor informing him that the contract was behind schedule and directed the contractor to take the necessary steps to put the project back on schedule. In this letter, the contractor was directed to take such steps including:

- additional shifts
- overtime
- longer work weeks
- increased construction plant

The contractor was directed to take these steps at no additional cost to the owner. No mention was made of the pending change orders which involved extension of time.

A similar letter was sent to the contractor by the owner at approximately the twelve-month mark.

In both cases, the contractor formally protested, mentioning the unresolved change orders, but agreed to comply.

At the completion of the project, the contractor filed a claim for:

• inefficiency due to acceleration	$573,197
• increased overhead	119,154
• price increases	
labor	8,200
materials	62,100
sub-contractors	211,000
• finance costs	100,000
• administrative costs 5%	48,682
• profit 15%	146,048
Subtotal	$1,268,381
• bond .5%	6,342
Total Claim	$1,274,723

This was in addition to the amount paid by the owner for the 65 change orders.

Method of Computing Acceleration Costs

Direct Labor. The contractor, based on the first letter from the owner directing him to accelerate, stated that during the first six months, he was in a pre-acceleration period and was working at the normal rate of efficiency for his organization.

The contractor used a standard estimating book to compute labor man-hours. The handbook was one accepted by contractors working in the same locale and performing work of a similar nature. The contractor computed the man-hours required to perform the actual work completed during the first six months of the contract. This work included:

- rough grading
- foundation excavation
- footing excavation
- pile driving
- forming, pouring, stripping pile caps, reinforcing
- forming, pouring, stripping grade beams
- excavating, placing and backfilling drains
- grade, form, pour slab on grade, form, pour, strip columns
- lay brick in walls

In the interest of simplicity, the contractor separated the man-hours into two classifications: skilled labor; and unskilled labor. He computed 15,200 man-hours of skilled labor, and 6,100 man-hours of unskilled labor.

Then using job time cards and other records, covering the same time period and the same work, the contractor found that he had spent 21,700 man-hours of skilled labor and 10,200 man-hours of unskilled labor.

Dividing the handbook man-hours by the actual man-hours expended by the contractor, he arrived at the following:

Skilled Labor $\dfrac{15,200}{21,700} = 70\%$

Unskilled Labor $\dfrac{6,100}{10,200} = 59.8\%$

The contractor states that these percentage figures are his factors of efficiency as compared to the handbook figures for ideal productivity. This is for a period during which the contractor claims that he is working at his normal rate of efficiency.

This process was repeated for the remaining work on the project during the time the contractor stated that he had been accelerating.

From the handbook, the contractor computed 30,100 man-hours of skilled labor, and 21,400 man-hours of unskilled labor as the labor theoretically required to perform the work.

Then, applying the efficiency factors previously computed, he obtains:

Skilled: 30,100 divided by 70% = 43,000 man-hours
Unskilled: 21,400 divided by 59.8% = 35,790 man-hours

The contractor states that this is what it would have taken to complete the project if he were not forced into the inefficiencies of acceleration.

When he went to his time cards and other records for the same period, he found that the project had used 93,150 man-hours of skilled labor, and 54,400 man-hours of unskilled labor.

The difference between the time card figures and the adjusted handbook figures were as follows:

Skilled Labor	Unskilled Labor
93,150 man-hours	54,400 man-hours
43,000 man-hours	35,790 man-hours
50,150 man-hours	18,610 man-hours

The contractor computed his average labor rates for skilled and unskilled labor including all add-ons applicable to labor for insurance, FOAB, union payments, unemployment, and vacation fund (but no labor rate increases). These figures are $9.50 and $5.20, respectively, which are applied as follows:

Skilled   50,150 MH $\times$ $9.50 = $476,425
Unskilled   18,610 MH $\times$ $5.20 =   96,772
                            Total   573,197

This, the contractor states, is the increase in direct labor cost due to the inefficiency of acceleration. (This is the first item on the claim listed earlier in this section.)

Increased Overhead

By audit of his books, the contractor found that during the first six months (pre-acceleration period) his overhead was $350.00 per day based on a seven-day week. This was made up of 31 items, which included: travel expense, postage, utilities, job photographs, overhead salaries, watchmen, and office supplies.

For the original 18-month (547 days) project, his overhead would have been:

$350.00 $\times$ 547 days = $191,450.

By audit of his actual costs for the original 18 months, plus 193 days overrun for a total of 547 days, the contractor found his actual overhead was $621,200.

He subtracts: $621,200
               −   191,450
               $429,750

with the net figure being his increase in overhead due to acceleration and delay.

However, the change orders issued by the owner included overhead costs totaling $310,596. He subtracts:

He subtracts: $429,750
              $-$ 310,596
                 $119,154

The result is the net claim for overhead due to acceleration. (Refer back to the claim on page 97 of this section.)

Price Increases

Labor.   The average labor rates used in previous computations did not include any wage increases. Therefore, this portion of the claim is arrived at by calculating the number of man-hours expended in a later wage period than had been originally contemplated, by the labor escalation, including add-ons, in each such period. This would include labor performed both during the contract period and afterwards to the extent that it was performed in a higher wage period than it should have been, had it not been for the delay.

Material.   This includes the cost of any increase in material costs after original completion date, using audited invoices and previous sales contracts or quotations. If the CPM spot-points the delivery of materials and there was sufficient delay due to change orders or other causes, and material prices increased significantly during the delay, these also are included.

Subcontracts.   Subcontractors compute increased labor and material cost as above, and include overhead and profit.

Finance charges.   These include the cost of financing the additional work due to the change orders, together with delayed payments and cash flow accounts. An audit of the contractor's bank statements should support this.

Administrative Cost.   This refers to main office costs which are applicable to the project and which are based on the main office work load and estimate of involvement in the additional work claimed, or the use of a formula such as the Eichleay Formula.

Profit.   This would be the normal percentage applied by contractors.

Bond.   This is based on terms of the bonding agreement between the contractor and the bonding company.

WORKSHOP PROBLEM: DELAYS, ACCELERATION

The following problem is used as a classroom exercise during the Construction Claims course taught by the authors of this book. The example, involving highway construction, illustrates some principles about delay and acceleration, and is used in the course to elicit discussion. Therefore there are no absolute "right" answers to the questions posed. However, the problems and the solutions offered provide some useful insights and the exercise is a valuable one.

Workshop Problem

THE PROJECT

During the past ten years, the City of Warden had been constructing a six-lane urban highway across the southern portion of the city. Appropriately named Southern Parkway, the remaining segment needed to complete the route which was across a narrow 50'-deep rock gully through which the Jones Falls stream flows.

The project consisted of the folowing:

(1) From Martin Avenue to Garden Drive (see pages 106 and 107).

(2) Project length - Sta. 50+25 to Sta. 59+10 = 885 lf.

(3) Six-lane divided urban highway.

(4) Triple-cell 15'-span × 9'-rise concrete box culvert.

(5) Relocation of a 36" high-pressure water line and construction of a pumping station.

The City of Warden retained the services of a consultant engineering firm to design the project, develop specifications and constructions estimate. The project was to be advertised by the Department of Public Works.

Although short in length, the project required a sequence of operations which must accommodate the temporary relocaton of a major stream and existing 36" high-pressure water line (HPWL) through solid rock, the construction of a triple-cell concrete box culvert and new pumping station for the water line. Since this project was to be advertised in the Spring of 1971, the following completion dates were included in the contracts.

(1) Completion of the temporary relocation of a stream and HPWL. March 10, 1972.

(2) Completion of concrete box culvert and pumping station foundation—December 1, 1972.

(3) Completion of embankment and paving for the highway, and completion and testing of HPWL—December 15, 1972.

(4) Balance of work under contract—June 1, 1974.

The contract contained the following liquidated damages provisions:
(a) For failure to meet the March 10, 1972 date .... $ 200
(b) For failure to meet the December 1, 1972 date   200
(c) For failure to meet the December 15, 1973 date   1,000
(d) For failure to meet the June 1, 1974 date   100

The City of Warden budgeted the necessary funds and proceeded to advertise the contract for public bids on March 1, 1971, with bids to be received on April 14, 1971. Due to problems of coordination with the City of Warden's sewerage bond program, the bid opening was rescheduled for May 14, 1971.

The Gamma Construction Co. was the certified low bidder.

CONSTRUCTION PROGRESS

NOTICE TO PROCEED

Gamma was awarded the contract (using the EJDCC forms) and given Notice to Proceed on August 2, 1971.

CRITICAL PATH METHOD

In accordance with the contract proposal, Gamma submitted its preliminary CPM network schedule to the Department of Public Works on August 7, 1971, (see page 108) within 5 days of the Notice to Proceed.

This was a General Schedule, covering the major items of work, and was to be supplemented within 60 days by a detailed schedule containing at least 200 events.

Department of Public Works reviewed the schedule and returned it to Gamma on August 12, 1971, bearing the stamp, "Reviewed and Accepted."

The engineer, in a transmittal letter, raised certain questions and asked for specifics to be included in the detailed schedule to follow.

CONSTRUCTION OF TEMPORARY RELOCATION OF HPWL AND STREAM

On August 12, Gamma moved drilling and blasting equipment to the site which would be used to construct the temporary relocated HPWL and temporary relocated stream which traversed a rock face. Work commenced on August 12, but was stopped on August 15, because of lack of right-of-way clearance. Although the contract stated all rights-of-way were available, a condemnation case became protracted over a title clearance of a property wherein lay most of the temporary relocation of HPWL and the stream.

The General Schedule submitted by Gamma and accepted by the Department of Public Works, had shown Gamma beginning excavation of both of the temporary relocations August 12, 1971. Although Gamma had proceeded with its mobilization and moved its drilling-blasting equipment on the site, its power shovel, loader, and back dump trucks did not arrive on the site until September 1, 1971.

The City obtained a clear title to the land on October 3, 1971. On October 4, 1971, Gamma was allowed to continue work. Gamma wrote the Department of Public Works informing them of their intentions to make a claim for additional time and damages because of failure of the City to turn over the property for the period of August 15, 1971, thru October 3, 1971.

Gamma's rock excavation proceeded at the rate indicated on the CPM. They were unable to improve on their progress as a result of the limited space within the gully. These conditions precluded adding additional equipment.

The temporary relocation of the HPWL was to be located on a bench cut into the west slope of the relocated stream channel. To maintain the horizontal and vertical alignment of the temporary relocated HPWL, the plans indicated vertical strap anchors every 50 feet and horizontal strap anchors every 100 feet. The straps were to be secured to anchors consisting of holes drilled 6 feet in the rock, filled with grout, in which a #6 bar was embedded. An item of "HPWL Anchors" was provided in the proposal bid on an "each" basis. No delineation was made between vertical and horizontal anchorages.

During the rock excavation, it became evident that the rock was more fractured and not as hard as anticipated. This condition resulted in a design change. Gamma was advised on November 15, 1971, that rock conditions required that "anchors" be placed vertically and horizontally every 25 feet.

Since the contract was a unit price contract, the Department of Public Works proposed to pay for the additional anchors at the existing price for "HPWL anchors". In the letter transmitting drawings to Gamma showing the changes, the Department of Public Works requested the contractor concur with these changes at the existing prices. Gamma did not concur, however, saying that its preliminary examination of the drawings indicated that there were changes which materially increased the unit price of the work. Gamma indicated it intended to submit a claim for added cost when it completed a thorough study.

Gamma's study indicated that the original conditions required twice as many "vertical" as "horizontal" anchors, with the construction operations for a "vertical" anchor not as time consuming as that of a "horizontal" anchor. The change conditions increased both items, however, and there were now as many "horizontal" as "vertical" anchors.

Gamma notified the Department of Public Works that its cost had increased materially, citing the conditions as stated above and requesting a time extension to be determined. The engineer denied the request of added cost, again noting the unit price for "HPWL anchors" and stated that any request for time extension appeared to be without merit.
To expedite operations for the "HPWL anchors", Gamma mobilized two Crane and Drill Rigs and one "Jury Rig," when compared with the initial rig, which was specifically designed for the operation.

The specifications for the contract had set a completion date of March 10, 1972, for the temporary relocation of the HPWL and stream. This completion date was predicted on the requirements of the State's Department of Wildlife Agency, which included a prohibition against working the stream during the trout fish spawning period from March 15, and June 15, of each year.

In December, 1971, Gamma realized that their present schedule of operations must be accelerated in order to meet the March 10, 1972 completion date. In light of the project's delayed start and the design changes for the "HPWL anchors", Gamma instituted a 6-day per week schedule, stretching work day by the use of flood lights. Gamma notified the Department of Public Works on January 2, 1972, of the delays and its added costs of premium time and special lighting equipment required.

This accelerated schedule resulted in the completion of the relocation of the HPWL on February 14, 1972. The HPWL was tested and accepted on February 18, 1972. The relocation of stream was completed on March 8, 1972.

CONSTRUCTION OF THE TRIPLE CELL CONCRETE BOX CULVERT AND PUMPING STATION FOUNDATION

Simultaneously with the construction of the temporary relocation of the HPWL and the stream, Gamma began drilling, blasting and excavation of the alignment of the box culvert and pumping station foundation.

Gamma had submitted its shop drawings for the box culvert to the Department of Public Works on October 10, 1971, in anticipation of approval by October 20, 1971, which would allow a possible 8 weeks of concrete placement, weather permitting.

The engineer advised Gamma of the approval of the shop drawings for the steel fabrication on October 19, 1971. Gamma advised its fabricator to proceed as rapidly as possible, in order that concrete might be placed as soon as possible.

On November 10, 1971, the engineering office of the Department of Public Works advised that a plan error had been discovered in the top slab transverse reinforcing. In an apparent drafting error, the plan indicated #6 bars @8" center to center, when it should have shown #8 bar @6" center to center. This fact was verified by the consultant's design computations.

Gamma had not as yet installed any of the incorrect reinforcing, and immediately advised their fabricator of the error. The fabricator advised that he had completed 10 percent of the top slab re-bars. Gamma advised the Department of Public Works of an anticipated time delay and the need to replace the incorrectly fabricated re-bars.

On November 12, 1971, the Department of Public Works advised Gamma that a design change would be made for the top slab where the lighter fabricated re-bars would be alternated with #10 bars on 6" center to center.

On November 13, 1971, Gamma resubmitted the revised shop drawings and received approval of the modified re-bars design on November 15, 1971.

On December 1, 1971, the weather turned extremely cold and it snowed the entire day. Several days later the weather warmed up and made working site extremely difficult. When it snowed again on December 8, Gamma petitioned for a partial shutdown, as it did not intend to concrete through the winter.

With the completion of the temporary relocation of the stream and the HPWL on March 8, 1972, Gamma now had the entire alignment of the box culvert ready for construction.

In order to meet the December 1, 1972 completion date for the concrete box culvert, it was necessary to get a good jump on the concrete operation. Weather conditions allowed work to begin on March 12, 1972.

The December 1, 1972 completion date was critical for several reasons. Gamma had lost 4 weeks of concrete time in the fall of 1971, and needed a coordinated effort to complete this phase of the operation.

Although the winter temperatures in the Jones Falls Valley were such that excavation and some limited backfilling could be carried on in the daytime, temperatures at night dropped well below freezing between December 1 and March 1. Therefore, if concrete was to be placed during the period, winter protection would be necessary during mixing, transporting, placing, finishing and curing. Gamma felt that its schedule allowed sufficient time to cover normal problems that might arise and that it could avoid the added costs connected with winter concrete.

Gamma, in the spring and summer of 1972, worked the box culvert operations 6 days per week, with two shifts. In general, form work was performed during the first shift and concrete placement during the second shift.

On July 8, 1972, the project site was swept by the worst flood that the Jones Falls Valley had experienced in over 40 years. Gamma's haul roads, stream crossings were washed out, and the work area inundated in spite of Gamma's diversion ditching and diking.

It was not until July 15, 1972, that Gamma was able to reestablish construction operations. Gamma notified the Department of Public Works of the delay by letter of July 16, 1972.

On October 16, 1972, the carpenters, who had been working without a labor contract, went on strike until October 23, 1972, when an agreement was reached. While they were on strike, all concrete operations came to a halt. Gamma notified the Department of Public Works of this delay in accordance with the contract.

As December 1, 1972 approached, it became quite evident that the contractor would still have some concrete to place.

On November 15, 1972, Gamma wrote the engineer informing him that it proposed to shut down concrete operations between December 1, 1972, and March 1, 1973. It further requested that the box culvert completion date and final completion date be extended each 64 days, citing as excusable reasons for the extension (1) failure of the owner to provide access, 50 days; (2) error in re-bar design and bad weather, 20 days; (3) storm in July 1972, 7 days; (4) carpenter strike, October 1972, 7 days.

The engineer denied the request for extension of time, saying that the specified completion dates were final and that Gamma must organize and schedule its remaining work so as to meet them. Gamma saw no alternative to working concrete through the winter and proceeded to mobilize for winter concrete. By December 1, 1972, Gamma had placed approximately 75 percent of the box culvert concrete; the pump station foundation was complete.

Gamma continued on after December 1, 1972, but with noticeable reduction in production. The box culvert was completed on March 12, 1973. Gamma again requested an extension of time, this time requesting an additional 27 days for winter work. The engineer replied as before, that the specified completion dates must be met.

On March 15, 1973, the box culvert was inspected and accepted by the engineer. Diversion of the stream was not accomplished until June 16, 1973, in conformance with regulations of the State Wildlife Agency.

RELOCATION OF HPWL AND PUMPING STATION

On June 17, 1973, Gamma began excavation for the HPWL, utilizing the existing stream bed and the relocation channel for the temporary stream. This alignment required very little additional excavation and the first sections of pipe were laid from the upstream end. Gamma also commenced the construction of the pump station.

On July 2, 1973, the welders and pipe fitters walked off the job and remained on strike 5 days until July 7, 1973. During this period, no work was performed on the pipe line or the pump station.

Once the welders and pipe fitters returned to the site, the work progressed smoothly and the pipe line was completed on August 15, 1973, with the pump station completed on August 30, 1975. The HPWL was tested and accepted on September 9, 1973.

EMBANKMENT AND PAVING FOR THE HIGHWAY

When it became apparent that it was not going to be able to divert the stream thru the box culvert until June 16, 1973, Gamma made plans to start the major roadway embankment on either side of the stream, leaving a gap in the center. Gamma began embankment operations on March 15, 1973, but instead of a single run working from the bottom up, it was limited to two sections. The preliminary embankment was completed on May 15, 1973.

Gamma commenced to close the embankment gap on September 10, 1973, and completed the embankment on October 21, 1973.

Gamma began its paving operations on October 1, 1973, and completed same by December 1, 1973.

LANDSCAPING

Following the winter, the top soil and landscaping were completed by May 15, 1974, well in advance of the specified completion date.

LIQUIDATED DAMAGES

The Department of Public Works withheld $20,800 (104 days @ $200 per day) "pending final determination of the extent of liability for liquidated damages" connected with Gamma's failure to complete the concrete box culvert and pumping station foundation on December 1, 1972, as required.

Problem Number 1

a. List each of the excusable delays under the Gamma Construction Company contract.

b. Identify each excusable delay as warranting an extension of time, or as concurrent.

c. Identify each excusable delay as being compensable or noncompensable.

d. Where enough information is given in the problem, determine the total time extension, if any, to which Gamma is entitled.

Problem Number 2

a. Identify all areas where Gamma incurred damages from causes for which the engineer and/or owner are responsible.

b. For each of the claim areas above, list the kinds of damages for which Gamma is entitled to receive compensation, i.e., labor escalation, loss of production, etc.

c. Describe the methods to be used in establishing the various items of damage, and the records that would be required to compute the amount.

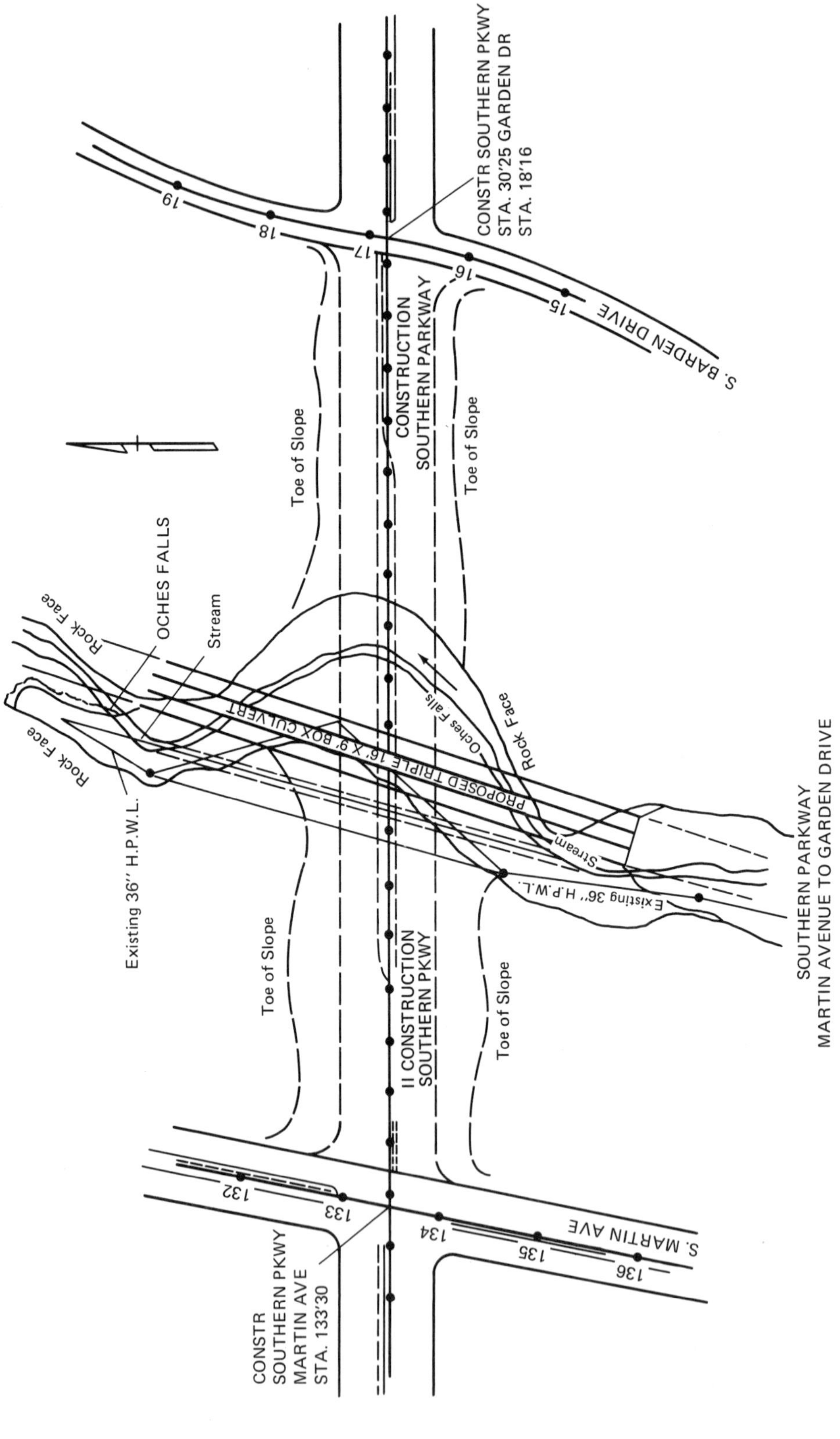

CONSTR SOUTHERN PKWY
STA. 30'25 GARDEN DR
STA. 18'16
S. BARDEN DRIVE
19
18
17
16
15
CONSTRUCTION
SOUTHERN PARKWAY
Toe of Slope
Toe of Slope
OCHES FALLS
Stream
Rock Face
Rock Face
Rock Face
Oches Falls
PROPOSED TRIPLE 16' X 9' BOX CULVERT
Stream
Existing 36" H.P.W.L.
Existing 36'' H.P.W.L.
SOUTHERN PARKWAY
MARTIN AVENUE TO GARDEN DRIVE
Toe of Slope
Toe of Slope
II CONSTRUCTION
SOUTHERN PKWY
132
133
134
135
136
S. MARTIN AVE
CONSTR
SOUTHERN PKWY
MARTIN AVE
STA. 133'30

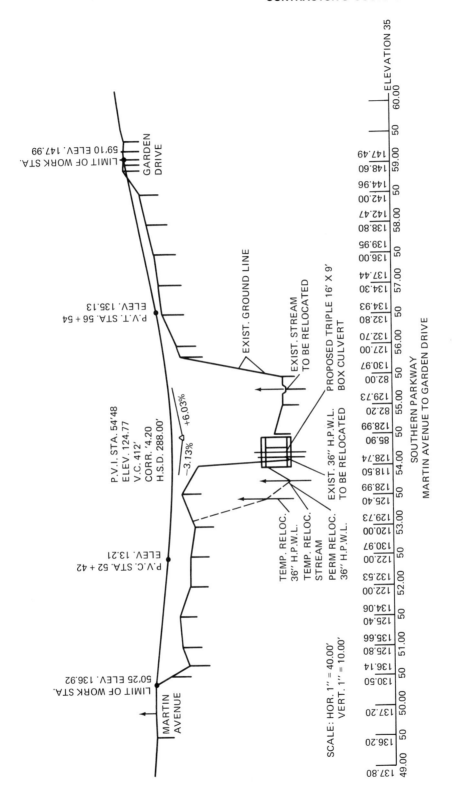

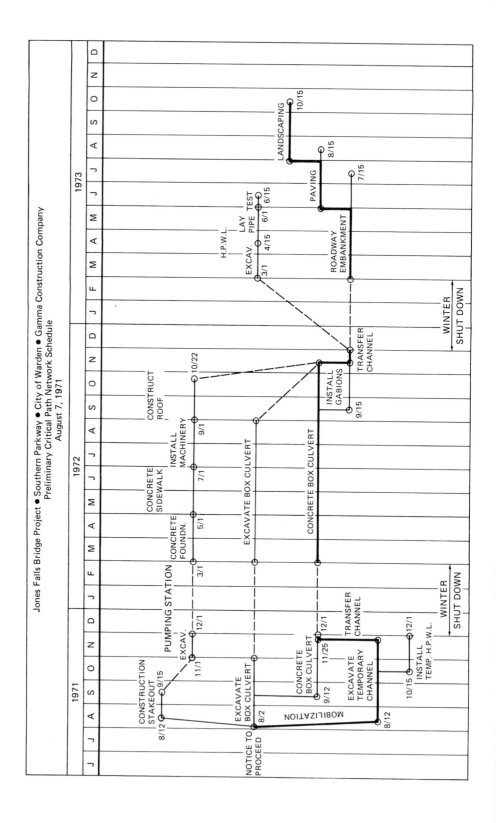

SOLUTION

In general, there is insufficient information to make a conclusive determination. One purpose of the exercise is to determine what additional information is required.

Excusable Delays

Excusable Delays on the Critical Path

All delays on the critical path warrant an extension of time. They are additive and determine the job total time extension.

(1) Lack of Right-of-Way Clearance

Although the contract stated all right-of-way was available and although Gamma had scheduled the excavation of the temporary channel to begin on August 12, 1971, Gamma did not get the necessary equipment on site until September 1, 1971. From August 12, 1971, until September 1, 1971, there were concurrent nonexcusable and excusable delays.

From September 1, to October 3, 1971, the responsibility for delay lies wholly with the owner.

Proper notice was given.

August 12-September 1,	17 days excusable but noncompensable
September 1-October 3	33 days excusable and compensable
TOTAL EXCUSABLE DELAY	50 days

(2) Additional Time Required to Install Additional Anchor Bars for the HPWL

Originally the anchor bars were not on the critical path and therefore not an excusable delay. However, the critical path may have shifted to put the anchor bars on the critical path. If so any delay is both excusable and compensable. Assuming the critical path did shift, there is not enough information given on the CPM to determine how much additional time is justified due to the additional bars. You would have to go to the detailed CPM to make such a determination. The main point is the unit price is no longer applicable after the ratio of horizontal to vertical bars is changed.

Excusable and compensable

(3) Plan Error in the Top Slab Transverse Reinforcing for the Box Culvert

The same question here as in (2) above: Is this activity on the critical path? This is clearly the fault of the owner, and the contractor is entitled to an adjustment in time if on the critical path and damages if they can be proven. One approach on the time adjustment would be the number of days required from the time the error was discovered until the solution is found and the contractor's progress is back to normal. Again not enough information is given to determine time or damages.

(4) Storm—July 8-15, 1972

(Unusually severe weather conditions beyond the contractor's control)

Excusable, but noncompensable   7 days

(5) Carpenter's Strike—October 16-23, 1972

(Act by others beyond the contractor's control)

Excusable, but noncompensable   8 days

(6) Ironworker's Strike—July 2-7, 1973

Although this 5-day delay is excusable, it affects work in a noncritical path operation and does not delay the project as a whole. It is concurrent, noncompensable, and does not warant time.

(7) Delays Due to Winter Concrete

This is a complex one to figure. First we have to find out where Gamma was on December 1, 1972. We know there were the following excusable delays which the owner refused to grant.

Lack of ROW	50 days
Added Anchor Bars	Undeterminable
Rebar Error	Undeterminable
Storm	7
Carpenter's Strike	8
	65 + days

The first thing is to get enough additional information to evaluate the anchor bar and rebar error delays. Had the owner granted the time extensions, the contractor would not have been forced to place concrete during the winter.

One way to determine how far behind schedule the contractor was at what would have been the winter shutdown is to compare production rates to see if he had more days of concrete placing left than he had excusable delay. If he did, then part of the acceleration costs would be his. Assume that the contractor had more time coming than he was behind schedule and that the owner pays the acceleration costs. The owner has in effect bought back the excusable delay and Gamma is no longer entitled to those days of excusable delay.

Now to the question of liquidated damages for missing completion of the culvert on December 1, 1972, prior to the winter shutdown. We have established that Gamma has 65 + days of excusable delay as the winter shutdown approached. Days of time extensions must be given during the construction season, that is, you must replace good working days with good working days. If a time extension had been given, the 48 + days extension would begin at the spring start-up but it would be shortened by those days from December 1, 1972, to the winter shutdown.

Since the culvert was completed on March 15, 1973, no liquidated damages are assessable.

(8) Disruption in the Embankment Operation

By failing to acknowledge excusable delays in a timely manner, the owner forced Gamma into starting embankment before the area was ready. Therefore, the owner is responsible for this acceleration.

Damages

1. Claim No. 1

a.   Damages to Gamma resulting from failure of the Owner to provide entry to the property between September and October 3, 1971, 33 days.

b.   Types of damages involved:

(1)   Equipment standby costs;

(2)   Standby labor (labor brought in expressedly for this operation and for which no alternate work could be found);

(3)   Labor escalation;

(4)   Indirect costs;

(5) Extended period costs;

(6) Impact (see claim no. 3).

2. Claim No. 2

a. Additional costs due to revisions in anchor bars.

b. Types of damages involved:

(1) Additional costs due to change in the ratio of vertical to horizontal bars;

(2) Additional costs arising from loss of production in jury rig operation (acceleration cost)

(3) Labor escalation;

(4) Additional premium time;

(5) Indirect costs;

(6) Impact.

3. Claim No. 3

a. Plan error in re steel

b. Types of damages involved:

(1) Refabrication cost

(2) Resubmittal cost;

(3) Equipment and labor standby costs;

(4) Indirect costs;

(5) Loss of production, inefficiency;

(6) Impact.

4. Claim No. 7

a. Wrongful denial of extension of time requiring acceleration in the form of winter concrete.

b. Types of damages involved:

(1) Winterization costs (i.e., forms, buckets, batch plant, etc);

(2) Heating and protection costs;

(3) Concrete additives (more cement, calcium chloride, etc.);

(4) Loss of production; inefficiency;

(5) Labor escalation;

(6) Additional premium time;

(7) Indirect costs;

(8) Impact.

6. Owner's Damages for Delays

Most construction contracts contain a provision for liquidated damages. Such clauses amount to a charge against the contractor for not completing the work within the time specified in the contract. A reasonable liquidated damage sum provides added incentive for timely completion and at the same time puts a ceiling on the contractor's liability. For the owner, liquidated damages afford protection and reimbursement in the event of late completion.

The great advantage of liquidated damages is that the amount is set beforehand. It is not necessary to calculate actual damages. In many cases where actual damages would be difficult to prove, this is an expedient method for the owner to recover those damages arising from tardy completion.

The liquidated damages figure sets a reasonable forecast of the harm that will result to the owner from the delay in completion. The courts have held that liquidated damages may not be used as a penalty. Where the damages figure has been proven to be a penalty against the contractor, the courts have held these unenforceable. In other words, liquidated damages should not be a club with which to beat the contractor over the head.

When liquidated damages are challenged, the usual test of fairness hangs on the reasonableness of the estimate of damage at the time the contract was entered into. This is an important concept. If, after the fact, the owner's damages are actually greater or less than that estimate, courts have held that irrelevant. If the amount was reasonable at the time, both parties must abide by those estimates. Naturally, a contractor is not likely to challenge liquidated damages unless he believes the owner has *not* incurred as much damage as the contractor has to pay.

Liquidated damages are, or can be, an effective tool in construction. The problem is one of fixing on a reasonable figure. This is the owner's problem and one that should be approached carefully. Disputes over liquidated damages are likely to surface after the fact of a delay when a contractor is forced to consider having to pay those damages. At that time, it is not surprising that he should question the amount and the causes of the delay, i.e., that he should try to establish that the delay was due to the owner's actions or other excusable causes. So, while we advocate liquidated damages, there is a certain amount of built-in conflict. No one ever wants to pay.

CONTRACT PROVISIONS

The place to begin with any kind of construction problem is with the contract. Here is a liquidated damages clause from the New York City Department of Public Works.

"Article 16. Liquidated Damages. "In case the contractor shall fail to complete the work within the time fixed for such completion in the General Conditions . . ., or within the time to which such completion may have been extended, the contractor must pay to the City the sum fixed in the General Conditions.., for each and every calendar day that the time consumed in completing the work exceed the time allowed therefor; which said sum, in view of the difficulty of accurately ascertaining the loss which the City shall suffer by reason of delay in the completion of the work hereunder is hereby fixed and agreed as the liquidated damages that the City will suffer by reason of such delay, and not as a penalty. The Comptroller will deduct and retain out of the moneys which may become due hereunder, the amount of any such liquidated damages; and in case the amount which may become due hereunder shall be less than the amount of liquidated damages suffered by the City, the Contractor shall be liable to pay the difference upon demand by the Comptroller."

The liquidated damages clause of the federal government standard form 23A states the following:

"If fixed and agreed liquidated damages are provided in the contract and if the government so terminates the contractor's right to proceed, the resulting damage will consist of such liquidated damages until such reasonable time as may be required for final completion of the work together with any increased costs occasioned the government in completing the work. [(23A, 5 (b)]

If fixed and agreed liquidated damages are provided in the contract and if the government does not so terminate the contractor's right to proceed, the resulting damage will consist of such liquidated damages until the work is completed or accepted. [23A 5 (c)]

The contractor's right to proceed shall not be so terminated nor the contractor charged with resulting damage if:

(1) The delay in the completion of the work arises from unforeseeable causes beyond the control and without the fault or negligence of the contractor, including but not restricted to, acts of God, acts of the public enemy, acts of the government in its sovereign or contractual capacity, acts of another contractor in the performance of a contract with the government, fires, floods, epidemics, quarantine restrictions, strikes, freight embargoes, unusually severe weather, or delays of subcontractors or suppliers arising from unforeseeable causes beyond the control and without the fault or negligence of both the contractor and such subcontractors or suppliers;

(2) The contractor within 10 days from the beginning of any such delay (unless the contracting officer grants a further period of time before the date of final payment under the contract), notifies the contracting officer in writing of the causes of delay. [23A 5 (a) 1 and 2]"

The Contracting Officer then must determine whether the delay warrants a time extension. If not, the possibility of assessing liquidated damages looms. The owner must make an analysis of all job delays to determine how many days of delay are excusable, i.e., beyond the contractor's control. Liquidated damages are not assessable if there are excusable delays that the owner has not granted yet. (See Chapter 4.) Sometimes in a complicated project there are overlapping, concurrent delays, some of which may be attributed to either side. These must be sorted out before the owner can be certain that damages are due him. Some courts have held that damages will not be apportioned; that is, if the owner causes some delay, he may not recover any liquidated damages. This is not the modern point of view, however. With increasing frequency, courts are apportioning delay to the guilty party.

One advantage of liquidated damages clauses is that both parties know exactly what a day of delay in completion of a job will cost, assuming the contractor is at fault. For the contractor, this can amount to a sword over his head. When a delay occurs, the first thing both parties should do is to determine who is responsible. Naturally, each side will wish to see the responsibility placed elsewhere. So, as we have stressed continually, accurate records must be kept and schedules maintained and updated to reflect the impact of delays, and changes and their impacts must be incorporated in those schedules.

Generally, owners do not assess liquidated damages unless the contractor's delay is flagrant or unless the contractor asserts a delay claim against the owner. Then the owner is likely to resort to liquidated damages as a defensive tactic. In the public sector, this is less likely to be true. If the job is late and there are no excusable delays, liquidated damages will be assessed.

When disputes reach the courts, most jurisdictions will not grant both liquidated and actual damages. In fact, this is almost unheard of, so an owner should not allow himself to be persuaded that his case would be an exception. One exception, however, is where the liquidated damages clause on its face is limited to certain types of owner damages such as extended engineering, interest, taxes, and where other damages are specifically excluded such as the claims of other contractors affected by this contractor's delay. In such an event, both liquidated and specified actual damages may be recoverable. Moreover, the amount of the liquidated damages previously agreed on can be challenged on the grounds that it constitutes a penalty rather than a fair assessment of the damages owing to the delay. Upon a finding that the liquidated damages set were a penalty, or were unreasonable, then only provable, actual damages are recoverable.

In the absence of a liquidated damages clause, the contractor will be liable for the owner's proven actual damages due to unexcused late completion. These damages may be enormous in relation to the dollar amount of the contract. A contractor should consider what these damages may be before seeking to negotiate a deletion of a liquidated damages clause from his contract. Often contractors will object to liquidated damages clauses without considering the extent of their own exposure to the owner's actual damages absent such provisions.

A prime contractor can hold a subcontractor responsible for liquidated damages assessed by the owner to the extent of subcontractor-caused delay. The prime can, in addition, assess his sub for his actual damages such as extended supervision, overhead, etc., attributable to the delay, depending, of course, on the provisions of the subcontract.

The period of time for which those liquidated damages must be paid is usually the time between the date specified in the contract for completion and the time by which the job can be "substantially complete" or when the owner takes "beneficial occupancy." Clearly, if the contractor has to pay a sizable sum for each day of delay, it is important, and sometimes controversial, to fix that time period.

SETTING LIQUIDATED DAMAGE FIGURES

How does an owner establish his liquidated damages figure? The following are some considerations:

1. Extra rental of other buildings that might be required because the one being built is not completed.
2. Extra maintenance and utility costs that may be incurred either in the continued use of old high-cost buildings or equipment or in the maintenance of a new area before beneficial use.
3. Interest on the investment or borrowed capital.
4. Extra training required to maintain worker skills pending availability of the building or equipment.
5. Extended supervision cost.
6. Additional operating costs that may result from the continued use of inefficient facility or equipment.
7. Extra costs of split operations resulting from partial occupancy or use of equipment.
8. Loss of revenue, e.g., bridge tolls, sale of power from a power plant, building rentals, etc.
9. Impact costs relating to follow-on contracts.

As we pointed out earlier, the amount of the liquidated damages must be reasonable and not a penalty. In addition to that legal consideration, there is a more practical reason for setting a fair damages figure. Too high an amount may scare contractors away. A high liquidated damages figure could also cause contractors to include a high contingency figure in their bids in order to cover the possibility of paying those damages later on. In such cases, the owner bears that extra cost whether or not the job is delayed.

However, parties don't usually enter into a contract with the idea that they will have to assess or pay liquidated damages. On the other hand, there may be contractors who prefer to gamble on a windfall profit if they finish on time; if not, they feel they can go to court to try to prove that the liquidated damages figure was not reasonable, or that delays were excusable.

REASONABLE COMPLETION DATES

Of course, disputes might be avoided altogether if the completion date were a reasonable one to begin with. If the owner has set an unrealistic date and has set a high liquidated damages figure, he might be letting himself in for litigation or at least for claims and requests for time extensions. A contractor might accept a job with that combination of terms because he needs the work or because he believes he can recover through claims and changes. Neither approach is recommended.

During performance of the work, each party should be liable for his own delays. The liquidated damages should not be used to threaten the contractor, nor should the contractor's actions inspire such threats.

The contractor should keep in mind that as unpleasant as it might be to pay liquidated damages, the fact that the figure was set earlier puts a ceiling on his liability. He knows throughout the job exactly what he must pay if he delays the job. Even though no one likes to pay, knowing the amount beforehand eliminates uncertainty.

7. Bonding

TERMINOLOGY

Throughout this chapter we use language special to the bonding world. *Surety* means the bonding company. The party who furnishes the bond, for example, the contractor, is the *principal*. The party—usually, the owner—benefitting from the bond is the *obligee*. The person who agrees to reimburse, or indemnify, the surety for any money the surety is required to pay out on the bond is called an *indemnitor*. The principal, for example, the contractor, is always an indemnitor. Frequently, when the surety feels that the principal has insufficient assets, the surety requires others to sign up as indemnitors. These persons might be corporate officers of the contracting firm (and their wives), or a parent corporation may be asked to be an indemnitor. (The surety could also ask for a pledge of stock or a mortgage on real property.)

Most public and many private construction contracts require that the contractor be bonded. For a fee of a dollar or two per hundred dollars of the contract price, a bonding company "guarantees" the contractor's performance and payment by him of subcontractors and suppliers.

"Guarantee" appears in quotation marks because the bond provides insurance of a highly qualified sort. In fact, a surety bond is not insurance in the traditional sense. Insurance premiums are calculated actuarially based on losses and risks. Bond premiums are not. They are calculated as a fee for the extension of credit, much as a bank would charge a fee for issuing a letter of credit if it believes the customer has the resources to repay the bank when the letter is called in. The bank assumes there is no real risk of loss; otherwise, it would not extend credit.

Similarly, a surety will only write a bond if it believes that the contractor has sufficient financial resources and the technical competence to perform the work and pay his bills. The surety assumes there will be no significant risk of loss.

This difference applies to the manner in which bonding companies deal with claims, as compared with insurance companies. When an insurance company receives a claim covered under the policy it has issued, the company expects to pay without recourse against the insured party.

When a bonding company receives a claim, it turns to the contractor for a response, since the contractor has agreed to completely indemnify the bonding company against any loss.

The bonding company will only consider satisfying the claim once it is convinced that its contractor is unable to do so and that there is no legitimate defense to the claim.

Another aspect of this complicated arrangement is that the contractor is anxious that the bonding company not receive any claims against his performance. Bonds are becoming increasingly more difficult to obtain, and yet they are so often required by owners that a contractor will usually do whatever he can to prevent his bonding capability from being jeopardized.

Practically speaking, then, what does the bond mean?

In order to obtain bonding, a financial investigation of the contractor is made. In addition, the surety checks the contractor's technical credentials for performing the work in question.

Issuance of the bond also places the financial resources of the surety behind the contractor. Contractors come and go; sureties go on forever, or at least for a long enough time. However, recovery is not a simple process. If an owner must actually press for recovery under a bond, he should know that the law regarding bonding is extremely complex. If a default situation seems to be in the making, an owner should retain a lawyer knowledgeable in this field, and as soon as possible. Recovery is more likely to result from a lawsuit than from a telephone call or a letter describing the contractor's failings.

The bonding company, as we have stated, will not pay until it is convinced that the contractor will not respond to the claim and that there is no legitimate defense of that claim.

We recommend avoiding litigation as a means of recourse under all but extraordinary circumstances. The reason is that the legal battle will substantially reduce any benefits and the delay will be more costly than attempting other courses of action.

THE OWNER'S POINT OF VIEW

When should the owner declare the contractor in default? Should the owner permit the contractor to drag the job to completion? Obviously, if the contractor walks off the job, and after adequate notice from the owner he fails to return, there is no choice but to declare him in default.

However, if it is a question of slowness, continuing delays, or an undermanned project—but work *is* progressing—there are some points to consider.

If the project is 95% complete, the default process (including negotiations with the bonding company, obtaining new bids and contracting out, preparation of new contract documents, etc.) in most instances will be more time-consuming than would be permitting the lagging contractor to proceed at his own pace.

The question is, how far down the percentage scale of completion would it make sense for an owner to default a contractor? As a rule of thumb, it hardly ever pays to default when the job is over 75% complete, unless the job is at a complete standstill.

Between 50% and 75% there must be a judgment made. In usual cases of slowness on the part of the contractor, or work stoppage due to lack of financial resources, a discussion with the bonding company is in order. The surety may decide to provide financial support. The owner must judge how long it will take to complete the project at the present rate of progress versus the time to complete if the default, rebid, and award steps are taken. The owner, in making this decision, must also guess whether the contractor on the job will continue at the same slow rate, or will get worse, or better.

Even when the slowdown or other difficulty occurs below the 50% completion mark, the owner has to make some serious judgments, but the chance here is better that the default process will in the end gain time.

Generally speaking, if the bonding company learns early enough about the difficulties, its posture as a guarantor rather than in insurer can take a constructive turn. The surety will often lend a helping hand by offering the contractor financial aid or managerial assistance if such actions are thought to prevent default.

In this sense, the owner is protected in an indirect manner. The bonding company will help out to avoid being put in the position of being called on by the owner to complete the work, or to pay.

The contractor will most likely work harder to avoid losing his status with the bonding company. In fact, a contractor who is performing both bonded and unbonded work will most likely put his bonded work first if difficulties arise or if his resources become scarce. The contractor will not want to risk his standing with the surety nor run the risk of being called on to make personal indemnification to the surety. Typically, the surety will seek indemnity to the full extent of its potential exposure under the bonds.

THE PENAL SUM

The amount for which the bond is written, called the penal sum, is the maximum amount for which the surety agrees to be liable. Ordinarily, the penal sum is set at 100% of the contract price. Sometimes, especially on very large contracts, the penal sum is set at between 50% and 100% of the contract price. (It can also be less.)

When default occurs, the surety can either come in and finish the job itself, or can pay. How is the amount to be paid determined? The surety is liable for the cost to complete the work *minus* the unpaid balance on the construction contract and *plus* liquidated damages, if any are established. Those costs cannot exceed the penal sum. If they do, the penal sum is all the surety must pay in all but the most rare instances.

If the surety decides to finish the work, this is usually accomplished in one of two ways. The surety can hire a completing contractor. In this case, if the final cost exceeds the penal sum, the surety must still pay. The surety may also provide the owner with a lump-sum contract with another contractor acceptable to the owner. The surety pays the owner the amount of that contract less the unpaid amount on the defaulted contract up to the penal sum of the bond. In some cases, the owner lets a completion contract and is reimbursed by the surety on the same basis.

The surety's decision is usually based on what it believes is the least-cost approach. Often it is not possible to find a contractor willing to complete the project for a lump sum, as the second contractor would have to assume responsibility for unknown conditions in the work begun by another.

The surety, if it is assuming responsibility for the default, generally prefers to make a lump-sum payment in order to put a cap on its loss rather than to have a continuing exposure. That cap is arrived at through negotiations between the owner and the surety. The owner, naturally, would like to complete the project with the surety's money rather than its own and would also prefer to avoid litigation. If the surety does pay up front, then some sort of release is required from the owner. That release covers the risk of problems with the completing contractor. Consequently, the owner would be well advised to insist that the completing contractor be bonded as a condition of giving the surety the release. It should be obvious that agreement is not reached swiftly in such cases.

COMMON TYPES OF BONDS

1. Bid Bonds.   These guarantee that the contractor will honor his bid price for the work described in the contract documents, will sign the contract if it is awarded to him, and furnish performance, as well as labor and material payment bonds if required.

A contractor could bid low, be awarded the work, then try to negotiate for more money. The owner would, of course, have the right to take legal action to enforce the bid. However, the time and money involved might be considered so great that he would accede to the contractor's demands. So the bid bond, in the main, is a sort of insurance when owners are dealing with unknown contractors. The bid bond requirement tends to exclude all but serious qualified bidders. If a private sector owner is dealing with a pool of bidders he knows well, the bid bond might seem superfluous. In any case, the guarantee is not unqualified. The bonding company is relieved of liability if the owner makes any modification or addition in going from the bid documents to the contract documents, for example, changes the design, time of performance, general conditions, and so on. The same applies if the owner fails to live up to any of his obligations under the bid documents, such as the time for making an award.

The amount of the bid bond (called the penal sum) is specified in the bidding documents. It is usually in the range of 5% to 20% of the bid price, depending on the size of the project.

There are two common types of bid bonds: (1) liquidated damages; and (2) difference-in-cost. The liquidated damages type requires forfeiture of the entire penal sum as "liquidated damages." This is to cover the owner's cost of rebidding, delay in the start of the project, and any difference in cost upon rebidding. The difference-in-cost type requires payment, up to the penal sum of the bond, of the owner's actual rebidding cost and the actual differences in cost on rebidding, assuming it is higher. If on rebid, the low bid is sufficiently lower so that it covers the owner's rebid costs, then, under this type of bond, there would be no liability. But this rarely happens.

2. Performance Bonds.   As the name suggests, the performance bond guarantees that the contractor will live up to his obligations under the contract. The bonding company's liability is, however, conditional on the owner living up to *his* contract obligations. Many owners fail to appreciate the significance of this latter condition.

This point illustrates clearly the distinction between a bond and an insurance policy. In most cases, it is understood that the insured did not start the fire or cause the flood, or otherwise contribute to the cause that gave rise to the claim. On the other hand, with the bond the question becomes a matter of degree on both sides. Were the contractor's breaches so substantial as to warrant default by the owner? Were the owner's breaches so substantial as to relieve the surety of liability?

Since the surety was not on the job, it does not have first-hand knowledge of the facts. The surety investigates the situation to assess the performance of contract obligations by both parties. That situation is rarely as clear as asking "was there a fire?" as in the case of an insurance claim.

Even when the surety listens to the contractor's version and the owner's version of the events that led to the slowdown or financial problems, the surety cannot be a totally impartial judge. The surety, after all, wishes to be indemnified by those indemnitors mentioned earlier. Therefore, the surety is more than likely to side with the contractor unless it appears that the contractor's contentions are substantially without merit. In most cases, out of duty to those indemnitors, the surety will let the contractor have his day in court.

Most owners fail to understand this point and are incensed when the surety sides with the contractor. In paying for the bond, directly or indirectly, what the owner buys is the security of knowing that if he is right, and can prove it, he will ultimately be compensated for his damages.

This is a far cry from getting a check from one's insurance company. However, bond premiums would be much higher were they to provide protection comparable to that of an insurance policy.

3. A Joint-Obligee Bond. A Joint-Obligee performance bond is one where there are two obligees, typically the owner and a lending institution. This form of bond makes the bank which has been providing the construction financing, the beneficiary of the bond along with the owner.

4. Labor and Material Payment Bonds. This category of bonds covers those people who supply labor and material for the project (including subcontractors, suppliers, renters of equipment, etc.). A performance bond may also cover these items; however, a performance bond does not give direct rights to such persons. If the owner pays for labor and materials and obtains reimbursement under the performance bond, this cuts into the penal sum. An owner may not wish to diminish that sum. Subs and suppliers cannot claim and recover under the performance bond. They can do so only under a labor and material payment bond.

Therefore, it makes sense for an owner to require both kinds of bonds. The penal sum of the performance bond is in addition to the penal sum of the payment bond. The owner should consider these points:

1. The premium for the two bonds is generally the same as for one.
2. The penal sums are greater: they are the sum of the two bonds. But the premium, remember, is the same.
3. Subcontractors and suppliers may not wish to rely on the contractor's credit, or may do so only at a premium price. The owner may believe that the payment bond will result in savings in sub and supplier prices that will be passed along to the owner by the contractor.

4. Under the lien laws in some states, the owner can be directly liable to subs and suppliers unless a payment bond has been posted by the general contractor.

5. For public relations reasons, some owners may prefer to have payment bonds. They can then satisfy a moral obligation (even if there is no legal obligation) to make sure that subs and suppliers are paid. If the subs or suppliers contact them, they can merely send a copy of the payment bond and recommend that a remedy under the bond conditions be pursued.

The Federal Government Miller Act

The federal government, through the Miller Act, requires payment bonds for all construction undertaken by federal agencies. There are two principal reasons for this:

1. There is no right to file a lien on a federal project.
2. It is an avowed public policy to insure that subs and suppliers on federal projects are paid.

Many states have enacted "little Miller Acts" that apply to state public works projects. These do not extend to private construction within the state.

In general, the owner has no contract with the subs and suppliers. Unless the jurisdiction in which the project is located has a statute (for example a lien law) providing otherwise, the owner has no obligation to the subs and suppliers, since they are not in privity of contract, i.e., a party to the contract. If they are not paid by the contractor, they cannot recover from the owner.

1. Single Instrument Payment and Performance Bonds. Typically, the performance bond and the payment bond are two separate instruments; their penal sums are cumulative. Sometimes, the performance bond and the payment bond are in a single instrument. In such a case, there is a single penal sum for both obligations. Some courts have so held. In such event, the owner is better protected if he gets two separate bonds, especially if the premium charged is the same in both cases.

2. Completion Bonds. This is a variation of the performance bond. In general, sureties do not like to write them because they (a) guarantee completion regardless of the cost (without the limitation of a penal sum) and (b) they require the surety to complete the project, without the option of merely paying money or providing a satisfactory completing contractor.

3. Guarantee Bonds. Often these are guarantees in the contract documents that extend beyond the life of the performance bond (generally one to two years after acceptance of the work). These typically apply to guarantees on paving, roofing, or specialized equipment. It can be desirable to require specific bonds to secure these guarantees.

As an alternative, owners will often hold a sum of money to secure these obligations for their duration. This must be provided for in the contract documents. Sometimes the contract will allow a choice: the contractor will allow $ X for X years to secure the paving guarantee, or he will provide the guarantee bond.

Many of these bonds, especially those offered by manufacturers, are very restrictive in their language. Recovery is not easy. Wording should be reviewed carefully to see if the owner is getting anything of value.

Claims under these bonds are difficult to establish. Once the contractor has left and the facility is operating, defects can be laid to poor maintenance, improper usage, and other causes beyond the contractor's control or responsibility, none of which would be covered by such a bond.

4. Lien Discharge Bonds. Under the lien laws of some states, the owner may not make further payments to a general contractor after a lien has been filed without running the risk of direct liability to the lienors, i.e., having to pay a second time. This bond, when provided by the general contractor, relieves the owner from that liability.

5. Subcontractor Performance and Payment Bonds. Often the contractor may require bonds of his subs. Sometimes the owner will insist on this for certain subs. This may be the case even if the contractor has himself furnished bonds to the owner. In doing so, the owner wishes to avoid potential trouble with key trades, such as the steel erector or the concrete sub. Default by a key sub on the critical path of a project can have a disastrous effect on the job. The owner or contractor will have to pay a little more to obtain this additional bond, but in some cases may find this requirement worth that expense.

PERFORMANCE BOND CLAIMS

Contractor defaults don't occur overnight. A vigilant owner should be aware of difficulties long before a contractor goes under and should try to remedy the situation. With the owner's cooperation, temporary problems can be overcome. In this book we have outlined good administrative practices. An adversary stance is to be avoided whenever possible.

However, if the owner has reason to think that the contractor is in real trouble, he should ask for explanations first; then and if necessary, he should tell the contractor that the bonding company will be informed.

Some common symptoms of trouble are these: payment inquiries from vendors and subcontractors, requests for accelerated payments, shortages of labor on the job, and inability to obtain responses from the principals of the contracting firm. As we said earlier, the contractor will probably make every effort to avoid notice to the surety.

Three standard lines of defense are available to the surety when a claim is made. These are:

- that the owner did not give the surety adequate notice;
- that the owner caused or contributed to the contractor's problems; and
- that the owner made cardinal, or major, changes in the contract provisions.

Any of these may obviate the surety's obligations under the bond.

The Owner's Position

The owner should know that these are standard defenses and should conduct himself accordingly. For example, the owner must give adequate notice. Most performance bonds have provisions regarding notice. This gives the surety the opportunity to head off a default. If the bond requires prior notice to the surety, an owner must not take the matter into his own hands and complete the project without giving such notice. If he does, he can forfeit recovery from the surety.

Unless the bond so states such notice requirements, the owner has no legal obligation to inform the surety. Sureties often make routine requests for information regarding project status and the adequacy of the contractor's performance. The owner should avoid a perfunctory sign-off if he does submit this information. If these reports do not indicate anything out of the ordinary, when in fact there is, the surety can claim that the owner misled it. Owners would be better off not responding at all than to do so incorrectly or incompletely.

Once the bonding company is informed of the problem, investigation may take many weeks or even several months. During this time, work on the project is slowed down or even stopped. So the owner must choose his timing carefully. He should not use the bonding company as a club to threaten the contractor. Nor should he wait too long to inform the surety of a major problem.

The owner can send the surety, for information purposes, carbon copies of letters stating concern about lack of progress. The owner might refer in such letters to the contract provisions relating to default, stating that this is a remedy if progress is not improved. Certified mail (return receipt requested) protects the owner by providing proof of receipt.

The Surety's Defenses

Under the legal theory of subrogation, the surety has available to it all the defenses the contractor has against the owner. In other words, the owner has no greater rights against the surety than he does against the contractor.

This means that the owner, guilty of delays and interferences to the contractor, cannot default the contractor and then look to the surety to complete the work and to pay liquidated damages.

The surety will pursue the same defenses as the contractor when dealing with delays and other construction problems. The bonding company will say that the owner prevented site access, delayed delivery of equipment, suspended work or in some other way interfered with the work and consequently caused the contractor hardship.

As elsewhere, diligent documentation, progress schedules, and other records are essential to the owner. It should be obvious that the contractor would have nothing to lose and everything to gain by assisting the surety in building his case. The surety also has other defenses available against the owner. It may claim that cardinal or material changes to the construction contract have been made, changes that have not been consented to by the surety. The contractor may have asked for these changes or the owner may have consented to them. This doesn't change things for the surety. If the bonding company did not consent to the change, the bonding agreement could be obviated.

Most construction contracts give the owner the right to make changes, and most bonds waive notice of these changes to the surety. However, such provisions do not extend to major changes. When in doubt as to whether a change is "major," the owner should get the surety's consent to a change to the construction contract. In most cases, that consent is routinely granted when requested before the fact.

Changes in Payment Procedures

Changes are not limited to physical changes in the scope of the work but can also include changes in payment procedures. An owner may agree to a contractor's request for accelerated payments. The owner may do this out of a desire to help the contractor out of temporary difficulty. If this assistance doesn't prevent a default, the surety will claim that this accelerated payment was a departure from the contract and that the owner consequently should forfeit part or all recovery.

DEALING WITH PERFORMANCE BOND SURETIES

The following is some practical advice for dealing with sureties when a claim is made by an owner.

1. Establish credibility early. When the notice of default is given to the surety by the owner, the surety will turn first to the contractor and other indemnitors to hear their position.

The contractor and those other indemnitors naturally have a vested interest in preventing the surety from paying since they are obligated to repay the surety for every dollar it pays out. Thus the surety is likely to hear two stories.

The surety will be inclined to believe the contractor's version. If the surety pays over the contractor's objections, the contractor will not indemnify the surety voluntarily. The surety will most likely have to sue to recover. Thus, the owner's principal objective should be to establish credibility with the surety early, to convince the surety that the contractor's defenses are not valid. This is achieved through candor and a manifest desire to give the surety the full story. It starts with early notice to the surety.

2. Be reasonable. Since the surety invariably has the option of letting the owner complete the project at his own expense and suing for recovery later, the owner should provide the surety a positive incentive to pay at the time the default is declared.

As we have mentioned, the surety will be under pressure from the indemnitors not to pay. The owner has a considerable burden here. He must convince the surety that it will be less costly to pay now than suffer a subsequent lawsuit when the project is completed. Exhorbitant or unreasonable claims by the owner will only serve to support the surety's inclination to defend rather than to pay.

On the other hand, if the surety is offered a bargain, or has the opportunity to put a cap on an otherwise indeterminate claim, the surety may leap at the chance. Also, if for no other reason than good public relations, sureties like to settle amicably when they are shown to have no valid defense. If they can settle for a reasonable amount, they probably will.

3. Do it right.   The laws and procedures affecting construction bonds are complex and not well understood.

Owners entering a prospective default situation are well advised to seek counsel and guidance from persons experienced in dealing with sureties. A surety is well within its legal rights to assert technical defenses and will often do so. Competent advice will minimize the likelihood of such defenses and will impress on the surety the owner's ability to successfully pursue the case should the surety decide to defend.

4. Consider alternatives to default.   Just as a divorce is not always the best solution to matrimonial problems and is usually the last resort, a default is not to be taken lightly. The owner must be aware above all that recovery from the surety is difficult at best. That final resort may be more time-consuming and costly than helping the contractor to avoid default. Initial proper selection procedures and good administration practices can help avoid this situation.

APPENDIX

What follows are sample bond forms published used by the American Institute of Architects. Note the apparent simplicity of these forms in contrast to the complexity of effecting recovery as described in this chapter.

THE AMERICAN INSTITUTE OF ARCHITECTS

AIA Document A311

Performance Bond

KNOW ALL MEN BY THESE PRESENTS: that

(Here insert full name and address or legal title of Contractor)

as Principal, hereinafter called Contractor, and,

(Here insert full name and address or legal title of Surety)

as Surety, hereinafter called Surety, are held and firmly bound unto
(Here insert full name and address or legal title of Owner)

as Obligee, hereinafter called Owner, in the amount of

Dollars ($),

for the payment whereof Contractor and Surety bind themselves, their heirs, executors, administrators, successors and assigns, jointly and severally, firmly by these presents.

WHEREAS,

Contractor has by written agreement dated   19   , entered into a contract with Owner for
(Here insert full name, address and description of project)

in accordance with Drawings and Specifications prepared by
(Here insert full name and address or legal title of Architect)

which contract is by reference made a part hereof, and is hereinafter referred to as the Contract.

AIA DOCUMENT A311 • PERFORMANCE BOND AND LABOR AND MATERIAL PAYMENT BOND • AIA ®
FEBRUARY 1970 ED. • THE AMERICAN INSTITUTE OF ARCHITECTS, 1735 N.Y. AVE., N.W., WASHINGTON, D. C. 20006

1

NOTE: Because AIA documents are revised from time to time, users should ascertain from the AIA the current editions of the documents reproduced herein.

PERFORMANCE BOND

NOW, THEREFORE, THE CONDITION OF THIS OBLIGATION is such that, if Contractor shall promptly and faithfully perform said Contract, then this obligation shall be null and void; otherwise it shall remain in full force and effect.

The Surety hereby waives notice of any alteration or extension of time made by the Owner.

Whenever Contractor shall be, and declared by Owner to be in default under the Contract, the Owner having performed Owner's obligations thereunder, the Surety may promptly remedy the default, or shall promptly

1) Complete the Contract in accordance with its terms and conditions, or

2) Obtain a bid or bids for completing the Contract in accordance with its terms and conditions, and upon determination by Surety of the lowest responsible bidder, or, if the Owner elects, upon determination by the Owner and the Surety jointly of the lowest responsible bidder, arrange for a contract between such bidder and Owner, and make available as Work progresses (even though there should be a default or a succession of defaults under the contract or contracts of completion arranged under this paragraph) sufficient funds to pay the cost of completion less the balance of the contract price; but not exceeding, including other costs and damages for which the Surety may be liable hereunder, the amount set forth in the first paragraph hereof. The term "balance of the contract price," as used in this paragraph, shall mean the total amount payable by Owner to Contractor under the Contract and any amendments thereto, less the amount properly paid by Owner to Contractor.

Any suit under this bond must be instituted before the expiration of two (2) years from the date on which final payment under the Contract falls due.

No right of action shall accrue on this bond to or for the use of any person or corporation other than the Owner named herein or the heirs, executors, administrators or successors of the Owner.

Signed and sealed this   day of   19

_____
(Witness)

{ (Principal)   (Seal)

   _____
   (Title)

_____
(Witness)

{ (Surety)   (Seal)

   _____
   (Title)

THE AMERICAN INSTITUTE OF ARCHITECTS

AIA Document A311

Labor and Material Payment Bond

THIS BOND IS ISSUED SIMULTANEOUSLY WITH PERFORMANCE BOND IN FAVOR OF THE OWNER CONDITIONED ON THE FULL AND FAITHFUL PERFORMANCE OF THE CONTRACT

KNOW ALL MEN BY THESE PRESENTS: that

(Here insert full name and address or legal title of Contractor)

as Principal, hereinafter called Principal, and,

(Here insert full name and address or legal title of Surety)

as Surety, hereinafter called Surety, are held and firmly bound unto

(Here insert full name and address or legal title of Owner)

as Obligee, hereinafter called Owner, for the use and benefit of claimants as hereinbelow defined, in the

amount of

(Here insert a sum equal to at least one-half of the contract price)   Dollars ($),

for the payment whereof Principal and Surety bind themselves, their heirs, executors, administrators, successors and assigns, jointly and severally, firmly by these presents.

WHEREAS,

Principal has by written agreement dated   19   , entered into a contract with Owner for

(Here insert full name, address and description of project)

in accordance with Drawings and Specifications prepared by

(Here insert full name and address or legal title of Architect)

which contract is by reference made a part hereof, and is hereinafter referred to as the Contract.

LABOR AND MATERIAL PAYMENT BOND

NOW, THEREFORE, THE CONDITION OF THIS OBLIGATION is such that, if Principal shall promptly make payment to all claimants as hereinafter defined, for all labor and material used or reasonably required for use in the performance of the Contract, then this obligation shall be void; otherwise it shall remain in full force and effect, subject, however, to the following conditions:

1. A claimant is defined as one having a direct contract with the Principal or with a Subcontractor of the Principal for labor, material, or both, used or reasonably required for use in the performance of the Contract, labor and material being construed to include that part of water, gas, power, light, heat, oil, gasoline, telephone service or rental of equipment directly applicable to the Contract.

2. The above named Principal and Surety hereby jointly and severally agree with the Owner that every claimant as herein defined, who has not been paid in full before the expiration of a period of ninety (90) days after the date on which the last of such claimant's work or labor was done or performed, or materials were furnished by such claimant, may sue on this bond for the use of such claimant, prosecute the suit to final judgment for such sum or sums as may be justly due claimant, and have execution thereon. The Owner shall not be liable for the payment of any costs or expenses of any such suit.

3. No suit or action shall be commenced hereunder by any claimant:

a) Unless claimant, other than one having a direct contract with the Principal, shall have given written notice to any two of the following: the Principal, the Owner, or the Surety above named, within ninety (90) days after such claimant did or performed the last of the work or labor, or furnished the last of the materials for which said claim is made, stating with substantial accuracy the amount claimed and the name of the party to whom the materials were furnished, or for whom the work or labor was done or performed. Such notice shall be served by mailing the same by registered mail or certified mail, postage prepaid, in an envelope addressed to the Principal, Owner or Surety, at any place where an office is regularly maintained for the transaction of business, or served in any manner in which legal process may be served in the state in which the aforesaid project is located, save that such service need not be made by a public officer.

b) After the expiration of one (1) year following the date on which Principal ceased Work on said Contract, it being understood, however, that if any limitation embodied in this bond is prohibited by any law controlling the construction hereof such limitation shall be deemed to be amended so as to be equal to the minimum period of limitation permitted by such law.

c) Other than in a state court of competent jurisdiction in and for the county or other political subdivision of the state in which the Project, or any part thereof, is situated, or in the United States District Court for the district in which the Project, or any part thereof, is situated, and not elsewhere.

4. The amount of this bond shall be reduced by and to the extent of any payment or payments made in good faith hereunder, inclusive of the payment by Surety of mechanics' liens which may be filed of record against said improvement, whether or not claim for the amount of such lien be presented under and against this bond.

Signed and sealed this _____ day of _____ 19____

_____
(Witness)

_____
(Principal)   (Seal)

_____
(Title)

_____
(Witness)

_____
(Surety)   (Seal)

_____
(Title)

PART II. PROSECUTING AND DEFENDING CLAIMS

8. Documentation and Record Keeping

The second half of this chapter carries certain legal overtones, the sense of documenting one's case in court. But if the first task, that of record keeping, is conscientiously conducted, many construction differences are likely never to reach the courtroom.

Ultimately, what is at stake in any claim is money. But as a matter of sound administrative practice on any project, records must be kept, filed in an orderly fashion, and referred to as the occasion demands. Memories become faulty with time. Verbal agreements entered into in good faith are not recalled in detail. The stage will have been set for a potential dispute or claim. Documentation should be maintained whether or not either party foresees a change or a claim. In particular, anything that might conceivably affect the cost of the project should be documented. Any changes, however inconsequential they may seem at the time, must be recorded. These may be typed or written memoranda; they may be photographs with notes; or they may be entries in the contract plans or specifications. This latter system provides an excellent method of recording technical changes. For example, a note on the footing plans might state that on a specific date the owner's representative, by name, directed that footing E-8 be enlarged one foot in a northerly direction with appropriate increases in the length of reinforcement. This note should be initialed and dated. It is not unusual on large and complex projects to have more than 500 changes. Obviously, these can have a synergistic effect; it's going to be a lot easier to plot the effects of one change or another and their total impact on the job if every change is clearly recorded.

No one wishes to go to court or to resort to other methods of formally settling disputes. Both sides incur risks in doing so, not the least of which is a reputation for litigiousness or claims consciousness. In the long run, court cases are expensive. In addition to the obvious legal fees, there are less visible expenses: for example, diverting personnel from other more productive activities to activities related to the lawsuit such as time spent in court, with attorneys, in checking documents, and so forth.

But disputes do reach litigation. When they do, the sheer weight of paper can overwhelm the opposition, bolster one's case, and prove one's point. What follows is a discussion of the types of things that need to be recorded, the significance of the paper paraphernalia that attaches itself to any construction project, and suggestions about the storing and retrieval of that paperwork.

First, some general admonitions. With the broad freedom-of-information laws and broader interpretation of "discovery," just about any scrap of paper is likely to be accessible to the parties in a lawsuit, and could become part of the legal proceedings. Double entendre, wisecracks, or personal remarks in the margin or text of job records could become acutely embarrassing years later in the judicial setting. However, embarrassing records are better than no records. It has been argued that a certain amount of scribbling in the corners adds authenticity to such records; it does, particularly if it clarifies or ties to another document. But, be aware; anything down on paper could be subject to further scrutiny. (See the inspector's report at the end of this chapter. The handwritten version is preferable to a subsequent typed version when a dispute is being settled if it is legible. Both, of course, may be submitted.)

STORAGE AND RETRIEVAL

We are talking about a considerable amount of paper in most cases. The volume of paper is in proportion to the size of the project and of the dispute. Before it piles up, a system for filing should be established. Records may be kept for years on a long-term project; workable categories should be sorted out. Which categories these might be is to some extent a personal matter. The important thing is accessibility and some degree of orderliness. It is imperative that at least one complete record of all paper related to the project should be kept intact.

Cross-files according to subject areas, (i.e., concrete, payroll, borings, progress meeting minutes, etc.) can be maintained according to preference. Copies of documents and correspondence having to do with specific segments of the work or with particular individuals may be kept separately by the appropriate persons who, in certain cases, may be in widely separated locations.

Originals of field records generally are kept in the project office until job completion. Originals of contract documents are kept either in a regional office or a headquarters office. Originals of other documents such as weather conditions and strikes may be kept in still another office, such as a divison office.

The important thing is that all top level personnel associated with a project must know where the originals are and, at the appropriate time, make them available for negotiation purposes or for court appearances. If documents are sent to warehouse storage, responsible project officers must know what has been sent, how it is filed, and who controls access.

The contract documents must always remain intact. These, signed by both parties, will include the plans, which in many cases are also signed or at least initialed by both parties. They should also contain the performance bonds. This point should be clear to all on the job: *No one* should remove a relevant page for his particular use, or be in a position to lose or misplace any part of those documents while using it for reference. Conformed documents can be made available and will serve all purposes, except that final appearance in court.

With projects now increasing in size and with claims following in number, complexity, and dollar volume, computers are now being used for cross-referencing and information storage. There are no rules of thumb about what is the optimum project size where the use of a computer in retrieval is effective. The claim size must certainly be in the multi-million dollar range, and the numbers of documents in the tens of thousands of pages.

In the absence of documentation, when both sides are working in a professional manner to negotiate and settle claims, both will attempt to reconstruct events and establish the validity of the claims. This is, unfortunately, a most unsatisfactory way to proceed because everything relies on memory, and a very valid claim can be lost because neither party can substantiate what should be a proper settlement. Further, if the documentation was done but couldn't be found, all those hours of careful record keeping were wasted.

CORRESPONDENCE

The importance of sending letters cannot be overemphasized. Unlike the other categories of records—notes, diaries, invoices, meeting minutes, etc.—letters convey the sense of "shared" information. The recipient cannot say at a later date that he was unaware of a troublesome situation. In some cases, unacknowledged receipt can be construed as acquiescence or as lack of cooperation. Where matters of top importance are being discussed through correspondence, the use of return receipt certified mail or the inclusion of a duplicate copy with a place for the recipient to note receipt is recommended.

Letters should be written about everything that could impact the project. Even in the most harmonious of working situations, verbal suggestions, changes, promises, or complaints should be put in letter form and copies of such letters sent to enough people in order to spread that knowledge around. This can be done in the briefest of letters, but it should be done with all correspondence dated. A serial number can be assigned to each letter. Each letter can then be logged into a central register. Keep the principles of good letter writing in mind. Inform the writer why you are writing the letter. Is it for his information? Is it a direction to him? Does it call for a reply? When do you expect a reply? If you are referring to a continuing situation, use the same basic descriptive terms in each letter and refer to previous correspondence on this subject by date.

Receipt of letters should always be acknowledged. Acknowledgement can be cursory and noncommittal, but should be made. For example, "we received your letter of xxx about yyyy and are reviewing the situation. We expect to give you a complete reply by . . ." Again, send copies of these letters to project principals. The more copies distributed, the less likely the problem will disappear through a crack in the floor only to reappear when it has grown into a catastrophe.

PHOTOGRAPHS

Photographs of the work should be taken at every stage by both the owner and the contractor. This starts with pre-bid visits to the site. Photographs should be taken on the date of the start of work. Specific progress photographs on a predetermined time basis should also be included. Any unusual conditions or situations must be photographed. Finally, photographs should be taken of the completed project. Several staff members can be assigned this task. It is imperative that all photographs should be dated, and the location and the photographer noted. It is also helpful to include a person or some object of known dimensions in the photo to give a sense of scale. Without this identification, such photos are of little use in documenting a claim or change. Obvious candidates for this photographic record are changed conditions, damaged equipment or materials, blocked access to the site, flooding, and heavy snow.

General work progress should also be photographed. At some future time, a dated photograph indicating some state of construction — the extent of a concrete pour in a certain area — can belie or back up someone's sketchy notes or memory. Random shots are also essential. Some detail in the background may buttress a point in contention years later, for example, that the steel rebars are placed at a particular date during the work. A photograph may clarify a condition of the work during construction that is not observable during a claim unless test holes are cut into the concrete.

For example, in one relevant case, a reinforced concrete building was being analyzed after construction as to adequacy under a new seismic code. The design drawings were not clear as to the penetration of the column reinforcing into the floor slab, and the shop drawings could not be located ten years afterwards. Fortunately, a set of photographs were found indicating that the column reinforcing projected into the slab.

Sophisticated cameras and professional photographers are not necessary; the most pedestrian of pictures might still be worth more than a witness's 1,000 words. A 35mm camera using fine grain film in the hands of an amateur photographer can provide inexpensive photographs which can be blown up into clear 8″×10″ glossies that will clearly define the status of the work when the photograph was taken. Polaroid cameras do not have similar benefits; nevertheless, a polaroid shot of a hole in the pavement or disintegrated pavement or a crack in a brick masonry wall may very well tell the story. Polaroids also have the advantage of giving the photographer immediate knowledge that he has a usable photograph. He doesn't have to wait until the film is developed, by which time a condition may have changed.

A RECORDS CHECKLIST

The preceding points on the storage of information, the need for correspondence on sensitive items, photos, and or the caveat on making personal comments in job records are all general precepts to be followed by both the owner and the contractor. What follows is a checklist of points to be covered in a typical job sequence. In all cases, dates, time of day, location if appropriate, and people in attendance, should be noted.

Pre-bid.   Records should be kept for the following: the Invitation to Bid (newspaper, commerce business daily, or letter), Dodge Reports, Browns Letters, site visit notes and photographs, minutes of any pre-bid meetings, proposed schedules, estimates including work sheets, project log, and all addenda and logs of telephone conversations.

Some owners have found pre-bid meetings of value in clearing up ambiguities or unclear sections of the plans and specifications. They can also be used to clarify site conditions and provide information concerning other contracts in the general vicinity. At the meeting, the knowledgeable owner will state that no information given at the meeting is binding, nor a part of the contract, until a written set of the pre-bid meeting minutes is distributed with questions and answers included. These should be made an addendum to the contract.

Bid.   The contractor should have copies of all papers submitted, together with all supporting bid calculations, quantity takeoffs, subcontractors' and suppliers' quotes, estimated productivity of labor and equipment, and proposed project schedule in detail. Where subcontractors' prices and supplier's prices were received by telephone, there should be a written memorandum of each quotation together with date, time, and names of all parties involved. There should be a record of the receipt of all addenda received and any consultant reports. The names of the other bidders and the amounts bid by each should be recorded and kept in the file.

The owner should record the names of each organization submitting a bid, the amount of the bid, and whether or not bonds and other required material are attached—together with any protests or statements that were made by bidders or attendees. The names of the owner's representatives present should be recorded by both the owner and the contractor.

Precontract. Records should be kept for the following items: minutes of negotiation meetings, minutes of qualification hearings where applicable, job schedules, and record of any changes in costs that were negotiated. Any decisions agreed upon by the owner/contractor/engineer should be included. As part of any change, all calculations should be maintained as a permanent job file. Photographs and notes of any site visits during this period should also be stored.

Contract. Keep the original contract documents in a secure file (not to be used as working copies); conformed contracts should be made available for the job.

Construction. Minutes of a preconstruction conference should definitely be included. Such conferences are generally held between the award of the contract and the start of work. (See Appendix for an example of such minutes.) Copies of job schedules (including revisions) should be stored. Records should be made of all verbal instructions and field orders.

Job diaries, including those of foremen, field superintendents, and management are also part of the record. These form a record of what happened on the job each day — visitors, weather, materials delivered, trades working, names of all men working and so on. All diaries, including personal diaries, should be readily accessible. Parties maintaining these should understand that under the freedom-of-information laws relating to the prelitigation process, the contents of those diaries are all available to the otherside.

The fact that a diary is kept at home does not preclude its being entered into evidence during a pre-trial questioning, court proceeding, or arbitration hearing. Essentially any record, in whatever form, kept in connection with the project, by anyone, is available to all parties. These can even include tape recorded job "diaries." If it can be established that such were a part of a systematic procedure on the job and not a random instance, it is possible to introduce such records under the doctrines of "business records" or otherwise as "past recollection recorded."

Shop Drawings. The shop drawing log should be maintained accurately, with any delays in approval duly noted and, where possible, explained. These drawings can be one of the more critical aspects of a project, and if improperly handled, they can create major problems and delay on the project.

Shop drawing reviews are subject to misuse. Contractors have been known to make changes to the work and the intent of the design without highlighting the point, or possibly, without recognizing that they have changed the design. In turn, architects and engineers have been known to effect design changes with resultant changes in construction costs in the process of approving shop drawings without acknowledging (or again, recognizing) that they have done so. Neither intentional action is professional unless it is spelled out to the other party and the change noted. If one party believes the other has made a change, it should be discussed at once.

The engineer should be aware of the legal significance of his signature on shop drawings. In spite of exculpatory language on the approval stamp, i.e., "approval for general conformance with design requirements, not as to details and dimensions," courts and administrative boards are loathe to enforce exculpatory language that protects only the author of a document.

As-built drawings should be kept up to date; seemingly minor field changes should not be filled in later when the memory is dim. These might prove to be particularly important in the claim situation that involves changed conditions, increased quantities, or a failure.

Job Schedules. Job schedules and actual progress can be charted in several ways, such as "S" curves that plot money against time, simple bar graphs that indicate progress in various separate categories of work, and the critical path method (CPM). Progress may also be recorded with the aid of a computer on large complex projects.

Particular effort should be made to maintain accurate files of these charts and of any revisions made. In the final preparation for defense of a claim, these charts can prove to be the most telling piece of evidence to prove or disprove a case. They are essentially the final product of all documentation. Actual work completed can be overlayed against the original schedule and the causal relationship between the segments analyzed. In this manner, ripple or impact effects can be plotted, and their effect upon costs down the line can be measured. For example, a steel strike may delay one segment upon which another depends. This in turn causes another portion of the work to be performed during the winter which in turn required different equipment than that originally considered. CPM charts are a sophisticated analysis method and deserve careful scrutiny and review. (See chapters on delays and costs of delays.)

Owner's Records. While the basic records kept by an owner or a contractor are essentially the same (except for fixed-price contracts where the owner doesn't have much incentive to keep cost records), the owner has additional records which he keeps as a matter of form. These include inspectors' reports, concrete form approvals, borrow pit approval, field direction or clarification, safety observations and direction, and administrative decisions (such as permits, easements, transmittal of shop drawings, approval of material, and payment calculations).

Change Order Files. For each change that occurs or is believed to have occurred during the course of the work, a separate self-contained file should be maintained that includes the order, relevant correspondence, a record of all negotiations concerning the change, estimate of cost, and the calculations on which the estimates are based. Where possible, xerox copies of the appropriate sections of the specifications and the contract drawings will make the file more complete and simplify work during negotiations. At the end of the chapter, we have included an auditor's report on the costs of a change. This kind of document should always be kept on file.

Daily Reports. Records should be kept for daily staffing of the project, divided into trades amd subcontractors, part of which should include the time cards kept on the project. Time cards are one of the basic sources of data concerning a project. The time card on the average project is coded by the labor classification of the workman and another code indicating the type of work done. Each worker has a particular code; for example, every carpenter will be in the 700 series with the carpenter's helpers in the 800 series and the laborers in the 900 series. (See sample time cards at the end of this chapter.)

Every time card should include the date, the shift, the code number and name of every workman in that particular crew, the number of hours worked, the items worked on, the location, and the equipment and materials used. The time card should provide a space for the foreman to make his estimate of production, any problems, visitors, weather, lost time, or inefficient time. As a cross-check, the timekeeper will certify that these men were on the project at that particular time, were performing that particular operation, and the number of hours they worked. The payroll clerk will also check numbers, and depending upon the project, a member of management will also check the work items.

When there is a claim situation, it is desirable to have both the owner and the contractor agree as the work progresses upon the classification of labor, the man-hours, the equipment used, and any material involved in the item in dispute.

Payment Requisitions. The methods of payment are covered by the contract, and while many methods of payment are provided for, the two most common are:
  a. payment at predetermined intervals of time, such as monthly, based on percentage of completion.
  b. payment at completion of a certain phase of the project or of a certain dollar amount of work, such as $100,000.

The payment is made on the basis of a requisition submitted by the contractor to the owner. Or the owner can make his own estimate of work and pay based on that estimate. In both cases, both the contractor and the owner ought to agree upon the work performed during the payment period. Calculations by which these estimates are obtained should be kept by the party who prepared them. They are one source of a future reconstruction of the job and the preparation of an as-built CPM chart.

Minutes of all Meetings. These should include time, place where meeting is held, and those in attendance. The minutes should indicate who each participant represents. If these are continuing meetings, it is desirable to number the minutes to avoid the possibility of a set being overlooked or mislaid. These minutes should be kept in the same form for each meeting. Prior to the meeting, an agenda should be prepared and distributed. (A sample of job meeting minutes appears at the end of this chapter.)

A job meeting should cover such items as progress, any delays, effect of strikes or of material delivery delays, staffing of project, start of a new operation, status of change orders, status of shop drawing review, information required from the owner, information required from the contractor, and the need for clarification of drawings or specifications.

Change orders or agreements can start at such job meetings. Their insertion in the minutes is the beginning of documentation on a particular change order or agreement. It is desirable, however, that change orders or agreements be followed up by letters or written orders. The final item in the minutes should be the date, time, and location of the next meeting.

Several methods may be used to obtain concurrence of the minutes by those in attendance. At the following meeting, the opening item on the agenda can be the approval or changes to the prior minutes. Or both parties can sign the minutes when they have been approved or concurred in. If the minutes are distributed to all parties attending, and no objections are received, it can be assumed that the parties concur in what the minutes contain. Hence, if a party receives minutes that are incorrect or incomplete, he should make sure his objections are recorded in writing somewhere. Otherwise, years later in a claims setting, it will be difficult to overcome the presumed correctness of the minutes.

Field Reports.   Daily records should be kept of such items as cubic yards of concrete delivered, truckloads of earth or rock removed, truckloads of sand fill, deliveries of structural steel, shift progress in a tunnel, and the inspectors' reports on the work—including the location that he inspected each day. Daily reports should also include areas where work was performed, estimate of production, problems, visitors, weather, lost time or reports on inefficiency, and similar remarks. Records of estimated production are invaluable in a claims situation, especially where comparisons can be made between production before, during, and after the period when problems arose. (See samples of Inspector's Daily Report at the end of this chapter.)

Weather.   Daily weather records should be kept. In cases of delays which are attributed to weather conditions, the U.S. Meteorological Service can provide reference point data. The general contract usually contains time extension clauses excusing delay for unusually severe weather. (This subject is dealt with in Chapter 4.)The effect of the weather upon the job should be indicated. A series of rainy days can have a severe effect upon an earth moving operation, while it would have no effect upon interior work in a building.

Material and Equipment Records.   Delivery dates for all materials should be kept. Where there are delays in the delivery of such material, they should be indicated. All quotations, purchase orders, invoices, and similar documents should be kept on file. A record should be kept of damaged material or unsuitable supplies. Photographs may be used to document such damage. Any storage required for materials or equipment should be noted, especially if related to a change or delay of work. Unavailability of material and the reason for it should be documented. Cost of equipment on the project should be recorded.

Idle or extra time for expensive equipment can be a major cost in a claim. Ripple effects of changes involving equipment can be a significant factor. Storage, removing such equipment from another job, work under adverse conditions (winter months) or simply the delay caused by moving bulky equipment to a different location on a site should be recorded. (Chapter 5 on the costs of delays deals with this subject in more detail.)

A record of the types of equipment used each day and the number of hours these are used should be kept. A full description of every piece of equipment should be available in an equipment register or a similar record. When equipment is being repaired, the nature of the breakdown and the repair work should be recorded, as well as the time and materials used for repair.

Accident Records. The circumstances and the details of each accident that occurs on a job should be described. The amount of detail in connection with each accident should be in direct proportion to the seriousness of the accident. In addition, a record should be made of measures taken to insure safety. These can include regular meetings, use of films, use of lectures.

Generally, accidents are entirely an internal problem of the contractor, but there can be situations where accidents or potential accidents involving employee safety can have a major effect upon job progress and provide the groundwork for potential delays and claims. For example, if a tunnel becomes unsafe to the extent that miners will not go into it, special rehabilitation work may provide the basis for a claim. This may involve the installation of special temporary steel support and cause not only a dispute as to the method of payment, but cause a further delay due to the time required to set such steel. During such a time, a sizable work crew, together with equipment, is not productively engaged in proceeding on the tunnel.

Delay Records. Any delays due to strikes, weather, lack of access to the site, late delivery of materials, unavailability to materials, accidents, or any other reason should be kept in a delay file. Specifics should be listed.

For instance, in the case of a strike, the dates when work stopped, when the strike was settled, and when the work was resumed—all should be spelled out in detail. Add to this what the effect of the strike was on the project. Did it affect the entire project or did it stop an operation? If it did stop an operation, what was the effect of this on the overall progress? Strikes elsewhere that affect the work should be recorded. A national steelworkers strike or a national teamsters strike could have an effect upon the project. (See Chapter 4 for more detail.)

Subcontractors. The owner and the contractor can require of major subcontractors that similar records be kept on labor, equipment, delays, and similar matters. Naturally, if the subcontractor is a party to the claim, his records would be part of the claim, and he would be responsible for his own record keeping.

Overhead. Records of overhead costs on the job over a period of time are necessary if a claim is filed. Therefore, they should be kept as a matter of routine. This includes the time of all personnel, whether they be at the job site or in a headquarters office when they are doing work related to the project. It will include the costs of trailers, light, heat, telephone, supplies, and postage. The items that can be considered to be overhead are numerous. Overhead can include any costs connected with the project that are not specifically chargeable to a specific item of work. Whether or not an item is overhead is usually dependent upon the manner in which a contractor keeps his books.

The Eichleay Formula is one of the methods used to allocate jobs overhead. This Formula and other methods of computing costs are discussed in Chapter 5.

Time Cards. The time card process starts when the employee is hired. The worker is assigned a craft-related employee number at that time. For example, all carpenters could be in a 5000 series.

Firms that have many projects, or even one with more than 200 employees are advised to use computers. In a computerized payroll and cost accounting system, basic data such as the employee's social security number, craft, employee number, pay rate, etc., are entered either into a computer or a cassette used with the computer. Anything that affects pay rates, overtime rates, tax deductions, union deductions, or other payments by the employer is entered into the computer or cassette.

Similarly, every operation on which the contractor wishes to keep a record of costs (labor in this case, but the system is used to record other costs as well) is assigned a code number. For example, forms for concrete may be subdivided into classifications of footings and slabs on earth, then into walls, beams, soffits for slabs and so on. In turn, these subdivisions can be subdivided into prefabricated forms, erect, strip, and clean and oil. So, concrete forms may have a 6000 designation. Within the series, we could have 6010 (footing forms), 6011 (erect footing forms), 6014 (strip footing forms), 6015 (clean and oil footing forms), 6020 (wall forms), and so forth.

These codes generally require fine tuning for each particular project. The foreman must know the codes and also the details of the system so that he can enter proper numbers and descriptions.

When a card is complete for a shift and turned in, it must be checked by a responsible member of the project administrative staff for accuracy. For example, depending on job size this can be the project manager, the superintendent, or the cost engineer.

The information on the time card, along with the basic information stored on a cassette is fed into the computer. This includes the employee's hours worked as a total as well as the hours worked that are designated under a particular coded item or items.

The computer then provides payroll data on a weekly basis. The output can be mailed to the job site, or if the computer is on site, a printout can be provided there. Checks are made out mechanically at either location.

Cost data may be printed on a weekly or a monthly basis. The responsibility rests with the estimator or the cost engineer to feed the necessary quantities of work prepared during the period into the computer. Thus, total stored labor costs can be distributed into total and costs per item of work.

On smaller projects all these calculations can be performed manually either on site or at the main office.

Some sample time cards follow.

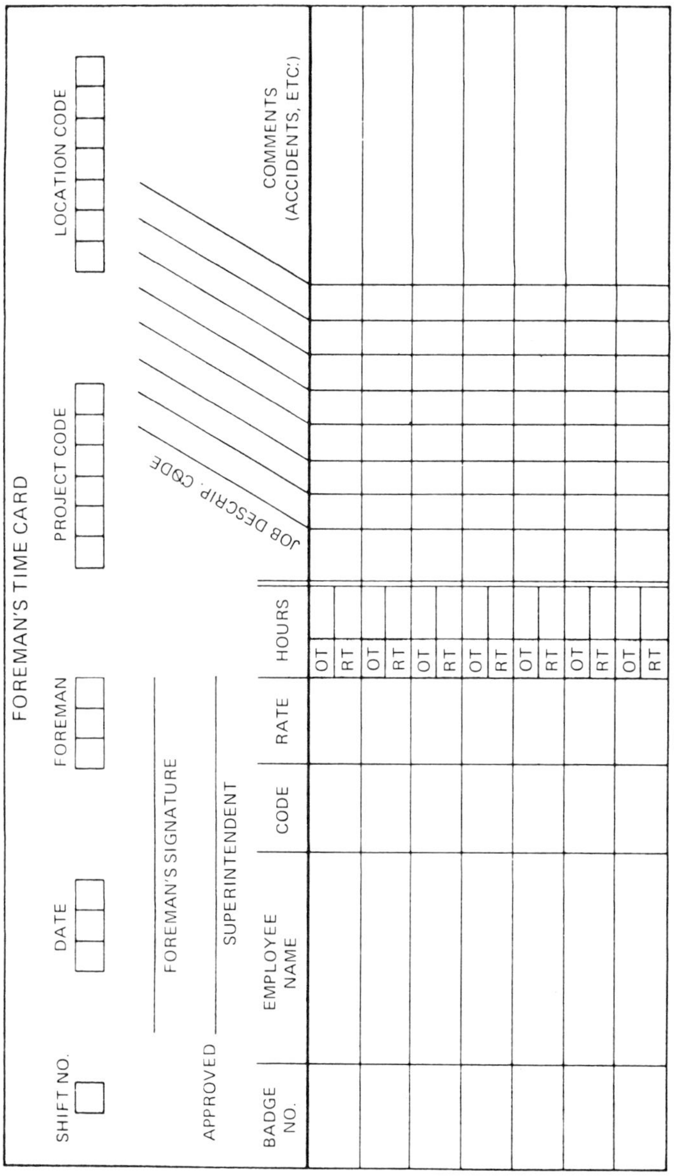

FOREMAN'S TIME CARD

SHIFT NO.

DATE

FOREMAN

PROJECT CODE

LOCATION CODE

FOREMAN'S SIGNATURE

APPROVED _____ SUPERINTENDENT

JOB DESCRIP. CODE

BADGE NO.	EMPLOYEE NAME	CODE	RATE	HOURS		COMMENTS (ACCIDENTS, ETC.)
				OT		
				RT		
				OT		
				RT		
				OT		
				RT		
				OT		
				RT		
				OT		
				RT		
				OT		
				RT		
				OT		
				RT		

This time card is generally used on computerized payrolls and cost accounting. Foreman enters data including employees' names, badge number, work description, work code, and craft code. Computer does the rest.

Foreman completes this section of card entering description of work being done by each man in his crew, e.g. Strip Col. Forms 1st fl, bldg 12.

Superintendent, project engineer or cost acc't enters job code for work described by foremen.

Foreman enters hours.

Clerk or cost acc't enters amount which is hours times pay rate.

Foreman enters badge number in numerical order for each man in his crew and enters hours work on each item

Clerk or cost acc't rates and amounts and makes cross check to verify that all figures check.

Time keeper checks foreman's hours entered against his field checks.

Foreman signs card and should turn in at close of work day.

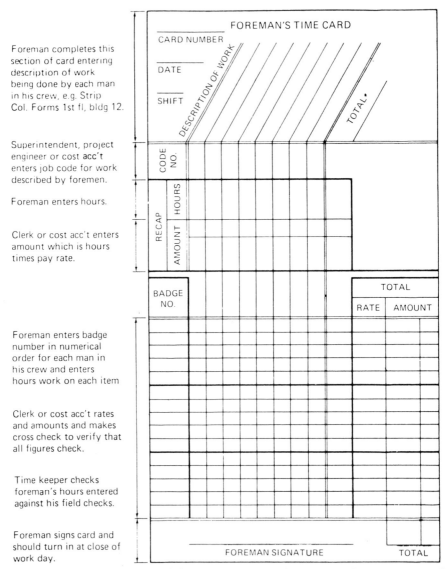

TIME CARD for a relatively small project and generally, but not necessarily for a non-computerized payroll and cost accounting system.

Summary.   Records are kept for many purposes on a construction project. A contractor requires cost records and productivity records for use in the preparation of item costs to be used in the preparation of future bids. As a matter of good business, as the job progresses, the contractor should determine how his actual expenses compare with his estimated expenses. He should be calculating what his anticipated profit is on a continuing basis compared to the profit he estimated when his bid was prepared. Payroll records must be kept so that the proper payroll taxes such as federal, state, and local income taxes can be deducted, together with social security and similar taxes and charges applicable to payroll.

The owner is generally interested as to whether or not the contractor is paying the prevailing wage rate and, at times, may be interested in keeping his own costs on particular items of work for reference in future projects. There are also records required by federal, state, or local regulations. For example, those relating to affirmative action, equal opportunity, minority hiring goals and so on.

Most important, in terms of this book, records are kept to document claims or to defend against claims or extra costs caused by a wide spectrum of delays or changes.

All parties to a project should be keeping records. Once it has been determined that a delay exists or that there is a change to the contract documents, the records should provide an equitable means of determining whatever additional costs are incurred. If records are not maintained or have been lost, one party or the other may suffer unjustly. Claimants may be forced to rely on experts' reasonable estimates, for example, or be forced to accept the other party's calculations of costs, or go to court.

The contractual documents are the obvious reference point for the start of a claim. It is the claimant's responsibility to prove not only that there was a deviation from the contract documents, but that the incurred additional expenses came either directly or indirectly as a result of this deviation. The proof of the claimant's position must rest with the documentation that he maintained and the documentation available under freedom-of-information laws, pre-trial disclosure, or through the good will of the party from whom he is requesting recompense.

MINUTES OF JOB MEETING

The following is a typical heading for a set of minutes for a job meeting, followed by the outline of business conducted during that meeting. In this fictional case, the project is being performed under a construction manager (CM), who is responsible for keeping the minutes.

ABC CONSTRUCTION MANAGEMENT CO.

	Meeting No.	_____
Minutes of Job Meeting	Page	_____
Owner: Fairfax Developers	Date	_____
Project: Timon Housing	Contract No.	_____

Phase II Grading and Road Paving
       DEF Construction Company

Present: Mssrs.

T. E. Smith	DEF Construction Co.	B. C. White	Timon Housing
R. A. Jones	DEF Construction Co.	D. F. Right	ABC Construction Management Co.
A. C. Black	Timon Housing		

Date: _____   Location: _____

Outline of basic entries:

1. General and Special Announcements
2. Review of Minutes of Last Meeting
3. Payment Requests—status, past and present.
4. Job progress by specific items with emphasis on critical path items
5. Job Administration
    Shop drawing status
    Change order status
    Owner furnished materials and equipment
    Quality control reports
    As-built drawings
    Progress photos
    Site control (access, parking, etc.)
6. County restrictions
7. Contract Item List—list of materials needed such as roadway base stone, cast iron inlets, road signs, manhole casting.
8. Safety Reports
9. Labor Conditions
10. Equal employment opportunity reports
11. Weekly payroll reports.
12. Date of next meeting, time and location.

Distribution list

    All present
    Others

Signed by _____
Title

INSPECTOR'S DAILY REPORTS

What follows are two samples of an Inspector's Daily Report. The first is hand-written; the second is the same report, but typed out. Although the typed version may be more legible, the handwritten copy lends more authenticity to the report.

SNCO-4

UNITED STATES
DEPARTMENT OF THE INTERIOR
BUREAU OF RECLAMATION
SOUTHERN NEVADA CONSTRUCTION OFFICE

INSPECTOR DAILY REPORT

PROJECT _____ S-N-C-O _____

ROUTING	INT
Chief Inspector	
Field Engineer	
Const. Engr.	
Office Engr.	
Contract Adm.	

Feature _PUMPING PLANTS_   Date _THURS. APRIL 10, 19__ Shift _DAY 6 AM - 3 PM_

Specs No. _DC7347_   Weather _CLEAR   COOL TO WARM_

Contractor _____   Contractor Rep. _____

Sub Contractor _____   Location of Work _HACIENDA PUMPING PLANT._

Safety _SATISFACTORY - 5 MIN. TAILGATE SAFETY MEETING CHANGED TO MON. OF EACH WEEK._

Description of Work _6 AM - 3" & 4" SUMP PUMPS OPERATED_

WHAT DURING PAST 24 HOURS. 6" DISCHARGE - 252 GPM ±

WHERE 9 AM - DISCHARGE MANIFOLD ENC. N° 5 E' PORTION OF

WHO NORTH WALL ELEV. 1846 42 TO ELEV. 1853 33 LINES 'B' & 'C'

WHY AND LINES '1 TO 5 WAS PLACED BY PLACEMENT

WHEN CREW. CONCRETE WAS REASONABLY CONSISTENT
AS TO WORKABILITY. BATCH 70 Y³ USED 69 3/4 Y³ 1/4 Y³
WASTE. 12 30 PM PLACEMENT COMPLETE.
2 CARPENTER CREWS CONTINUE WORK ON LEVEL
II SOUTHWALL N° 5 FORMS. GETTING FORMS
READY FOR WPRS SURVEY CREW CHECKOUT.
WPRS SURVEY CREW CHECKED OUT INSIDE
WALL FORM FOR LINE & PLUMB. WILL
COMPLETE CHECKOUT @ 7 30 AM FRIDAY 4/11/80
PLACEMENT OF 100 Y³ SCHEDULED FOR 9 00 AM
FRIDAY, 4/11/80.
2 CARPENTER CREWS CONTINUE WORKING
ON 2ND DECK FORMS & BEAM FORMS.
IRONWORKERS COMPLETED PLACING & TYING
REBAR FOR BEAMS & TOP & BOTTOM MATS IN II
DECK.

(OVER)

ELECTRICIANS CONTINUE CONDUIT & LIGHT
BOX INSTALLATIONS IN 2ND DECK
HOURS WORKED CRAIG $6\frac{5}{AM}$ - $7\frac{00}{PM}$
                    HART $7\frac{00}{AM}$ - $6\frac{30}{PM}$

PLUMBERS COMPLETED INSTALLATION OF
DRAIN SYSTEM FOR THIS AREA.
LABORERS CONTINUE CLEANUP &
BLOWDOWN OF FORMS AND MATERIALS
DIRT SPREAD - AIR CHAMBER TEE ENG. AREA.
   3 - 10 WHEEL DUMP TRUCKS & 2 SEMI
TRAILERS (END DUMPS) CONTINUE HAULING
BACKFILL MATERIAL FROM WASTE AREA
FOR USE AS COMPACTED EMBANKMENT
AROUND & ABOUT STRUCTURE.
SPREADING BY JD 450 DOZER & SPREADING
& COMPACTION BY CAT 825 B WHEEL
ROLLER. WACKER BEING USED FOR
COMPACTION AROUND AND AT STRUCTURE
WALLS
RETEST Nº 1 - COMPACTION BY WACKER
ELEV 1854$\frac{00}{}$ - LINE 14 & LINE 'a'
RESULTS 93.3% & .4 DRY - WILL REWORK &
RETEST.
TEST Nº 2 - COMPACTION BY WHEEL ROLLER
   ELEV 1864$\frac{00}{}$ LINE 'a' 15' NORTH & LINE 22 50' WEST
RESULTS - 99.8% - .4 WET ACCEPT
TEST Nº 3. COMPACTION BY WACKER
   ELEV 1864$\frac{00}{}$ LINE 'a' 5 FT. NORTH & LINE 22 40' WEST
RESULTS - 96.8% - 1.2 DRY ACCEPT
$3\frac{30}{PM}$
OPER & OILER w/ HC 138A CRANE; MASTER MECHANIC
w/ TRUCK, WELDER & TOOLS & 2 LABORERS STARTED
ADDING A 30' JT OF GCM PIPE TO SUMP OF
3" PUMP. WILL ALSO CHANGE PIPING &
ADD HOSE FOR ADDITIONAL DEPTH
$6\frac{30}{PM}$ JOB NOT COMPLETE - 3" SUMP PUMP NOT BACK IN
OPERATION. WILL START AT $6\frac{30}{AM}$ FRIDAY 4/11/80

SNCO 9

UNITED STATES
DEPARTMENT OF THE INTERIOR
BUREAU OF RECLAMATION
Southern Nevada Construction Office
CONCRETE INSPECTORS PLACEMENT REPORT

ROUTING	INIT.
CHIEF INSPECTOR	
FIELD ENGINEER	
CONST. ENGINEER	
OFFICE ENGINEER	
CONTRACT ADMIN	

HACIENDA PUMPING PLANT

FEATURE _____ CONTRACTOR *PETER KIEWIT SONS* SPEC. NO. *DC 7347*

FOREMAN *H. ARGABRIGHT* WEATHER *CLEAR-WARM* DATE *4/10/80* TNURS. DAY *30* SHIFT *7am-3pm*

PLM NO	STRUCTURE	STATION FROM	STATION TO	ELEVATION FROM	ELEVATION TO	TIME START	TIME END
1	DISCH. MANI. ENG #5 E	LINES 'A' TO 'C'	LINES 1 TO 5	1846-42	1853-33	9:10 AM	12:30 PM
2	NORTH WALL						
3							
4							

PLM NO	CY CONCRETE PLACED GROUT	3/4"	1-1/2"	3"	CY CONCRETE WASTED GVMNT	CONTR	MAX SIZE	REASON	PLACING TEMP NO TAK	MAX	MIN
1			69 3/4			1/4		OVERORDER		75°F	70°F
2											
3											
4											

PLM NO	METHOD OF: PLACING	CONSOLIDATING	PROTECTING	CURING
1	CRANE W/2Y³ BUCKET	INTERNAL VIBRATION	CLEAR É WHITE CURING COMPOUND	
2				
3				
4				

SAFETY & REMARKS *REBAR AS DETAILED AND AS PER SPEC. DWGS*

CONTINUE REMARKS ON BACK OF SHEET

RELIEVED _____ RELIEVED BY _____ INSPECTOR *Jules M. Craig*

SNCO-7

UNITED STATES
DEPARTMENT OF THE INTERIOR
BUREAU OF RECLAMATION
SOUTHERN NEVADA CONST. OFFICE

INSPECTORS DAILY REPORT FOR *THURS* DATE 4/10/80

LABOR AND EQUIPMENT

SPEC'S. NO. DC7347

INSPECTOR *[signature]*

LABOR

Name of Employee	Class	Rate	Hour	Description of Today's Work	Item
M. ROBERSON	GEN CARP FMN		11½		
~~L. EASTON~~	~~CARP~~			VACATION	
D. NERO	CARP FMN		10½	SUPERVISION	
G. GRAHAM	CARP FMN		10½		
C.P. JOHNSON	CARP FMN		8		
C.R. LEWIS	CARP FMN		11		
H. LOOSBROOCK	"		10½	BUILD FORMS	
J. GRAHAM	"		10½	SET FORMS	
D. COURTNEY	"		10½	STRIP FORMS	
G. STERRETT	"		10½	SET FALSE WORK	
J. McCULLAR	"		10½		
R. DOZIER	"		10½		
A. MAESTAS	"		8		
A. ANDERSON	"		8		

EQUIPMENT

Equipment	Model	Make	Hour	Capacity	Today's Work	Item

SNCO-7

UNITED   STATES
DEPARTMENT OF THE INTERIOR
BUREAU OF RECLAMATION
SOUTHERN NEVADA CONST. OFFICE

INSPECTORS DAILY REPORT FOR   *THURS* DATE *4/10/80*

LABOR   AND   EQUIPMENT

SPEC'S. NO. *OC7347*   INSPECTOR *Jules M. Craig*

LABOR

Name of Employee	Class	Rate	Hour	Description of Today's Work	Item
J. SALAZAR	CARP.		10½		
				BUILD FORMS	
D. BRADBURN	CARP APP		10½	SET FORMS	
W. HUGHES	" "		10½	STRIP FORMS	
K. LESTER	" "		8	BUILD SAFETY HANDRAILS,	
R. HOUSKA	" "		10½	STAIRS, ETC.	
R. KEEVER	" "		8	SET FALSEWORK	
AL WARD	CEM FIN FMN		8	SUPERVISON	
C. DUSHANE	C/F APP.		8	CONCRETE REPAIRS	
M. DELEO	CEM. FIN		8		

EQUIPMENT

Equipment	Model	Make	Hour	Capacity	Today's Work	Item

SNCO-7

UNITED   STATES
DEPARTMENT   OF   THE   INTERIOR
BUREAU OF RECLAMATION
SOUTHERN   NEVADA CONST.   OFFICE
INSPECTORS   DAILY   REPORT   FOR

THURS
DATE 4/10/80

LABOR   ~AND~   EQUIPMENT

SPEC'S. NO. _DC7347_

INSPECTOR Jules M. Craig

LABOR

Name of Employee	Class	Rate	Hour	Description of Today's Work	Item
L. SMITH	LABOR FMN		11¼	SUPERVISION	
E. SACHETTI	LABORER		8		
J. WATERS	''		8		
A. DELAROSA	''		8	SAND BLASTING	
W.H. WILSON	''		10½	BLOW DOWN	
I. LOGAN	''		11'	CLEAN UP	
M. ROBB	''		10½	HELP CARPENTERS	
M. REITH	''		8		
A. CHAVEZ	''		8		
P. SILVA	TMSTR		8	WATER TRUCK	
PHIL JUAREZ	MSTR, MECH,		6	WELD GCMPEXTENSION	

EQUIPMENT

Equipment	Model	Make	Hour	Capacity	Today's Work	Item

SNCO-7

UNITED   STATES
DEPARTMENT   OF   THE   INTERIOR
BUREAU   OF   RECLAMATION
SOUTHERN   NEVADA   CONST.   OFFICE

INSPECTORS   DAILY   REPORT   FOR

LABOR   *AND*   EQUIPMENT

THURS 4/10/80
DATE

SPEC'S. NO. _DC 7347_   INSPECTOR _Jules M. Craig_

LABOR

Name of Employee	Class	Rate	Hour	Description of Today's Work	Item
R. ALLISON	OPER.FMN		8		
J. MATTHEWS	OPER		8	LOAD TRUCKS	
L. ABRAMS	"		9	HAUL BACKFILL MATERIAL	
~~A. PATTAC~~				SPREAD BACKFILL MATERIAL	
~~J SAND LANTI~~	OPER "		8	COMPACT EMBANKMENT	
R. GABEL	TMSTR		8	HAUL é PLACE ROCK	
G. CHADWICK	"		8		
R. JAMES	"		8		
J. PERDON	"		8		
C. BAIRD	"		8		
J. LANCASTER	OPER.		12	CRANE WORK W/ FORMS	
J. DREW	OILER		11½	UNLOAD MATERIALS	
A. MATTHEWS	LABORER		8	COMPACT EMBANKMENT	
R. WAGNER	"		8	FLAGMAN - HANDWORK - DIRT	

EQUIPMENT

Equipment	Model	Make	Hour	Capacity	Today's Work	Item
CRANE	HC138A	LINKBELT	12 / 8	25 T	FORMS é MATERIALS	
DOZER	JD450C	JOHN DEERE	8		SPREAD BACKFILL	
VIBRATORY ROLLER (SHEEP FOOT		ESSICK)			COMPACTION	
WACKERS	SER. 300	MIKAYSA	8		"	
WATER TRUCK		FORD	6	1200GAL	DUST CONTROL	
LOADER	966C	CAT	8	$3/5 y^3$	LOAD TRUCKS	
BACKHOE	780	CASE	4	$2 y^3$	HAUL ROCK	
TRUCKS - 3 (10 WHEEL END DUMB é 2 - TRAILER					HAUL BACKFILL	
END DUMPS)			24		MATERIAL	

UNITED   STATES
DEPARTMENT OF THE INTERIOR
BUREAU OF RECLAMATION

SNCO-7

SOUTHERN NEVADA CONST. OFFICE

INSPECTORS DAILY REPORT FOR   THURS DATE 4/10/80

LABOR   AND   EQUIPMENT

SPEC'S. NO. _OC 7347_

INSPECTOR _Jules M. Craig_

LABOR

Name of Employee	Class	Rate	Hour	Description of Today's Work	Item
STEEL ENG'R'G.					
J. HUFFSTEDLER	I/W FMN		8		
R. CAMPBELL	I/W FMN		8		
DALE COWAN	I/W		8	PLACE é TIE REBAR	
JIM NELSON	I/W		8		
L. LAUNCIEAUX	I/W		8		
BOB RIPER	I/W		8		
ROSENDIN ELEC					
J. HEISHMAN	ELEC		8	PLACE é SECURE CONDUIT	
J. BUETTNER	ELEC		8		
B. P. WILLIAMS					
P. BROPHY	PLBR FMN		4	DRAINS	
M. VELENCE	"	"	4		

EQUIPMENT

Equipment	Model	Make	Hour	Capacity	Today's Work	Item

SNCO-4

UNITED STATES
DEPARTMENT OF THE INTERIOR
WATER AND POWER RESOURCES SERVICE

SOUTHERN NEVADA CONSTRUCTION OFFICE

INSPECTOR DAILY REPORT

ROUTING	INT
Chief Inspector	
Field Engineer	
Const. Engr.	
Office Engr.	
Contract Adm.	

PROJECT _____ SNCO _____

Feature Pumping Plants _____ **Date** Thurs. 4/10/80 **Shift** 6:15 A.M. – 3:30 P.M.

Specs No. DC-7347 _____ **Weather** Clear, Cool to Warm _____

Contractor ___ __ _____ **Contractor Rep** _____

Sub Contractor _____ **Location of Work** ___ __ _____

Safety Satisfactory – 5 min. tailgate safety meeting changed to Monday of
each week.

Description of Work 6:15 A.M. – 3" and 4" sump pumps operated during past 24 hours.

WHAT
WHERE
WHO
WHY
WHEN

6" discharge – 252 gmp^{+}. 9:10 A.M. – discharge manifold enc. No. 5 and portion
of north wall elev. 1846.42 to elev. 1853.33 lines 'a' and 'c' and lines 1 to 5
was placed by placement crew. Concrete was reasonably consistent as to
workability. Batch 70 y^3 used 69 3/4 y^3 1/4 y^3 waste. 12:30 P.M. placement
complete.

2 carpenter crews continue work on level II southwall No. 5 forms. Getting
forms ready for WPRS survey crew checkout. WPRS survey crew checked out inside
wall form for line and plumb. Will complete checkout at 7:30 A.M. Friday,
4/11/80. Placement of 100 y^3 scheduled for 9:00 A.M. Friday, 4/11/80.

2 carpenter crews continue working on 2nd deck forms and beam forms. Iron
workers completed placing and tying rebar for beams and top and bottom mats in II
deck.

Electricians continue conduit and light box installations in 2nd deck.

Plumbers completed installation of drain system for this area. Laborers continue
clean-up and blow down of forms and materials dirt spread – air chamber tee enc.
area. 3 – 10 wheel dump trucks and 2 semi trailers (end dumps) continue hauling
backfill material from waste area for use as compacted embankment around and about
structure.

Spreading by JD 450 Dozer and spreading and compaction by Cat 825B wheel roller.

Wacker being used for compaction around and at structure walls.

Retest No. 1 – compaction by wacker.

Elev. 1854.00 – line 14 and line 'a'.

Results: 93.3% and .4 dry – will rework and retest.

(OVER) **INSPECTOR**

Test No. 2 - Compaction by wheel roller,

Elev. 1864.00 - line 'a' 15' north and line 22 50' west

Results - 99.8% - .4 wet accept

Test No. 3 - compaction by wacker

Elev. 1864.00 - line 'a' 5 feet north and line 22 40' west

Results - 96.8% - 1.2 dry accept

3:30 P.M. - oper and oiler w/HC138A crane; master mechanic w/truck, welder

and tools and 2 laborers started adding a 30' jt of GCM pipe to sump of

3" pump. Will also change piping and add hose for additional depth.

6:30 P.M. - job not complete - 3" sump pump not back in operation. Will

start at 6:30 A.M., Friday 4/11/80.

SNCO 9

UNITED STATES
DEPARTMENT OF THE INTERIOR
BUREAU OF RECLAMATION
Southern Nevada Construction Office
CONCRETE INSPECTORS PLACEMENT REPORT

ROUTING	INIT.
CHIEF INSPECTOR	
FIELD ENGINEER	
CONST. ENGINEER	
OFFICE ENGINEER	
CONTRACT ADMIN.	

FEATURE __Pumping Plant__ CONTRACTOR _____ SPEC. NO __DC-7347__

FOREMAN _____ WEATHER __clear, warm__ DATE __4/10/80__ SHIFT __7 - 3:30__ Day

PLM NO	STRUCTURE	STATION FROM	STATION TO	ELEVATION FROM	ELEVATION TO	TIME START	TIME END
1	Disch. Mani. Enc. #5 &	Lines 'a' to	Lines 1 to 5	1846.42	1853.33	9:10 A	12:30 P
2	North wall	'c'					
3							
4							

PLM NO	GROUT	3/4"	1-1/2"	3"	GVMNT	CONTR	MAX SIZE	REASON	NO TAK	MAX	MIN
1			69 3/4			1/4		Overorder		75 F	70F
2											
3											
4											

CY CONCRETE PLACED — CY CONCRETE WASTED — PLACING TEMP

PLM NO	PLACING	CONSOLIDATING	PROTECTING	CURING
1	Crane w/2 Y^3 Bucket	Internal Vibration	Clear & White Curing Compound	
2				
3				
4				

METHOD OF:

SAFETY & REMARKS __Rebar as detailed and as per spec. drawings.__

CONTINUE REMARKS ON BACK OF SHEET

RELIEVED _____ RELIEVED BY _____ INSPECTOR _____

UNITED STATES
DEPARTMENT OF THE INTERIOR
WATER & POWER RESOURCES SERVICE

SNCO-7

SOUTHERN NEVADA CONST. OFFICE

INSPECTORS DAILY REPORT FOR

LABOR ⟋AND⟍ EQUIPMENT

Thurs.

DATE 4/10/80

SPEC'S. NO. DC-7347   INSPECTOR_____

LABOR

Name of Employee	Class	Rate	Hour	Description of Today's Work	Item
M. X	Gen Carp Fmn		11½		
D. X	Carp Fmn		10½	Supervision	
G. X	Carp Fmn		10½		
C. X	Carp Fmn		8		
C. X	Carp Fmn		11		
H. X	Carp Fmn		10½	Build Forms	
J. X	Carp Fmn		10½	Set Forms	
D. X	Carp Fmn		10½	Strip Forms	
G. X	Carp Fmn		10½	Set False Work	
J. X	Carp Fmn		10½		
R. X	Carp Fmn		10½		
A. X	Carp Fmn		8		
A. X	Carp Fmn		8		

EQUIPMENT

Equipment	Model	Make	Hour	Capacity	Today's Work	Item

SNCO-7

UNITED   STATES
DEPARTMENT OF THE INTERIOR
WATER & POWER RESOURCES SERVICE
SOUTHERN NEVADA CONST. OFFICE

INSPECTORS   DAILY   REPORT   FOR

LABOR   ~AND~   EQUIPMENT

Thurs.
DATE 4/10/80

SPEC'S. NO. DC-7347   INSPECTOR

LABOR

Name of Employee	Class		Rate	Hour	Description of Today's Work	Item
J. S	Carp.			10½		
					Build Forms	
D. B	Carp	App.		10½	Set Forms	
W. H	Carp	App.		10½	Strip Forms	
K. L	Carp	App.		8	Build Safety Hand Rails,	
R. H	Carp	App.		10½	Stairs, etc.	
R. K	Carp	App.		8	Set False Work	
Al	Cem	Fin Fmn		8	Supervision	
C. D	C/F	App.		8	Concrete Repairs	
M. D	Cem	Fin		8		

EQUIPMENT

Equipment	Model	Make	Hour	Capacity	Today's Work	Item

UNITED STATES
DEPARTMENT OF THE INTERIOR
WATER & POWER RESOURCES SERVICE
SNCO-7
SOUTHERN NEVADA CONST. OFFICE

INSPECTORS DAILY REPORT FOR

LABOR AND EQUIPMENT

Thurs.
DATE 4/10/80

SPEC'S. NO. DC-7347

INSPECTOR

LABOR

Name of Employee	Class	Rate	Hour	Description of Today's Work	Item
L. SS	Labor Fmn		11½	Supervision	
E. SS	Laborer		8		
J. WS	Laborer		8		
A. DS	Laborer		8	Sand Blasting	
W. HS.	Laborer		10½	Blow Down	
I. LS	Laborer		11	Clean-up	
M. IS	Laborer		10½	Help Carpenters	
M. IS	Laborer		8		
A. S	Laborer		8		
P. SS	TMSTR		8	Water Truck	
Phil JS	MSTR. MECH.		6	Weld GCMP Extension	

EQUIPMENT

Equipment	Model	Make	Hour	Capacity	Today's Work	Item

SNCO-7

UNITED STATES
DEPARTMENT OF THE INTERIOR
WATER & POWER RESOURCES SERVICE
SOUTHERN NEVADA CONST. OFFICE
INSPECTORS DAILY REPORT FOR
LABOR ⟵AND⟶ EQUIPMENT

Thurs.
DATE 4/10/80

SPEC'S. NO. DC-7347

INSPECTOR_____

LABOR

Name of Employee	Class	Rate	Hour	Description of Today's Work	Item
A X	Oper Fmn		8		
M X	Oper.		8	Load Trucks	
A X	Oper.		9	Haul Backfill Material	
S X	Oper.		8	Spread Backfill Material	
C X	TMSTR.		8	Compact Embankment	
C X	TMSTR.		8	Haul & Place Rock	
J X	TMSTR.		8		
P X	TMSTR.		8		
B X	TMSTR.		8		
L X	Oper.		12	Crane work w/forms	
D X	Oiler		11½	Unload Materials	
M X	Laborer		8	Compact Embankment	
W X	Laborer		8	Flagman - Hand work - Dirt	

EQUIPMENT

Equipment	Model	Make	Hour	Capacity	Today's Work	Item
Crane	HC138A	Linkbelt	12	75T	Forms & Materials	
Dozer	JO450C	John Deere	8		Spread Backfill	
Vibratory Roller	(Sheep Foot Essick)				Compaction	
Wackers	Ser. 300	Mikaysa	8		Compaction	
Water Truck		Ford	6	1200 GAL	Dust Control	
Loader	966C	Cat	8	3/5 Y^3	Load Trucks	
Backhoe	780	Case	4	24.3	Haul Rock	
Trucks - 3 (10 wheel end dumps and 2- trailer					Haul Backfill	
end dumps)			24		Material	

SNCO-7

UNITED STATES
DEPARTMENT OF THE INTERIOR
WATER & POWER RESOURCES SERVICE
SOUTHERN NEVADA CONST. OFFICE
INSPECTORS DAILY REPORT FOR
LABOR ⟨AND⟩ EQUIPMENT

Thurs.
DATE 4/10/80

SPEC'S. NO. DC-7347

INSPECTOR

LABOR

Name of Employee	Class	Rate	Hour	Description of Today's Work	Item
Steel Engr.					
J. HX	I/W Fmn		8		
R. CX	I/W Fmn		8		
Dale X	I/W		8	Place and Tie Rebar	
Jim X	I/W		8		
L. X	I/W		8		
Bob X	I/W		8		
Elec.					
J. X	Elec		8	Place and Secure Conduit	
J. X	Elec		8		
B.PX					
P. X	Plbr Fmn		4	Drains	
M. X	Plbr Fmn		4		

EQUIPMENT

Equipment	Model	Make	Hour	Capacity	Today's Work	Item

AUDIT REPORT

What follows is an audit report on a federal project.

II-C-IDA-LBR-13-75(R)

UNITED STATES DEPARTMENT of the INTERIOR
OFFICE OF THE SECRETARY
OFFICE OF AUDIT AND INVESTIGATION
CENTRAL REGION

1841 Wadsworth
Lakewood, Colorado 80215

MEMORANDUM AUDIT REPORT

January 21, 1975

Memorandum

To: Commissioner, Bureau of Reclamation

From: Regional Audit Manager

Subject: Audit of Change Order No. 2 (Powerhouse), Specifications No. DC-6910, Teton Dam, Power and Pumping Plant, Teton Basin Project

We have completed our audit of costs incurred under Order for Changes No. 2 (Powerhouse), Specifications No, DC-6910, Teton Dam, Power and Pumping Plant, Teton Basin Project. Field work was completed at the Contractor's (a joint venture between Morrison-Knudsen Company, Inc., and Peter Kiewit Sons' Company) construction site at Newdale, Idaho, on December 13, 1974.

Your request was for an audit of costs incurred under Order for Changes No. 2 (Powerhouse) and Order for Changes No. 4 (Riprap). Order for Changes No. 2 resulted from not encountering rock in the northwest corner of the foundation of the power and pumping plant at elevation 4980 as anticipated in the specifications. The change order, as revised by the Contractor and submitted to the Bureau of Reclamation (LBR) per Contractor's letter dated June 26, 1974, claimed costs (and profit) totaling $177,848. Costs claimed under this change order were incurred during October and November 1972.

Order for Changes No. 4 resulted from increased costs associated with a change in the designated riprap source; the original quarry failed to provide the larger sizes of rock required by specifications. The change in quarry sites resulted in an increased haul distance and nonproductive costs incurred in attempting to utilize the original quarry site.

The original contract price for supplying and placing a ton of riprap on the dam was $2.85 per ton. In the Contractor's letter dated July 2, 1974, a proposed price of $6.80 per ton to supply and place riprap on the dam was made. This figure was revised in a subsequent letter from the Contractor dated November 26, 1974. The revised figure was set by the Contractor at $10.31 per ton.

Following a discussion of the increased costs of riprap with the Contractor's representatives, including the assistant comptroller from the Boise, Idaho, home office, were informed by the assistant comptroller that he and his Boise office felt that Order for Changes No. 4 was not submitted with due consideration to appropriate contract provisions and relative correspondence and that resubmittal was in order. He stated that a resubmittal would be made at a later date, possibly by the lattter part of December 1974. Consequently, our audit was limited to costs claimed under Order for Changes No. 2.

AUDITED COSTS

The Contractor claimed costs totaling $177,848 under Order for Changes No. 2 (see attached exhibit). LBR has reimbursed the Contractor $7,900 under this change order. As a result of our audit we have questioned $16,336 of the 177,848 as follows:

Direct costs	$10,568
Indirect costs	5,768
	$16,336

Questioned costs are discussed in the remainder of this report under the captions direct costs and indirect costs.

DIRECT COSTS

Direct costs claimed under Order for Changes No. 2 and related questioned costs follow:

Items	Claimed costs	Questioned costs	Approved costs
Direct labor	$36,278	($4,718)	$31,560
Equipment ownership	20,151	(2,062)	18,089
Equipment operating expense	19,018	(3,044)	15,975
Materials	29,557	300	29,857
Escalation	15,277		15,277
Small tools	2,123	(242)	1,881
Plant operations	6,028	(688)	5,340
Overtime premium	2,166	(114)	2,051
Totals	$130,598	($10,568)	$120,030

Direct costs adjustments shown above resulted from a review made by LBR personnel (with minor audit adjustments) of hourly rates and utilizaton of labor and equipment. LBR has already discussed these adjustments with the Contractor's personnel.

INDIRECT COSTS

Indirect costs applicable to the change order were computed as follows:

	Per contractor	Per audit	Questioned costs
Direct costs	$130,598	$120,030	
Indirect rate	23.79%	21.09%	
Indirect costs	$31,082	$25,314	$5,768

The indirect cost rate per Contractor and per audit were computed as follows:

	Per contractor	Per audit
Total direct costs	$6,404,651	$6,404,651
Total indirect costs	1,523,464	1,350,471
Indirect rate	23.79%	21.09%

Audit adjustments to the Contractor's indirect cost accounts were as follows:

Accounts	Accounts balances as of 12/31/72	Audit adjustments	Accounts adjusted balances
Travel expense - job connected	$9,943	($77)	$9,866
Entertainment, donations and contributions	678	(678)	
Insurance - other than payroll	90,828	(90,828)	
Taxes - other than payroll	35,165	(35,165)	
Mobilization expenses paid:			
General expenses (excluding items listed above)	1,297,131	(1,018)	1,296,113
General plant	89,719	(45,227)	44,492
Totals	$1,523,464	($172,993)	$1,350,471

Following are explanations of indirect costs questioned.

Travel expense - job connected

We have questioned $77 in travel costs. Sixty-two dollars in airfare was incurred by an employee's wife to attend a convention and $15 for entertainment. Only costs incurred by an employee for official business are allowable per 41 CFR 1-15.205-46(a), and entertainment costs are unallowable per 41 CFR 1-15.205-11.

Entertainment, donations and contributions

We questioned the $678 balance in the entertainment, donations and contributions account. Entertainment costs are unallowable costs according to 41 CFR 1-15.205-11. Donations and contributions are unallowable costs according to 41 CFR 1-15.205.8.

Insurance and taxes

Insurance and tax expenses applicable to equipment were recorded in the Contractor's general expense accounts ($90,828 and $35,165) and were used by the Contractor in the computation of his indirect cost rate. In his claim as a direct charge, the Contractor computed equipment ownership costs using percentage rates published by the Associated General Contractors of America (AGC). The AGC rates include a factor for equipment insurance and tax expenses, thus resulting in a duplication of costs.

Since the Contractor was unable to furnish us with data showing the breakdown of insurance and tax expenses, we have deducted total insurance costs of $90,828 and total tax costs of $35,165 in computing the overhead rate. Information available to us indicates that substantially all of the Contractor's recorded costs for insurance and taxes are related to equipment in use at the site.

Mobilization expenses paid

In accordance with the advertised contract, the Contractor received payments for mobilization and preparatory work for plant and equipment in a lump sum of $3 million. The mobilization costs were recorded in deferred asset accounts and are being amortized over the contract period. A portion of the mobilization costs appeared in the general expenses and general plant expense accounts (indirect costs accounts) for the period under consideration and in turn were included in the Contractor's computation of the indirect rate. Since these costs are applicable to the advertised contract and not the negotiated change orders, we have identified and deducted such costs ($1,018 and $45,227) in our computation of the indirect cost rate. Order for Changes No. 2 did not involve any mobilization or preparatory work.

While the indirect cost rate of 21.09 percent is applicable to this change order, it should not be considered applicable to change orders involving costs incurred after Jauary 1974, because the Morrison-Knudsen

Company recently underwent a reorganization. The reorganization resulted in a redistribution of overhead costs to the various divisions within the organization. It is our belief that this redistribution of overhead costs to the division sponsoring the Teton Dam project will differ from the costs distributed to the division prior to the reorganization.

UNSUPPORTED COSTS

The 10 percent profit rate (margin) applied to this claim is a negotiable amount to be determined by agreement between the Contractor and LBR. We have therefore classified the entire amount of profit proposed by the Contractor ($16,168) as unsupported.

We have discussed the audit findings with appropriate representatives of LBR and the Contractor at the Newdale, Idaho site. In the event there is need for additional information, you should contact me at the above address. Copies of correspondence pertaining to the negotiation of this change order should be forwarded to this office.

cc: F. X. Smith, Chief
Division of Construction
Bureau of Reclamation

SUMMARY OF COSTS APPLICABLE TO CHANGE ORDER NO. 2 (POWERHOUSE) SPECIFICATION NO. DC-6910 TETON BASIN PROJECT

	Revised claim	Questioned costs	Unsupported costs	Approved by audit
Direct labor	$36,278	($4,718)		$31,560
Equipment ownership	20,151	(2,062)		18,089
Equipment operations expense	19,018	(3,044)		29,857
Materials	29,557	300		29,857
Escalation	15,277			15,277
Small tools	2,123	(242)		1,881
Plant operations	6,028	(688)		5,340
Overtime premium	2,166	(114)		2,051
Indirect costs	31,082	(5,768)		25,314
Profit	16,168		($16,168)	
Totals	$177,848	($16,168)	($16,168)	$145,344

9. Claims Presentation

Claims have a tendency to escalate with time. A principal point of this text has been that enlightened contracting practices and project management can avert time-consuming and costly claims.

The choice of contract type is the first step in establishing the environment in which claims are likely (or not) to be filed. As we have discussed, fixed-price contracts in which risk is placed on the contractor are more likely to result in claims than any other kind of contract. However, various provisions in those contracts can mitigate the claims potential. We have discussed such provisions as variation in quantity clauses, differing site conditions clauses, and others that work to spread risk equitably.

Prompt attention to requests for extensions of time and other actions on the part of the owner are sound project management practices that can also help prevent claims from escalating into disputes.

But assuming that a claim does arise, here is a typical sequence of events.

THE CLAIMS PROCEDURE

First a letter is written by the contractor to the owner, pointing out a problem or a potential problem on the project. This might be a temporary impediment to site access, or some other violation of the owner's obligation under the contract. The owner can immediately face the problem by holding a meeting with the contractor in which the parties discuss whether the contractor is due an extension of time and possibly additional payment because of this situation.

Or the owner can ignore the situation and the letter of notice and allow the minor problem to escalate into a major one. Obviously, there are possibilities between these two extremes. At this stage, letter-writing can also become a weapon. One side might send a barrage of letters designed to keep the other off guard and to build up the record. Knowing that a responsible owner or contractor will set up a claims file on the receipt of such a letter, the other side can count on triggering this record-keeping process. A lot of letters can keep the opponent so busy that the extent of real problems can become obfuscated. This is not an effective tactic, nor is it an effective way to solve problems and finish a project.

The proper approach is for the party who receives the letter to accept a potential claims notice in good faith. He should start his own file and then prepare and accumulate pertinent documentation.

The contractor, in making a claim, should give details and refer to the contract documents to show why his claim is legitimate. This need not be done in the first letter, but it should be done early in the proceedings.

The contractor should keep records of time, materials, and potential delay to the overall project as part of his documentation of the expense caused by the situation for which a claim is made and furnish copies of these to the owner.

To sum up the contractor's position at this point: he wants to establish two things in these letters and records: (1) that his claim is legitimate under the contract; and (2) that expenses have been incurred because of the claim situation.

MEETINGS

At this stage, meetings between the owner's representative—the architect or engineer—and the contractor can help achieve an early resolution of differences. Unfortunately, too many owners tend to postpone any corrective action while they study the claim. In some cases, this takes months and even years. Thus owners often contribute to the escalation process.

When claims escalate for whatever reason, attorneys will frequently attend meetings and take over the presentation of the parties case or defense. If resolution is not achieved, the case passes out of the hands of those original parties and goes to arbitration, the courtroom, an appeals board (in the case of some public bodies), or some other formal dispute forum.

Let's examine the sequence of events in more detail.

1. Notice. The first step is for the contractor to recognize that a claims situation exists. He should acknowledge the problem and realize that slippage at this stage could lead to further damage down the line. He will recognize and calculate those effects, both time and money, on the eventual completion of the contracted work. At this point those calculations are estimates based on the contractor's experience.

The contractor should send the owner a concise letter describing the situation and his opinion of its effect on the project. The letter should refer to that section of the contract concerning "notice."

The contractor should be certain that the notice is timely under that clause and that notice is presented to the proper individual. If all facts are not available when that first letter is written, others can be added in a follow-up letter. It is more important to get timely notice out than to include all relevant material by that deadline. The omission of this timely notice could preclude recovery by the contractor.

It is the owner's responsibility to acknowledge such letters promptly. Even if the reply only indicates that the matter is being looked into, or some other form of acknowledgement, the intent to cooperate has been established. This can be very important later on should the situation become more complicated.

All parties should keep separate files for each claim, and if possible, agree on a numbering or other identification system to facilitate correspondence and access to information in the future.

2. Preparation. The next step in this long process is the preparation of the claim itself by the contractor.

The contractor must accumulate the justification for the claim under the contract terms, and information on its material costs, labor costs, and all other costs, plus the effect of the claims situation on other phases of the project. There may be considerable time gap between the first step and the second. If the contractor can assemble his justification quickly, the owner sometimes agrees to make partial payments while the claims paperwork progresses. This is not unusual on major claims where a major delay in payment to a contractor could lead him to financial difficulties. Clearly, when this happens the owner is acknowledging to some extent that the claim is justified.

As the work progresses for which the contractor is claiming additional payment, copies of the appropriate labor time cards, additional materials, equipment, tools and supplies, overtime costs and other items outlined in the documentation chapter of this book, should be kept in the file. This information should be furnished to the owner through the appropriate party as provided in the contract.

At the same time, the contractor must continue buttressing the legal arguments for his claim.

3. Assembling the Claim.   Who puts the claim together? As we have seen, there are two elements to claims: the legal justification, and the cost data.

If the contractor has a sizable staff that handles large dollar volume construction work, much of the cost data can be assembled in-house. For smaller firms, or for complex claims, the contractor may employ a claims consultant.

On small claims, the staff can generally also provide the justification. But it is advisable that attorneys work on claims as they increase in complexity and size. These may be in-house counsel or outside attorneys who specialize in construction claims.

Assembling a claim is a team effort. If the claim is complex and an attorney is involved, he should assemble the final document, or at the very minimum, review the final work assembled by others.

The expense of having an attorney document and prepare a claim can be high. It is generally more economical to retain a claims consultant to assemble the data and then retain an attorney for the final product. As an alternative, the attorney may retain the claims consultant.

The level of documentation and justification assembled for a claim depends on several factors. The complexity of the claim and the dollars involved are most important. The needs and requirements of the owner are also important. Certain public agencies may demand more documentation than others.

The ability and resources of the owner are another consideration. Some owners don't have the manpower to analyze a massive amount of data. Others have the staff to adequately review a claim. For example, a large utility with major ongoing construction and a knowledgeable staff may require limited justification together with reasonable estimates of costs. The utility's own staff can verify this material. A municipality, for public accountability, may require extremely detailed justification and cost documentation.

Many contractors can assess the needs of the owner. However, claims consultants and attorneys who have processed claims for a particular owner in the past can be invaluable in this area.

Certain agencies, both municipal and federal, have better reputations than others in claims processing. A knowledgeable contractor will be aware of those reputations when he bids. He will, to a degree, provide for the cost of financing extra work when the agency has a poor reputation.

In prosperous times, contractors may even avoid such agencies, and as a result, those agencies can have difficulty attracting bids.

Ordinarily, the processing of a claim, timely or untimely, does not affect the progress of the work. There are exceptional cases where the lack of payment is a hardship to the contractor and can force him to slow down or into default or even bankruptcy. The basic contract agreement provides that a contractor must proceed with the work, invoking the contractually specified disputes resolution procedure as his sole means of relief.

To sum up, a well-prepared and complete claim is always a good idea. Here are some other points to keep in mind concerning the claims process.

1. The contract should be thoroughly understood. Too often contract provisions are regarded as a lot of boilerplate. The contract should be read carefully, and when a potential claims situation arises, it should be reread before embarking on the claims course. The "boilerplate" may decide the case before it begins.

2. The owner can reject the claim as unacceptable. This may happen whether or not the claim document is unsatisfactory, but grounds for such action should be avoided. Make the claim clear, concise, and thorough. The appearance of a claim document is not merely cosmetic. The presentation should indicate that the claimant means business, that he hasn't thrown together the equivalent of some scribbling on the back of an envelope. If the owner wants to send back a claim as a tactic in his battle campaign, he will; the contractor needn't provide ammunition in the form of careless documentation and presentation that will be used against him.

3. The opponent should be sized up carefully. We have already discussed this point in relation to the capability of the owner to analyze the claims justification and the cost data. However, to carry the analysis one step further, some owners may have a reputation for emphasizing certain aspects of claims. For example, an owner may be a stickler for exhaustive legal justification.

In discussion with the owner's job- and home-office staff, determine the kind of detail the owner requires on quantities, costs, productivity, labor, and equipment rates. What kind of documentation does he want? Does he need receipted invoices, or notarized, or certified payrolls? How does he pay for fuels and repairs, for tools and supplies? Is he willing to accept some percentage of the equipment rates cited in manuals prepared by equipment associations?

Does the owner have a litigious reputation? If so, prepare the claim with the thought that the judge and jury may be the final audience for your case.

This advice works for all parties. Each can, and will be, gearing up to deal on the basis of the other side's reputation.

4. Remember that the claim will likely be judged by someone who has not been on the job. That could be the mayor of the municipality or the head of a federal agency. If possible, have that person visit the job site.

Prepare an executive summary that is brief and persuasive. Depending on the case, anything from two to ten pages should do it. Put time and effort into this; it is the broad brush-stroke description of the claim. It should be convincing to that ultimate arbiter who, as we have said, may never have been on the job. The non-engineer, the person unaccustomed to dealing with contracts, will need all the assistance available when he reviews and judges the claim. The executive summary is the first impression of the claim; it should give the reader a clear concise picture of what the claimant wants and why he is entitled to it.

A good executive summary also makes a favorable impression on the top official who is familiar with the procedures. The claim may be settled expeditiously on the basis of a convincing summary. On the other hand, that top official may set it aside for a long period of time if it is confusing, disjointed, or contradictory.

The next section of the claim can be an enlargement of the summary, as much as ten times as long, with considerable detail but without all the minutia.

Finally, the last section of the claim should include all the calculations, backup material, correspondence, and other documentation in an appendix. This may even be a separate volume. There are no hard rules here. The claim should be structured based on one side's estimate of who will read it, and on who will make the final decision.

5. The claim presentation should include photographs, charts, copies of relevant correspondence, and any other appropriate visual evidence. These can be more persuasive than pages of text and will assist reviewers who have not been to the job site.

6. Avoid holding back any information with the idea of saving a compelling bit of evidence for the "perfect moment." If you believe that you have overwhelming proof of the merits of your case, present it as early as possible. The other party may concede immediately and save both sides a lot of time and money. It is, of course, rare that a single item can tip the scales so radically. It is also an understandable temptation to want to hold a trump card. But there is no point in marching everyone to the courtroom for a show-stopper presentation, when the case could have been resolved at an earlier stage.

A considerable amount of judgment about the parties and the case should go into the decision about when and where to present particular evidence.

7. The claims presentation should include statements, and if possible, documentation, of the steps taken to mitigate the condition that led to the claim. Telephone calls, letters sent, and meetings held should be outlined. Good project management and administration assumes that such steps were taken; therefore, these are a key part of the claims presentation.

8. Contractors should avoid the trap of thinking that certain agencies or owners are likely to pay so many cents on the dollar.

This leads to situations in which contractors overstate their claims to protect themselves. Unfortunately, however, there are some owners who operate this way. We reiterate: contractors should know as much as possible about the owner and his policies. Cost documentation must be credible, calculations logical and available to the owner. Pages of formulas may be impressive, but the end result must be reasonable. Much can be lost by having inflated figures exposed as being just that.

In each of the steps discussed here, there should be continued communications between the parties: telephone calls, letters, and meetings. This communication provides opportunities for early settlement. In a situation in which the dispute drags on, such communication provides opportunities for documenting that each side knew or was informed of the other side's actions. And at the very least, it provides the vehicle for both sides to check their positions on the facts and figures so that misunderstandings don't occur. The owner's file on the claim should be growing at the same rate as the contractor's. When the final decision and settlement are being debated, discussion should focus on the legitimacy of the claim, not on those facts and figures.

CALCULATING THE CLAIM

There are many approaches to calculating damages. Basically what the contractor wants to establish is how much additional cost he incurred. Put another way, he wants to establish the difference between what the job would have cost without the condition that gave rise to the claim, and what cost was due to the claims situation.

A contractor knows what the job actually cost if he kept basic cost records, and he should be able to document every amount spent. The problem is in determining what it would have cost without the claim situation, and in convincing the owner that these figures are accurate.

The difference between the bid price and the actual costs is not a sound basis for establishing damages. The bid price will rarely be accepted as gospel. The variations in bids presented by competing contractors for the same project show that there is a definite difference in opinion as to what a particular portion of the work will cost.

The contractor keeps cost records as a matter of routine. He compares his actual costs with the estimated costs with which he originally prepared the bid. Then, when these figures differ notably, he tries to determine why they do. The contractor attempts to determine if the difference is his own fault, either through inaccurate estimates, poor productivity, job delays which are not the responsibility of the owner, or other problems that are not under the owner's control. If, however, the problem does seem to be the owner's responsibility, then the contractor begins the claim process.

Even without cost records, the sophisticated contractor can recognize a condition that will increase his expense. Even so, to provide documentation he must go through the cost calculations and quantify the cost that can be attributed to the claim situation. More detail on these calculations will be provided in this chapter.

An important point to remember is that no one can know what the actual cost of the project would have been without the changes. There can be estimates, and in rare instances a contractor may have done the same kind of work elsewhere. If there were no changes on that other project, we have a comparison. However, it would be extremely rare that there would be an exact "control group" set of circumstances for another project. The weather and the season of year may have been different even if the work were the same; the level of expertise and the productivity of the workers might have been different.

Thus, to a certain extent, there is a subjective aspect to the financial calculations in any claim. Many owners will make a judgmental decision as to cost. They will even state that their decision is subjective in the final report. This is particularly true in cases where loss of efficiency and the resulting costs are discussed.

Ultimately, the acceptance and the settlement of a claim without recourse to the courts (or to other formal dispute resolution forums) may depend on, and be determined by, subjective factors. The skill of tacticians, the credibility of witnesses and experts, and the effect of these parties on the representative of the owner may count as much as do the facts in the case.

But those facts must be assembled with care. The caveat about subjectivity is merely that: preparation should be as factual and as thorough as possible.

The precedents in the case, either legal or those that can be used to calculate costs, should be made known.

We discuss costs of delays, acceleration, and changes in other chapters. Now in attributing costs to these items, the contractor has to find out which costs are allowable. His claims consultant and attorney can provide such information.

Here are some important points to consider.

1. There are objective aspects of the added costs that should be easy to quantify if good records have been kept: labor costs, supplies, materials, equipment costs, field office expense, etc.

2. There is a second category of costs that is less objective but that has been granted for by owners for a sufficient number of years so as to provide precedent. These might include allocation of job-site and main-office overhead to the costs of the work change, the inefficiencies of work forced into winter months or rainy seasons, limitations placed on access to the site, and occasionally the interest on capital borrowed by the contractor to perform this change in the work. (The federal government pays interest costs only in unusual circumstances.)

3. Finally, there are items for which calculations must be subjective or to put it another way, for which there are no precise calculations. Examples might be the determination of the cost of change in the quality of supervision, of lowered morale on the job, of a change in the learning curve of workers due to the change in the work, and of the need for increased manpower or equipment on the site due to the claims situation.

Another difficult area to quantify in the inability of the contractor to take on other profitable work. While there are precedents for recovery of such damages, they are usually held to be too speculative to be allowed. A convincing and imaginative analysis is essential if a significant portion of the claim depends on such items. The services of either a claims consultant or an attorney with experience in this field would be advisable. In some cases, the services of both might be needed. They would know which areas have been allowable and what methods of calculation should be acceptable. The contractor's staff and counsel should be capable of judging the validity of such approaches.

Thus actual labor costs, payroll records, and material expenses are only the beginning of the work needed to document a complex claim. The chapter on the contractor's costs of delays includes more on this subject, and a lengthy example of the calculations involved in claims.

RESPONSE TO A CLAIM

The owner must respond to the claim. The letter of acknowledgement can be brief; the response itself is a detailed reply to the claim that can take considerable time, regardless of the amounts of money involved. Lack of acknowledgement can be interpreted as lack of cooperation on the part of the owner.

That owner, having had previous notification of a potential claims situation, should have long since begun to accumulate his own file on the claim. He should also have met with the contractor. Even so, the analysis and the detailed response can take six months or longer.

A slow reaction on the part of the owner can be a tactic, albeit unethical. An owner may wish to gain leverage by dragging his feet with the idea that when the contractor reaches the negotiating table, he will be so eager for settlement that he will accept less. On the other hand, the owner risks arousing the ire of the contractor who may then push the claim as a matter of principle to the bitter end, which could be a prolonged lawsuit.

Ultimately, though, both parties will sit down at the negotiating table. There are a minority in the construction industry who relish these skirmishes. The industry, however, would be better served if this expenditure of energy and intelligence were directed elsewhere. One such direction would be an expeditious settlement of problems along the way before they reach the crisis stage, with top contractor and owner personnel involved.

THE INITIAL MEETING

The first meeting during the negotiating stage is usually an informal one. Both sides will try to evaluate the position of the other and the degree of seriousness which that side attributes to the particular claim.

The principal purpose of this first meeting is to establish procedures, state positions, and work toward a meeting of minds. Major areas of agreement should be determined, major areas of disagreement should be highlighted, and a middle ground where neither side is convinced should be ascertained.

Coming to the negotiating table may be the beginning of an extended process where experts with different purposes and viewpoints act in good faith in order to arrive at an equitable and legal settlement. Parties should avoid playing games and trying to escalate the discussion into a battle of wits. If the negotiations fail and the claim does escalate to another level, the ultimate judge in the case will be less interested in personalities and tactics than in the facts.

At this initial meeting, both sides walk through the claim. There should be a serious attempt to agree on the facts. If the facts cannot be agreed upon, an acceptable method of determining those facts should be established. For example, if weather is an important factor, there are several sources such as job records and the U.S. Weather Bureau that can provide documentation. The parties should agree on which data they will accept. If the type and use of equipment on the site at a specific time is important, parties could agree on a method of determination acceptable to all. They can also agree to have that information available for the next meeting.

A second and important function of that first meeting is that it allows each group to evaluate the other. Parties can attempt to analyze the other side's strategy. Here are some points to keep in mind:

1. **Be prepared.** Even at the first meeting, it is important to be thoroughly prepared. Have a game plan. Decide beforehand who is going to speak and when. A team leader should be selected. Make sure everyone on the team knows who that person is.

   An outline should be prepared, listing the important items that should be covered at this meeting. As we have stressed, each side is evaluating the other; appearing to be unprepared can leave an unfavorable impression.

2. **Who comes to the meeting?** It is courteous to inform the other side of the approximate number of people that will attend the meeting. It is also appropriate to indicate who they are. If one side brings an attorney without telling the other side, or if the top brass descends on the meeting for one side, while the other has sent only lower rank people, the impact is obvious. It is well worth the effort to send a list of the people who plan to attend the meeting. If the owner will be represented by a vice-president, then the contractor should certainly have the opportunity to have representation of equal rank.

   Two people are essential. One is the person who can speak for the firm with authority. The other is someone who has actually been on the job site. Failing the latter, there must be someone who is intimately involved with the project, and knowledgeable about the problems.

3. **Know what you will settle for.** Both sides should know before that first meeting how much or how little they will settle for. Have a high and a low figure in mind from the start.

4. **Be flexible.** As the meeting progresses, be capable of adjusting the presentation according to your evaluation and perception of the other group. Do they seem to want a fast, concise overview, or do they plan on an all-day meeting to discuss details?

5. **Is there a personality conflict?** If there is, regroup forces as quickly as possible—definitely before the next meeting, and if possible, during this one. A private meeting between the two principals can also resolve this sort of conflict by removing the sources of friction, or by other mutually agreeable means.

6. **Be tactful.**   Strong words, accusations, and finger pointing will not be helpful. In fact, such actions are counter-productive. The personal approach with re-criminations frequently forces the parties into court. A more amicable—yet still factual—approach may resolve the matter in less time and at less expense.

FORMAL NEGOTIATIONS

The closing item of the initial meeting should be to establish the time, place, and the agenda for the next meeting. There should have been some agreement about who will attend that next meeting. An agenda should be at least outlined.

Parties should aim at resolving the claim in that second meeting. At the very least, they should aim at deciding at that time whether agreement can or cannot be reached. If it cannot, the claim should move to the next level of decision-making.

In big money and more complex claims categories, it is not unusual for a series of meetings to be held. Many of these will be at staff level for the purpose of agreeing on data and matters of fact. The final negotiations will be in the hands of the principals.

These formal negotiations represent the final effort to come to agreement before submitting to a higher, outside authority. In the case of the federal government, this usually means going to the agency's board of contract appeals after which the claim can go to the claims court and ultimately, though rarely, to the U.S. Supreme Court. With other owners, the case may go to arbitration or to local or state courts. All are time-consuming processes, and ones in which the final judgment is out of the parties' hands.

Thus the stakes are high. The participants need to be skillful tacticians operating under some prearranged strategy. Ideally, project management practices and en-lightened contract arrangements should prevent disputes from reaching this "United Nations Security Council" stage. However, having reached that stage, parties should be prepared.

Each has had an opportunity to size up the other at that initial meeting. But in addition to that first impression that the principal participants have of one another, it's a good idea to do some research. What are the reputations and backgrounds of these people. If the owner is a public agency, is the principal present in a position to make the final decision, or is he subject to being overruled by a higher authority. Could his yielding on the claim jeopardize an opportunity he might have for promotion. Could it lead to a transfer. Is there an election coming up that could influence his actions. Could this case become a political issue that might be blown out of proportion by the incumbent's political opponents.

Both sides should investigate the financial aspects of the claim. Will the settlement of this claim force the owner to find new financing? Will the owner have to return to a political body, such as a city council, for approval to spend the additional money? If the claim is settled at a lower figure, does the owner have the financing immediately available to pay the claim? In the case of the contractor, does he need the cash for immediate financing, or does the claim in any way affect his ability to obtain a bond on new work?

Find out if the other party has retained outside counsel and a claims consultant. If so, check out the reputations of these individuals, too. Neither side knows what facts the other has in its arsenal. Parties to the negotiations including counsel and consultants may have written papers themselves on similar subjects that could be relevant to the claim. This would be so if the information in such papers (in technical journals, etc.) appears to contradict statements made by those individuals during negotiations.

With freedom-of-information laws, the contractor can research the files of the public owner in matters pertaining to the case. Similarly, contract clauses may give the owner the right to see much of a contractor's documentation. In addition, an owner has a certain leverage. If, for example, he calls up a contractor and says that he needs to see certain documents in order to evaluate the contractor's claim, few contractors would be likely to deny the owner access to those documents.

In negotiation, advantage is a psychological matter, and a great deal depends on one's perspective. Contractors think the owner has the advantage at the beginning of the negotiations. The owner's staff have read and carefully studied the contractor's claim. The contractor has no idea what discrepancies or flaws have been found. Yet owners think the contractor has the advantage. He is on the offensive; he can call the shots. Probably both points of view are valid under certain circumstances.

The following are principles that apply to the later stages of negotiation:

1. Much of what has been said during the initial meeting applies to subsequent meetings. Have an agenda and a game plan. Designate a team leader. Preparation is very important.

2. At the meeting, a spokesman for either side may run through what was agreed on at prior meetings. This gives the participants a chance to start out on a amicable basis, agreeing on something. Of course, in some cases there may be a different interpretation of what happened previously.

3. Minutes should be kept of everything that is agreed on at these meetings. Thus, in addition to that verbal run-through, there is a document to which the parties have agreed or which they may amend. All parties present at the meeting should read and sign off on those minutes, particularly if agreement was reached on any sub-items. Parties may have a great reluctance to signing off on anything at this point, feeling that such action will close off options later on in the bargaining. However, parties negotiating with candor and in good faith should be willing to stand by agreements that they have reached.

If final agreement is not reached at this meeting, the time, date, and site should be set for the next.

Time and timing are very important. While holding frequent meetings does not guarantee that the dispute will be settled quickly, if they are not held at regular intervals, the dispute is bound to last longer. Months and even years have been required to reach settlement in many cases. Obviously, however, a definite period of time is required between meetings in order for parties to mull things over and to prepare factual analyses in response to points made at the previous meeting.

The passage of time apparently inspires some confidence in the justice of the decision. That optimum period of time "tells" each party that reasonable thought, analysis, and careful consideration were given to the problem. While this view of the time it takes for proper judgment is far from exact, it seems to be a fact of negotiating life.

What is that optimum period? It varies from case to case. But time means different things to different groups in the industry. A large federal agency, with staff to match and respectable resources including engineers and attorneys, has almost infinite time compared to a contractor who, in the worst of cases, could be on the brink of bankruptcy. Agencies will be there "forever" and have their own regular pace of accomplishing business. The Contract Disputes Act of 1978 (see Appendix) has several provisions for hastening that pace; that law is discussed in Chapter 10.

Contractors, unless they are giants, are often working with borrowed money and have cash flow problems. It can be assumed that some will settle as quickly as possible and for less than what they have asked for, in order to obtain fluid capital.

Time, in most cases, is on the side of the owner. For example, he is rarely required to pay realistic interest charges on the money due the contractor. Government at all levels borrows money at a lower rate of interest than that of inflation. So with or without interest, the contractor is paid with dollars of lesser value when a dispute takes a long time to resolve. There is, therefore, the likelihood that the owner is saving money if the dispute goes on for years.

Unless there is a complete stoppage of work as a result of the claim, and these are rare, inflation works to the advantage of the owner. Most construction contracts provide that the work must continue while claims are being negotiated or adjudicated. For a contractor to threaten work stoppage amounts to an idle threat. If the contractor should carry out such a threat, he risks default and loss of his bonding.

4. Negotiating strategy is a personal matter. There are more or less standard approaches, and these may work for one individual and not for another. One member of the group is tough and firm, while another member of the team talks about compromise and argues the other side's case. If he doesn't actually argue, he may appear to be a sympathetic to certain points made by the other side. The object is to make the opponents think that they had better accept the "white hat's" offer or they'll be stuck with the "black hat's" harsher demands.

Playing "dumb" is another approach that may lure the adversary team into revealing more information than they intended.

Scornful accusations sometimes can be effective with some personality types. In other cases, such an approach can create hostilities and alienate parties so that settlement is effectively blocked. The use of such tactics relies to some extent on intuition and subjective judgments.

More often than not, there is no correlation between the sophistication of the negotiators and the size and complexity of the claim.

The more sophisticated participants in a negotiation proceeding, regardless of the size of the claim, have heard everything and will probably dismiss the tactics we have just described as time-wasters. The skilled and seasoned negotiator is more impressed by facts and the quality of the presentation, written and oral, than by role-playing. (We point out, in the next chapter on courtroom resolution of disputes, that most judges are equally unimpressed by dramatic strategems.)

On the other hand, a city engineer who hears one claim a year, may react in quite a different way to such negotiation tactics. And the claim may be enormous. In addition, at the local level, no matter what the size of the claim, newspaper publicity, the interference of public officials and the public will all be factors. The same factors will affect the contractor. His reputation could well suffer as the result of adverse publicity.

If the contractor wants repeat business with any owner, he should avoid the stance of the tough, unyielding claims negotiator. Nor should he ever leave the impression that he is excessively claims-conscious. In the private sector, this may cost him the opportunity for future contracts. In the public sector, an owner may have no choice but to accept his bid, if it is the lowest, but his projects will be monitored very carefully.

To sum up, negotiating can be something of an art. The stakes are important, but so are the players. It's relatively easy to make a mistake about the personality or temperament of the adversaries. In any case, thorough preparation and documentation are the best tools to begin with.

5. Prolonged negotiations have ramifications other than the financial ones mentioned earlier. After long delays, all parties need to be re-educated on the facts of the claim. Attorneys, witnesses, the staff, the principals—all have to take the time to re-immerse themselve into the case. Some parties lose interest, others become discouraged. The staffs of the parties can change; people are transferred, or they retire, leave for jobs elsewhere, or even die. Continuity becomes a problem, even when copious minutes are maintained on all negotiations and other meetings.

6. Visual aids are most effective and persuasive. Scale models of a dam, a cross-section of a tunnel, CPMs, schedules, graphs, blown-up photographs—anything that depicts the claim situation will be convincing to both the expert negotiator or the tyro.

These can get the point across more effectively than pages of text, no matter how well expressed. A large four-color chart done by a skilled draftsman or graphic artist, can be a blockbuster. Such a chart can show, for example, how a site was blocked and precisely where and how men and machines had to be deployed around the impediment.

In another example, such illustrations can be used to show rock conditions in tunnels. Photographs and a series of cross-sections showing locations of previously unknown fault planes can be very convincing.

If the written text of the claim closely explains the same facts the illustrations can be more dramatic and convincing at the negotiating table.

The critical path chart is one of the basics of the delay claim display arsenal. Use it to establish and dramatize the effect of delay on the job. However, the chart can also be used against the maker if flaws in logic or errors in input are discovered.

7. Outside parties may be brought in to bolster one's case during the negotiation phase. (These parties will ultimately be called in as witnesses in the case reaches an

appeals board or other formal dispute resolution forum.) Choose these persons with care. An expert in a field may be a poor speaker. He may wander off the point or open doors one would not wish to open. Such persons should be reliable and available when they are needed. Such "witnesses" should be prepared: they should know how the case is being argued, what the strategy is, and what points are being made that relate to him. There may be regional prejudices to be considered. For example, a witness from the north may arouse certain undesirable reactions in a negotiating session in the south.

Prior to the meeting at which he appears, there should be a meeting between the members of the negotiating team and a witness so that no contradictory or harmful statements are likely to be made.

If the credibility of a witness is damaged at the negotiating table, the damage to the case can be considerable.

SUMMARY

To sum up, it is clear that a great deal of time, energy, and money go into these negotiation proceedings. The process has certain dramatic aspects, complete with role-playing and rehearsals and visual aids.

There can be many styles of negotiating as there are negotiations. Similarly, there are many tactics that can be used. We have tried to describe those styles and tactics that we have found to be the most successful over the long run.

As we pointed out earlier, it would be better for the industry if this energy were transferred to avoiding large scale conflict. But the realities of the industry dictate that parties be prepared to negotiate effectively. That being the case, the ideas in this chapter aim at effective, informed, and ethical strategies.

10. Formal Dispute Resolution

FORUMS

Once negotiations have failed, the next step is to bring the dispute to an outside party of avowed impartiality. The principal forums for resolution of construction disputes are the courts, arbitration, and administrative boards of appeal. It must be remembered that until this stage is reached, control of the situation remains with the parties. Once a claim is lodged under one of these formal methods, control passes out of the hands of those involved. It is an axiom in the industry that a poor settlement during negotiation is better than a good lawsuit.

While some the time-honored formal methods fall short of the lawsuit, it is still true that control has passed to an outside party. All methods have some drawbacks, and it's important to understand the pros and cons of each. Parties should be able to choose the best method, or failing that, to be prepared for whatever shortcomings each method may have. Sometimes the formal disputes forum will have been written into the contract; in other instances, the parties might want to determine which forum they want to use according to the size and complexity of the project, or according to the nature of the dispute.

We will discuss the principal methods the courts, arbitration, and boards of appeal-at some length.

CONSTRUCTION INDUSTRY ARBITRATION

More and more, parties to disputes of all sorts are turning to arbitration as a means of resolving disputes short of the courtroom. The procedure itself is quasi-legal. An impartial panel of arbitrators hears both sides of the dispute. Parties may be represented by counsel. Witnesses may be called in to testify, and other formal courtroom procedures can be incorporated. However, many of the time-consuming legal niceties are bypassed. While this is intended to save precious time, the significant protection afforded by the formal judicial apparatus is missing because the forum is not a court of law, nor the arbitrator a judge, or even necessarily a lawyer. Yet the arbitrators' decision is in most states legally binding.

Agreeing to arbitration under such conditions deserves some thought. Arbitration is different from the other dispute resolution mechanisms in that parties agree before hand to submit to this procedure by including a binding arbitration clause in the contract documents. No one needs to insert such a clause about the courtroom; it is implicit that the judicial system provides the final ruling. However, arbitration is final and precludes going to a higher level unless fraud or conflict of interest on the part of an arbitrator can be proved.

How does arbitration work? The American Arbitration Association maintains the machinery for the arbitration of disputes in many fields including construction. The AAA has developed a standard "all disputes" arbitration clause similar to that in the AIA General Conditions.

The AAA has established procedures for selection of arbitrators experienced in appropriate areas. Record keeping and coordination are also performed by the AAA, as well as some training for arbitrators. Fees go to the Association for these services, and to the arbitrators for their time and travel expenses. These costs can be substantial, in many instances more than for a prolonged court trial. Most cases are settled with three or four days of hearings. However, these may be widely spaced in time. Some complicated cases have gone on for years.

The construction industry is a relatively new arena for formal arbitration. In 1966 only 600 cases involving construction disputes went to arbitration under the auspices of the AAA. In 1978, 2400 construction industry disputes were resolved through AAA arbitration. The AAA estimates that over half the construction contracts in force in the U.S. today might include arbitration clauses. These would mostly be in the private sector. Most large public-sector agencies and state government bodies rely on the courts or their own administrative procedures for the disposition of disputes. Local public bodies have adopted arbitration in recent years. However, there are unresolved legal questions about committing a public body to binding arbitration. In some states, enabling legislation might be required.

In the private sector, enabling legislation exists in most states. This gives the forum some considerable force, and makes it incumbent on the parties to approach arbitration very seriously. The proceeding is not just one skirmish in a long battle. The decision is final. No one can be compelled to arbitrate unless he has agreed to do so, but once he has, he must abide by the finding. To be realistic, when contracts are drawn up, contractors may agree to all sorts of things including arbitration, because they want the work, or because some other aspect of the contract seems more important at the time. The important thing here, as we have discussed throughout this book, is that parties should thoroughly understand the meaning of that contract. In the case of binding arbitration, *parties are surrendering the protection of the formal legal machinery.*

There is one out. If both sides agree when the dispute arises that they do not want to resolve the difference through arbitration, they can resort to other means. But both must agree. Action cannot be taken unilaterally if arbitration is provided for in the contract.

(It should be noted that in a few states, when there is no contractual agreement as to arbitration, one party can write and "demand" arbitration of a dispute. If there is no response in a given number of days, the second party can be drawn into arbitration.)

An advantage of arbitration over other methods of dispute resolution is the expertise of the individuals who act as arbitrators. The AAA provides parties with a list of potential arbitrators from names recommended to the Association.

The two parties then select the arbitrators. Knowledgeable arbitrators should be able to come to just decisions. In many courts of law, the judge may have heard a divorce suit one day, an accident case the next, and a construction dispute the next. The judge can't be expected to be familiar with the intricacies of the industry, nor with what is acknowledged common practice. Much time and explanations are thus saved in arbitration; arbitrators don't need to have elementary construction procedures and practices explained to them. As industry leaders, which most would be, their sympathies lie with their fellow practitioners (on both sides of the disputes). They are less likely to render a punitive award than are many juries who feel the need to find a villain in the piece. Even in public agency boards of contract appeal, the board may not have as full a knowledge of industry practices as many arbitrators have. What's more, arbitration is private and it is not conducted in the public arena as is a court proceeding.

The arbitrator has a vested interest in an equitable resolution; he is part of the construction industry establishment. He wants both parties to go away satisfied if that is at all possible. At the very least, arbitrators are likely to want both parties to feel that they got a fair shake.

Disadvantages.

Arbitration has several notable disadvantages, too. Expert, respected arbitrators are usually busy people. Their schedules have to mesh with the disputants. Thus, resolution can be prolonged. Once a court trial begins, it proceeds without interruption, in most cases. (Of course, it may take a long while to begin that trial.) But arbitration hearings can be scheduled at great intervals of time, due mainly to the volunteer nature of the arbitrator's duties. Materials for presentations and witnesses have to be assembled and prepared again each time. This repetition of effort can be counter-productive. If the dispute is not complicated, this may not be an issue.

However, a more serious shortcoming is the lack of legal safeguard. A court ruling can be appealed. An arbitration award cannot, in most instances. The letter of the law, no matter how nit-picking it may appear to some, is designed to protect the rights of the litigants. But resort to those legal precedents is foregone in arbitration.

Other time-consuming procedures are eliminated in the interest of expeditious resolution. Pre-trial disclosure is one of these. Without being too technical, this kind of examination before a trial can clear the air and eliminate disputes or discrepancies of fact before the parties go before the judge. Courts grant this right, and over half the time, disputes are settled out of court during this pre-trial disclosure period.

In arbitration, most disclosures are made during the course of hearings. In short, and paradoxically, this can prolong the arbitration hearing.

There is probably an optimum degree of complexity in a construction dispute up to which point arbitration is the best means of resolution. After that point, formal litigation may have advantages. There have been suggestions that a top-dollar limit be set on arbitration cases and that those above this limit go to the court process. In practice, relatively few cases of over one million dollars have gone to arbitration. Statistics supplied by the American Arbitration Association show that most claims settled by this practice are of lower dollar amounts. This may change.

Deciding on Arbitration

The decision to go the courtroom route has to be mutual if an arbitration clause has been included in the contract, as we have pointed out. When disputes occur, it's human nature for each side to seek a means to gain the upper hand. The party who thinks he has the most equitable case might prefer to go to arbitration where the fairness of his position will be recognized. On the other hand, a party who thinks he has the law on his side, no matter how unfair it may seem, would probably want to go to court.

However these decisions are made, it is clear that there is a construction industry trend to arbitration, or to variations thereof. The growing numbers of industry cases that go to arbitration is one proof of acceptance.

The trend is guarded, however. There are substantial numbers of industry practitioners who believe the process takes as long as, or longer than, litigation and lacks the protection that formal litigation provides. At a 1979 conference on risk and liability in the construction industry, sponsored by the American Society of Civil Engineers, participants were surveyed on this and other questions. The respondents, a mix of high-level owners, contractors and attorneys, disfavored AAA arbitration by a percentage of 54 percent. (See Survey in the Appendix.)

On the other hand, the National Academy of Science's U.S. National Committee on Tunneling Technology, another prestigious group, recommended in their 1977 report that underground construction disputes be resolved by a special board of arbitrators. Their suggestion, however, would be a departure from the AAA procedures; the arbitrators would be a permanent group selected by industry experts and given the authority to settle all disputes on a given project.

The AAA itself monitors and makes recommendations on the process through a construction industry committee. Two variations have been put forward in recent years. These, mediation and mediation/arbitration are both so new as to have virtually no track record in the construction industry. But they are efforts to improve or to simplify the disputes resolution process other than through the courts.

None of these methods solves the basic lack of legal protection described here. Parties with complex disputes involving large amounts of money will probably be best advised to seek satisfaction within the shelter of the judicial system, if their contract permits.

Procedures

Disputes involving lesser amounts will probably continue to seek resolution through arbitration. For those who will use the method, here are points to consider.

1. **Fees.** The American Arbitration Association maintains a fee schedule based on the amount of damages sought in the given case. The Association gets this amount no matter what the outcome of the case. This fee covers basic overhead costs that the AAA incurs in monitoring arbitration cases—staff devoted to the case, paperwork, maintaining the arbitration machinery and so on.

    Fees for arbitrators are considered an honorarium, according to the AAA. Arbitrators have their expenses paid and receive $50 to $350 per day for their services. However, parties have been known to stipulate a higher fee on the grounds that they want the best possible arbitrators. Those "best" people are busy and deserve more renumeration for a case that may be prolonged, etc. But once an individual has agreed to be an arbitrator, he accepts the fact that the fee will not compensate him in the manner to which he has become accustomed. Fees negotiated beyond the $350/day mark presumably still fall short of any realistic compensation.

2. **Contracts.** The contract should spell out the various ways in which arbitration is to be applicable and the procedures involved. The number of days required before a claimant must file for arbitration may be noted. The exact duties of the arbitrators may be set forth. This can become important; if it can be proved that the arbitrators exceeded their scope, it is possible to appeal an arbitration finding on those grounds. The contract may set forth exactly which kinds of disputes and claims can be submitted to the arbitrators, and will probably refer to the rules of the American Arbitration Association or some other group that has arbitration rules.

3. **Laws.** States have differing laws pertaining to arbitration. A contractor should find out what those are before he enters into a contract that includes an arbitration clause. It is assumed that the owner, who formulated the contract, knows those laws. But this is not necessarily true. Both sides should know the law in the state that applies.

4. **Witnesses.** Witness preparation is more difficult for arbitration than for traditional legal proceedings. This is so because the more relaxed procedures can make the witness more vulnerable. In the courtroom, attorneys know the rules; in arbitration, some of those rules are foregone in the interest of hastening the procedure. So a witness has to be prepared for any eventuality. The flexibility of the hearing does not preclude certain lines of questioning as might be true in the more formal setting. Keeping in mind that the arbitrators need not be attorneys, witnesses have to be carefully prepared. Similarly, parties to the arbitration can talk at length about what the opponents consider irrelevancies. The arbitrators can, unfortunately, through lack of experience or confidence fail to maintain a firm hand on the proceedings. Evidence may be admitted that would not be permitted in a courtroom under the rules of evidence and the arbitrators' decision may be based on such evidence.

In some cases, parties to the arbitration will set ground rules for procedures during the hearings.

5. **Arbitrators.** Arbitrators are listed by the AAA. Anyone wishing to serve as an arbitrator may write to the AAA and will be sent an application form. The AAA then adds the person's name to the panel upon verifying references. As we have mentioned, the parties to the arbitration hearing consult the list and select mutually agreeable arbitrators.

When a dispute goes to arbitration, the AAA prepares a list of 10 to 20 persons who, based on background information they have filed, appear to have some expertise in the subject of the dispute. The parties strike the names of unacceptable arbitrators and list the remaining names in order of preference. The AAA then attempts to match the preferences of the parties. If this cannot be done from the first list, then a second list may be sent. Otherwise, the selection can be made by the AAA.

6. Arbitration Among Parties Themselves.   Parties can elect to arbitrate a dispute themselves and proceed along AAA or similar guidelines without working through the Association. There is undoubtedly less control of the situation in this case. The presence of an experienced outside group such as the AAA increases the likelihood of orderliness in the proceedings.

VARIATIONS ON ARBITRATION

There are some fairly recent variations on arbitration procedures that attempt to bypass short comings we have mentioned. A brief description of several follows:

1. Mediation.   The mediator is an outside party, usually of some reputation in the industry. Both parties agree to listen to this individual whose principal duty is to provide an atmosphere of reason and impartiality. He would attempt to find solutions for their problems, and may or may not recommend a settlement. However, his recommendation, if he makes one, is not binding. Parties usually decide to try this method after a dispute has arisen. This is the least formal of the methods available after negotiation, and it has not yet been widely used.

2. Mediation/Arbitration.   This is an innovative method for resolving disputes and is a combination of mediation and arbitration, wherein the parties agree to move on to arbitration if the first stage doesn't work. "Med/Arb" is an innovation that has not been yet tested by time in the construction industry.

3. Independent Board of Consultants.   Rarely used, and one still in the evolutionary stages, this method involves a procedure built into the contract. Parties agree on a board of impartial experts who will sit in this board. The consultants meet periodically, and attempt to head off problems before they mature into disputes. Their recommendations may be binding; this can be set forth in the contract, or not, as parties see fit. The one well-known application of this innovation has been on the Eisenhower Tunnel in Colorado, where the method has apparently been successful.

At the Eisenhower Tunnel, owned by the Colorado Division of Highways, the contract provided for a three-man review board. This board was to be made up of tunneling experts who would settle any contract disagreements that staff could not agree on. The owner chose one expert, the contractor another, and the owner and contractor together selected the third. All bidders were required to submit with their bid every piece of information used in arriving at the bid price. These documents were reviewed by the owner and the bidder at the time of the award. Documents were then sealed and placed in escrow. When disputes arose, the contractor and the chief engineer were empowered to order

FOR USE IN NEW YORK STATE

American Arbitration Association

CONSTRUCTION INDUSTRY ARBITRATION RULES

DEMAND FOR ARBITRATION

DATE:_____

TO: (Name) _____
(of party upon whom the Demand is made)

(Address) _____

(City and State) _____

(Telephone) _____

Named claimant, a party to an arbitration agreement contained in a written contract,

dated _____, providing for arbitration, under the Construction Industry Arbitration Rules, hereby demands arbitration thereunder.

NATURE OF DISPUTE:

CLAIM OR RELIEF SOUGHT: (amount, if any)

PLEASE TAKE FURTHER NOTICE, that unless within 20 days after service of this Notice of Intention to Arbitrate, you apply to stay the arbitration herein, you shall thereafter be precluded from objecting that a valid agreement was not made or has not been complied with and from asserting in court the bar of a limitation of time.

Please indicate industry category for each party.

Claimant:
☐ Owner ☐ Architect ☐ Engineer ☐ Contractor ☐ Subcontractor, Specify_____,
Other_____ .

Respondent:
☐ Owner ☐ Architect ☐ Engineer ☐ Contractor ☐ Subcontractor, Specify_____,
Other_____ .

HEARING LOCALE REQUESTED:_____
(City and State)

You are hereby notified that copies of our Arbitration Agreement and of this Demand are being filed with the American Arbitration Association at its_____
Regional Office, with the request that it commence the administration of the arbitration. Under Section 7 of the Arbitration Rules, you may file an answering statement within seven days after notice from the Administrator.

Signed_____ Title_____
(May be Signed by Attorney)

Name of Claimant_____

Address(to be used in connection with this case)_____

City and State_____ Zip Code_____

Telephone_____

Name of Attorney_____

Address _____

City & State _____ Zip Code_____

Telephone_____

To institute proceedings, please send three copies of this Demand and the arbitration agreement, with the filing fee, as provided in Section 47 of the Rules, to the AAA. Send original Demand to Respondent.

FORM C3CR-2M-1-78

these opened and the documents studied. The review board also had access to the documents when the order to open was given.

When the review board was asked to settle a dispute, its finding was subject to the chief engineer's review and final decision. It was felt, apparently, that the reputation of the board would be such that the chief engineer would rarely disagree with those findings.

The standard form used by the AAA appears on page 187.

FEDERAL GOVERNMENT DISPUTES RESOLUTION

The federal government has had a formal mechanism for resolving contract disputes for decades. Contract appeals boards have been set up within the various federal agencies engaging in construction to hear contract disputes. These have evolved in response to need and have been codified into law over the years. The procedures were last updated and refined in the Contract Disputes Act of 1978, which appears in the Appendix of this book.

The contract appeals boards are made up of appointed officials who are considered knowledgeable and impartial judges, capable of ruling on contract disputes. They are supposed to be experts in construction practices as well, although the boards hear other kinds of contract disputes. The main idea has been to reduce the number of cases going to the courts. The boards are able to hear disputes on a more timely basis than are the courts. The system also has the advantage of having specialized judges.

The 1978 law allows claimants to bypass the boards and go directly to the U.S. Court of Claim if they choose. At this writing, the effect of this change is not yet known. Most think that the case load of agency boards will be only minimally affected and that few cases will go directly to court.

The boards have generally worked well over the years. However, some inevitable criticisms resulted in the changes contained in the 1978 law. One example of a change, of course, is the direct access to the courts. How many people use that right remains to be seen, given the general good reputation of the boards. Another criticism that has not been addressed, and possibly can never be addressed, is that the judges may be partial to the agency that appointed them. They certainly know the practices of their agency and the personalities of the agency personnel involved. However, in practice this issue has rarely been raised in a contract dispute. The judges are more conversant with construction practices than are most courtroom judges. One consideration may outweigh the other.

The federal boards have great advantages over most state and local government forums. One is that the procedures are fairly uniform. The rules are the same, too; however, practices in different agencies may vary somewhat. As we point out in the next section, the methods at state and local levels of government vary greatly. Some are a good deal more effective and free from local influence than are others. The federal boards conduct hearings in a quasi-legal atmosphere. Many of the formalities and the rights that one would have in the courts obtain, such as the right to subpoena. Another legalistic aspect in that the findings of the boards may be appealed.

Contractors who deal with the federal government should be familiar with the workings of these boards or should have staff or consultants who are. The federal agencies naturally have staff schooled in these procedures:

Some important points about the federal board procedures follow:

1. Each agency that lets contracts must set up an appeals procedure. Each must have a case load that justifies three full-time board members. Those agencies that do not have a sufficient case load refer disputes to another agency board, or to the Office of Federal Procurement Policy.

2. The boards must have a minimum of three full-time members. Each member must have five years experience in public contract law. The 1978 law has a grandfather clause, so this five-year rule might not wholly obtain. The board members are appointed by the head of the agency.

3. The boards have jurisdiction over contracts that deal with the procurement of property and services. Services include construction, alteration, repair and maintenance of real property, and the disposal of personal property.

4. All disputes relating to contracts may be heard before an agency board. The claim may be under the provisions of the contract, or it may arise from an alleged breach of contract.

5. A government contract may include a clause—and virtually all do—that states that the contractor must proceed with work while disputes are pending. In other words, the contractor has no grounds on which to stop work while the dispute is being resolved.

6. Agency boards have procedures similar to those of the courts. They can authorize depositions, administer oaths, and subpoena witnesses and books and papers relevant to the case. If a witness refuses to obey a subpoena, an appropriate U.S. District Court can order the appearance of that person before the board. Failure to comply can result in a citation for contempt of court.

7. A contractor is permitted to bypass the appeals board. He may take the case directly to the Court of Claims. An attorney is the best adviser in such cases.

8. Both parties may appeal the decision of the appeals board. Conclusions of law may be appealed as a matter of right. Findings of fact can be appealed only if they are not supported by sufficient evidence. The case would then go to the Court of Claims and possibly to the U.S Supreme Court as the ultimate appeal.

9. The 1978 law includes anti-fraud provisions. In addition, the contractor must certify that his information is accurate and complete and accept the consequences. The government thus places the liability for error or misstatement on the contractor.

   The government is entitled to recovery of the amount of the claim proved to be unsupported if misrepresentation can be shown. The government can also recover the cost of reviewing the claim.

10. The payment of interest on damages has been a controversial issue for years. As we have noted in this book, it is often to the benefit of the owner not to settle a claim promptly. The owner sometimes pays no interest on damages or

pays so little compared to prevailing rates that he has little incentive to act quickly.

The 1978 law governing the federal boards and their procedures states that interest will be paid from the date that the contracting officer receives the claim until payment if the board finds money due the claimant. The law, however, is not specific as to what constitutes a claim from which date the interest accrues. Therefore it is advisable, in order to be scrupulous, to send a complete and certified document, i.e., an official claim. That way there can be little doubt about the commencement of interest.

The interest rate is established by the Secretary of the Treasury and is revised every six months. That interest rate has thus provided some compensation for claimants and some incentive for the government to act expeditiously. However, the new rates cannot be said to be quite comparable to prevailing rates.

To sum up, the boards are conducted in much the same manner as a courtroom proceeding and with many of the same rules. The decisions of the boards can be cited as legal precedent and they can also be appealed. The boards may be bypassed, and cases can go directly to the Court of Claims. While many board hearings are conducted in Washington, D.C., there is no requirement that this be the case. In the interest of saving travel money for witnesses and others involved, hearings are occasionally conducted outside the capital.

PROCEDURES—TIME LIMITATIONS

Once a contractor has made a claim there are certain procedures that must be observed, and there are time limits for subsequent actions.

First, the contractor must submit his claim in writing to the contracting officer. That officer is identified in the contract documents.

The contracting officer must respond within sixty days of receiving the claim. At that time, if the claim is for less than $50,000, he must make a decision in the case. If the claim is for more than $50,000, the contracting officer has two choices: he can rule on the claim, or he can inform the contractor of the time within which he will make a decision.

If the contractor finds the time period unreasonable, he can appeal to the contract board to direct the officer to rule in more timely fashion. Of course, the board may agree with the contracting officer and leave the matter as it was.

When the contracting officer makes his decision, he must state the basis upon which it was made and include a description of the administrative appeals process. If he does not respond to the claim at all within the sixty-day limit, it is tantamount to a denial of the claim. The appeals process then commences.

Appealing a Decision

The contractor must file his appeal with the agency board within ninety days of the receipt of the contracting officer's decision (or after sixty days pass with no response).

At this point, the contractor may decide to go directly to the U.S. Court of Claims. In this case, he has twelve months in which to act.

If the dispute goes to the appeal board, the decision of that body may be appealed. Either party can do this, and both must act within 120 days. The contractor would seek the advice of his attorney before appealing the board's decision. The federal agencies would, as we have noted, seek the concurrence of both the agency head and the U.S. Attorney General before filing an appeal of its own board's ruling. Such an appeal has rarely been sought.

Under the law, claims under $10,000 can be settled by a single member of the board and within 120 days. The 1978 law also provides that each agency can establish its own rules for achieving this end.

Some federal agencies have developed such procedures. The U.S. Postal Service, for example, has rules governing claims under $10,000, those under $25,000 and those under $50,000. All, of course, comply with the provisions of the federal laws governing disputes resolution.

STATE AND LOCAL LEVEL DISPUTES RESOLUTION

Sovereign immunity is the principle that the entitiy that makes the laws cannot be sued under those laws. The idea goes back to early Anglo-Saxon times and to the concept that the king is above the law. The principle is still honored in that the federal government and states now "consent" to be sued. The limited grounds on which they may be sued are usually set forth in statutes. The federal government in consenting to be sued has, as we have seen, set forth an orderly method for resolving construction claims. The contracting officer makes a decision that can be appealed to an agency board of contract appeals or to the Court of Claims. The Supreme Court would hear the ultimate appeal in such cases.

The fifty states, however, have developed many different approaches to the recovery process. A wise contractor will find out what the law is in his own state and in others where he might be involved in a public works project.

In most instances, the first step at the state level is the same as that at the federal level. The contracting officer or whoever is named in the contract, makes the first-line decision. The next step, if that initial ruling proves unsatisfactory, can vary considerably.

In some states, the claim must be appealed to the state comptroller; in others, the claim is filed with a local court or with the state court of claims. A description of some other variations follows.

Administrative Boards.   A few states have instituted administrative boards of appeals, and these vary from state to state where they do exist. Most are patterned after the federal boards of contract appeals, but the test of time has not yet been applied. One criticism is that state boards are likely to be made up of political appointees and therefore to have political overtones. Another criticism is that the individuals appointed have little or no experience in the field of construction and contract law.

Rulings of these boards may be final by statute in some cases. In other states, judicial appeal may be permitted or required. Procedures may be more or less formal in the legal sense. The boards meet at intervals and may have jurisdiction only over certain kinds of disputes.

Review Boards. In some cases, a review panel is appointed to oversee certain categories of public expenditures: highways and roads, for example, or water and sewage waste disposal. These bodies may be the first line of appeal when a construction claim is likely.

In short, it is important to know what kind of relief can be obtained in a particular state. When a claim arises, it is important, even crucial, to retain an attorney early. Of course, the involvement of an attorney depends in part on the complexity and the dollar value of the case and on the contractor's knowledge of the processes in that state. However, if proper procedures are not followed within the proper time-frame, recovery for either the owner or the contractor could be time-barred.

Awards of Damages

If damages are awarded on the state level, a legislative act could be required to settle those claims. Funds might have to be appropriated to pay the contractor. The governor of the state ultimately has to sign such bills, and political considerations may enter into his decisions. If a court has not directed the state to pay, but instead the directive comes from a panel or other administrative body, the legislature may act differently. Again, political matters may influence their decision to abide by the board's ruling, or whether or not they decide to pay, and if they do, how much. It is possible, in other words, that the legislature will be more attentive to the court's ruling.

State panels, boards, and legislatures, even those with competent individuals sitting, are generally not familiar with contract law or with the practices of the construction industry. They may be reluctant or not permitted to award great sums of public funds to contractors. By the same token, they may place onerous penalties on contractors out of misplaced zeal, lack of knowledge about the construction process and its problems, or even out of a wish to be punitive on behalf of the state. This can occur even when the individuals believe the claim reasonable or justified.

The American Bar Association has developed a model procurement code, approved in 1979, which was intended as a guide for government bodies other than federal. One recommendation within this model code was that states and other governmental entities set up contract appeals boards similar to those of the federal government. Maryland has adopted a contract appeals board in accordance with those recommendations. As the model code is more widely promulgated, other states may follow suit. As we have mentioned, there are now other states with some sort of appeal board, or panel, but none except those following the ABA code recommendations, can be expected to bear close resemblance to the federal procedures described in this book.

Cities and other Local Government Bodies

Many of the statements we have made about states apply to local-level government: cities, towns, counties, or regional authorities. One major difference is this:

sovereign immunity does not apply at the local level, so the government body, whichever it is, may be sued.

Some cities and other government bodies have review panels. A commissioner may have the authority to appoint such panels for cases involving his department. In some cases, the local commissioner of public works or another designated city official hears all disputes. These people may be lacking in any experience in, or knowledge of, the construction field. The possibilities are tied to some extent to the size of the governmental unit in question.

There is no right to trial by jury in a claim against the state. Generally, however, this right *does* apply to claims against local governments. The right may be waived in the contract or by the parties in litigation who may prefer to have the judge hear the case alone. Again this requires specialized knowledge of the laws and regulations of local government.

Out-of-State Contractors

Generally, a contractor can only sue a local government body in a federal court if he is incorporated in a state other than the one in which the claim arose. Many contractors follow this procedure whenever they can because they have greater faith in the impartiality and the competency of the federal court system than they do in the local or state courts. These federal district courts provide for trial by jury unless the litigants agree to waive this right.

Clearly, the advice of an attorney should be sought before making such decisions.

Summary

Here, then, are some important points that bear on dealing with state and local governments in contract disputes.

1. The city or state may not have funds on hand to settle the construction claim. Taxes may have to be increased or a bond floated. Such considerations will certainly have an effect on the judgment of those individuals deliberating on the claim, especially if they sit on an administrative panel, or they even will have an effect on a local court if it is hearing the case. However, if sufficient funds are available and have been appropriated or earmarked for the project, claims are apt to be settled more swiftly.

   The matter of sufficient funds is increasingly complicated by the great number of public works projects that are funded on a sharing basis with a grantee. For example, costs may be shared on a 90-10, or a 75-25, basis. Providing for payment of damages with limited funds and another layer of restrictions can be a complicated and lengthy procedure.

2. Public bodies are generally not in a rush to settle a claim. The reason is that little, or no, interest is paid on such claims. In most cases, the public body saves money by waiting as long as possible to settle, while the contractor loses not only the use of his settlement cash, but of substantial interest as well. Cases against a state have been known to stretch on for ten years, with interest

on the ultimate award lower than half the going rate. In addition, inflation eats away at the recovery figure. The federal government pays higher interest on claims than do most states or cities, but even the federal rate is below market rates.

3. If a claim does go to court, the level of defense raised by the state or local municipality may vary from the superb to the terrible. The same may apply to the contractor's presentation, of course, but he has some control over that level. He chooses his attorney; a local government may be restricted to using staff counsel.

    In cases involving large sums of money or matters that may establish precedents for future cases, it is not unusual for the state or city to retain, at considerable expense, the services of a law firm with expertise in this area. On the other hand, the government body in most cases will continue to exist regardless of the outcome of the case, and this may account for a less than spectacular defense. There are exceptions. Several major cities have been on the brink of default, and in those instances, a major settlement against those cities might have had serious repercussions. Again, the advice of one's attorney on the level of defense to be expected is useful.

    The contractor does have great incentive to invest in legal fees and to retain the top contract claims lawyer he can afford. His staying in business may well depend on the outcome of the case. Yet some contractors, operating under severe financial restrictions believe that they cannot afford the "best" counsel.

    A larger contractor generally has the in-house staff to deal with claims such as attorneys whose principal responsibility is the review of contracts, analysis of claims, and the prosecution of such claims through boards and courts. Even so, such a contractor may engage a local attorney because that individual knows local procedures, laws and regulations, and in some cases, the reputation of the personalities involved.

4. Both parties should know the reputation of the other, especially in matters of claims and their resolution. If a contractor is contemplating bidding on a major project for a government body, he should find out whether that body has been known to fight for years before paying on legitimate claims. The contractor, after all, has the choice of not bidding at all. Or he can bid high enough to cover the risk of a slow-pay or no-pay situation.

    The public body is obliged to accept the lowest bid, no matter if the contractor has a litigious reputation or not, so long as he has the technical and financial capabilities to do the job. But the public owner should know about that reputation in order to deal effectively with the contractor on the project. The owner can be prepared; he can try to head off potential claims situations.

ATTORNEY-CLIENT RELATIONSHIPS

Throughout this book, the term "knowledgeable attorney" has been used. Naturally, both parties to a dispute want to retain an attorney likely to obtain a favorable result. The first step is to retain an attorney who has experience in the construction industry, with a particular emphasis on contracts and claims. A second step might be to assure that the attorney has argued before a federal contract appeals board, if that is the resolution forum. It's a good idea, though not essential, that the attorney have experience in the particular forum chosen.

Once the dispute has reached the litigation stage, however, parties will definitely want a lawyer with courtroom experience. This poses a "Catch-22" situation. Everyone wants an attorney with trial experience. How does a lawyer begin to get that experience? The set of such attorneys is rather small. More than 80% of construction cases are settled before they reach the courtroom, in pre-trial phases.

Of course, an attorney needs experience to maneuver successfully here, too. In addition, firms specializing in contract law want to win. They are just as reluctant to assign an attorney without courtroom experience to a case as most clients are to retain such an individual. So the number of attorneys who have actually argued a substantial construction case before a tribunal is not a large one.

Attorneys can gain experience by acting as assistants to trial attorneys. Experience is also gained by working on smaller cases. So there are suitable substitutes for an attorney with a lengthy courtroom record. The reputation of a firm carries some weight, too. A young attorney with a top-notch firm who has been an assistant to a trial attorney might be superior to someone else with a lengthy court-room track record.

The scarcity of experienced trial attorneys in the contract field is reflected in fees. They can be high. Both owners and contractors face the problem of selecting the "right" attorney from that limited pool. Some public owners are restricted by law to using staff attorneys and are thus relieved of the task of seeking outside counsel. There are exceptions. When the dollars are considerable or if there could be an important precedent set in the case, public bodies have retained outside counsel to supplement their in-house capability.

How does one find a suitable attorney? Mainly through word of mouth. Since the pool of firms that deal in construction law is not a large one, and the construction industry is relatively close-knit, reputations are not difficult to ascertain.
Here are three points to bear in mind:

1. Actual trial experience should be weighed along with the lawyer's construction industry and contract law background. The advice a lawyer can offer based on his knowledge of attitudes, customs, and political considerations within a jurisdiction must also be taken into account. For example, the attorney might suggest moving the case to another jurisdiction (if that is possible) because of local political situations. Obviously, attorneys also know the temperament and reputations of judges in their district who might be assigned to the case.

2. The reputations and strengths of a law firm may change. A firm well-thought of for years may be experiencing a stale period. A top attorney may have left the firm, or there may be internal conflict in the firm. A firm with a lesser reputation may have acquired an outstanding new attorney. Sometimes it's a good idea to hire the attorney and the firm that comes with him (or her) than to hire the firm.

3. How can one find out what courtroom experience an attorney has? It is possible (but extraordinary) to obtain transcripts of previous trials and to read these.

One can also seek the opinion of other attorneys, including house counsel if that applies. Finally, one can ask the attorney what cases he has handled and the names of persons that can be contacted about these cases: the judge, the parties, and other attorneys.

All this research may seem excessive, but depending on the magnitude of the stakes, it can be worthwhile.

Once an attorney and that firm are retained, it's a good idea to monitor the proceedings. Here are some things to remember about law firms.

1. Ask if the attorney retained will also be the person in charge of billing your account. This establishes a clear line of responsibility in the firm. Sometimes a partner is assigned to bringing in new business; that "star" may turn the cases over to another attorney and not necessarily follow the progress of the litigation, except to send the bills. This is an extreme example, but one that should be avoided. If it is made clear that the firm has been retained because of the reputation of attorney X, more of the responsibility of the case will reside with X. That means billing, too. This serves to centralize the firm's attention to the case.

2. Are large firms better than small ones? There are pros and cons to both. Larger firms may have greater resources; smaller firms can guarantee that the case won't get lost in the shuffle. However, make sure that the resources of any firm are adequate and that you are satisfied with the attorneys handling the case. There is probably nothing else that can be done in deciding the merits of a large or a small firm.

3. In general, it is considered more "professional" to retain an attorney on a time compensation basis rather than on a contingency basis. However, this provides no incentive for the attorney to move expeditiously. There is a trend toward modifying time compensation arrangements by reducing the hourly rate and adding a bonus, which is a percentage of recovery or the savings resulting from the final ruling. The idea is to provide incentive to prosecute the case in a timely manner.

4. Fees for attorneys are rarely recoverable. Such a clause may be put in the contract at the outset, as can almost any kind of clause if the parties agree. However, this is very unusual.

If the case is extremely complicated and looks as though it will be costly to pursue—depositions requiring great distances for travel, etc.—it could be worthwhile to examine the billing policy on these items. The firm's procedures on travel allowances and related expenses may be very liberal. Therefore, resentment over mounting costs may be avoided if these items are understood from the start. Of course, if the case is won, the memory of one's attorney "wining and dining" at the client's expense will dim quickly.

It makes sense to ask that the lowest professional level feasible prepare appropriate portions of the case. It is unreasonable and extremely costly to insist that the senior partner or trial attorney perform research that an associate attorney can accomplish. The trial attorney's special skills and experience should be rationed out judiciously.

The Premise of Honesty

The best approach to settling any disputes is to be honest and straightforward. It should be understood by the attorney from the start that this is what the client wants. The client sets the tone in the attorney relationship. Most attorneys are eager to please the client and will conduct themselves in the manner they perceive to be what the client expects from them. This does not mean that an attorney will immediately fall in with the attitudes of an unscrupulous client. On the contrary, the relationship will be tortured and difficult. If the client makes it clear that he wants the case to be conducted in the most honest and credible manner possible, most attorneys will breathe a sigh of relief. The case will be easier to prosecute, and juries will more likely be convinced. If the client believes his case has merit, this shouldn't be difficult. As we walk through the next stage of litigation, it will be apparent why a straightforward approach must be maintained.

Preparation

Preparation for litigation is the most crucial stage of the process. The documents are the skeleton of the case; the witnesses are the flesh. The typical construction claims litigation is highly dependent on those documents. These include correspondence, meeting memos, invoices, time cards, daily reports—all the paper that accumulated in the course of a project. The attorney may have to read, organize, and absorb thousands of documents. There may be several sets in each category of documents; the contractor, the owner, and the engineer or architect may have maintained separate records, especially if each knew a dispute was brewing.

All documents must be read and understood. The attorney must know of every document. If one piece of paper is introduced at trial and the attorney has not seen it, something is wrong. This is part of the open and honest approach. The case may be lost on just one such omission, intentional or not. A client may hope the other side will not find a particular document and take his lawyer into his confidence. This is unacceptable, unfair to one's attorney, and, of course, in the end the client may lost on the basis of that single unrevealed document. Still, there can be honest mistakes. A document can be lost in the mists of time, or it can surface because one side kept meticulous records and the other kept sloppy records. It doesn't matter how this happens; it shouldn't happen.

No one can rely on anything remaining "secret." With today's discovery laws as to pre-trial examination, almost every document will be accessible to both sides in the case. Clients must make certain that their attorneys see everything.

The same thorough preparation applies to witnesses. It is almost axiomatic that there are no bad witnesses, only bad attorneys. Witnesses must be well prepared and instructed to handle any contingency. Nothing should be left to chance. The courtroom is no place for off-the-cuff remarks. In fact, only part of that intense preparation will be needed. There is no way of knowing, however, just what part the opposition will concentrate on, or what response will convince a jury. It's good sense to be prepared for anything.

During this preparation stage, witnesses should be instructed that jargon will only obscure the information they have to offer. Technical language is becoming a problem in jury trials. Newspapers have cited instances of lengthy antitrust or banking lawsuits where many highly educated persons could barely make sense out of the technical aspects, let alone a jury selected more or less at random.

The danger in a construction claim case is that a jury may make judgments on grounds of sympathy or prejudice if testimony is unclear to them. Witnesses with fairly esoteric specialties, say in earthquake engineering, or in a narrow area of soils or geology, may be world-renowned. But they won't do any good if the jury can't comprehend their points. On a less esoteric level, construction industry jargon can be confusing, too.

Finally, the judge and jury will want to hear the witness, not the attorney. Preparation should focus on an effective presentation by the witness, not on dramatic packaging by the attorney.

Pre-Trial Disclosure

Pre-trial disclosure is not available in all the formal dispute resolution forums. But procedural rules in most courts grant this right, which allows each side to see documents in possession of the adversary and to question that adversary orally before a court stenographer.

In arbitration, for example, surprises can be sprung in the presence of the arbitrators, often to the detriment of one side's case. At best, an unexpected document or bit of information throws one's attorney off-balance during the procedings. The federal government boards of contract appeal permit pre-trial disclosure; the various dispute forums at that state and local level may not. The attorney should know.

If some evidence that could jeopardize one side's position surfaces during the pre-trial disclosure, the parties have the option of settling the case out of court. Of course, parties can always back out of other dispute resolution forums and decide to settle, but the earlier this information is disclosed the easier that settlement may be. Once formal proceedings, say of arbitration, have begun, it becomes less easy to back out. The party whose case is strengthened by the disclosure may possibly want to continue with the proceeding; their case may result in a larger award than the settlement otherwise would have been. In pre-trial disclosure, the final formal proceedings of the courtroom have not yet begun, and in most cases, both parties would prefer to avoid the expense and time of a lawsuit if this is possible.

This pre-trial process can take years. If no settlement is forthcoming, it could take years to set a trial date, and even more time to complete the trial. Under the rules of discovery, collecting and presenting all documents take time. Of course, in public contracts, the claimant contractor could ask for all documents under the freedom-of-information laws much earlier in the dispute since he is dealing with a public body. Often, however, the contractor does not do this while the parties are still at the negotiating table, out of fear of offending the other side by invoking these procedures.

But once litigation is formally commenced, it's official. All and everything must be presented to both sides.

At this point, the attorney, depending on the information disclosed, will advise the client on whether to proceed to trial or to try to settle. Recommendation to settle may be made on grounds other than that the other side possesses damning evidence. It's often cheaper to settle than to risk a more onerous court-mandated result. The time saved is saved for both parties.

THE COURTROOM

Once the decision has been made to move to trial, the advice given earlier about the straightforward, credible approach becomes even more important. Juries, especially, will be suspicious or offended by a ranting, raving, insinuating attorney. Clients don't have much to say once the attorney has behaved in such a fashion. But the client should previously have set the tone of the approach. If it has been made clear that an academy-award winning performance is not the client's style, the attorney will probably avoid the histrionics. Juries often interpret attacks and delays in the courtroom as evidence of concealment or even of guilt. Similarly, dramatic courtroom maneuvers can be interpreted as purposeful distractions from the facts, an attempt to gloss over shaky facts.

Reasonableness is less risky, and apparently more convincing. After all, the judge and jury are assessing the "reasonableness" of the damage figure and the degree of fault. While judges are accustomed to courtroom dramatics and are less likely to regard such tactics with the suspicion a jury might have, the judge is also more likely to see through a showy performance and to stick to the facts.

If the facts are on the side of the ranting attorney, the judge will see that too, whether or not the performance is dramatic. It may sound naive, but the reasonable, honest approach works best in the courtroom.

Appendix—Construction Claims: Analysis; Presentation; Defense

1. Standard Contract Conditions, Engineers Joint Contract Documents Committee.
2. a. Federal Government Standard Contract Form 23A.
   b. Additional Supplement to General Provisions.
3. Contract Disputes Act of 1978.
4. a. Associated General Contractors of America, Contractors Equipment Manual (excerpts).
   b. Rental Rate Blue Book, Equipment Guide-Book Co. (excerpts).
5. Findings of Fact and Decision by the contracting officer on a claim under a federal contract.
6. Decision by a Federal Board of Contract Appeals.
7. Minutes of a Preconstruction Conference—federal government project.
8. Report on construction contract risks, Los Angeles Department of Public Works.
9. Risk and Liability Survey, American Society of Civil Engineers.

1. Standard Contract Conditions, Engineer's Joint Contract Documents Committee

NOTE: These general conditions are now issued under the aegis of the Engineer's Joint Contract Documents Committee (EJCDC), which includes ASCE along with the organizations listed above. A number of standard contract forms are alluded to in the text, using EJCDC terminology.

STANDARD
GENERAL CONDITIONS
OF THE
CONSTRUCTION CONTRACT

Jointly Issued by

PROFESSIONAL ENGINEERS IN PRIVATE PRACTICE

A practice division of the

NATIONAL SOCIETY OF PROFESSIONAL ENGINEERS

and by

AMERICAN CONSULTING ENGINEERS COUNCIL

and by

CONSTRUCTION SPECIFICATIONS INSTITUTE

© 1978 National Society of Professional Engineers
2029 K Street, N.W., Washington, D.C. 20006

American Consulting Engineers Council
1015 15th Street, N.W., Washington, D.C. 20005

Construction Specifications Institute
1150 17th Street, N.W., Washington, D.C. 20036

TABLE OF CONTENTS OF GENERAL CONDITIONS

INDEX TO GENERAL CONDITIONS

GENERAL CONDITIONS

ARTICLE 1—DEFINITIONS _____

Wherever used in these General Conditions or in the other Contract Documents, the following terms have the meanings indicated which are applicable to both the singular and plural thereof:

Addenda—Written or graphic instruments issued prior to the opening of Bids which clarify, correct or change the bidding documents or the Contract Documents.

Agreement—The written agreement between OWNER and CONTRACTOR covering the Work to be performed; other Contract Documents are attached to the Agreement and made a part thereof as provided therein.

Application for Payment—The form accepted by ENGINEER which is to be used by CONTRACTOR in requesting progress or final payment and which is to include such supporting documentation as is required by the Contract Documents.

Bid—The offer or proposal of the Bidder submitted on the prescribed form setting forth the prices for the Work to be performed.

Bonds—Bid, performance and payment bonds and other instruments of security.

Change Order—A written order to CONTRACTOR signed by OWNER authorizing an addition, deletion or revision in the Work, or an adjustment in the Contract Price or the Contract Time issued after the effective date of the Agreement.

Contract Documents—The Agreement, Addenda (which pertain to the Contract Documents), CONTRACTOR's Bid (including documentation accompanying the Bid and any post-Bid documentation submitted prior to the Notice of Award) when attached as an exhibit to the Agreement, the Bonds, these General Conditions, the Supplementary Conditions, the Specifications, the Drawings as the same are more specifically identified in the Agreement, together with all Modifications issued after the execution of the Agreement.

Contract Price—The moneys payable by OWNER to CONTRACTOR under the Contract Documents as stated in the Agreement.

Contract Time—The number of days (computed as provided in paragraph 17.2) or the date stated in the Agreement for the completion of the Work.

CONTRACTOR—The person, firm or corporation with whom OWNER has entered into the Agreement.

day—A calendar day of twenty-four hours measured from midnight to the next midnight.

defective—An adjective which when modifying the word Work refers to Work that is unsatisfactory, faulty or deficient, or does not conform to the Contract Documents or does not meet the requirements of any inspection, test or approval referred to in the Contract Documents, or has been damaged prior to ENGINEER's recommendation of final payment.

Drawings—The drawings which show the character and scope of the Work to be performed and which have been prepared or approved by ENGINEER and are referred to in the Contract Documents.

effective date of the Agreement—The date indicated in the Agreement on which it becomes effective, but if no such date is indicated it means the date on which the Agreement is signed and delivered by the last of the two parties to sign and deliver.

ENGINEER—The person, firm or corporation named as such in the Agreement.

Field Order—A written order issued by ENGINEER which orders minor changes in the Work in accordance with paragraph 10.2 but which does not involve a change in the Contract Price or the Contract Time.

General Requirements—Sections of Division 1 of the Specifications.

Modification—(a) A written amendment of the Contract Documents signed by both parties, (b) a Change Order, or (c) a Field Order. A modification may only be issued after the effective date of the Agreement.

Notice of Award—The written notice by OWNER to the apparent successful Bidder stating that upon compliance by the apparent successful Bidder with the conditions precedent enumerated therein, within the time specified, OWNER will sign and deliver the Agreement.

Notice to Proceed—A written notice given by OWNER to CONTRACTOR (with a copy to ENGINEER) fixing the date on which the Contract Time will commence to run and on which CONTRACTOR shall start to perform his obligation under the Contract Documents.

OWNER—The public body or authority, corporation, association, partnership, or individual with whom CONTRACTOR has entered into the Agreement and for whom the Work is to be provided.

Project—The total construction of which the Work to be provided under the Contract Documents may be the whole, or a part as indicated elsewhere in the Contract Documents.

Resident Project Representative—The authorized representative of ENGINEER who is assigned to the site or any part thereof.

Shop Drawings—All drawings, diagrams, illustrations, schedules and other data which are specifically prepared by CONTRACTOR, a Subcontractor, manufacturer, fabricator, supplier or distributor to illustrate some portion of the Work and all illustrations, brochures, standard schedules, performance charts, instructions, diagrams and other information prepared by a manufacturer, fabricator, supplier or distributor and submitted by CONTRACTOR to illustrate material or equipment for some portion of the Work.

Specifications—Those portions of the Contract Documents consisting of written technical descriptions of materials, equipment, construction systems, standards and workmanship as applied to the Work and certain administrative details applicable thereto.

Subcontractor—An individual, firm or corporation having a direct contract with CONTRACTOR or with any other Subcontractor for the performance of a part of the Work at the site.

Substantial Completion—The Work (or a specified part thereof) has progressed to the point where, in the opinion of ENGINEER as evidenced by his definitive certificate of Substantial Completion, it is sufficiently complete, in accordance with the Contract Documents, so that the Work (or specified part) can be utilized for the purposes for which it was intended; or if there be no such certificate issued, when final payment is due in accordance with paragraph 14.13. The terms "substantially complete" and "substantially completed" as applied to any Work refer to Substantial Completion thereof.

Work—The entire completed construction or the various separately identifiable parts thereof required to be furnished under the Contract Documents. Work is the result of performing services, furnishing labor and furnishing and incorporating materials and equipment into the construction, all as required by the Contract Documents.

ARTICLE 2—PRELIMINARY MATTERS

Delivery of Bonds:

2.1.   When CONTRACTOR delivers the executed Agreements to OWNER, CONTRACTOR shall also deliver to OWNER such Bonds as CONTRACTOR may be required to furnish in accordance with paragraph 5.1.

Copies of Documents:

2.2.   OWNER shall furnish to CONTRACTOR up to ten copies (unless otherwise specified in the General Requirements) of the Contract Documents as are reasonably necessary for the execution of the Work. Additional copies will be furnished, upon request, at the cost of reproduction.

Commencement of Contract Time; Notice to Proceed:

2.3.   The Contract Time will commence to run on the thirtieth day after the effective date of the Agreement, or, if a Notice to Proceed is given, on the day indicated in the Notice to Proceed; but in no event shall the Contract Time commence to run later than the ninetieth day after the day of Bid opening or the thirtieth day after the effective date of the Agreement. A Notice to Proceed may be given at any time within thirty days after the effective date of the Agreement.

Starting the Project:

2.4.   CONTRACTOR shall start to perform the Work on the date when the Contract Time commences to run, but no Work shall be done at the site prior to the date on which the Contract Time commences to run.

Before Starting Construction:

2.5.   Before undertaking each part of the Work, CONTRACTOR shall carefully study and compare the Contract Documents and check and verify pertinent figures shown thereon and all applicable field measurements. CONTRACTOR shall promptly report in writing to ENGINEER any conflict, error or discrepancy which CONTRACTOR may discover; however, CONTRACTOR shall not be liable to OWNER or ENGINEER for failure to report any conflict, error or discrepancy in the Drawings or Specifications, unless CONTRACTOR had actual knowledge thereof or should reasonably have known thereof.

2.6.   Within ten days after the effective date of the Agreement (unless otherwise specified in the General Requirements), CONTRACTOR shall submit to ENGINEER for review and acceptance an estimated progress schedule indicating the starting and completion dates of the various stages of the Work, a preliminary schedule of Shop Drawing submissions, and a preliminary schedule of values of the Work.

2.7.   Before any Work at the site is started, CONTRACTOR shall deliver to OWNER, with a copy to ENGINEER, certificates (and other evidence of insurance requested by OWNER) which CONTRACTOR is required to purchase and maintain in accordance with paragraphs 5.3 and 5.4, and OWNER shall deliver to CONTRACTOR certificates (and other evidence of insurance requested by CONTRACTOR) which OWNER is required to purchase and maintain in accordance with paragraphs 5.6 and 5.7.

Preconstruction Conference:

2.8.   Within twenty days after the effective date of the Agreement, but before CONTRACTOR starts the Work at the site, a conference will be held for review and acceptance of the schedules referred to in paragraph 2.6, to establish procedures for handling Shop Drawings and other submittals and for processing Applications for Payment, and to establish a working understanding among the parties as to the Work.

ARTICLE 3—CONTRACT DOCUMENTS: INTENT AND REUSE

Intent:

3.1.   The Contract Documents comprise the entire Agreement between OWNER and CONTRACTOR concerning the Work. They may be altered only by a Modification.

3.2.   The Contract Documents are complementary; what is called for by one is as binding as if called for by all. If, during the performance of the Work, CONTRACTOR finds a conflict, error or discrepancy in the Contract Documents, he shall report it to ENGINEER in writing at once and before proceeding with the Work affected thereby; however, CONTRACTOR shall not be liable to OWNER or ENGINEER for failure to report any conflict, error or discrepancy in the Specifications or Drawings unless CONTRACTOR had actual knowledge thereof or should reasonably have known thereof.

3.3.   It is the intent of the Specifications and Drawings to describe a complete project (or part thereof) to be constructed in accordance with the Contract Documents. Any Work that may reasonably be inferred from the Specifications or Drawings as being required to produce the intended result shall be supplied whether or not it is specifically called for. When words which have a well-known technical or trade meaning are used to describe Work, materials or equipment such words shall be interpreted in accordance with such meaning. Reference to standard specifications, manuals or codes of any technical society, organization or association, or to the code of any governmental authority, whether such reference be specific or by implication, shall mean the latest standard specification, manual or code in effect at the time of opening of Bids (or, on the effective date of the Agreement if there were no Bids), except as may be otherwise specifically stated. However, no provision of any referenced standard specification, manual or code (whether or not specifically incorporated by reference in the Contract Documents) shall change the duties and responsibilities of OWNER, CONTRACTOR or ENGINEER, or any of their agents or employees from those set forth in the Contract Documents. Clarifications and interpretations of the Contract Documents shall be issued by ENGINEER as provided for in paragraph 9.3.

3.4.   The Contract Documents will be governed by the law of the place of the Project.

Reuse of Documents:

3.5.   Neither CONTRACTOR nor any Subcontractor, manufacturer, fabricator, supplier or distributor shall have or acquire any title to or ownership rights in any of the Drawings, Specifications or other documents (or copies of any thereof) prepared by or bearing the seal of ENGINEER; and they shall not reuse any of them on extensions of the Project or any other project without written consent of OWNER and ENGINEER and specific written verification or adaptation by ENGINEER.

ARTICLE 4—AVAILABILITY OF LANDS; PHYSICAL CONDITIONS; REFERENCE POINTS

Availability of Lands:

4.1.   OWNER shall furnish, as indicated in the Contract Documents, the lands upon which the Work is to be performed, rights-of-way for access thereto, and such other lands which are designated for the use of CONTRACTOR. Easements for permanent structures or permanent changes in existing facilities will be obtained and paid for by OWNER, unless otherwise provided in the Contract Documents. If CONTRACTOR believes that any delay in OWNER's furnishing these lands or easements entitles him to an extension of the Contract Time, CONTRACTOR may make a claim therefor as provided in Article 12. CONTRACTOR shall provide for all additional lands and access thereto that may be required for temporary construction facilities or storage of materials and equipment.

Physical Conditions—Investigations and Reports:

4.2.   Reference is made to the Supplementary Conditions for identification of those reports of investigations and tests of subsurface and latent physical conditions at the site or otherwise affecting cost, progress or performance of the Work which have been relied upon by ENGINEER in preparation of the Drawings and Specifications. Such reports are not guaranteed as to accuracy or completeness and are not part of the Contract Documents.

Unforeseen Physical Conditions:

4.3.   CONTRACTOR shall promptly notify OWNER and ENGINEER in writing of any subsurface or latent physical conditions at the site or in an existing structure differing materially from those indicated or referred to in the Contract Documents. ENGINEER will promptly review those conditions and advise OWNER in writing if further investigation or tests are necessary. Promptly thereafter, OWNER shall obtain the necessary additional investigations and tests and furnish copies to ENGINEER and CONTRACTOR. If ENGINEER finds that the results of such investigations or tests indicate that there are subsurface or latent physical conditions which differ materially from those intended in the Contract Documents, and which could not reasonably have been anticipated by CONTRACTOR, a Change Order shall be issued incorporating the necessary revisions.

Reference Points:

4.4.   OWNER shall provide engineering surveys for construction to establish reference points which in his judgment are necessary to enable CONTRACTOR to proceed with the Work. CONTRACTOR shall be responsible for laying out the Work (unless otherwise specified in the General Requirements), shall protect and preserve the established reference points and shall make no changes or relocations without the prior written approval of OWNER. CONTRACTOR shall report to ENGINEER whenever any reference point is lost or destroyed or requires relocation because of necessary changes in grades or locations, and shall be responsible for replacement or relocation of such reference points by professionally qualified personnel.

ARTICLE 5—BONDS AND INSURANCE

Performance and Other Bonds:

5.1. CONTRACTOR shall furnish performance and payment Bonds, each in an amount at least equal to the Contract Price as security for the faithful performance and payment of all CONTRACTOR's obligations under the Contract Documents. These Bonds shall remain in effect at least until one year after the date of final payment, except as otherwise provided by law. CONTRACTOR shall also furnish such other Bonds as are required by the Supplementary Conditions. All Bonds shall be in the forms prescribed by the bidding documents or Supplementary Conditions and be executed by such Sureties as (i) are licensed to conduct business in the state where the Project is located, and (ii) are named in the current list of "Companies Holding Certificates of Authority as Acceptable Sureties on Federal Bonds and as Acceptable Reinsuring Companies" as published in Circular 570 (amended) by the Audit Staff Bureau of Accounts, U.S. Treasury Department. All Bonds signed by an agent must be accompanied by a certified copy of the authority to act.

5.2. If the Surety on any Bond furnished by CONTRACTOR is declared a bankrupt or becomes insolvent or its right to do business is terminated in any state where any part of the Project is located or it ceases to meet the requirements of clauses (i) and (ii) of paragraph 5.1, CONTRACTOR shall within five days thereafter substitute another Bond and Surety, both of which shall be acceptable to OWNER.

Contractor's Liability Insurance:

5.3. CONTRACTOR shall purchase and maintain such comprehensive general liability and other insurance as will provide protection from claims set forth below which may arise out of or result from CONTRACTOR's performance of the Work and CONTRACTOR's other obligations under the Contract Documents, whether such performance is by CONTRACTOR, by any Subcontractor, by anyone directly or indirectly employed by any of them, or by anyone for whose acts any of them may be liable:

5.3.1. Claims under workers' or workmen's compensation, disability benefits and other similar employee benefit acts;

5.3.2. Claims for damages because of bodily injury, occupational sickness or disease, or death of CONTRACTOR's employees;

5.3.3. Claims for damages because of bodily injury, sickness or disease, or death of any person other than CONTRACTOR's employees;

5.3.4. Claims for damages insured by personal injury liability coverage which are sustained (i) by any person as a result of an offense directly or indirectly related to the employment of such person by CONTRACTOR, or (ii) by any other person for any other reason;

5.3.5. Claims for damages, other than to the Work itself, because of injury to or destruction of tangible property, including loss of use resulting therefrom; and

5.3.6. Claims for damages because of bodily injury or death of any person or property damage arising out of the ownership, maintenance or use of any motor vehicle.

The insurance required by this paragraph 5.3 shall include the specific coverages and be written for not less than the limits of liability and coverages provided in the Supplementary Conditions, or required by law, whichever is greater. The comprehensive general liability insurance shall include completed operations insurance. All such insurance shall contain a provision that the coverage afforded will not be cancelled, materially changed or renewal refused until at least thirty days' prior written notice has been given to OWNER and ENGINEER. All such insurance shall remain in effect until final payment and at all times thereafter when CONTRACTOR may be correcting, removing or replacing defective Work in accordance with paragraph 13.12. In addition, CONTRACTOR shall maintain such completed operations insurance for at least two years after final payment and furnish OWNER with evidence of continuation of such insurance at final payment and one year thereafter.

Contractual Liability Insurance:

5.4. The comprehensive general liability insurance required by paragraph 5.3 will include contractual liability insurance applicable to CONTRACTOR's obligations under paragraphs 6.30 and 6.31.

Owner's Liability Insurance:

5.5. OWNER shall be responsible for purchasing and maintaining his own liability insurance and, at his option, may purchase and maintain such insurance as will protect OWNER against claims which may arise from operations under the Contract Documents.

Property Insurance:

5.6. Unless otherwise provided in the Supplementary Conditions, OWNER shall purchase and maintain property insurance upon the Work at the site to the full insurable value thereof (subject to such deductible amounts as may be provided in the Supplementary Conditions or required by law). This insurance shall include the interests of OWNER, CONTRACTOR and Subcontractors in the Work, shall insure against the perils of fire and extended coverage and shall include "all risk" insurance for physical loss and damage including theft, vandalism and malicious mischief, collapse and water damage, and such other perils as may be provided in the Supplementary Conditions, and shall include damages, losses and expenses arising out of or resulting from any insured loss or incurred in the repair or replacement of any insured property (including fees and charges of engineers, architects, attorneys and other professionals). If not covered under the "all risk" insurance or otherwise provided in the Supplementary Conditions, CONTRACTOR shall purchase and maintain similar property insurance on portions of the Work stored on and off the site or in transit when such portions of the Work are to be included in an Application for Payment. The policies of insurance required to be purchased and maintained by OWNER in accordance with paragraphs 5.6 and 5.7 shall contain a provision that the coverage afforded will not be cancelled or materially changed until at least thirty days' prior written notice has been given to CONTRACTOR.

5.7.   OWNER shall purchase and maintain such boiler and machinery insurance as may be required by the Supplementary Conditions or by law. This insurance shall include the interests of OWNER, CONTRACTOR and Subcontractors in the Work.

5.8.   OWNER shall not be responsible for purchasing and maintaining any property insurance to protect the interests of CONTRACTOR or Subcontractors in the Work to the extent of any deductible amounts that are provided in the Supplementary Conditions. If CONTRACTOR wishes property insurance coverage within the limits of such amounts, CONTRACTOR may purchase and maintain it at his own expense.

5.9.   If CONTRACTOR requests in writing that other special insurance be included in the property insurance policy, OWNER shall, if possible, include such insurance, and the cost thereof shall be charged to CONTRACTOR by appropriate Change Order. Prior to commencement of the Work at the site, OWNER will in writing advise CONTRACTOR whether or not such other insurance has been procured by OWNER.

Waiver of Rights:

5.10.   OWNER and CONTRACTOR waive all rights against each other and the Subcontractors and their agents and employees and against ENGINEER and separate contractors (if any) and their subcontractors' agents and employees, for damages caused by fire or other perils to the extent covered by insurance provided under paragraphs 5.6 and 5.7, inclusive, or any other property insurance applicable to the Work, except such rights as they may have to the proceeds of such insurance held by OWNER as trustee. OWNER shall require similar written waivers by ENGINEER and from each separate contractor, and CONTRACTOR shall require similar written waivers from each Subcontractor (in accordance with paragraph 6.11 as applicable); each such waiver will be in favor of all other parties enumerated in this paragraph 5.10.

Receipt and Application of Proceeds:

5.11.   Any insured loss under the policies of insurance required by paragraphs 5.6 and 5.7 shall be adjusted with OWNER and made payable to OWNER as trustee for the insureds, as their interests may appear, subject to the requirements of any applicable mortgage clause and of paragraph 5.12. OWNER shall deposit in a separate account any

money so received, and he shall distribute it in accordance with such agreement as the parties in interest may reach. If no other special agreement is reached the damaged Work shall be repaired or replaced, the moneys so received applied on account thereof and the Work and the cost thereof covered by an appropriate Change Order.

5.12.   OWNER as trustee shall have power to adjust and settle any loss with the insurers unless one of the parties in interest shall object in writing within fifteen days after the occurrence of loss to OWNER's exercise of this power. If such objection be made, OWNER as trustee shall make settlement with the insurers in accordance with such agreement as the parties in interest may reach. If required in writing by any party in interest, OWNER as trustee shall upon the occurrence of an insured loss, give bond for the proper performance of his duties.

Acceptance of Insurance:

5.13.   If OWNER has any objection to the coverage afforded by or other provisions of the insurance required to be purchased and maintained by CONTRACTOR in accordance with paragraphs 5.3 and 5.4 on the basis of its not complying with the Contract Documents, OWNER will notify CONTRACTOR in writing thereof within ten days of the date of delivery of such certificates to OWNER in accordance with paragraph 2.7. If CONTRACTOR has any objection to the coverage afforded by or other provisions of the policies of insurance required to be purchased and maintained by OWNER in accordance with paragraphs 5.6 and 5.7 on the basis of their not complying with the Contract Documents, CONTRACTOR will notify OWNER in writing thereof within ten days of the date of delivery of such certificates to CONTRACTOR in accordance with paragraph 2.7. OWNER and CONTRACTOR will each provide to the other such additional information in respect of insurance provided by him as the other may reasonably request. Failure by OWNER or CONTRACTOR to give any such notice of objection within the time provided shall constitute acceptance of such insurance purchased by the other as complying with the Contract Documents.

Partial Utilization—Property Insurance:

5.14.   If OWNER finds it necessary to occupy or use a portion or portions of the Work prior to Substantial Completion of all the Work, such use or occupancy may be accomplished in accordance with paragraph 14.10; provided that no such use or occupancy shall commence before the insurers providing the property insurance have acknowledged notice thereof and in writing effected the changes in coverage necessitated thereby. The insurers providing the property insurance shall consent by endorsement on the policy or policies, but the property insurance shall not be cancelled or lapse on account of any such partial use or occupancy.

ARTICLE 6—CONTRACTOR'S RESPONSIBILITIES

Supervision and Superintendence:

6.1.   CONTRACTOR shall supervise and direct the Work competently and efficiently, devoting such attention thereto and applying such skills and expertise as may be necessary to perform the Work in accordance with the Contract Documents. CONTRACTOR shall be solely responsible for the means, methods, techniques, sequences and procedures of construction, but CONTRACTOR shall not be solely responsible for the negligence of others in the design or selection of a specific means, method, technique, sequence or procedure of construction which is indicated in and required by the Contract Documents. CONTRACTOR shall be responsible to see that the finished Work complies accurately with the Contract Documents.

6.2. CONTRACTOR shall keep on the Work at all times during its progress a competent resident superintendent, who shall not be replaced without written notice to OWNER and ENGINEER except under extraordinary circumstances. The superintendent will be CONTRACTOR's representative at the site and shall have authority to act on behalf of CONTRACTOR. All communications given to the superintendent shall be as binding as if given to CONTRACTOR.

Labor, Materials and Equipment:

6.3. CONTRACTOR shall provide competent, suitably qualified personnel to survey and lay out the Work and perform construction as required by the Contract Documents. CONTRACTOR shall at all times maintain good discipline and order at the site. Except in connection with the safety or protection of persons or the Work or property at the site or adjacent thereto, and except as otherwise indicated in the Supplementary Conditions, all Work at the site shall be performed during regular working hours, and CONTRACTOR will not permit overtime work or the performance of Work on Saturday, Sunday or any legal holiday without OWNER's written consent given after prior written notice to ENGINEER.

6.4. CONTRACTOR shall furnish all materials, equipment, labor, transportation, construction equipment and machinery, tools, appliances, fuel, power, light, heat, telephone, water and sanitary facilities and all other facilities and incidentals necessary for the execution, testing, initial operation and completion of the Work.

6.5. All materials and equipment shall be of good quality and new, except as otherwise provided in the Contract Documents. If required by ENGINEER, CONTRACTOR shall furnish satisfactory evidence (including reports of required tests) as to the kind and quality of materials and equipment.

6.6. All materials and equipment shall be applied, installed, connected, erected, used, cleaned and conditioned in accordance with the instructions of the applicable manufacturer, fabricator, supplier or distributor, except as otherwise provided in the Contract Documents.

Equivalent Materials and Equipment:

6.7. Whenever materials or equipment are specified or described in the Drawings or Specifications by using the name of a proprietary item or the name of a particular manufacturer, fabricator, supplier or distributor, the naming of the item is intended to establish the type, function and quality required. Unless the name is followed by words indicating that no substitution is permitted, materials or equipment of other manufacturers, fabricators, suppliers or distributors may be accepted by ENGINEER if sufficient information is submitted by CONTRACTOR to allow ENGINEER to determine that the material or equipment proposed is equivalent to that named. The procedure for review by ENGINEER will be as set forth in paragraphs 6.7.1 and 6.7.2 below as supplemented in the General Requirements.

6.7.1. Requests for review of substitute items of material and equipment will not be accepted by ENGINEER from anyone other than CONTRACTOR. If CONTRACTOR wishes to furnish or use a substitute item of material or equipment CONTRACTOR shall make written application to ENGINEER for acceptance thereof, certifying that the proposed substitute will perform adequately the functions called for by the general design, be similar and of equal substance to that specified and be suited to the same use and capable of performing the same function as that specified. The application will state whether or not acceptance of the substitute for use in the Work will require a change in the Drawings or Specifications to adapt the design to the substitute and whether or not incorporation or use of the substitute in connection with the Work is subject to payment of any license fee or royalty. All variations of the proposed substitute from that specified shall be identified in the application and available maintenance, repair and replacement service will be indicated. The application will also contain an itemized estimate of all costs that will result directly or indirectly from acceptance of such substitute, including costs of redesign and claims of other contractors affected by the resulting change, all of which shall be considered by ENGINEER in evaluating the proposed substitute. ENGINEER may require CONTRACTOR to furnish at CONTRACTOR's expense additional data about the proposed substitute. ENGINEER will be the sole judge of acceptability, and no substitute will be ordered or installed without ENGINEER's prior written acceptance. OWNER may require CONTRACTOR to furnish at CONTRACTOR's expense a special performance guarantee or other surety with respect to any substitute.

6.7.2. ENGINEER will record time required by ENGINEER and ENGINEER's consultants in evaluating substitutions proposed by CONTRACTOR and in making changes in the Drawings or Specifications occasioned thereby. Whether or not ENGINEER accepts a proposed substitute, CONTRACTOR shall reinburse OWNER for the charges of ENGINEER and ENGINEER's consultants for evaluating any proposed substitute.

Concerning Subcontractors:

6.8. CONTRACTOR shall not employ any Subcontractor or other person or organization (including those who are to furnish the principal items of materials or equipment), whether initially or as a substitute, against whom OWNER or ENGINEER may have reasonable objection. A Subcontractor or other person or organization identified in writing to OWNER and ENGINEER by CONTRACTOR prior to the Notice of Award and not objected to in writing by OWNER or ENGINEER prior to the Notice of Award will be deemed acceptable to OWNER and ENGINEER. Acceptance of any Subcontractor, other person or organization by OWNER or ENGINEER shall not constitute a waiver of any right of OWNER or ENGINEER to reject defective Work. If OWNER or ENGINEER after due investigation has reasonable objection to any Subcontractor, other person or organization proposed by CONTRACTOR after the Notice of Award, CONTRACTOR shall submit an acceptable substitute and the Contract Price shall be increased or decreased by the difference in cost occasioned by such substitution, and an appropriate Change Order shall be issued. CONTRACTOR shall not be required to employ any Subcontractor, other person or organization against whom CONTRACTOR has reasonable objection.

6.9. CONTRACTOR shall be fully responsible for all acts and omissions of his Subcontractors and of persons and organizations directly or indirectly employed by them and of persons and organizations for whose acts any of them may be liable to the same extent that CONTRACTOR is responsible for the acts and omissions of persons directly employed by CONTRACTOR. Nothing in the Contract Documents shall create any contractual relationship between OWNER or ENGINEER and any Subcontractor or other person or organization having a direct contract with CONTRACTOR, nor shall it create any obligation on the part of OWNER or ENGINEER to pay or to see to the payment of any moneys due any Subcontractor or other person or organization, except as may otherwise be required by law. OWNER or ENGINEER may furnish to any Subcontractor or other person or organization, to the extent practicable, evidence of amounts paid to CONTRACTOR on account of specific Work done.

6.10. The divisions and sections of the Specifications and the identifications of any Drawings shall not control CONTRACTOR in dividing the Work among Subcontractors or delineating the Work to be performed by any specific trade.

6.11. All Work performed for CONTRACTOR by a Subcontractor will be pursuant to an appropriate agreement between CONTRACTOR and the Subcontractor which specifically binds the Subcontractor to the applicable terms and conditions of the Contract Documents for the benefit of OWNER and ENGINEER and contains waiver provisions as required by paragraph 5.10. CONTRACTOR shall pay each Subcontractor a just share of any insurance moneys received by CONTRACTOR on account of losses under policies issued pursuant to paragraphs 5.6 through 5.8.

Patent Fees and Royalties:

6.12. CONTRACTOR shall pay all license fees and royalties and assume all costs incident to the use in the performance of the Work or the incorporation in the Work of any inven-

tion, design, process, product or device which is the subject of patent rights or copyrights held by others. If a particular invention, design, process, product or device is specified in the Contract Documents for use in the performance of the Work and if to the actual knowledge of OWNER or ENGINEER its use is subject to patent rights or copyrights calling for the payment of any license fee or royalty to others, the existence of such rights shall be disclosed by OWNER in the Contract Documents. CONTRACTOR shall indemnify and hold harmless OWNER and ENGINEER and anyone directly or indirectly employed by either of them from and against all claims, damages, losses and expenses (including attorneys' fees) arising out of any infringement of patent rights or copyrights incident to the use in the performance of the Work or resulting from the incorporation in the Work of any invention, design, process, product or device not specified in the Contract Documents, and shall defend all such claims in connection with any alleged infringement of such rights.

Permits:

6.13. Unless otherwise provided in the Supplementary Conditions, CONTRACTOR shall obtain and pay for all construction permits and licenses. OWNER shall assist CONTRACTOR, when necessary, in obtaining such permits and licenses. CONTRACTOR shall pay all governmental charges and inspection fees necessary for the prosecution of the Work, which are applicable at the time of opening of Bids. CONTRACTOR shall pay all charges of utility service companies for connections to the Work, and OWNER shall pay all charges of such companies for capital costs related thereto.

Laws and Regulations:

6.14. CONTRACTOR shall give all notices and comply with all laws, ordinances, rules and regulations applicable to the Work. If CONTRACTOR observes that the Specifications or Drawings are at variance therewith, CONTRACTOR shall give ENGINEER prompt written notice thereof, and any necessary changes shall be adjusted by an appropriate Modification. If CONTRACTOR performs any Work knowing or having reason to know that it is contrary to such laws, ordinances, rules and regulations, and without such notice to ENGINEER, CONTRACTOR shall bear all costs arising therefrom; however, it shall not be CONTRACTOR's primary responsibility to make certain that the Specifications and Drawings are in accordance with such laws, ordinances, rules and regulations.

Taxes:

6.15. CONTRACTOR shall pay all sales, consumer, use and other similar taxes required to be paid by him in accordance with the law of the place of the Project.

Use of Premises:

6.16. CONTRACTOR shall confine construction equipment, the storage of materials and equipment and the operations of workmen to areas permitted by law, ordinances, permits or the requirements of the Contract Documents, and shall not unreasonably encumber the premises with construction equipment or other materials or equipment.

6.17. During the progress of the Work, CONTRACTOR shall keep the premises free from accumulations of waste materials, rubbish and other debris resulting from the Work. At the completion of the Work CONTRACTOR shall remove all waste materials, rubbish and debris from and about the premises as well as all tools, appliances, construction equipment and machinery, and surplus materials, and shall leave the site clean and ready for occupancy by OWNER. CONTRACTOR shall restore to their original condition those portions of the site not designated for alteration by the Contract Documents.

6.18. CONTRACTOR shall not load nor permit any part of any structure to be loaded in any manner that will endanger the structure, nor shall CONTRACTOR subject any part of the Work or adjacent property to stresses or pressures that will endanger it.

Record Documents:

6.19. CONTRACTOR shall keep one record copy of all Specifications, Drawings, Addenda, Modifications, Shop Drawings and samples at the site, in good order and annotated to show all changes made during the construction process. These shall be available to ENGINEER for examination and shall be delivered to ENGINEER for OWNER upon completion of the Work.

Safety and Protection:

6.20. CONTRACTOR shall be responsible for initiating, maintaining and supervising all safety precautions and programs in connection with the Work. CONTRACTOR shall take all necessary precautions for the safety of, and shall provide the necessary protection to prevent damage, injury or loss to:

6.20.1. all employees on the Work and other persons who may be affected thereby,

6.20.2. all the Work and all materials or equipment to be incorporated therein, whether in storage on or off the site, and

6.20.3. other property at the site or adjacent thereto, including trees, shrubs, lawns, walks, pavements, roadways, structures and utilities not designated for removal, relocation or replacement in the course of construction.

CONTRACTOR shall comply with all applicable laws, ordinances, rules, regulations and orders of any public body having jurisdiction for the safety of persons or property or to protect them from damage, injury or loss; and shall erect and maintain all necessary safeguards for such safety and protection. CONTRACTOR shall notify owners of adjacent property and utilities when prosecution of the Work may affect them. All damage, injury or loss to any property referred to in paragraph 6.20.2 or 6.20.3 caused, directly or indirectly, in whole or in part, by CONTRACTOR, any Subcontractor or anyone directly or indirectly employed by any of them or anyone for whose acts any of them may be liable, shall be remedied by CONTRACTOR (except damage or loss attribut-

able to the fault of Drawings or Specifications or to the acts or omissions of OWNER or ENGINEER or anyone employed by either of them or anyone for whose acts either of them may be liable, and not attributable, directly or indirectly, in whole or in part, to the fault or negligence of CONTRACTOR). CONTRACTOR's duties and responsibilities for the safety and protection of the Work shall continue until such time as all the Work is completed and ENGINEER has issued a notice to OWNER and CONTRACTOR in accordance with paragraph 14.13 that the Work is acceptable.

6.21. CONTRACTOR shall designate a responsible member of his organization at the site whose duty shall be the prevention of accidents. This person shall be CONTRACTOR's superintendent unless otherwise designated in writing by CONTRACTOR to OWNER.

Emergencies:

6.22. In emergencies affecting the safety or protection of persons or the Work or property at the site or adjacent thereto, CONTRACTOR, without special instruction or authorization from ENGINEER or OWNER, is obligated to act to prevent threatened damage, injury or loss. CONTRACTOR shall give ENGINEER prompt written notice of any significant changes in the Work or deviations from the Contract Documents caused thereby.

Shop Drawings and Samples:

6.23. After checking and verifying all field measurements, CONTRACTOR shall submit to ENGINEER for review and approval, in accordance with the accepted schedule of Shop Drawing submissions (see paragraph 2.8), five copies (unless otherwise specified in the General Requirements) of all Shop Drawings, which shall have been checked by and stamped with the approval of CONTRACTOR and identified as ENGINEER may require. The data shown on the Shop Drawings will be complete with respect to dimensions, design criteria, materials of construction and like information to enable ENGINEER to review the information as required.

6.24. CONTRACTOR shall also submit to ENGINEER for review and approval with such promptness as to cause no delay in Work, all samples required by the Contract Documents. All samples will have been checked by and stamped with the approval of CONTRACTOR, identified clearly as to material, manufacturer, any pertinent catalog numbers and the use for which intended.

6.25. At the time of each submission, CONTRACTOR shall in writing call ENGINEER's attention to any deviations that the Shop Drawings or samples may have from the requirements of the Contract Documents.

6.26. ENGINEER will review and approve with reasonable promptness Shop Drawings and samples, but ENGINEER's review and approval shall be only for conformance with the design concept of the Project and for compliance with the information given in the Contract Documents and shall not extend to means, methods, sequences, techniques or procedures of construction or to safety precautions or programs incident thereto. The review and approval of a separate item as such will not indicate approval of the assembly in which the item functions. CONTRACTOR shall make any corrections required by ENGINEER and shall return the required number of corrected copies of Shop Drawings and resubmit new samples for review and approval. CONTRACTOR shall direct specific attention in writing to revisions other than the corrections called for by ENGINEER on previous submittals. CONTRACTOR's stamp of approval on any Shop Drawing or sample shall constitute a representation to OWNER and ENGINEER that CONTRACTOR has either determined and verified all quantities, dimensions, field construction criteria, materials, catalog numbers, and similar data or assumes full responsibility for doing so, and that CONTRACTOR has reviewed or coordinated each Shop Drawing or sample with the requirements of the Work and the Contract Documents.

6.27.   Where a Shop Drawing or sample is required by the Specifications, no related Work shall be commenced until the submittal has been reviewed and approved by ENGINEER.

6.28.   ENGINEER's review and approval of Shop Drawings or samples shall not relieve CONTRACTOR from responsibility for any deviations from the Contract Documents unless CONTRACTOR has in writing called ENGINEER's attention to such deviation at the time of submission and ENGINEER has given written concurrence and approval to the specific deviation, nor shall any concurrence or approval by ENGINEER relieve CONTRACTOR from responsibility for errors or omissions in the Shop Drawings.

Continuing the Work:

6.29.   CONTRACTOR shall carry on the Work and maintain the progress schedule during all disputes or disagreements with OWNER. No Work shall be delayed or postponed pending resolution of any disputes or disagreements, except as CONTRACTOR and OWNER may otherwise agree in writing.

Indemnification:

6.30.   To the fullest extent permitted by law, CONTRACTOR shall indemnify and hold harmless OWNER and ENGINEER and their agents and employees from and against all claims, damages, losses and expenses including but not limited to attorneys' fees arising out of or resulting from the performance of the Work, provided that any such claim, damage, loss or expense (a) is attributable to bodily injury, sickness, disease or death, or to injury to or destruction of tangible property (other than the Work itself) including the loss of use resulting therefrom and (b) is caused in whole or in part by any negligent act or omission of CONTRACTOR, any Subcontractor, anyone directly or indirectly employed by any of them or anyone for whose acts any of them may be liable, regardless of whether or not it is caused in part by a party indemnified hereunder.

6.31.   In any and all claims against OWNER or ENGINEER or any of their agents or employees by any employee of CONTRACTOR, any Subcontractor, anyone directly or indirectly employed by any of them or anyone for whose acts any of them may be liable, the indemnification obligation under paragraph 6.30 shall not be limited in any way by any limitation on the amount or type of damages, compensation or benefits payable by or for CONTRACTOR or any Subcontractor under workers' or workmen's compensation acts, disability benefit acts or other employee benefit acts.

6.32.   The obligations of CONTRACTOR under paragraph 6.30 shall not extend to the liability of ENGINEER, his agents or employees arising out of the preparation or approval of maps, drawings, opinions, reports, surveys, Change Orders, designs or specifications.

ARTICLE 7—WORK BY OTHERS

7.1.   OWNER may perform additional work related to the Project by himself, or have additional work performed by utility service companies, or let other direct contracts therefor which shall contain General Conditions similar to these. CONTRACTOR shall afford the utility service companies and the other contractors who are parties to such direct contracts (or OWNER, if OWNER is performing the additional work with OWNER's employees) reasonable opportunity for the introduction and storage of materials and equipment and the execution of work, and shall properly connect and coordinate his Work with theirs.

7.2.   If any part of CONTRACTOR's Work depends for proper execution or results upon the work of any such other contractor or utility service company (or OWNER), CONTRACTOR shall inspect and promptly report to ENGINEER in writing any patent or apparent defects or deficiencies in such work that render it unsuitable for such proper execution and results. CONTRACTOR's failure so to report shall constitute an acceptance of the other work as fit and proper for integration with CONTRACTOR's Work except for latent or non-apparent defects and deficiencies in the other work.

7.3.   CONTRACTOR shall do all cutting, fitting and patching of his Work that may be required to make its several parts come together properly and integrate with such other work. CONTRACTOR shall not endanger any work of others by cutting, excavating or otherwise altering their work and will only cut or alter their work with the written consent of ENGINEER and the others whose work will be affected.

7.4.   If the performance of additional work by other contractors or utility service companies or OWNER was not noted in the Contract Documents, written notice thereof shall be given to CONTRACTOR prior to starting any such additional work. If CONTRACTOR believes that the performance of such additional work by OWNER or others involves additional expense to CONTRACTOR or requires an extension of the Contract Time, CONTRACTOR may make a claim therefor as provided in Articles 11 and 12.

ARTICLE 8—OWNER'S RESPONSIBILITIES

8.1. OWNER shall issue all communications to CONTRACTOR through ENGINEER.

8.2. In case of termination of the employment of ENGINEER, OWNER shall appoint an engineer against whom CONTRACTOR makes no reasonable objection, whose status under the Contract Documents shall be that of the former ENGINEER. Any dispute in connection with such appoinment shall be subject to arbitration.

8.3. OWNER shall furnish the data required of OWNER under the Contract Documents promptly and shall make payments to CONTRACTOR promptly after they are due as provided in paragraphs 14.4 and 14.13.

8.4. OWNER's duties in respect of providing lands and easements and providing engineering surveys to establish reference points are set forth in paragraphs 4.1 and 4.4 Paragraph 4.2 refers to OWNER's identifying and making available to CONTRACTOR copies of reports of investigations and tests of subsurface and latent physical conditions at the site or otherwise affecting performance of the Work which have been relied upon by ENGINEER in preparing the Drawings and Specifications.

8.5. OWNER's responsibilities in respect of purchasing and maintaining liability and property insurance are set forth in paragraphs 5.5 through 5.7.

8.6. In connection with OWNER's rights to request changes in the Work in accordance with Article 10, OWNER (especially in certain instances as provided in paragraph 10.4) is obligated to execute Change Orders.

8.7. OWNER's responsibility in respect of certain inspections, tests and approvals is set forth in paragraph 13.4.

8.8. In connection with OWNER's right to stop Work or suspend Work, see paragraphs 13.10 and 15.1. Paragraph 15.2 deals with OWNER's right to terminate services of CONTRACTOR under certain circumstances.

ARTICLE 9—ENGINEER'S STATUS DURING CONSTRUCTION

Owner's Representative:

9.1. ENGINEER will be OWNER's respresentative during the construction period. The duties and responsibilities and the limitations of authority of ENGINEER as OWNER's representative during construction are set forth in the Contract Documents and shall not be extended without written consent of OWNER and ENGINEER.

Visits to Site:

9.2. ENGINEER will make visits to the site at intervals appropriate to the various stages of construction to observe the progress and quality of the executed Work and to determine, in general, if the Work is proceeding in accordance with the Contract Documents. ENGINEER will not be required to make exhaustive or continuous on-site inspections to check the quality or quantity of the Work. ENGINEER's efforts will be directed toward providing for OWNER a greater degree of confidence that the completed Work will conform to the Contract Documents. On the basis of such visits and on-site observations as an experienced and qualified design professional, ENGINEER will keep OWNER informed of the progress of the Work and will endeavor to guard OWNER against defects and deficiencies in the Work.

Clarifications and Interpretations:

9.3. ENGINEER will issue with reasonable promptness such written clarifications or interpretations of the Contract Documents (in the form of Drawings or otherwise) as ENGINEER may determine necessary, which shall be consistent with or reasonably inferable from the overall intent of the Contract Documents. If CONTRACTOR believes that a written clarification or interpretation justifies an increase in the Contract Price or Contract Time, CONTRACTOR may make a claim therefor as provided in Article 11 or Article 12.

Rejecting Defective Work:

9.4. ENGINEER will have authority to disapprove or reject Work which is defective, and will also have authority to require special inspection or testing of the Work as provided in paragraph 13.9, whether or not the Work is fabricated, installed or completed.

Shop Drawings, Change Orders and Payments:

9.5. In connection with ENGINEER's responsibility for Shop Drawings and samples, see paragraphs 6.23 through 6.29 inclusive.

9.6. In connection with ENGINEER's responsibilities as to Change Orders, see Articles 10, 11 and 12.

9.7. In connection with ENGINEER's responsibilities in respect of Applications for Payment, etc., see Article 14.

Project Representation:

9.8. If OWNER and ENGINEER agree, ENGINEER will furnish a Resident Project Representative to assist ENGINEER in observing the performance of the Work. The duties, responsibilities and limitations of authority of any such Resident Project Representative and assistants will be as provided in the Supplementary Conditions. If OWNER designates another agent to represent him at the site who is not ENGINEER's agent or employee, the duties, responsibilities and limitations of authority of such other person will be as provided in the Supplementary Conditions.

Decisions on Disagreements:

9.9. ENGINEER will be the initial interpreter of the requirements of the Contract Documents and judge of the acceptability of the Work thereunder. Claims, disputes and other matters relating to the acceptability of the Work or the interpretation of the requirements of the Contract Documents pertaining to the execution and progress of the Work shall be referred initially to ENGINEER in writing with a request for a formal decision in accordance with this paragraph, which ENGINEER will render in writing within a reasonable time. Written notice of each such claim, dispute and other matter shall be delivered by the claimant to ENGINEER and the other party to the Agreement within fifteen days of the occurrence of the event giving rise thereto, and written supporting data will be submitted to ENGINEER and the other party within forty-five days of such occurrence unless ENGINEER allows an additional period of time to ascertain more accurate data. In his capacity as interpreter and judge ENGINEER will not show partiality to OWNER or CONTRACTOR and will not be liable in connection with any interpretation or decision rendered in good faith in such capacity.

9.10.   The rendering of a decision by ENGINEER pursuant to paragraph 9.9 with respect to any such claim, dispute or other matter (except any which have been waived by the making or acceptance of final payment as provided in paragraph 14.16) will be a condition precedent to any exercise by OWNER or CONTRACTOR of such rights or remedies as either may otherwise have under the Contract Documents or at law in respect of any such claim, dispute or other matter.

Limitations on ENGINEER's Responsibilities:

9.11.   Neither ENGINEER's authority to act under this Article 9 or elsewhere in the Contract Documents nor any decision made by ENGINEER in good faith either to exercise or not exercise such authority shall give rise to any duty or responsibility of ENGINEER to CONTRACTOR, any Subcontractor, any manufacturer, fabricator, supplier or distributor, or any of their agents or employees or any other person performing any of the Work.

9.12.   Whenever in the Contract Documents the terms "as ordered", "as directed", "as required", "as allowed" or terms of like effect or import are used, or the adjectives "reasonable", "suitable", "acceptable", "proper" or "satisfactory" or adjectives of like effect or import are used, to describe requirement, direction, review or judgment of ENGINEER as to the Work, it is intended that such requirement, direction, review or judgment will be solely to evaluate the Work for compliance with the Contract Documents (unless there is a specific statement indicating otherwise). The use of any such term or adjective never indicates that ENGINEER shall have authority to supervise or direct performance of the Work or authority to undertake responsibility contrary to the provisions of paragraphs 9.13 or 9.14.

9.13.   ENGINEER will not be responsible for CONTRACTOR's means, methods, techniques, sequences or procedures of construction, or the safety precautions and programs incident thereto, and ENGINEER will not be responsible for CONTRACTOR's failure to perform the Work in accordance with the Contract Documents.

9.14.   ENGINEER will not be responsible for the acts or omissions of CONTRACTOR or of any Subcontractors, or of the agents or employees of any CONTRACTOR or Subcontractor, or of any other persons at the site or otherwise performing any of the Work.

ARTICLE 10—CHANGES IN THE WORK

10.1.   Without invalidating the Agreement, OWNER may, at any time or from time to time, order additions, deletions or revisions in the Work; these will be authorized by Change Orders. Upon receipt of a Change Order, CONTRACTOR shall proceed with the Work involved. All such Work shall be executed under the applicable conditions of the Contract Documents. If any Change Order causes an increase or decrease in the Contract Price or an extension or shortening of the Contract Time, an equitable adjustment will be made as provided in Article 11 or Article 12 on the basis of a claim made by either party.

10.2.   ENGINEER may authorize minor changes in the Work not involving an adjustment in the Contract Price or the Contract Time, which are consistent with the overall intent of the Contract Documents. These may be accomplished by a Field Order and shall be binding on OWNER, and also on CONTRACTOR who shall perform the change promptly. If CONTRACTOR believes that a Field Order justifies an increase in the Contract Price or Contract Time, CONTRACTOR may make a claim therefor as provided in Article 11 or Article 12.

10.3.   Additional Work performed without authorization of a Change Order will not entitle CONTRACTOR to an increase in the Contract Price or an extension of the Contract Time, except in the case of an emergency as provided in paragraph 6.22 and except as provided in paragraphs 10.2 and 13.9.

10.4.   OWNER shall execute appropriate Change Orders prepared by ENGINEER covering changes in the Work which are required by OWNER, or required because of unforeseen physical conditions or emergencies, or because of uncovering Work found not to be defective, or as provided in paragraphs 11.9 or 11.10, or because of any other claim of CONTRACTOR for a change in the Contract Time or the Contract Price which is recommended by ENGINEER.

10.5.   If notice of any change affecting the general scope of the Work or change in the Contract Price is required by the provisions of any Bond to be given to the Surety, it will be CONTRACTOR's responsibility to so notify the Surety, and the amount of each applicable Bond shall be adjusted accordingly. CONTRACTOR shall furnish proof of such adjustment to OWNER.

ARTICLE 11—CHANGE OF CONTRACT PRICE

11.1.   The Contract Price constitutes the total compensation (subject to authorized adjustments) payable to

CONTRACTOR for performing the Work. All duties, responsibilities and obligations assigned to or undertaken by CONTRACTOR shall be at his expense without change in the Contract Price.

11.2.   The Contract Price may only be changed by a Change Order. Any claim for an increase in the Contract Price shall be based on written notice delivered to OWNER and ENGINEER within fifteen days of the occurrence of the event giving rise to the claim. Notice of the amount of the claim with supporting data shall be delivered within forty-five days of such occurrence unless ENGINEER allows an additional period of time to ascertain accurate cost data. All claims for adjustment in the Contract Price shall be determined by ENGINEER if OWNER and CONTRACTOR cannot otherwise agree on the amount involved. Any change in the Contract Price resulting from any such claim shall be incorporated in a Change Order.

11.3.   The value of any Work covered by a Change Order or of any claim for an increase or decrease in the Contract Price shall be determined in one of the following ways:

11.3.1.   Where the Work involved is covered by unit prices contained in the Contract Documents, by application of unit prices to the quantities of the items involved (subject to the provisions of paragraph 11.9).

11.3.2.   By mutual acceptance of a lump sum.

11.3.3.   On the basis of the Cost of the Work (determined as provided in paragraphs 11.4 and 11.5) plus a Contractor's Fee for overhead and profit (determined as provided in paragraph 11.6).

Cost of the Work:

11.4.   The term Cost of the Work means the sum of all costs necessarily incurred and paid by CONTRACTOR in the proper performance of the Work. Except as otherwise may be agreed to in writing by OWNER, such costs shall be in amounts no higher than those prevailing in the locality of the Project, shall include only the following items and shall not include any of the costs itemized in paragraph 11.5:

11.4.1.   Payroll costs for employees in the direct employ of CONTRACTOR in the performance of the Work under schedules of job classifications agreed upon by OWNER and CONTRACTOR. Payroll costs for employees not employed full time on the Work shall be apportioned on the basis of their time spent on the Work. Payroll costs shall include, but not be limited to, salaries and wages plus the cost of fringe benefits which shall include social security contributions, unemployment, excise and payroll taxes, workers' or workmen's compensation, health and retirement benefits, bonuses, sick leave, vacation and holiday pay applicable thereto. Such employees shall include superintendents and foremen at the site. The expenses of performing Work after regular working hours, on Sunday or legal holidays, shall be included in the above to the extent authorized by OWNER.

11.4.2.   Cost of all materials and equipment furnished and incorporated in the Work, including costs of transportation and storage thereof, and manufacturers' field services required in connection therewith. All cash discounts shall accrue to CONTRACTOR unless OWNER deposits funds with CONTRACTOR with which to make payments, in which case the cash discounts shall accrue to OWNER. All trade discounts, rebates and refunds, and all returns from sale of surplus materials and equipment shall accrue to OWNER and CONTRACTOR shall make provisions so that they may be obtained.

11.4.3.   Payments made by CONTRACTOR to the Subcontractors for Work performed by Subcontractors. If required by OWNER, CONTRACTOR shall obtain competitive bids from Subcontractors acceptable to CONTRACTOR and shall deliver such bids to OWNER who will then determine, with the advice of ENGINEER, which bids will be accepted. If a subcontract provides that the Subcontractor is to be paid on the basis of Cost of the Work Plus a Fee, the Subcontractor's Cost of the Work shall be determined in the same manner as CONTACTOR's Cost of the Work. All subcontracts shall be subject to the other provisions of the Contract Documents insofar as applicable.

11.4.4.   Costs of special consultants (including, but not limited to, engineers, architects, testing laboratories, surveyors, lawyers and accountants) employed for services specifically related to the Work.

11.4.5.   Supplemental costs including the following:

11.4.5.1.   The proportion of necessary transportation, travel and subsistence expenses of CONTRACTOR's employees incurred in discharge of duties connected with the Work.

11.4.5.2.   Cost, including transportation and maintenance, of all materials, supplies, equipment, machinery, appliances, office and temporary facilities at the site and hand tools not owned by the workmen, which are consumed in the performance of the Work, and cost less market value of such items used but not consumed which remain the property of CONTRACTOR.

11.4.5.3.   Rentals of all construction equipment and machinery and the parts thereof whether rented from CONTRACTOR or others in accordance with rental agreements approved by OWNER with the advice of ENGINEER, and the costs of transportation, loading, unloading, installation, dismantling and removal thereof—all in accordance with terms of said rental agreements. The rental of any such equipment, machinery or parts shall cease when the use thereof is no longer necessary for the Work.

11.4.5.4.   Sales, use or similar taxes related to the Work, and for which CONTRACTOR is liable, imposed by any governmental authority.

11.4.5.5.   Deposits lost for causes other than CON-TRACTOR's negligence, royalty payments and fees for permits and licenses.

11.4.5.6.   Losses and damages (and related expenses), not compensated by insurance or otherwise, to the Work or otherwise sustained by CONTRACTOR in connection with the execution of the Work, provided they have resulted from causes other than the negligence of CONTRACTOR, any Subcontractor, or anyone directly or indirectly employed by any of them or for whose acts any of them may be liable. Such losses shall include settlements made with the written consent and approval of OWNER. No such losses, damages and expenses shall be included in the Cost of the Work for the purpose of determining Contractor's Fee. If, however, any such loss or damage requires reconstruction and CONTRACTOR is placed in charge thereof, CON-TRACTOR shall be paid for services a fee proportionate to that stated in paragraph 11.6.2.

11.4.5.7.   The cost of utilities, fuel and sanitary facilities at the site.

11.4.5.8.   Minor expenses such as telegrams, long distance telephone calls, telephone service at the site, expressage and similar petty cash items in connection with the Work.

11.4.5.9.   Cost of premiums for additional Bonds and insurance required because of changes in the Work.

11.5.   The term Cost of the Work shall not include any of the following:

11.5.1.   Payroll costs and other compensation of CON-TRACTOR's officers, executives, principals (of partnership and sole proprietorships), general managers, engineers, architects, estimators, lawyers, auditors, accountants, purchasing and contracting agents, expeditors, timekeepers, clerks and other personnel employed by CONTRACTOR whether at the site or in his principal or a branch office for general administration of the Work and not specifically included in the agreed upon schedule of job classifications referred to in subparagraph 11.4.1—all of which are to be considered administrative costs covered by the Contractor's Fee.

11.5.2.   Expenses of CONTRACTOR's principal and branch offices other than CONTRACTOR's office at the site.

11.5.3.   Any part of CONTRACTOR's capital expenses, including interest on CONTRACTOR's capital employed for the Work and charges against CON-TRACTOR for delinquent payments.

11.5.4.   Cost of premiums for all Bonds and for all insurance whether or not CONTRACTOR is required by the Contract Documents to purchase and maintain the same (except for additional Bonds and insurance required because of changes in the Work).

11.5.5.   Costs due to the negligence of CONTRAC-TOR, any Subcontractor, or anyone directly or indirectly employed by any of them or for whose acts any of them may be liable, including but not limited to, the correction of defective Work, disposal of materials or equipment wrongly supplied and making good any damage to property.

11.5.6.   Other overhead or general expense costs of any kind and the costs of any item not specifically and expressly included in paragraph 11.4.

Contractor's Fee:

11.6.   The Contractor's Fee allowed to CONTRACTOR for overhead and profit shall be determined as follows:

11.6.1.   a mutually acceptable fixed fee; or if none can be agreed upon,

11.6.2.   a fee based on the following percentages of the various portions of the Cost of the Work:

11.6.2.1.   for costs incurred under paragraphs 11.4.1 and 11.4.2, the Contractor's Fee shall be ten percent,

11.6.2.2.   for costs incurred under paragraph 11.4.3, the Contractor's Fee shall be five percent; and if a subcontract is on the basis of Cost of the Work Plus a Fee, the maximum allowable to the Subcontractor as a fee for overhead and profit shall be ten percent, and

11.6.2.3.   no fee shall be payable on the basis of costs itemized under paragraphs 11.4.4, 11.4.5 and 11.5.

11.7.   The amount of credit to be allowed by CONTRAC-TOR to OWNER for any such change which results in a net decrease in cost, will be the amount of the actual net decrease. When both additions and credits are involved in any one change, the combined overhead and profit shall be figured on the basis of the net increase, if any.

Adjustment of Unit Prices:

11.8.   Whenever the cost of any Work is to be determined pursuant to paragraphs 11.4 and 11.5, CONTRACTOR will submit in form acceptable to ENGINEER an itemized cost breakdown together with supporting data.

11.9.   Where the quantity of Work with respect to any item that is covered by a unit price differs materially and significantly from the quantity of such Work indicated in the Contract Documents, an appropriate Change Order shall be issued on recommendation of ENGINEER to adjust the unit price.

Cash Allowances:

11.10. It is understood that CONTRACTOR has included in the Contract Price all allowances so named in the Contract Documents and shall cause the Work so covered to be done by such Subcontractors, manufacturers, fabricators, suppliers or distributors and for such sums within the limit of the allowances as may be acceptable to ENGINEER. Upon final payment, the Contract Price shall be adjusted as required and an appropriate Change Order issued. CONTRACTOR agrees that the original Contract Price includes such sums as CONTRACTOR deems proper for costs and profit on account of cash allowances. No demand for additional cost or profit in connection therewith will be valid.

ARTICLE 12—CHANGE OF THE CONTRACT TIME

12.1. The Contract Time may only be changed by a Change Order. Any claim for an extension in the Contract Time shall be based on written notice delivered to OWNER and ENGINEER within fifteen days of the occurrence of the event giving rise to the claim. Notice of the extent of the claim with supporting data shall be delivered within forty-five days of such occurrence unless ENGINEER allows an additional period of time to ascertain more accurate data. All claims for adjustment in the Contract Time shall be determined by ENGINEER if OWNER and CONTRACTOR cannot otherwise agree. Any change in the Contract Time resulting from any such claim shall be incorporated in a Change Order.

12.2. The Contract Time will be extended in an amount equal to time lost due to delays beyond the control of CONTRACTOR if a claim is made therefor as provided in paragraph 12.1. Such delays shall include, but not be limited to, acts or neglect by OWNER or others performing additional Work as contemplated by Article 7, or to fires, floods, labor disputes, epidemics, abnormal weather conditions, or acts of God.

12.3. All time limits stated in the Contract Documents are of the essence of the Agreement. The provisions of this Article 12 shall not exclude recovery for damages (including compensation for additional professional services) for delay by either party.

ARTICLE 13—WARRANTY AND GUARANTEE; TESTS AND INSPECTIONS; CORRECTION, REMOVAL OR ACCEPTANCE OF DEFECTIVE WORK

Warranty and Guarantee:

13.1. CONTRACTOR warrants and guarantees to OWNER and ENGINEER that all Work will be in accordance with the Contract Documents and will not be defective. Prompt notice of all defects shall be given to CONTRACTOR. All defective Work, whether or not in place, may be rejected, corrected or accepted as provided in this Article 13.

Access to Work:

13.2. ENGINEER and ENGINEER's representatives, other representatives of OWNER, testing agencies and governmental agencies with jurisdictional interests will have access to the Work at reasonable times for their observation, inspection and testing. CONTRACTOR shall provide proper and safe conditions for such access.

Tests and Inspections:

13.3. CONTRACTOR shall give ENGINEER timely notice of readiness of the Work for all required inspections, tests or approvals.

13.4. If any law, ordinance, rule, regulation, code, or order of any public body having jurisdiction requires any Work (or part thereof) to specifically be inspected, tested or approved, CONTRACTOR shall assume full responsibility therefor, pay all costs in connection therewith and furnish ENGINEER the required certificates of inspection, testing or approval. CONTRACTOR shall also be responsible for and shall pay all costs in connection with any inspection or testing required in connection with OWNER's or ENGINEER's acceptance of a manufacturer, fabricator, supplier or distributor of materials or equipment proposed to be incorporated in the Work, or of materials or equipment submitted for approval prior to CONTRACTOR's purchase thereof for incorporation in the Work. The cost of all other inspections, tests and approvals required by the Contract Documents shall be paid by OWNER (unless otherwise specified).

13.5. All inspections, tests or approvals other than those required by law, ordinance, rule, regulation, code or order of any public body having jurisdiction shall be performed by organizations acceptable to OWNER and CONTRACTOR (or by ENGINEER if so specified).

13.6. If any Work that is to be inspected, tested or approved is covered without written concurrence of ENGINEER, it must, if requested by ENGINEER, be uncovered for observation. Such uncovering shall be at CONTRACTOR's expense unless CONTRACTOR has given ENGINEER timely notice of CONTRACTOR's intention to cover such Work and ENGINEER has not acted with reasonable promptness in response to such notice.

13.7. Neither observations by ENGINEER nor inspections, tests or approvals by others shall relieve CONTRACTOR from his obligations to perform the Work in accordance with the Contract Documents.

Uncovering Work:

13.8. If any Work is covered contrary to the written request of ENGINEER, it must, if requested by ENGINEER, be uncovered for ENGINEER's observation and replaced at CONTRACTOR's expense.

13.9. If ENGINEER considers it necessary or advisable that covered Work be observed by ENGINEER or inspected or tested by others, CONTRACTOR, at ENGINEER's request, shall uncover, expose or otherwise make available for observation, inspection or testing as ENGINEER may require, that portion of the Work in question, furnishing all necessary labor, material and equipment. If it is found that such Work is defective, CONTRACTOR shall bear all the expenses of such uncovering, exposure, observation, inspection and testing and of satisfactory reconstruction, including compensation for additional professional services, and an appropriate deductive Change Order shall be issued. If, however, such Work is not found to be defective, CONTRACTOR shall be allowed an increase in the Contract Price or an extension of the Contract Time, or both, directly attributable to such uncovering, exposure, observation, inspection, testing and reconstruction if he makes a claim therefor as provided in Articles 11 and 12.

Owner May Stop the Work:

13.10.   If the Work is defective, or CONTRACTOR fails to supply sufficient skilled workmen or suitable materials or equipment, OWNER may order CONTRACTOR to stop the Work, or any portion thereof, until the cause for such order has been eliminated; however, this right of OWNER to stop the Work shall not give rise to any duty on the part of OWNER to exercise this right for the benefit of CONTRACTOR or any other party.

Correction or Removal of Defective Work:

13.11.   If required by ENGINEER, CONTRACTOR shall promptly, without cost to OWNER and as specified by ENGINEER, either correct any defective Work, whether or not fabricated, installed or completed, or, if the Work has been rejected by ENGINEER, remove it from the site and replace it with nondefective Work.

One Year Correction Period:

13.12.   If within one year after the date of Substantial Completion or such longer period of time as may be prescribed by law or by the terms of any applicable special guarantee required by the Contract Documents or by any specific provision of the Contract Documents, any Work is found to be defective, CONTRACTOR shall promptly, without cost to OWNER and in accordance with OWNER's written instructions, either correct such defective Work, or, if it has been rejected by OWNER, remove it from the site and replace it with nondefective Work. If CONTRACTOR does not promptly comply with the terms of such instructions, or in an emergency where delay would cause serious risk of loss or damage, OWNER may have the defective Work corrected or the rejected Work removed and replaced, and all direct and indirect costs of such removal and replacement, including compensation for additional professional services, shall be paid by CONTRACTOR.

Acceptance of Defective Work:

13.13.   If, instead of requiring correction or removal and replacement of defective Work, OWNER (and, prior to ENGINEER's recommendation of final payment, also ENGINEER) prefers to accept it, OWNER may do so. In such case, if acceptance occurs prior to ENGINEER's recommendation of final payment, a Change Order shall be issued incorporating the necessary revisions in the Contract Documents, including appropriate reduction in the Contract Price; or, if the acceptance occurs after such recommendation, an appropriate amount shall be paid by CONTRACTOR to OWNER.

OWNER May Correct Defective Work:

13.14.   If CONTRACTOR fails within a reasonable time after written notice of ENGINEER to proceed to correct and to correct defective Work or to remove and replace rejected Work as required by ENGINEER in accordance with paragraph 13.11, or if CONTRACTOR fails to perform the Work in accordance with the Contract Documents (including any requirements of the progress schedule), OWNER may, after seven days' written notice to CONTRACTOR, correct and remedy any such deficiency. In exercising his rights under this paragraph OWNER shall proceed expeditiously. To the extent necessary to complete corrective and remedial action, OWNER may exclude CONTRACTOR from all or part of the site, take possession of all or part of the Work, and suspend CONTRACTOR's services related thereto, take possession of CONTRACTOR's tools, appliances, construction equipment and machinery at the site and incorporate in the Work all materials and equipment stored at the site or for which OWNER has paid CONTRACTOR but which are stored elsewhere. CONTRACTOR shall allow OWNER, OWNER's representatives, agents and employees such access to the site as may be necessary to enable OWNER to exercise his rights under this paragraph. All direct and indirect costs of OWNER in exercising such rights shall be charged against CONTRACTOR in an amount verified by ENGINEER, and a Change Order shall be issued incorporating the necessary revisions in the Contract Documents and a reduction in the Contract Price. Such direct and indirect costs shall include, in particular but without limitation, compensation for additional professional services required and all costs of repair and replacement of work of others destroyed or damaged by correction, removal or replacement of CONTRACTOR's defective Work. CONTRACTOR shall not be allowed an extension of the Contract Time because of any delay in performance of the Work attributable to the exercise by OWNER of OWNER's rights hereunder.

ARTICLE 14—PAYMENTS TO CONTRACTOR AND COMPLETION

Schedules:

14.1   At least ten days prior to submitting the first Application for a progress payment, CONTRACTOR shall (except as otherwise specified in the General Requirements) submit to ENGINEER a progress schedule, a final schedule of Shop Drawing submission and where applicable a schedule of values of the Work. These schedules shall be satisfactory in form and substance to ENGINEER. The schedule of values shall include quantities and unit prices aggregating the Contract Price, and shall subdivide the Work into component parts in sufficient detail to serve as the basis for progress payments during construction. Upon acceptance of the schedule of values by ENGINEER, it shall be incorporated into a form of Application for Payment acceptable to ENGINEER.

Application for Progress Payment:

14.2.   At least ten days before each progress payment falls due (but not more often than once a month), CONTRACTOR shall submit to ENGINEER for review an Application for Payment filled out and signed by CONTRACTOR covering the Work completed as of the date of the Application and accompanied by such supporting documentation as is required by the Contract Documents and also as ENGINEER may reasonably require. If payment is requested on the basis of materials and equipment not incorporated in the Work but delivered and suitably stored at the site or at another location agreed to in writing, the Application for Payment shall also be accompanied by such data, satisfactory to OWNER, as will establish OWNER's title to the material and equipment and protect OWNER's interest therein, including applicable insurance. Each subsequent Application for Payment shall include an affidavit of CONTRACTOR stating that all previous progress payments received on account of the Work have been applied to discharge in full all of CONTRACTOR's obligations reflected in prior Applications for Payment. The amount of retainage with respect to progress payments will be as stipulated in the Agreement.

CONTRACTOR's Warranty of Title:

14.3.   CONTRACTOR warrants and guarantees that title to all Work, materials and equipment covered by any Application for Payment, whether incorporated in the Project or not, will pass to OWNER at the time of payment free and clear of all liens, claims, security interests and encumbrances (hereafter in these General Conditions referred to as "Liens").

Review of Applications for Progress Payment:

14.4.   ENGINEER will, within ten days after receipt of each Application for Payment, either indicate in writing a recommendation of payment and present the Application to OWNER, or return the Application to CONTRACTOR indicating in writing ENGINEER's reasons for refusing to recommend payment. In the latter case, CONTRACTOR may make the necessary corrections and resubmit the Application. OWNER shall, within ten days of presentation to him of the Application for Payment with ENGINEER's recommendation pay CONTRACTOR the amount recommended.

14.5.   ENGINEER's recommendation of any payment requested in an Application for Payment will constitute a representation by ENGINEER to OWNER, based on ENGINEER's on-site observations of the Work in progress as an experienced and qualified design professional and on ENGINEER's review of the Application for Payment and the accompanying data and schedules that the Work has progressed to the point indicated; that, to the best of ENGINEER's knowledge, information and belief, the quality of the Work is in accordance with the Contract Documents (subject to an evaluation of the Work as a functioning Project upon Substantial Completion, to the results of any subsequent tests called for in the Contract Documents and any qualifications stated in the recommendation) and that CONTRACTOR is entitled to payment of the amount recommended.

However, by recommending any such payment ENGINEER will not thereby be deemed to have represented that exhaustive or continuous on-site inspections have been made to check the quality or the quantity of the Work, or that the means, methods, techniques, sequences, and procedures of construction have been reviewed or that any examination has been made to ascertain how or for what purpose CONTRACTOR has used the moneys paid or to be paid to CONTRACTOR on account of the Contract Price, or that title to any Work, materials or equipment has passed to OWNER free and clear of any Liens.

14.6.   ENGINEER's recommendation of final payment will constitute an additional representation by ENGINEER to OWNER that the conditions precedent to CONTRACTOR's being entitled to final payment as set forth in paragraph 14.13 have been fulfilled.

14.7.   ENGINEER may refuse to recommend the whole or any part of any payment if, in his opinion, it would be incorrect to make such representations to OWNER. He may also refuse to recommend any such payment, or, because of subsequently discovered evidence or the results of subsequent inspections or tests, nullify and such payment previously recommended to such extent as may be necessary in ENGINEER's opinion to protect OWNER from loss because:

14.7.1.   the Work is defective, or completed Work has been damaged requiring correction or replacement,

14.7.2.   written claims have been made against OWNER or Liens have been filed in connection with the Work,

14.7.3.   the Contract Price has been reduced because of Modifications,

14.7.4.   OWNER has been required to correct defective Work or complete the Work in accordance with paragraph 13.14,

14.7.5.   of CONTRACTOR's unsatisfactory prosecution of the Work in accordance with the Contract Documents, or

14.7.6.   CONTRACTOR's failure to make payment to Subcontractors, or for labor, materials or equipment.

Substantial Completion:

14.8.   When CONTRACTOR considers the entire Work ready for its intended use CONTRACTOR shall, in writing to OWNER and ENGINEER, certify that the entire Work is substantially complete and request that ENGINEER issue a certificate of Substantial Completion. Within a reasonable time thereafter, OWNER, CONTRACTOR and ENGINEER shall make an inspection of the Work to determine the status of completion. If ENGINEER does not consider the Work substantially complete, ENGINEER will notify CONTRACTOR in writing giving his reasons therefor. If ENGINEER considers the Work substantially complete, ENGINEER will prepare and deliver to OWNER a tentative certificate of Substantial Completion which shall fix the date of Substantial Completion. There shall be attached to the certificate a tentative list of items to be completed or corrected before final payment. OWNER shall have seven days after receipt of the tentative certificate during which he may make written objection to ENGINEER as to any provisions of the certificate or attached list. If, after considering such objections, ENGINEER concludes that the Work is not substantially complete, ENGINEER will within fourteen days after submission of the tentative certificate to OWNER notify CONTRACTOR in writing, stating his reasons therefor. If, after consideration of OWNER's objections, ENGINEER considers the Work substantially complete, ENGINEER will within said fourteen days execute and deliver to OWNER and CONTRACTOR a definitive certificate of Substantial Completion (with a revised tentative list of items to be completed or corrected) reflecting such changes from the tentative certificate as he believes justified after consideration of any objections from OWNER. At the time of delivery of the tentative certificate of Substantial Completion ENGINEER will deliver to OWNER and CONTRACTOR a written recommendation as to division of responsibilities pending final payment between OWNER and CONTRACTOR with respect to security, operation, safety, maintenance, heat, utilities and insurance. Unless OWNER and CONTRACTOR agree otherwise in writing and so inform ENGINEER prior to his issuing the definitive certificate of Substantial Completion ENGINEER's aforesaid recommendation will be binding on OWNER and CONTRACTOR until final payment.

14.9. OWNER shall have the right to exclude CONTRACTOR from the Work after the date of Substantial Completion, but OWNER shall allow CONTRACTOR reasonable access to complete or correct items on the tentative list.

Partial Utilization:

14.10. Use by OWNER of completed portions of the Work may be accomplished prior to Substantial Completion of all the Work subject to the following:

14.10.1. OWNER at any time may request CONTRACTOR in writing to permit OWNER to use any part of the Work which OWNER believes to be substantially complete and which may be so used without significant interference with construction of the other parts of the Work. If CONTRACTOR agrees, CONTRACTOR will certify to OWNER and ENGINEER that said part of the Work is substantially complete and request ENGINEER to issue a certificate of Substantial Completion for that part of the Work. Within a reasonable time thereafter OWNER, CONTRACTOR and ENGINEER shall make an inspection of that part of the Work to determine its status of completion. If ENGINEER does not consider that part of the Work to be substantially complete, ENGINEER will notify OWNER and CONTRACTOR in writing giving his reasons therefor. If ENGINEER considers that part of the Work to be substantially complete, ENGINEER will execute and deliver to OWNER and CONTRACTOR a certificate to that effect, fixing the date

of Substantial Completion as to that part of the Work, attaching thereto a tentative list of items to be completed or corrected before final payment. Prior to issuing a certificate of Substantial Completion as to part of the Work ENGINEER will deliver to OWNER and CONTRACTOR a written recommendation as to the division of responsibilities pending final payment between OWNER and CONTRACTOR with respect to security, operation, safety, maintenance, utilities and insurance for that part of the Work which shall become binding upon OWNER and CONTRACTOR at the time of issuing the definitive certificate of Substantial Completion as to that part of the Work unless OWNER and CONTRACTOR shall have otherwise agreed in writing and so informed ENGINEER. OWNER shall have the right to exclude CONTRACTOR from any part of the Work which ENGINEER has so certified to be substantially complete, but OWNER shall allow CONTRACTOR reasonable access to complete or correct items on the tentative list.

14.10.2. In lieu of the issuance of a certificate of Substantial Completion as to part of the Work, OWNER may take over operation of a facility constituting part of the Work whether or not it is substantially complete if such facility is functionally and separately useable; provided that prior to any such takeover, OWNER and CONTRACTOR have agreed as to the division of responsibilities between OWNER and CONTRACTOR for security, operation, safety, maintenance, correction period, heat, utilities and insurance with respect to such facility.

14.10.3. No occupancy of part of the Work or taking over of operations of a facility will be accomplished prior to compliance with the requirements of paragraph 5.14 in respect of property insurance.

Final Inspection:

14.11. Upon written notice from CONTRACTOR that the Work is complete, ENGINEER will make a final inspection with OWNER and CONTRACTOR and will notify CONTRACTOR in writing of all particulars in which this inspection reveals that the Work is incomplete or defective. CONTRACTOR shall immediately take such measures as are necessary to remedy such deficiencies.

Final Application for Payment:

14.12. After CONTRACTOR has completed all such corrections to the satisfaction of ENGINEER and delivered all maintenance and operating instructions, schedules, guarantees, Bonds, certificates of inspection, marked-up record documents and other documents—all as required by the Contract Documents, and after ENGINEER has indicated that the Work is acceptable (subject to the provisions of paragraph 14.16), CONTRACTOR may make application for final payment following the procedure for progress payments. The final Application for Payment shall be accompanied by all documentation called for in the Contract Documents and such other data and schedules as ENGINEER may reasonably require, together with complete and legally effective releases or waivers (satisfactory to OWNER) of all Liens arising out of or filed in connection with the Work. In lieu thereof and as approved by OWNER, CONTRACTOR may furnish receipts or releases in full; an affidavit of CONTRACTOR that the releases and receipts include all labor, services, material and equipment for which a Lien could be filed, and that all payrolls, material and equipment bills, and other indebtedness connected with the Work for which OWNER or his property might in any way be responsible, have been paid or otherwise satisfied; and consent of the Surety, if any, to final payment. If any Subcontractor, manufacturer, fabricator, supplier or distributor fails to furnish a release or receipt in full, CONTRACTOR may furnish a Bond or other collateral satisfactory to OWNER to indemnify OWNER against any Lien.

Final Payment and Acceptance:

14.13. If, on the basis of ENGINEER's observation of the Work during construction and final inspection, and ENGINEER's review of the final Application for Payment and accompanying documentation—all as required by the Contract Documents, ENGINEER is satisfied that the Work has been completed and CONTRACTOR has fulfilled all of his obligations under the Contract Documents, ENGINEER will, within ten days after receipt of the final Application for Payment, indicate in writing his recommendation of payment and present the Application to OWNER for payment. Thereupon ENGINEER will give written notice to OWNER and CONTRACTOR that the Work is acceptable subject to the provisions of paragraph 14.16. Otherwise, ENGINEER will return the Application to CONTRACTOR, indicating in writing the reasons for refusing to recommend final payment, in which case CONTRACTOR shall make the necessary corrections and resubmit the Application. If the Application and accompanying documentation are appropriate as to form and substance, OWNER shall, within thirty days after receipt thereof pay CONTRACTOR the amount recommended by ENGINEER.

14.14. If, through no fault of CONTRACTOR, final completion of the Work is significantly delayed thereof and if ENGINEER so confirms, OWNER shall, upon receipt of CONTRACTOR's final Application for Payment and recommendation of ENGINEER, and without terminating the Agreement, make payment of the balance due for that portion of the Work fully completed and accepted. If the remaining balance to be held by OWNER for Work not fully completed or corrected is less than the retainage stipulated in the Agreement, and if Bonds have been furnished as required in paragraph 5.4, the written consent of the Surety to the payment of the balance due for that portion of the Work fully completed and accepted shall be submitted by CONTRACTOR to ENGINEER with the Application for such payment. Such payment shall be made under the terms and conditions governing final payment, except that it shall not constitute a waiver of claims.

Contractor's Continuing Obligation:

14.15. CONTRACTOR's obligation to perform and complete the Work in accordance with the Contract Documents shall be absolute. Neither recommendation of any progress or final payment by ENGINEER, nor the issuance of a certificate of Substantial Completion, nor any payment by OWNER to CONTRACTOR under the Contract Documents, nor any use or occupancy of the Work or any part thereof by OWNER, nor any act of acceptance by OWNER nor any failure to do so, nor the issuance of a notice of acceptability by ENGINEER pursuant to paragraph 14.13, nor any correction of defective Work by OWNER shall constitute an acceptance of Work not in accordance with the Contract Documents or a release of CONTRACTOR's obligation to perform the Work in accordance with the Contract Documents.

Waiver of Claims:

14.16. The making and acceptance of final payment shall constitute:

14.16.1. a waiver of all claims by OWNER against CONTRACTOR, except claims arising from unsettled Liens, from defective Work appearing after final inspection pursuant to paragraph 14.11 or from failure to comply with the Contract Documents or the terms of any special guarantees specified therein; however, it shall not constitute a waiver by OWNER of any rights in respect of CONTRACTOR's continuing obligations under the Contract Documents; and

14.16.2. a waiver of all claims by CONTRACTOR against OWNER other than those previously made in writing and still unsettled.

ARTICLE 15—SUSPENSION OF WORK AND
TERMINATION

Owner May Suspend Work:

15.1. OWNER may, at any time and without cause, suspend the Work or any portion thereof for a period of not more than ninety days by notice in writing to CONTRACTOR and ENGINEER which shall fix the date on which Work shall be resumed. CONTRACTOR shall resume the Work on the date so fixed. CONTRACTOR will be allowed an increase in the Contract Price or an extension of the Contract Time, or both, directly attributable to any suspension if he makes a claim therefor as provided in Articles 11 and 12.

Owner May Terminate:

15.2. Upon the occurrence of any one or more of the following events:

15.2.1. if CONTRACTOR is adjudged a bankrupt or insolvent,

15.2.2. if CONTRACTOR makes a general assignment for the benefit of creditors,

15.2.3. if a trustee or receiver is appointed for CONTRACTOR or for any of CONTRACTOR's property,

15.2.4. if CONTRACTOR files a petition to take advantage of any debtor's act, or to reorganize under the bankruptcy or similar laws,

15.2.5. if CONTRACTOR repeatedly fails to supply sufficient skilled workmen or suitable materials or equipment,

15.2.6. if CONTRACTOR repeatedly fails to make prompt payments to Subcontractors or for labor, materials or equipment,

15.2.7. if CONTRACTOR disregards laws, ordinances, rules, regulations or orders of any public body having jurisdiction,

15.2.8. if CONTRACTOR disregards the authority of ENGINEER, or

15.2.9. if CONTRACTOR otherwise violates in any substantial way any provisions of the Contract Documents,

OWNER may after giving CONTRACTOR and his Surety seven days' written notice, terminate the services of CONTRACTOR, exclude CONTRACTOR from the site and take possession of the Work and of all CONTRACTOR's tools, appliances, construction equipment and machinery at the site and use the same to the full extent they could be used by CONTRACTOR (without liability to CONTRACTOR for trespass or conversion), incorporate in the Work all materials and equipment stored at the site or for which OWNER has paid CONTRACTOR but which are stored elsewhere, and finish the Work as OWNER may deem expedient. In such case CONTRACTOR shall not be entitled to receive any further payment until the Work is finished. If the unpaid balance of the Contract Price exceeds the direct and indirect costs of completing the Work, including compensation for additional professional services, such excess shall be paid to CONTRACTOR. If such costs exceed such unpaid balance, CONTRACTOR shall pay the difference to OWNER. Such costs incurred by OWNER shall be verified by ENGINEER and incorporated in a Change Order, but in finishing the Work OWNER shall not be required to obtain the lowest figure for the Work performed.

15.3. Where CONTRACTOR's services have been so terminated by OWNER, the termination shall not affect any rights of OWNER against CONTRACTOR then existing or which may thereafter accrue. Any retention or payment of moneys due CONTRACTOR by OWNER will not release CONTRACTOR from liability.

15.4. Upon seven days' written notice to CONTRACTOR and ENGINEER, OWNER may, without cause and without prejudice to any other right or remedy, elect to abandon the Work and terminate the Agreement. In such case, CONTRACTOR shall be paid for all Work executed and any expense sustained plus reasonable termination expenses.

Contractor May Stop Work or Terminate:

15.5. If, through no act or fault of CONTRACTOR, the Work is suspended for a period of more than ninety days by OWNER or under an order of court or other public authority, or ENGINEER fails to act on any Application for Payment within thiry days after it is submitted, or OWNER fails for thirty days to pay CONTRACTOR any sum finally determined to be due, then CONTRACTOR may, upon seven days' written notice to OWNER and ENGINEER, terminate the Agreement and recover from OWNER payment for all Work executed and any expense sustained plus reasonable termination expenses. In addition and in lieu of terminating the Agreement, if ENGINEER has failed to act on an Application for Payment or OWNER has failed to make any payment as aforesaid, CONTRACTOR may upon seven days' notice to OWNER and ENGINEER stop the Work until payment of all amounts then due. The provisions of this paragraph shall not relieve CONTRACTOR of his obligations under paragraph 6.29 to carry on the Work in accordance with the progress schedule and without delay during disputes and disagreements with OWNER.

ARTICLE 16—ARBITRATION

16.1. All claims, disputes and other matters in question between OWNER and CONTRACTOR arising out of, or relating to the Contract Documents or the breach thereof except for claims which have been waived by the making or acceptance of final payment as provided by paragraph 14.16, shall be decided by arbitration in accordance with the Construction Industry Arbitration Rules of the American Arbitration Association then obtaining subject to the limitations of this Article 16. This agreement so to arbitrate and any other agreement or consent to arbitrate entered into in accordance herewith as provided in this Article 16 will be specifically enforceable under the prevailing arbitration law of any court having jurisdiction.

16.2. No demand for arbitration of any claim, dispute or other matter that is required to be referred to ENGINEER initially for decision in accordance with paragraph 9.9 shall be made until the earlier of (a) the date on which ENGINEER has rendered a decision or (b) the tenth day after the parties have presented their evidence to ENGINEER if a written decision has not been rendered by ENGINEER before that date. No demand for arbitration of any such claim, dispute or other matter shall be made later than thirty days after the date on which ENGINEER has rendered a written decision in respect thereof in accordance with paragraph 9.9; and the failure to demand arbitration within said thirty days' period shall result in ENGINEER's decision being final and binding upon OWNER and CONTRACTOR. If ENGINEER renders a decision after arbitration proceedings have been initiated, such decision may be entered as evidence but shall not supersede the arbitration proceedings, except where the decision is acceptable to the parties concerned.

16.3. Notice of the demand for arbitration shall be filed in writing with the other party to the Agreement and with the

American Arbitration Association, and a copy shall be sent to ENGINEER for information. The demand for arbitration shall be made within the thirty-day period specified in paragraph 16.2 where applicable, and in all other cases within a reasonable time after the claim, dispute or other matter in question has arisen, and in no event shall any such demand be made after institution of legal or equitable proceedings based on such claim, dispute or other matter in question would be barred by the applicable statute of limitations.

16.4.   No arbitration arising out of or relating to the Contract Documents shall include by consolidation, joinder or in any other manner any other person or entity (including ENGINEER, his agents, employees or consultants) who is not a party to this Agreement unless:

16.4.1.   the inclusion of such other person or entity is necessary if complete relief is to be afforded among those who are already parties to the arbitration,

16.4.2.   such other person or entity is substantially involved in a question of law or fact which is common to those who are already parties to the arbitration and which will arise in such proceedings, and

16.4.3.   the written consent of the other person or entity sought to be included and of OWNER and CONTRACTOR has been obtained for such inclusion, which consent shall make specific reference to this paragraph; but no such consent shall constitute consent to arbitration of any dispute not specifically described in such consent or to arbitration with any party not specifically identified in such consent.

16.5.   The award rendered by the arbitrators will be final, judgment may be entered upon it in any court having jurisdiction thereof, and will not be subject to modification or appeal except to the extent permitted by Sections 10 and 11 of the Federal Arbitration Act (9 U.S.C. §§10, 11).

ARTICLE 17—MISCELLANEOUS

Giving Notice:

17.1.   Whenever any provision of the Contract Documents requires the giving of written notice it shall be deemed to have been validly given if delivered in person to the individual or to a member of the firm or to an officer of the corporation for whom it is intended, or if delivered at or sent by registered or certified mail, postage prepaid, to the last business address known to the giver of the notice.

Computation of Time:

17.2.   When any period of time is referred to in the Contract Documents by days, it shall be computed to exclude the first and include the last day of such period. If the last day of any such period falls on a Saturday or Sunday or on a day made a legal holiday by the law of the applicable jurisdiction, such day shall be omitted from the computation.

General:

17.3.   Should OWNER or CONTRACTOR suffer injury or damage to his person or property because of any error, omission or act of the other party or of any of the other party's employees or agents or others for whose acts the other party is legally liable, claim shall be made in writing to the other party within a reasonable time of the first observance of such injury or damage.

17.4.   The duties and obligations imposed by these General Conditions and the rights and remedies available hereunder to the parties hereto, and, in particular but without limitation, the warranties, guarantees and obligations imposed upon CONTRACTOR by paragraphs 6.30, 13.1, 13.11, 13.14, 14.3 and 15.2 and all of the rights and remedies available to OWNER and ENGINEER thereunder, shall be in addition to, and shall not be construed in any way as a limitation of, any rights and remedies available to any or all of them which are otherwise imposed or available by law or contract, by special warranty or guarantee or by other provisions of the Contract Documents, and the provisions of this paragraph shall be as effective as if repeated specifically in the Contract Documents in connection with each particular duty, obligation, right and remedy to which they apply. All representations, warranties and guarantees made in the Contract Documents shall survive final payment and termination or completion of this Agreement.

2a. Federal Government Standard Contract Form 23A

GENERAL PROVISIONS

(Construction Contract)

1. DEFINITIONS

(a) The term "head of the agency" or "Secretary" as used herein means the Secretary, the Under Secretary, any Assistant Secretary, or any other head or assistant head of the executive or military department or other Federal agency; and the term "his duly authorized representative" means any person or persons or board (other than the Contracting Officer) authorized to act for the head of the agency or the Secretary.

(b) The term "Contracting Officer" as used herein means the person executing this contract on behalf of the Government and includes a duly appointed successor or authorized representative.

2. SPECIFICATIONS AND DRAWINGS

The Contractor shall keep on the work a copy of the drawings and specifications and shall at all times give the Contracting Officer access thereto. Anything mentioned in the specifications and not shown on the drawings, or shown on the drawings and not mentioned in the specifications, shall be of like effect as if shown or mentioned in both. In case of difference between drawings and specifications, the specifications shall govern. In case of discrepancy either in the figures, in the drawings, or in the specifications, the matter shall be promptly submitted to the Contracting Officer, who shall promptly make a determination in writing. Any adjustment by the Contractor without such a determination shall be at his own risk and expense. The Contracting Officer shall furnish from time to time such detail drawings and other information as he may consider necessary, unless otherwise provided.

3. CHANGES

(a) The Contracting Officer may, at any time, without notice to the sureties, by written order designated or indicated to be a change order, make any change in the work within the general scope of the contract, including but not limited to changes:

(1) In the specifications (including drawings and designs);

(2) In the method or manner of performance of the work;

(3) In the Government-furnished facilities, equipment, materials, services, or site; or

(4) Directing acceleration in the performance of the work.

(b) Any other written order or an oral order (which terms as used in this paragraph (b) shall include direction, instruction, interpretation, or determination) from the Contracting Officer, which causes any such change, shall be treated as a change order under this clause, provided that the Contractor gives the Contracting Officer written notice stating the date, circumstances, and source of the order and that the Contractor regards the order as a change order.

(c) Except as herein provided, no order, statement, or conduct of the Contracting Officer shall be treated as a change under this clause or entitle the Contractor to an equitable adjustment hereunder.

(d) If any change under this clause causes an increase or decrease in the Contractor's cost of, or the time required for, the performance of any part of the work under this contract, whether or not changed by any order, an equitable adjustment shall be made and the contract modified in writing accordingly: *Provided, however,* That except for claims based on defective specifications, no claim for any change under (b) above shall be allowed for any costs incurred more than 20 days before the Contractor gives written notice as therein required: *And provided further,* That in the case of defective specifications for which the Government is responsible, the equitable adjustment shall include any increased cost reasonably incurred by the Contractor in attempting to comply with such defective specifications.

(e) If the Contractor intends to assert a claim for an equitable adjustment under this clause, he must, within 30 days after receipt of a written change order under (a) above or the furnishing of a written notice under (b) above, submit to the Contracting Officer a written statement setting forth the general nature and monetary extent of such claim,

unless this period is extended by the Government. The statement of claim hereunder may be included in the notice under (b) above.

(f) No claim by the Contractor for an equitable adjustment hereunder shall be allowed if asserted after final payment under this contract.

4. DIFFERING SITE CONDITIONS

(a) The Contractor shall promptly, and before such conditions are disturbed, notify the Contracting Officer in writing of: (1) Subsurface or latent physical conditions at the site differing materially from those indicated in this contract, or (2) unknown physical conditions at the site, of an unusual nature, differing materially from those ordinarily encountered and generally recognized as inhering in work of the character provided for in this contract. The Contracting Officer shall promptly investigate the conditions, and if he finds that such conditions do materially so differ and cause an increase or decrease in the Contractor's cost of, or the time required for, performance of any part of the work under this contract, whether or not changed as a result of such conditions, an equitable adjustment shall be made and the contract modified in writing accordingly.

(b) No claim of the Contractor under this clause shall be allowed unless the Contractor has given the notice required in (a) above; provided, however, the time prescribed therefor may be extended by the Government.

(c) No claim by the Contractor for an equitable adjustment hereunder shall be allowed if asserted after final payment under this contract.

5. TERMINATION FOR DEFAULT—DAMAGES FOR DELAY—TIME EXTENSIONS

(a) If the Contractor refuses or fails to prosecute the work, or any separable part thereof, with such diligence as will insure its completion within the time specified in this contract, or any extension thereof, or fails to complete said work within such time, the Government may, by written notice to the Contractor, terminate his right to proceed with the work or such part of the work as to which there has been delay. In such event the Government may take over the work and prosecute the same to completion, by contract or otherwise, and may take possession of and utilize in completing the work such materials, appliances, and plant as may be on the site of the work and necessary therefor. Whether or not the Contractor's right to proceed with the work is terminated, he and his sureties shall be liable for any damage to the Government resulting from his refusal or failure to complete the work within the specified time.

(b) If fixed and agreed liquidated damages are provided in the contract and if the Government so terminates the Contractor's right to proceed, the resulting damage will consist of such liquidated damages until such reasonable time as may be required for final completion of the work together with any increased costs occasioned the Government in completing the work.

(c) If fixed and agreed liquidated damages are provided in the contract and if the Government does not so terminate the Contractor's right to proceed, the resulting damage will consist of such liquidated damages until the work is completed or accepted.

(d) The Contractor's right to proceed shall not be so terminated nor the Contractor charged with resulting damage if:

(1) The delay in the completion of the work arises from unforeseeable causes beyond the control and without the fault or negligence of the Contractor, including but not restricted to, acts of God, acts of the public enemy, acts of the Government in either its sovereign or contractual capacity, acts of another contractor in the performance of a contract with the Government, fires, floods, epidemics, quarantine restrictions, strikes, freight embargoes, unusually severe weather, or delays of subcontractors or suppliers arising from unforeseeable causes beyond the control and without the fault or negligence of both the Contractor and such subcontractors or suppliers; and

(2) The Contractor, within 10 days from the beginning of any such delay (unless the Contracting Officer grants a further period of time before the date of final payment

STANDARD FORM 23-A (Rev. 4-75)
Prescribed by GSA, FPR (41-CFR) 1-16.401

under the contract), notifies the Contracting Officer in writing of the causes of delay.

The Contracting Officer shall ascertain the facts and the extent of the delay and extend the time for completing the work when, in his judgment, the findings of fact justify such an extension, and his findings of fact shall be final and conclusive on the parties, subject only to appeal as provided in Clause 6 of these General Provisions.

(e) If, after notice of termination of the Contractor's right to proceed under the provisions of this clause, it is determined for any reason that the Contractor was not in default under the provisions of this clause, or that the delay was excusable under the provisions of this clause, the rights and obligations of the parties shall, if the contract contains a clause providing for termination for convenience of the Government, be the same as if the notice of termination had been issued pursuant to such clause. If, in the foregoing circumstances, this contract does not contain a clause providing for termination for convenience of the Government, the contract shall be equitably adjusted to compensate for such termination and the contract modified accordingly; failure to agree to any such adjustment shall be a dispute concerning a question of fact within the meaning of the clause of this contract entitled "Disputes."

(f) The rights and remedies of the Government provided in this clause are in addition to any other rights and remedies provided by law or under this contract.

(g) As used in Paragraph (d)(1) of this clause, the term "subcontractors or suppliers" means subcontractors or suppliers at any tier.

6. DISPUTES

(a) Except as otherwise provided in this contract, any dispute concerning a question of fact arising under this contract which is not disposed of by agreement shall be decided by the Contracting Officer, who shall reduce his decision to writing and mail or otherwise furnish a copy thereof to the Contractor. The decision of the Contracting Officer shall be final and conclusive unless, within 30 days from the date of receipt of such copy, the Contractor mails or otherwise furnishes to the Contracting Officer a written appeal addressed to the head of the agency involved. The decision of the head of the agency or his duly authorized representative for the determination of such appeals shall be final and conclusive. This provision shall not be pleaded in any suit involving a question of fact arising under this contract as limiting judicial review of any such decision to cases where fraud by such official or his representative or board is alleged: *Provided, however,* That any such decision shall be final and conclusive unless the same is fraudulent or capricious or arbitrary or so grossly erroneous as necessarily to imply bad faith or is not supported by substantial evidence. In connection with any appeal proceeding under this clause, the Contractor shall be afforded an opportunity to be heard and to offer evidence in support of his appeal. Pending final decision of a dispute hereunder, the Contractor shall proceed diligently with the performance of the contract and in accordance with the Contracting Officer's decision.

(b) This Disputes clause does not preclude consideration of questions of law in connection with decisions provided for in paragraph (a) above. Nothing in this contract, however, shall be construed as making final the decision of any administrative official, representative, or board on a question of law.

7. PAYMENTS TO CONTRACTOR

(a) The Government will pay the contract price as hereinafter provided.

(b) The Government will make progress payments monthly as the work proceeds, or at more frequent intervals as determined by the Contracting Officer, on estimates approved by the Contracting Officer. If requested by the Contracting Officer, the Contractor shall furnish a breakdown of the total contract price showing the amount included therein for each principal category of the work, in such detail as requested, to provide a basis for determining progress payments. In the preparation of estimates the Contracting Officer, at his discretion, may authorize material delivered on the site and preparatory work done to be taken into consideration. Material delivered to the Contractor at locations other than the site may also be taken into consideration (1) if such consideration is specifically authorized by the contract and (2) if the Contractor furnishes satisfactory evidence that he has acquired title to such material and that it will be utilized on the work covered by this contract.

(c) In making such progress payments, there shall be retained 10 percent of the estimated amount until final com-

pletion and acceptance of the contract work. However, if the Contracting Officer, at any time after 50 percent of the work has been completed, finds that satisfactory progress is being made, he may authorize payment in full of each progress payment for work performed beyond the 50 percent stage of completion. Also, whenever the work is substantially complete, the Contracting Officer, if he considers the amount retained to be in excess of the amount adequate for the protection of the Government, at his discretion, may release to the Contractor all or a portion of such excess amount. Furthermore, on completion and acceptance of each separate building, public work, or other division of the contract, on which the price is stated separately in the contract, payment may be made therefor without retention of a percentage.

(d) All material and work covered by progress payments made shall thereupon become the sole property of the Government, but this provision shall not be construed as relieving the Contractor from the sole responsibility for all material and work upon which payments have been made or the restoration of any damaged work. or as waiving the right of the Government to require the fulfillment of all of the terms of the contract.

(e) Upon completion and acceptance of all work, the amount due the Contractor under this contract shall be paid upon the presentation of a properly executed voucher and after the Contractor shall have furnished the Government with a release of all claims against the Government arising by virtue of this contract, other than claims in stated amounts as may be specifically excepted by the Contractor from the operation of the release. If the Contractor's claim to amounts payable under the contract has been assigned under the Assignment of Claims Act of 1940, as amended (31 U.S.C. 203, 41 U.S.C. 15), a release may also be required of the assignee.

8. ASSIGNMENT OF CLAIMS

(a) Pursuant to the provisions of the Assignment of Claims Act of 1940, as amended (31 U.S.C. 203, 41 U.S.C. 15), if this contract provides for payments aggregating $1,000 or more, claims for moneys due or to become due the Contractor from the Government under this contract may be assigned to a bank, trust company, or other financing institution, including any Federal lending agency, and may thereafter be further assigned and reassigned to any such institution. Any such assignment or reassignment shall cover all amounts payable under this contract and not already paid, and shall not be made to more than one party, except that any such assignment or reassignment may be made to one party as agent or trustee for two or more parties participating in such financing. Unless otherwise provided in this contract, payments to an assignee of any moneys due or to become due under this contract shall not, to the extent provided in said Act, as amended, be subject to reduction or setoff. (The preceding sentence applies only if this contract is made in time of war or national emergency as defined in said Act; and is with the Department of Defense, the General Services Administration, the Energy Research and Development Administration, the National Aeronautics and Space Administration, the Federal Aviation Administration, or any other department or agency of the United States designated by the President pursuant to Clause 4 of the proviso of section 1 of the Assignment of Claims Act of 1940, as amended by the Act of May 15, 1951, 65 Stat. 41.)

(b) In no event shall copies of this contract or of any plans, specifications, or other similar documents relating to work under this contract, if marked "Top Secret," "Secret," or "Confidential," be furnished to any assignee of any claim arising under this contract or to any other person not entitled to receive the same. However, a copy of any part or all of this contract so marked may be furnished, or any information contained therein may be disclosed, to such assignee upon the prior written authorization of the Contracting Officer.

9. MATERIAL AND WORKMANSHIP

(a) Unless otherwise specifically provided in this contract, all equipment, material, and articles incorporated in the work covered by this contract are to be new and of the most suitable grade for the purpose intended. Unless otherwise specifically provided in this contract, reference to any equipment, material, article, or patented process. by trade name, make, or catalog number. shall be regarded as establishing a standard of quality and shall not be construed as limiting competition, and the Contractor may, at his option, use any equipment, material. article, or process, which, in the judgment of the Contracting Officer, is equal to that named. The Contractor shall furnish to the Contracting Officer for his approval the name of the manufacturer, the model number, and other identifying data and information respecting the performance, capacity, nature, and rating of the machinery and mechanical and other equipment which the Contractor contemplates incorporating in the work. When required by this contract or when called for by the Contracting Officer, the Contractor shall furnish the Contracting Officer for approval full information concerning the material or articles which he contemplates incorporating in the work. When so directed, samples shall be submitted for approval at the Contractor's expense, with all shipping charges prepaid. Machinery, equipment, material, and articles installed or used without required approval shall be at the risk of subsequent rejection.

(b) All work under this contract shall be performed in a skillful and workmanlike manner. The Contracting Officer may, in writing, require the Contractor to remove from the work any employee the Contracting Officer deems incompetent, careless or otherwise objectionable.

10. INSPECTION AND ACCEPTANCE

(a) All work (which term includes but is not restricted to materials, workmanship, and manufacture and fabrication of components) shall be subject to inspection and test by the Government at all reasonable times and at all places prior to acceptance. Any such inspection and test is for the sole benefit of the Government and shall not relieve the Contractor of the responsibility of providing quality control measures to assure that the work strictly complies with the contract requirements. No inspection or test by the Government shall be construed as constituting or implying acceptance. Inspection or test shall not relieve the Contractor of responsibility for damage to or loss of the material prior to acceptance, nor in any way affect the continuing rights of the Government after acceptance of the completed work under the terms of paragraph (f) of this clause, except as hereinabove provided.

(b) The Contractor shall, without charge, replace any material or correct any workmanship found by the Government not to conform to the contract requirements, unless in the public interest the Government consents to accept such material or workmanship with an appropriate adjustment in contract price. The Contractor shall promptly segregate and remove rejected material from the premises.

(c) If the Contractor does not promptly replace rejected material or correct rejected workmanship, the Government (1) may, by contract or otherwise, replace such material or correct such workmanship and charge the cost thereof to the Contractor, or (2) may terminate the Contractor's right to proceed in accordance with the clause of this contract entitled "Termination for Default—Damages for Delay—Time Extensions."

(d) The Contractor shall furnish promptly, without additional charge, all facilities, labor, and material reasonably needed for performing such safe and convenient inspection and test as may be required by the Contracting Officer. All inspection and test by the Government shall be performed in such manner as not unnecessarily to delay the work. Special, full size, and performance tests shall be performed as described in this contract. The Government reserves the right to charge to the Contractor any additional cost of inspection or test when material or workmanship is not ready at the time specified by the Contractor for inspection or test or when reinspection or retest is necessitated by prior rejection.

(e) Should it be considered necessary or advisable by the Government at any time before acceptance of the entire work to make an examination of work already completed, by removing or tearing out same, the Contractor shall, on request, promptly furnish all necessary facilities, labor, and material. If such work is found to be defective or nonconforming in any material respect, due to the fault of the Contractor or his subcontractors, he shall defray all the expenses of such examination and of satisfactory reconstruction. If, however, such work if found to meet the requirements of the contract, an equitable adjustment shall be made in the contract price to compensate the Contractor for the additional services involved in such examination and reconstruction and, if completion of the work has been delayed thereby, he shall, in addition, be granted a suitable extension of time.

(f) Unless otherwise provided in this contract, acceptance by the Government shall be made as promptly as practicable after completion and inspection of all work required by this contract, or that portion of the work that the Contracting Officer determines can be accepted separately. Acceptance shall be final and conclusive except as regards latent defects, fraud, or such gross mistakes as may amount to fraud, or as regards the Government's rights under any warranty or guarantee.

11. SUPERINTENDENCE BY CONTRACTOR

The Contractor, at all times during performance and until the work is completed and accepted, shall give his personal superintendence to the work or have on the work a competent superintendent, satisfactory to the Contracting Officer and with authority to act for the Contractor.

12. PERMITS AND RESPONSIBILITIES

The Contractor shall, without additional expense to the Government, be responsible for obtaining any necessary licenses and permits, and for complying with any applicable Federal, State, and municipal laws, codes, and regulations, in connection with the prosecution of the work. He shall be similarly responsible for all damages to persons or property that occur as a result of his fault or negligence. He shall take proper safety and health precautions to protect the work, the workers, the public, and the property of others. He shall also be responsible for all materials delivered and work performed until completion and acceptance of the entire construction work, except for any completed unit of construction thereof which theretofore may have been accepted.

13. CONDITIONS AFFECTING THE WORK

The Contractor shall be responsible for having taken steps reasonably necessary to ascertain the nature and location of the work, and the general and local conditions which can affect the work or the cost thereof. Any failure by the Contractor to do so will not relieve him from responsibility for successfully performing the work without additional expense to the Government. The Government assumes no responsibility for any understanding or representations concerning conditions made by any of its officers or agents prior to the execution of this contract, unless such understanding or representations by the Government are expressly stated in the contract.

14. OTHER CONTRACTS

The Government may undertake or award other contracts for additional work, and the Contractor shall fully cooperate with such other contractors and Government employees and carefully fit his own work to such additional work as may be directed by the Contracting Officer. The Contractor shall not commit or permit any act which will interfere with the performance of work by any other contractor or by Government employees.

15. SHOP DRAWINGS

(a) The term "shop drawings" includes drawings, diagrams, layouts, schematics, descriptive literature, illustrations, schedules, performance and test data, and similar materials furnished by the Contractor to explain in detail specific portions of the work required by the contract.

(b) If this contract requires shop drawings, the Contractor shall coordinate all such drawings, and review them for accuracy, completeness, and compliance with contract requirements and shall indicate his approval thereon as evidence of such coordination and review. Shop drawings submitted to the Contracting Officer without evidence of the Contractor's approval may be returned for resubmission. The Contracting Officer will indicate his approval or disapproval of the shop drawings and if not approved as submitted shall indicate his reasons therefor. Any work done prior to such approval shall be at the Contractor's risk. Approval by the Contracting Officer shall not relieve the Contractor from responsibility for any errors or omissions in such drawings, nor from responsibility for complying with the requirements of this contract, except with respect to variations described and approved in accordance with (c) below.

(c) If shop drawings show variations from the contract requirements, the Contractor shall describe such variations in writing, separate from the drawings, at the time of submission. If the Contracting Officer approves any such variation(s), he shall issue an appropriate contract modification, except that, if the variation is minor and does not involve a change in price or in time of performance, a modification need not be issued.

16. USE AND POSSESSION PRIOR TO COMPLETION

The Government shall have the right to take possession of or use any completed or partially completed part of the work. Prior to such possession or use, the Contracting Officer shall furnish the Contractor an itemized list of work remaining to be performed or corrected on such portions of the project as are to be possessed or used by the Government, provided that failure to list any item of work shall not relieve the Contractor of responsibility for compliance with the terms of the contract. Such possession or use shall not be deemed an acceptance of any work under the contract. While the Government has such possession or use, the Contractor, notwithstanding the provisions of the clause of this contract entitled "Permits and Responsibilities," shall be relieved of the responsibility for the loss or damage to the work resulting from the Government's possession or use. If such prior possession or use by the Government delays the progress of the work or causes additional expense to the Contractor, an equitable adjustment in the contract price or the time of completion will be made and the contract shall be modified in writing accordingly.

17. SUSPENSION OF WORK

(a) The Contracting Officer may order the Contractor in writing to suspend, delay, or interrupt all or any part of the work for such period of time as he may determine to be appropriate for the convenience of the Government.

(b) If the performance of all or any part of the work is, for an unreasonable period of time, suspended, delayed, or interrupted by an act of the Contracting Officer in the administration of this contract, or by his failure to act within the time specified in this contract (or if no time is specified, within a reasonable time), an adjustment shall be made for any increase in the cost of performance of this contract (excluding profit) necessarily caused by such unreasonable suspension, delay, or interruption and the contract modified in writing accordingly. However, no adjustment shall be made under this clause for any suspension, delay, or interruption to the extent (1) that performance would have been so suspended, delayed, or interrupted by any other cause, including the fault or negligence of the Contractor or (2) for which an equitable adjustment is provided for or excluded under any other provision of this contract.

(c) No claim under this clause shall be allowed (1) for any costs incurred more than 20 days before the Contractor shall have notified the Contracting Officer in writing of the act or failure to act involved (but this requirement shall not apply as to a claim resulting from a suspension order), and (2) unless the claim, in an amount stated, is asserted in writing as soon as practicable after the termination of such suspension, delay, or interruption, but not later than the date of final payment under the contract.

18. TERMINATION FOR CONVENIENCE OF THE GOVERNMENT

If not physically incorporated elsewhere, the clause in Section 1–8.703 of the Federal Procurement Regulations, or paragraph 7–602.29(a) of the Armed Services Procurement Regulation, as applicable, in effect on the date of this contract is hereby incorporated by reference as fully as if set forth at length herein.

19. PAYMENT OF INTEREST ON CONTRACTORS' CLAIMS

(a) If an appeal is filed by the Contractor from a final decision of the Contracting Officer under the Disputes clause of this contract, denying a claim arising under the contract, simple interest on the amount of the claim finally determined owed by the Government shall be payable to the Contractor. Such interest shall be at the rate determined by the Secretary of the Treasury pursuant to Public Law 92–41, 85 Stat. 97, from the date the Contractor furnishes to the Contracting Officer his written appeal under the Disputes clause of this contract, to the date of (1) a final judgment by a court of competent jurisdiction, or (2) mailing to the Contractor of a supplemental agreement for execution either confirming completed negotiations between the parties or carrying out a decision of a board of contract appeals.

(b) Notwithstanding (a) above, (1) interest shall be applied only from the date payment was due, if such date is later than the filing of appeal; and (2) interest shall not be paid for any period of time that the Contracting Officer determines the Contractor has unduly delayed in pursuing his remedies before a board of contract appeals or a court of competent jurisdiction.

20. PRICING OF ADJUSTMENTS

When costs are a factor in any determination of a contract price adjustment pursuant to the Changes clause or any other provision of this contract, such costs shall be in accordance with the contract cost principles and procedures in Part 1–15 of the Federal Procurement Regulations, (41 CFR 1–15) or Section XV of the Armed Services Procurement Regulation, as applicable, which are in effect on the date of this contract.

21. PATENT INDEMNITY

Except as otherwise provided, the Contractor agrees to indemnify the Government and its officers, agents, and employees against liability, including costs and expenses, for infringement upon any Letters Patent of the United States (except Letters Patent issued upon an application which is now or may hereafter be, for reasons of national security, ordered by the Government to be kept secret or otherwise withheld from issue) arising out of the performance of this contract or out of the use or disposal by or for the account of the Government of supplies furnished or construction work performed hereunder.

22. ADDITIONAL BOND SECURITY

If any surety upon any bond furnished in connection with this contract becomes unacceptable to the Government, or if any such surety fails to furnish reports as to his financial condition from time to time as requested by the Government, or if the contract price is increased to such an extent that the penal sum of any bond becomes inadequate in the opinion of the Contracting Officer, the Contractor shall promptly furnish such additional security as may be required from time to time to protect the interests of the Government and of persons supplying labor or materials in the prosecution of the work contemplated by this contract.

23. EXAMINATION OF RECORDS BY COMPTROLLER GENERAL

(a) This clause is applicable if the amount of this contract exceeds $10,000 and was entered into by means of negotiation, including small business restricted advertising, but is not applicable if this contract was entered into by means of formal advertising.

(b) The contractor agrees that the Comptroller General of the United States or any of his duly authorized representatives shall, until the expiration of 3 years after final payment under this contract or such lesser time specified in either Appendix M of the Armed Services Procurement Regulation or the Federal Procurement Regulations Part 1–20, as appropriate, have access to and the right to examine any directly pertinent books, documents, papers, and records of the contractor involving transactions related to this contract.

(c) The Contractor further agrees to include in all his subcontracts hereunder a provision to the effect that the subcontractor agrees that the Comptroller General of the United States or any of his duly authorized representatives shall, until the expiration of 3 years after final payment under the subcontract or such lesser time specified in either Appendix M of the Armed Services Procurement Regulation or the Federal Procurement Regulations Part 1–20, as appropriate, have access to and the right to examine any directly pertinent books, documents, papers, and records of such subcontractor, involving transactions related to the subcontract. The term "subcontract" as used in this clause excludes (1) purchase orders not exceeding $10,000 and (2) subcontracts or purchase orders for public utility services at rates established for uniform applicability to the general public.

(d) The periods of access and examination described in (b) and (c), above, for records which relate to (1) appeals under the "Disputes" clause of this contract, (2) litigation or the settlement of claims arising out of the performance of this contract, or (3) costs and expenses of this contract as to which exception has been taken by the Comptroller General or any of his duly authorized representatives, shall continue until such appeals, litigation, claims, or exceptions have been disposed of.

24. BUY AMERICAN

(a) *Agreement.* In accordance with the Buy American Act (41 U.S.C. 10a–10d), and Executive Order 10582, December 17, 1954 (3 CFR, 1954–58 Comp., p. 230), as amended by Executive Order 11051, September 27, 1962 (3 CFR, 1959–63 Comp., p. 635), the Contractor agrees that only domestic construction material will be used (by the Contractor, subcontractors, materialmen, and suppliers) in the performance of this contract, except for nondomestic material listed in the contract.

(b) *Domestic construction material.* "Construction material" means any article, material, or supply brought to the construction site for incorporation in the building or work. An unmanufactured construction material is a "domestic construction material" if it has been mined or produced in the United States. A manufactured construction material is a "domestic construction material" if it has been manufactured in the United States and if the cost of its components which have been mined, produced, or manufactured in the United States exceeds 50 percent of the cost of all its components. "Component" means any article, material, or supply directly incorporated in a construction material.

(c) *Domestic component.* A component shall be considered to have been "mined, produced, or manufactured in the

United States" (regardless of its source in fact) if the article, material, or supply in which it is incorporated was manufactured in the United States and the component is of a class or kind determined by the Government to be not mined, produced, or manufactured in the United States in sufficient and reasonably available commercial quantities and of a satisfactory quality.

25. Equal Opportunity
(The following clause is applicable unless this contract is exempt under the rules, regulations, and relevant orders of the Secretary of Labor (41 CFR, ch. 60).)

During the performance of this contract, the Contractor agrees as follows:

(a) The Contractor will not discriminate against any employee or applicant for employment because of race, color, religion, sex, or national origin. The Contractor will take affirmative action to ensure that applicants are employed, and that employees are treated during employment, without regard to their race, color, religion, sex, or national origin. Such action shall include, but not be limited to, the following: Employment, upgrading, demotion, or transfer; recruitment or recruitment advertising; layoff or termination; rates of pay or other forms of compensation; and selection for training, including apprenticeship. The Contractor agrees to post in conspicuous places, available to employees and applicants for employment, notices to be provided by the Contracting Officer setting forth the provisions of this Equal Opportunity clause.

(b) The Contractor will, in all solicitations or advertisements for employees placed by or on behalf of the Contractor, state that all qualified applicants will receive consideration for employment without regard to race, color, religion, sex, or national origin.

(c) The Contractor will send to each labor union or representative of workers with which he has a collective bargaining agreement or other contract or understanding, a notice, to be provided by the agency Contracting Officer, advising the labor union or workers' representative of the contractor's commitments under this Equal Opportunity clause, and shall post copies of the notice in conspicuous places available to employees and applicants for employment.

(d) The Contractor will comply with all provisions of Executive Order No. 11246 of September 24, 1965, as amended by Executive Order No. 11375 of October 13, 1967, and of the rules, regulations, and relevant orders of the Secretary of Labor.

(e) The Contractor will furnish all information and reports required by Executive Order No. 11246 of September 24, 1965, as amended by Executive Order No. 11375 of October 13, 1967, and by the rules, regulations, and orders of the Secretary of Labor, or pursuant thereto, and will permit access to his books, records, and accounts by the contracting agency and the Secretary of Labor for purposes of investigation to ascertain compliance with such rules, regulations, and orders.

(f) In the event of the Contractor's noncompliance with the Equal Opportunity clause of this contract or with any of the said rules, regulations, or orders, this contract may be canceled, terminated, or suspended, in whole or in part, and the Contractor may be declared ineligible for further Government contracts in accordance with procedures authorized in Executive Order No. 11246 of September 24, 1965, as amended by Executive Order No. 11375 of October 13, 1967, and such other sanctions may be imposed and remedies invoked as provided in Executive Order No. 11246 of September 24, 1965, as amended by Executive Order No. 11375 of October 13, 1967, or by rule, regulation, or order of the Secretary of Labor, or as otherwise provided by law.

(g) The Contractor will include the provisions of paragraphs (a) through (g) in every subcontract or purchase order unless exempted by rules, regulations, or orders of the Secretary of Labor issued pursuant to Section 204 of Executive Order No. 11246 of September 24, 1965, as amended by Executive Order No. 11375 of October 13, 1967, so that such provisions will be binding upon each subcontractor or vendor. The Contractor will take such action with respect to any subcontract or purchase order as the contracting agency may direct as a means of enforcing such provisions, including sanctions for noncompliance: *Provided, however*, that in the event the Contractor becomes involved in, or is threatened with, litigation with a subcontractor or vendor as a result of such direction by the contracting agency, the Contractor may request the United States to enter into such litigation to protect the interests of the United States.

26. Covenant Against Contingent Fees
The Contractor warrants that no person or selling agency has been employed or retained to solicit or secure this contract upon an agreement or understanding for a commission, percentage, brokerage, or contingent fee, excepting bona fide employees or bona fide established commercial or selling agencies maintained by the Contractor for the purpose of securing business. For breach or violation of this warranty the Government shall have the right to annul this contract without liability or in its discretion to deduct from the contract price or consideration, or otherwise recover, the full amount of such commission, percentage, brokerage, or contingent fee.

27. Officials Not to Benefit
No member of or delegate to Congress or resident Commissioner shall be admitted to any share or part of this contract, or to any benefit that may arise therefrom; but this provision shall not be construed to extend to this contract if made with a corporation for its general benefit.

28. Convict Labor
In connection with the performance of work under this contract, the Contractor agrees not to employ any person undergoing sentence of imprisonment at hard labor except as provided by Public Law 89-176, September 10, 1965 (18 U.S.C. 4082(c)(2)) and Executive Order 11755, December 29, 1973.

29. Utilization of Small Business Concerns
(a) It is the policy of the Government as declared by the Congress that a fair proportion of the purchases and contracts for supplies and services for the Government be placed with small business concerns.

(b) The Contractor agrees to accomplish the maximum amount of subcontracting to small business concerns that the Contractor finds to be consistent with the efficient performance of this contract.

30. Utilization of Minority Business Enterprises
(a) It is the policy of the Government that minority business enterprises shall have the maximum practicable opportunity to participate in the performance of Government contracts.

(b) The Contractor agrees to use his best efforts to carry out this policy in the award of his subcontracts to the fullest extent consistent with the efficient performance of this contract. As used in this contract, the term "minority business enterprise" means a business, at least 50 percent of which is owned by minority group members or, in case of publicly-owned businesses, at least 51 percent of the stock of which is owned by minority group members. For the purposes of this definition, minority group members are Negroes, Spanish-speaking American persons, American-Orientals, American-Indians, American-Eskimos, and American-Aleuts. Contractors may rely on written representations by subcontractors regarding their status as minority business enterprises in lieu of an independent investigation.

31. Federal, State, and Local Taxes
(a) Except as may be otherwise provided in this contract, the contract price includes all applicable Federal, State and local taxes and duties.

(b) Nevertheless, with respect to any Federal excise tax or duty on the transactions or property covered by this contract, if a statute, court decision, written ruling, or regulation takes effect after the contract date, and—

(1) Results in the Contractor being required to pay or bear the burden of any such Federal excise tax or duty or increase in the rate thereof which would not otherwise have been payable on such transactions or property, the contract price shall be increased by the amount of such tax or duty or rate increase: *Provided*, That the Contractor if requested by the Contracting Officer, warrants in writing that no amount for such newly imposed Federal excise tax or duty or rate increase was included in the contract price as a contingency reserve or otherwise; or

(2) Results in the Contractor not being required to pay or bear the burden of, or in his obtaining a refund or drawback of, any such Federal excise tax or duty which would otherwise have been payable on such transactions or property or which was the basis of an increase in the contract price, the contract price shall be decreased by the amount of the relief, refund, or drawback, or that amount shall be paid to the Government, as directed by the Contracting Officer. The contract price shall be similarly decreased if the Contractor, through his fault or negligence or his failure to follow instructions of the Contract-

ing Officer, is required to pay or bear the burden of, or does not obtain a refund or drawback of, any such Federal excise tax or duty.

(c) No adjustment pursuant to paragraph b above will be made under this contract unless the aggregate amount thereof is or may reasonably be expected to be over $100.00.

(d) As used in paragraph b above, the term "contract date" means the date set for the bid opening, or if this is a negotiated contract, the date of this contract. As to additional supplies or services procured by modification to this contract, the term "contract date" means the date of such modification.

(e) Unless there does not exist any reasonable basis to sustain an exemption, the Government, upon request of the Contractor, without further liability, agrees, except as otherwise provided in this contract, to furnish evidence appropriate to establish exemption from any tax which the Contractor warrants in writing was excluded from the contract price. In addition, the Contracting Officer may furnish evidence to establish exemption from any tax that may, pursuant to this Clause, give rise to either an increase or decrease in the contract price. Except as otherwise provided in this contract, evidence appropriate to establish exemption from duties will be furnished only at the discretion of the Contracting Officer.

(f) The Contractor shall promptly notify the Contracting Officer of matters which will result in either an increase or decrease in the contract price, and shall take action with respect thereto as directed by the Contracting Officer.

7-1605 (10-78)
Supplement to SF-23A
Bureau of Reclamation
(Construction)

SUPPLEMENT TO GENERAL PROVISIONS
(Standard Form 23-A, April 1975 Edition)

a. Clause No. 4A.—The following is added as Clause No. 4A of the General Provisions:

"4A.   ADMINISTRATION OF THE
DIFFERING SITE
CONDITIONS CLAUSE

"(a) Nature of the clause. The Differing Site Conditions clause provides for an equitable adjustment to the Contractor or the Government which reflects the increases or decreases in a Contractor's cost of and time for performance that result from a differing site condition (as that term is defined in the clause) encountered by the Contractor. However, an equitable adjustment is only available to the Contractor if he gives the Contracting Officer a prompt notice in writing before disturbing the conditions (or secures an extension of the time for giving such notice) and asserts the claim before final payment under the contract.

"(b) Notice of differing site conditions. When a Contractor believes that a differing site condition has been encountered, the clause requires that a prompt written notice be given to the Contracting Officer so that the condition of the site can be investigated, the facts can be ascertained, and a determination can be made regarding the presence or absence of a differing site condition. The prompt notice requirement enables the Government to examine the condition of the site and, if necessary, (1) to modify the contract so that it will reflect the increased or decreased cost of and time for performance or (2) to develop records concerning any increase or decrease in the cost of and time for performance. Cost and time information is essential for an independent Government judgment regarding an equitable adjustment of the contract. A failure to give a timely notice could seriously prejudice the Government's ability to determine the extent to which the Contractor or the Government is entitled to an equitable adjustment. Since the existence of a differing site condition is not always recognizable immediately, the clause provides that the Contracting Officer may extend the time for the submission of the required notice. The purpose of the authority to extend the time for the notice is to ensure that Contractors are not deprived of the remedy provided by the clause because of an inadvertent failure to give the required notice. However, this authority to extend the time for the notice does not entitle a Contractor to a time extension beyond the time when he knew, or reasonably should have known, of the existence of a differing site condition. If the Contractor gives the required notice at the time he knew, or reasonably should have known, of the existence of the differing site condition, he is entitled to an equitable adjustment which reflects the increased costs and time required for performance that result from the differing site condition. If the Contractor fails to submit the required notice to the Contracting Officer by the time he knew, or reasonably should have known, of the existence of a differing site condition, he is not entitled to an equitable adjustment which reflects the increased costs and time required for performance prior to the time when he gave the notice or the time when the Government had actual notice of the existence of a differing site condition.

"(c) Processing of claims.

"(1) Since the time required by the Contractor to ascertain the amount of his claim varies with the circumstances, no specific time for the submission of a claim is specified in the clause or in this section. The clause simply states that no claim will be allowed if asserted after final payment. However, Contractors should not unnecessarily postpone the submission of claims for equitable adjustments.

"(2) To prevent Contractors from unnecessarily postponing the submission of claims, Contracting Officers shall take the following actions.

"(i) When a Contractor gives a prompt written notice of a differing site condition but has not submitted a claim for an equitable adjustment, although there has been a reasonable opportunity to ascertain the amount of the adjustment involved, the Contracting Officer shall send a written request to the Contractor (by registered or certified mail) that he submit within a specified period of time either a written claim or a request for an extension of the time for submission of the claim together with the reasons why the additional time is needed.

"(ii) In the event that the Contractor fails to submit a claim within the time specified in the request, or an approved time extension, the Contracting Officer shall make a unilateral determination of the amount of the equitable adjustment which the Contractor is entitled to and shall notify the Contractor of the determination. Such unilateral determinations may not be appealed under the Disputes clause of the contract."

b. Clause No. 5.—At the end of Paragraph 5(d)(2) the period after the word "delay" is deleted, a colon is substituted therefor, and the following is added:

"Provided, That the Contractor shall be excused for delays of suppliers only if the Contracting Officer shall determine that the materials or supplies to be furnished are not procurable in the open market."

c. Clause No. 7.—Paragraph 7(c) is deleted and the following Paragraph 7(c) is substituted therefor:

"(c) In making such progress payments, there shall be retained 10 percent of the estimated amount until final completion and acceptance of the contract work. However, if the Contracting Officer, finds that satisfactory progress was achieved during any period for which a progress payment is to be made, he may authorize such payment to be made in full without retention of a percentage. Also, whenever the work is substantially complete, the Contracting Officer shall retain an amount he considers adequate for protection of the Government and, at his discretion, may release to the Contractor all or a portion of any excess amount. Furthermore, on completion and acceptance of each separate building, public work, or other division of the contract, on which the price is stated separately in the contract, payment may be made therefor without retention of a percentage."

d. Clause No. 12.—At the end of Clause No. 12 the following is added:

"Upon completion of the contract, or final acceptance of any completed unit thereof, the work shall be delivered complete and undamaged."

e. Clause No. 21.—At the end of Clause No. 21 the following is added:

"Any patented invention, the use of which by these specifications is required or permitted in the alternative to be used and which the United States has the right to use royalty free, shall be available to the contractor without the payment of the royalty."

f. Clause No. 28.—In the third line of Clause No. 28, the words "at hard labor" are deleted.

g. Clause No. 32.—The following is added as Clause No. 32 of the General Provisions:

"32. AFFIRMATIVE ACTION FOR
    DISABLED VETERANS AND
    VETERANS OF THE VIETNAM
    ERA

"(This clause is applicable pursuant to 41 CFR 60-250.)

"(a) The Contractor will not discriminate against any employee or applicant for employment because he or she is a disabled veteran or veteran of the Vietnam Era in regard to any position for which the employee or applicant for employment is qualified. The Contractor agrees to take affirmative action to employ, advance in employment, and otherwise treat qualified disabled veterans and veterans of the Vietnam Era without discrimination based upon their disability or veterans status in all employment practices such as the following: employment upgrading, demotion or transfer, recruitment, advertising, layoff or termination, rates of pay or other forms of compensation, and selection for training, including apprenticeship.

"(b) The Contractor agrees that all suitable employment openings of the Contractor which exist at the time of the execution of this contract and those which occur during the performance of this contract, including those not generated by this contract and including those occurring at an establishment of the Contractor other than the one wherein the contract is being performed but excluding those of independently operated corporate affiliates, shall be listed at an appropriate local office of the State employment service system wherein the opening occurs. The Contractor further agrees to provide such reports to such local office regarding employment openings and hires as may be required.

"State and local government agencies holding Federal contracts of $10,000 or more shall also list all their suitable openings with the appropriate office of the State employment service, but are not required to provide those reports set forth in Paragraphs (d) and (e).

"(c) Listing of employment openings with the employment service system pursuant to this clause shall be made at least concurrently with the use of any other recruitment source or effort and shall involve the normal obligations which attach to the placing of a bona fide job order, including the acceptance of referrals of veterans and nonveterans. The listing of employment openings does not require the hiring of any particular job applicant or from any particular group of job applicants, and nothing herein is intended to relieve the Contractor from any requirements in Executive Orders or regulations regarding nondiscrimination in employment.

"(d) The reports required by Paragraph (b) of this clause shall include, but not be limited to, periodic reports which shall be filed at least quarterly with the appropriate local office or, where the Contractor has more than one hiring location in a State, with the central office of that State employment service. Such reports shall indicate for each hiring location (1) the number of individuals hired during the reporting period, (2) the number of nondisabled veterans of the Vietnam Era hired, (3) the number of disabled veterans of the Vietnam Era hired, and (4) the total number of disabled veterans hired. The reports should include covered veterans hired for on-the-job training under 38 U.S.C. 1787. The Contractor shall submit a report within 30 days after the end of each reporting period wherein any performance is made on this contract identifying data for each hiring location. The Contractor shall maintain at each hiring location copies of the reports submitted until the expiration of 1 year after final payment under the contract, during which time these reports and related documentation shall be made available, upon request, for examination by any authorized representatives of the Contracting Officer or of the Secretary of Labor. Documentation would include personnel records respecting job openings, recruitment, and placement.

"(e) Whenever the Contractor becomes contractually bound to the listing provisions of this clause, he shall advise the employment service system in each State where he has establishments of the name and location of each hiring location in the State. As long as the Contractor is contractually bound to these provisions and has so advised the State system, there is no need to advise the State system of subsequent contracts. The Contractor may advise the State system when he is no longer bound by this contract clause.

"(f) This clause does not apply to the listing of employment openings which occur and are filled outside of the 50 States, the District of Columbia, Puerto Rico, Guam, and the Virgin Islands.

"(g) The provisions of Paragraphs (b), (c), (d), and (e) of this clause do not apply to openings which the Contractor proposes to fill from within his own organization or to fill pursuant to a customary and traditional employer-union hiring arrangement. This exclusion does not apply to a particular opening once an employer decides to consider applicants outside of his own organization or employer-union arrangement for that opening.

"(h) As used in this clause:

"(1) 'All suitable employment openings' includes, but is not limited to, openings which occur in the following job categories: Production and nonproduction; plant and office; laborers and mechanics; supervisory and nonsupervisory; technical; and executive, administrative, and professional openings as are compensated on a salary basis of less than $25,000 per year. This term includes full-time employment, temporary employment of more than 3 days duration, and part-time employment. It does not include openings which the Contractor proposes to fill from within his own organization or to fill pursuant to a customary and traditional employer-union hiring arrangement nor openings in an educational institution which are restricted to students of that institution. Under the most compelling circumstances, an employment opening may not be suitable for listing, including such situations where the needs of the Government cannot reasonably be otherwise supplied, where listing would be contrary to national security, or where the requirement of listing would otherwise not be for the best interest of the Government.

"(2) 'Appropriate office of the State employment service system' means the local office of the Federal-State national system of public employment offices with assigned responsibility for serving the area where the employment opening is to be filled, including the District of Columbia, Guam, Puerto Rico, and the Virgin Islands.

"(3) 'Openings which the Contractor proposes to fill from within his own organization' means employment openings for which no consideration will be given to persons outside the Contractor's organization (including any affiliates, subsidiaries, and the parent companies), and includes any openings which the Contractor proposes to fill from regularly established 'recall' lists.

"(4) 'Openings which the Contractor proposes to fill pursuant to a customary and traditional employer-union hiring arrangement' means employment openings which the Contractor proposes to fill from union halls, which is part of the customary and traditional hiring relationship which exists between the Contractor and representatives of his employees.

"(i) The Contractor agrees to comply with the rules, regulations, and relevant orders of the Secretary of Labor issued pursuant to the Act.

"(j) In the event of the Contractor's noncompliance with the requirements of this clause, actions for noncompliance may be taken in accordance with the rules, regulations, and relevant orders of the Secretary of Labor issued pursuant to the Act.

"(k) The Contractor agrees to post in conspicuous places, available to employees and applicants for employment, notices in a form to be prescribed by the Director, provided by or through the Contracting Officer. Such notice shall state the Contractor's obligation under the law to take affirmative action to employ and advance in employment qualified disabled veterans and veterans of the Vietnam Era for employment, and the rights of applicants and employees.

"(l) The Contractor will notify each labor union or representative of workers with which it has a collective bargaining agreement or other contract understanding, that the Contractor is bound by the terms of the Vietnam Era Veterans Readjustment Assistance Act, and is committed to take affirmative action to employ and advance in employment qualified disabled veterans and veterans of the Vietnam Era.

"(m) The Contractor will include the provisions of this clause in every subcontract or purchase order of $10,000 or more unless exempted by rules, regulations, or orders of the Secretary issued pursuant to the Act, so that such provisions will be binding upon each subcontractor or vendor. The Contractor will take such action with respect to any subcontract or purchase order as the Director of the Office of Federal Contract Compliance Programs may direct to enforce such provisions, including action for noncompliance."

h. Clause No. 33.—The following is added as Clause No. 33 of the General Provisions:

"33. EMPLOYMENT OF THE HANDICAPPED

"(a) The Contractor will not discriminate against any employee or applicant for employment because of physical or mental handicap in regard to any position for which the employee or applicant for employment is qualified. The Contractor agrees to take affirmative action to employ, advance in employment, and otherwise treat qualified handicapped individuals without discrimination based upon their physical or mental handicap in all employment practices such as the following: employment, upgrading, demotion or transfer, recruitment, advertising, layoff or termination, rates of pay or other forms of compensation, and selection for training including apprenticeship.

"(b) The Contractor agrees to comply with the rules, regulations, and relevant orders of the Secretary of Labor issued pursuant to the Rehabilitation Act of 1973, as amended.

"(c) In the event of the Contractor's noncompliance with the requirements of this clause, actions for noncompliance may be taken in accordance with the rules, regulations, and relevant orders of the Secretary of Labor issued pursuant to the Act.

"(d) The Contractor agrees to post in conspicuous places, available to employees and applicants for employment, notices in a form to be prescribed by the Director, Office of Federal Contract Compliance Programs, Department of

Labor, provided by or through the contracting officer. Such notices shall state the Contractor's obligation under the law to take affirmative action to employ and advance in employment qualified handicapped employees and applicants for employment, and the rights of applicants and employees.

"(e) The Contractor will notify each labor union or representative of workers with which it has a collective bargaining agreement or other contract understanding, that the Contractor is bound by the terms of Section 503 of the Act and is committed to take affirmative action to employ and advance in employment physically and mentally handicapped individuals.

"(f) The Contractor will include the provisions of this clause in every subcontract or purchase order of $2,500 or more unless exempted by rules, regulations, or orders of the Secretary of Labor issued pursuant to Section 503 of the Act, so that such provisions will be binding upon each subcontractor or vendor. The Contractor will take such action with respect to any subcontract or purchase order as the Director, Office of Federal Contract Compliance Programs, may direct to enforce such provisions, including action for noncompliance."

i. Clause No. 34.—The following is added as Clause No. 34 of the General Provisions:

"34. CLEAN AIR AND WATER

"(Applicable only if the contract exceeds $100,000 or the Contracting Officer has determined that the orders under an indefinite quantity contract in any one year will exceed $100,000, or a facility to be used has been the subject of a conviction under the Clean Air Act (42 U.S.C. 1857c-8(c)(1)) or the Federal Water Pollution Control Act (33 U.S.C. 1319(c)) and is listed by EPA, or the contract is not otherwise exempt.)

"(a) The Contractor agrees as follows:

"(1) To comply with all the requirements of Section 114 of the Clean Air Act, as amended (42 U.S.C. 1857, et seq., as amended by Public Law 91-604) and Section 308 of the Federal Water Pollution Control Act (33 U.S.C. 1251 et seq., as amended by Public Law 92-500), respectively, relating to inspection, monitoring, entry, reports, and information, as well as other requirements specified in Section 114 and Section 308 of the Air Act and the Water Act, respectively, and all regulations and guidelines issued thereunder before the award of this contract.

"(2) That no portion of the work required by this prime contract will be performed in a facility listed on the Environmental Protection Agency List . of Violating Facilities on the date when this contract was awarded unless and until the EPA eliminates the name of such facility or facilities from such listing.

"(3) To use his best efforts to comply with clean air standards and clean water standards at the facility in which the contract is being performed.

"(4) To insert the substance of the provisions of this clause in any nonexempt subcontract, including this Paragraph (a)(4).

"(b) The terms used in this clause have the following meanings:

"(1) The term "Air Act" means the Clean Air Act, as amended (42 U.S.C. 1857 et seq., as amended by Public Law 91-604).

"(2) The term "Water Act" means Federal Water Pollution Control Act, as amended (33 U.S.C. 1251 et seq., as amended by Public Law 92-500).

"(3) The term "clean air standards" means any enforceable rules, regulations, guidelines, standards, limitations, orders, controls, prohibitions, or other requirements which are contained in, issued under, or otherwise adopted pursuant to the Air Act or Executive Order No. 11738, an applicable implementation plan as described in Section 110(d) of the Clean Air Act (42 U.S.C. 1857c-5(d)), an approved implementation procedure or plan under Section 111(c) or Section 111(d), respectively, of the Air Act (42 U.S.C. 1857c-6(c) or (d)), or an approved implementation procedure under Section 112(d) of the Air Act (42 U.S.C. 1857c-7(d)).

"(4) The term "clean water standards" means any enforceable limitation, control, condition, prohibition, standard, or other requirement which is promulgated pursuant to the Water Act or contained in a permit issued to a discharger by the Environmental Protection Agency or by a state under an approved program, as authorized by Section 402 of the Water Act (33 U.S.C. 1342), or by a local government to ensure compliance with pretreatment regulations as required by Section 307 of the Water Act (33 U.S.C. 1317).

"(5) The term "compliance" means compliance with clean air or water standards. Compliance shall also mean compliance with a schedule or plan ordered or approved by a court of competent jurisdiction, the Environmental Protection Agency, or an air or water pollution control agency in accordance with the requirements of the Air Act or Water Act and regulations issued pursuant thereto.

"(6) The term "facility" means any building, plant, installation, structure, mine, vessel, or other floating craft, location, or site of operations, owned, leased, or supervised by a contractor or subcontractor, to be utilized in the performance of a contract or subcontract. Where a location or site of operations contains or includes more than one building, plant, installation, or structure, the entire location or site shall be deemed to be a facility except where the Director, Office of Federal Activities, Environmental Protection Agency, determines that independent facilities are colocated in one geographical area."

2b. Additional Supplement to General Provisions

(Standard Form 23-A, April 1975 Edition)

a. Clause No. 6.—Clause No. 6 of the General Provisions is deleted in its entirety and the following is substituted therefor:

"6.   DISPUTES CLAUSE:

"(a) This contract is subject to the Contract Disputes Act of 1978 (Pub. L. 95-563).

"(b) Except as provided in the Act, all disputes arising under or relating to this contract shall be resolved in accordance with this clause.

"(c) (i) As used herein, "claim" means a written demand or assertion by one of the parties seeking, as a legal right, the payment of money, adjustment or interpretation of contract terms, or other relief, arising under or relating to this contract.

"(ii) A voucher, invoice, or request for payment that is not in dispute when submitted is not a claim for the purposes of the Act. However, where such submission is subsequently not acted upon in a reasonable time, or disputed either as to liability or amount, it may be converted to a claim pursuant to the Act.

"(iii) A claim by the contractor shall be made in writing and submitted to the contracting officer for decision. A claim by the Government against the contractor shall be subject to a decision by the contracting officer.

"(d) For contractor claims of more than $50,000, the contractor shall submit with the claim a certification that the claim is made in good faith; the supporting data are accurate and complete to the best of the contractor's knowledge and belief; and the amount requested accurately reflects the contract adjustment for which the contractor believes the Government is liable. The certification shall be executed by the contractor if an individual. When the contractor is not an individual, the certification shall be executed by a senior company official in charge at the contractor's plant or location involved, or by an officer or general partner of the contractor having overall responsibility for the conduct of the contractor's affairs.

"(e) For contractor claims of $50,000 or less, the contracting officer must render a decision within 60 days. For contractor claims in excess of $50,000, the contracting officer must decide the claim within 60 days or notify the contractor of the date when the decision will be made.

"(f) The contracting officer's decision shall be final unless the contractor appeals or files a suit as provided in the Act.

"(g) The authority of the contracting officer under the Act does not extend to claims or disputes which by statue or regulation other agencies are expressly authorized to decide.

"(h) Interest on the amount found due on a contractor claim shall be paid from the date the claim is received by the contracting officer until the date of payment.

"(i) Except as the parties may otherwise agree, pending final resolution of a claim by the contractor arising under the contract, the contractor shall proceed diligently with the performance of the contract in accordance with the contracting officer's decision."

b. Clause No. 7.—Paragraph 7.(e) of the General Provisions is redesignated as paragraph 7.(f) and the following is added as paragraph 7.(e):

"(e) If Miller Act (40 U.S.C. 270a-270e) performance or payment bonds are required under this contract, the Government shall pay to the Contractor the total premiums paid by the contractor to obtain the bonds. This payment shall be paid at one time to the contractor together with the first progress payment otherwise due after the contractor has (1) furnished the bonds (including coinsurance and reinsurance agreements, when applicable), (2) furnished evidence of full payment to the surety company, and (3) submitted a request for such payment. The payment by the Government of the bond premiums to the contractor shall not be made as increments of the individual progress payments and shall not be in addition to the contract price.

c. Clause No. 19.—Clause No. 19 of the General Provisions is deleted in its entirety.

d. Clause No. 25.—Clause No. 25 of the General Provisions is deleted in its entirety and the following is substituted therefor:

"25. EQUAL OPPORTUNITY

"(The following clause is applicable unless this contract is exempt under the rules, regulations, and relevant orders of the Secretary of Labor (41 CFR, ch. 60).)

"During the performance of this contract, the Contractor agrees as follows:

"(a) The contractor will not discriminate against any employee or applicant for employment because of race, color, religion, sex, or national origin. The contractor will take affirmative action to ensure that applicants are employed, and that employees are treated during employment, without regard to their race, color, religion, sex, or national origin. Such action shall include, but not be limited to, the following: Employment, upgrading, demotion, or transfer; recruitment or recruitment advertising; layoff or termination; rates of pay or other forms of compensation; and selection for training, including apprenticeship. The contractor agrees to post in conspicuous places, available to employees and applicants for employment, notices to be provided by the contracting officer setting forth the provisions of this nondiscrimination clause.

"(b) The contractor will, in all solicitations or advertisements for employees placed by or on behalf of the contractor, state that all qualified applicants will receive consideration for employment without discrimination because of race, color, religion, sex, or national origin.

"(c) The contractor will send to each labor union or representative of workers, with which it has a collective bargaining agreement or other contract or understanding, a notice, to be provided by the Contracting Officer, advising the said labor union or workers' representative of the contractor's commitments under Section 202 of Executive Order No. 11246 of September 24, 1965, and shall post copies of the notice in conspicuous places available to employees and applicants for employment.

"(d) The contractor will comply with all provisions of Executive Order No. 11246 of September 24, 1965, as amended, and of the rules, regulations, and relevant orders of the Secretary of Labor.

"(e) The contractor will furnish all information and reports required by said amended Executive Order and by the rules, regulations, and orders of the Secretary of Labor, or pursuant thereto, and will permit access to its books, records, and accounts by the contracting officer and the Secretary of Labor for purposes of investigation to ascertain compliance with such rules, regulations, and orders.

"(f) In the event of the contractor's noncompliance with the nondiscrimination clauses of this contract or with any of the such rules, regulations, or orders, this contract may be canceled, terminated, or suspended, in whole or in part, and the contractor may be declared ineligible for further Government contracts in accordance with procedures authorized in said amended Executive Order, and such other sanctions may be imposed and remedies invoked as provided in said Executive Order, or by rule, regulation, or order of the Secretary of Labor, or as otherwise provided by law.

"(g) The contractor will include the provisions of paragraphs (a) through (g) in every subcontract or purchase order unless exempted by the rules, regulations, or orders of the

Secretary of Labor issued pursuant to Section 204 of said amended Executive Order, so that such provisions will be binding upon each subcontractor or vendor. The contractor will take such action with respect to any subcontract or purchase order as may be directed by the Secretary of Labor as a means of enforcing such provisions, including sanctions for non-compliance: Provided, however, That in the event a contractor becomes involved in, or is threatened with, litigation with a subcontractor or vendor as a result of such direction, the contractor may request the United States to enter into such litigation to protect the interests of the United States.

Note: Equal Employment Opportunity provisions are directed by Executive Order No. 11246 of September 24, 1965, (3 CFR page 167, 1965 Supplement), as amended by Executive Order No. 11375 of October 13, 1967, (3 CFR page 320, 1967 Compilation) and Executive Order No. 12086 of October 5, 1978."

e. Clauses No. 29 and 30.—Clauses No. 29 and 30 of the General Provisions are deleted in their entirety and the following clause No. 29 is substituted therefor:

"29. UTILIZATION OF SMALL BUSINESS CONCERNS AND SMALL BUSINESS CONCERNS OWNED AND CONTROLLED BY SOCIALLY AND ECONOMICALLY DISADVANTAGED INDIVIDUALS

The following clause is applicable if the contract is over $10,000 except (1) contracts for services which are personal in nature and (2) contracts which will be performed entirely (including all subcontracts) outside any State, territory, or possession of the United States, the District of Columbia, or the Commonwealth of Puerto Rico: Subcontracting plans are not required of small business concerns.

"(a) It is the policy of the United States that small business concerns and small business concerns owned and controlled by socially and economically disadvantaged individuals shall have the maximum practicable opportunity to participate in the performance of contracts let by any Federal agency.

"(b) The contractor hereby agrees to carry out this policy in the awarding of subcontracts to the fullest extent consistent with the efficient performance of this contract. The contractor further agrees to cooperate in any studies or surveys that may be conducted by the Small Business Administration or the contracting agency which may be necessary to determine the extent of the contractor's compliance with this clause.

"(c) (1) As used in this contract, the term "small business concern" shall mean a small business as defined pursuant to Section 3 of the Small Business Act and in relevant regulations promulgated pursuant thereto.

"(2) The term "small business concern owned and controlled by socially and economically disadvantaged individuals" shall mean a small business concern—

"(i) which is at least 51 per centum owned by one or more socially and economically disadvantaged individuals; or in the case of any publicly owned business, at least 51 percentum of the stock of which is owned by one or more socially and economically disadvantaged individuals; and

"(ii) whose management and daily business operations are controlled by one or more of such individuals.

The contractor shall presume that socially and economically disadvantaged individuals include Black Americans, Hispanic Americans, Native Americans, Asian Pacific Americans, and other minorities, or any other individual found to be disadvantaged by the Small Business Administration pursuant to section 8(a) of the Small Business Act.

"(d) Contractors acting in good faith may rely on written representations by their subcontractors regarding their status as a small business concern or a small business concern owned and controlled by socially and economically disadvantaged individuals."

f. Clause No. 35.—The following is added as Clause No. 35 of the General Provisions:

"35. UTILIZATION OF WOMEN-OWNED BUSINESS CONCERNS (Over $10,000)

"The following clause is applicable if the contract is over $10,000 except (i) contracts which, including all subcontracts thereunder, are to be performed entirely outside the United States, its possessions, Puerto Rico and the Trust Territory of the Pacific Islands, and (ii) contracts for services which are personal in nature.

"(a) It is the policy of the United States Government that women-owned businesses shall have the maximum practicable opportunity to participate in the performance of contracts awarded by any Federal agency.

"(b) The contractor agrees to use his best efforts to carry out this policy in the award of subcontracts to the fullest extent consistent with the efficient performance of this contract. As used in this contract, a "woman-owned business" concern means a business that is at least 51 percent owned by a woman or women who also control and operate it. "Control" in this context means exercising the power to make policy decisions. "Operate" in this context means being actively involved in the day-to-day management. "Women" mean all women business owners."

3. Contract Disputes Act of 1978

NINETY-FIFTH CONGRESS
OF THE UNITED STATES OF AMERICA

At The Second Session

Begun and held at the City of Washington on Thursday, the nineteenth day of January, one thousand nine hundred and seventy-eight

An Act

To provide for the resolution of claims and disputes relating to Government contracts awarded by executive agencies

"The Contract Disputes Act of 1978" (Pub. L. 95-563)

DEFINITIONS

SEC. 2. As used in this Act—

(1) the term "agency head" means the head and any assistant head of an executive agency, and may "upon the designation by" the head of an executive agency include the chief official of any principal division of the agency;

(2) the term "executive agency" means an executive department as defined in section 101 of title 5, United States Code, an independent establishment as defined by section 104 of title 5, United States Code, (except that it shall not include the General Accounting Office): a military department as defined by section 102 of title 5, United States Code, and a wholly owned Government corporation as defined by section 846 of title 31, United States Code, the United States Postal Service, and the Postal Rate Commission;

(3) The term "contracting officer" means any person who, by appointment in accordance with applicable regulations, has the authority to enter into and administer contracts and make determinations and findings with respect thereto. The term also includes the authorized representative of the contracting officer, acting within the limits of his authority;

(4) the term "contractor" means a party to a Government contract other than the Government;

(5) The term "Administrator" means the Administrator for Federal Procurement Policy appointed pursuant to the Office of Federal Procurement Policy Act;

(6) The term "agency board" means an agency board of contract appeals established under section 8 of this Act; and

(7) The term "misrepresentation of fact" means a false statement of substantive fact, or any conduct which leads to a belief of a substantive fact material to proper understanding of the matter in hand, made with intent to deceive or mislead.

APPLICABILITY OF LAW

SEC. 3. (a) Unless otherwise specifically provided herein, this Act applies to any express or implied contract (including those of the nonappropriated fund activities described in sections 1346 and 1491 of title 2S, United States Code) entered into by an executive agency for—

(1) the procurement of property, other than real property in being;

(2) the procurement of services;

(3) the procurement of construction, alteration, repair or maintenance of real property; or,

(4) the disposal of personal property.

(b) With respect to contracts of the Tennessee Valley Authority, the provisions of this Act shall apply only to those contracts which contain a disputes clause requiring that a contract dispute be resolved through an agency administrative process. Notwithstanding any other provision of this Act, contracts of the Tennessee Valley Authority for the sale of fertilizer or electric power or related to the conduct or operation of the electric power system shall be excluded from the Act.

(c) This Act does not apply to a contract with a foreign government, or agency thereof, or international organization, or subsidiary body thereof, if the head of the agency determines that the application of the Act to the contract would not be in the public interest.

MARITIME CONTRACTS

SEC. 4. Appeals under paragraph (g) of section 8 and suits under section 10, arising out of maritime contracts, shall be governed by the Act of March 9, 1920, as amended (41 Stat. 525, as amended; 46 U.S.C. 741-752) or the Act of March

3, 1925, as amended (43 Stat. 1112, as amended; 46 U.S.C. 781-790) as applicable, to the extent that those Acts are not inconsistent with this Act.

FRAUDULENT CLAIMS

SEC. 5. If a contractor is unable to support any part of his claim and it is determined that such inability is attributable to misrepresentation of fact or fraud on the part of the contractor, he shall be liable to the Government for an amount equal to such unsupported part of the claim in addition to all costs to the Government attributable to the cost of reviewing said part of his claim. Liability under this section shall be determined within six years of the commission of such misrepresentation of fact or fraud.

DECISION BY THE CONTRACTING OFFICER

SEC. 6. (a) All claims by a contractor against the government relating to a contract shall be in writing and shall be submitted to the contracting officer for a decision. All claims by the government against a contractor relating to a contract shall be the subject of a decision by the contracting officer. The contracting officer shall issue his decision in writing, and shall mail or otherwise furnish a copy of the decision to the contractor. The decision shall state the reasons for the decision reached, and shall inform the contractor of his rights as provided in this Act. Specific findings of fact are not required, but, if made, shall not be binding in any subsequent proceeding. The authority of this subsection shall not extend to a claim or dispute for penalties or forfeitures prescribed by statute or regulation which another Federal agency is specifically authorized to administer, settle, or determine. This section shall not authorize any agency head to settle, compromise, pay, or otherwise adjust any claim involving fraud.

(b) The contracting officer's decision on the claim shall be final and conclusive and not subject to review by any forum, tribunal, or Government agency, unless an appeal or suit is timely commenced as authorized by this Act. Nothing in this Act shall prohibit executive agencies from including a clause in government contracts requiring that pending final decision of an appeal, action, or final settlement, a contractor shall proceed diligently with performance of the contract in accordance with the contracting officer's decision.

(c) (1) A contracting officer shall issue a decision on any submitted claim of $50,000 or less within sixty days from his receipt of a written request from the contractor that a decision be rendered within that period. For claims of more than $50,000, the contractor shall certify that the claim is made in good faith, that the supporting data are accurate and complete to the best of his knowledge and belief, and that the amount requested accurately reflects the contract adjustment for which the contractor believes the government is liable.

(2) A contracting officer shall, within sixty days of receipt of a submitted certified claim over $50,000—

(A) issue a decision; or

(B) notify the contractor of the time within which a decision will be issued.

(3) The decision of a contracting officer on submitted claims shall be issued within a reasonable time, in accordance with regulations promulgated by the agency, taking into account such factors as the size and complexity of the claim and the adequacy of the information in support of the claim provided by the contractor.

(4) A contractor may request the agency board of contract appeals to direct a contracting officer to issue a decision in a specified period of time, as determined by the board, in the event of undue delay on the part of the contracting officer.

(5) Any failure by the contracting officer to issue a decision on a contract claim within the period required will be deemed to be a decision by the contracting officer denying the claim and will authorize the commencement of the appeal or suit on the claim as otherwise provided in this Act. However, in the event an appeal or suit is so commenced in the absence of a prior decision by the contracting officer, the tribunal concerned may, at its option, stay the proceedings to obtain a decision on the claim by the contracting officer.

CONTRACTORS' RIGHT OF APPEAL TO BOARD OF CONTRACT APPEALS

SEC. 7. Within ninety days from the date of receipt of a contracting officer's decision under section 6, the contractor may appeal such decision to an agency board of contract appeals, as provided in section 8.

AGENCY BOARDS OF CONTRACT APPEALS

SEC. 8(a) (1) Except as provided in paragraph (2) an agency board of contract appeals may be established within an executive agency when the agency head, after consultation with the Administrator, determines from a workload study that the volume of contract claims justifies the establishment of a full-time agency board of at least three members who shall have no other inconsistent duties. Workload studies will be updated at least once every three years and submitted to the Administrator.

(2) The Board of Directors of the Tennessee Valley Authority may establish a board of contract appeals for the Authority of an indeterminate number of members.

(b) (1) Except as provided in paragraph (2), the members of agency boards shall be selected and appointed to serve in the same manner as hearing examiners appointed pursuant to section 3105 of title 5 of the United States Code, with an additional requirement that such members shall have had not fewer than five years' experience in public contract law. Full-time members of agency boards serving as such on the effective date of this Act shall be considered qualified. The chairman and vice chairman of each board shall be designated by the agency head from members so appointed. The chairman of each agency board shall receive compensation at a rate equal to that paid a GS-18 under the General Schedule contained in section 5332, United States Code, the vice chairman shall receive compensation at a rate equal to that paid a GS-17 under such General Schedule, and all other members shall receive compensation at a rate equal to that paid a GS-16 under such General Schedule. Such positions shall be in addition to the number of positions which may be placed in GS-16, GS-17, and GS-18 of such General Schedule under existing law.

(2) The Board of Directors of the Tennessee Valley Authority shall establish criteria for the appointment of members to its agency board of contract appeals established in subsection (a) (2), and shall designate a chairman of such board. The chairman of such board shall receive compensation at a rate equal to the daily rate paid a GS-18 under the General Schedule contained in section 5332, United States Code, for each day he is engaged in the actual performance of his duties as a member of such board. All other members of such board shall receive compensation at a rate equal to the daily rate paid a GS-16 under such General Schedule for each day they are engaged in the actual performance of their duties as members of such board.

(c) If the volume of contract claims is not sufficient to justify an agency board under subsection (a) or if he otherwise considers it appropriate, any agency head shall arrange for appeals from decisions by contracting officers of his agency to be

decided by a board of contract appeals of another executive agency. In the event an agency head is unable to make such an arrangement with another agency, he shall submit the case to the Administrator for placement with an agency board. The provisions of this subsection shall not apply to the Tennessee Valley Authority.

(d) Each agency board shall have jurisdiction to decide any appeal from a decision of a contracting officer (1) relating to a contract made by its agency, and (2) relating to a contract made by any other agency when such agency or the Administrator has designated the agency board to decide the appeal. In exercising this jurisdiction, the agency board is authorized to grant any relief that would be available to a litigant asserting a contract claim in the Court of Claims.

(e) An agency board shall provide to the fullest extent practicable, informal, expeditious, and inexpensive resolution of disputes, and shall issue a decision in writing or take other appropriate action on each appeal submitted, and shall mail or otherwise furnish a copy of the decision to the contractor and the contracting officer.

(f) The rules of each agency board shall include a procedure for the accelerated disposition of any appeal from a decision of a contracting officer where the amount of dispute is $50,000 or less. The accelerated procedure shall be applicable at the sole election of only the contractor. Appeals under the accelerated procedure shall be resolved, whenever possible, within one hundred and eighty days from the date the contractor elects to utilize such procedure.

(g) (1) The decision of an agency board of contract appeals shall be final, except that—

(A) a contractor may appeal such a decision to the Court of Claims within one hundred twenty days after the date of receipt of a copy of such decision, or

(B) the agency head, if he determines that an appeal should be taken, and with the prior approval of the Attorney General, transmits, the decision of the board of contract appeals to the United States Court of Claims for judicial review, under section 2510 of title 28, United States Code, as amended herein, within one hundred twenty days from the date of the agency's receipt of a copy of the board's decision.

(2) Notwithstanding the provisions of paragraph (1), the decision of the board of contract appeals of the Tennessee Valley Authority shall be final, except that—

(A) a contractor may appeal such a decision to a United States district court pursuant to the provisions of section 1337 of title 28, United States Code, within one hundred twenty days after the date of receipt of a copy of such decision, or

(B) The Tennessee Valley Authority may appeal the decision to a United States district court pursuant to the provisions of section 1337 of title 28, United States Code, within one hundred twenty days after the date of the decision in any case.

(h) Pursuant to the authority conferred under the Office of Federal Procurement Policy Act, the Administrator is authorized and directed, as may be necessary or desirable to carry out the provisions of this Act, to issue guidelines with respect to criteria for the establishment, functions, and procedures of the agency boards: (except for a board established by the Tennessee Valley Authority).

(i) Within one hundred twenty days from the date of enactment of this Act, all agency boards, except that of the Tennessee Valley Authority, of three or more full-time members shall develop workload studies for approval by the agency head as specified in section 8 (a) (1).

SMALL CLAIMS

SEC. 9. (a) The rules of each agency board shall include a procedure for the expedited disposition of any appeal from a decision of a contracting officer where the amount in dispute is $10,000 or less. The small claims procedure shall be applicable at the sole election of the contractor.

(b) The small claims procedure shall provide for simplified rules of procedure to facilitate the decision of any appeal thereunder. Such appeals may be decided by a single member of the agency board with such concurrences as may be provided by rule or regulation.

(c) Appeals under the small claims procedure shall be resolved, whenever possible, within one hundred twenty days from the date on which the contractor elects to utilize such procedure.

(d) A decision against the Government or the contractor reached under the small claims procedure shall be final and conclusive and shall not be set aside except in cases of fraud.

(e) Administrative determinations and final decisions under this section shall have no value as precedent for future cases under this Act.

(f) The Administrator is authorized to review at least every three years, beginning with the third year after the enactment of the Act, the dollar amount defined in section 9 (a) as a small claim, and based upon economic indexes selected by the Administrator, adjust that level accordingly.

ACTIONS IN COURT: JUDICIAL REVIEW OF BOARD DECISIONS

SEC. 10. (a) (1) Except as provided in paragraph (2), and in lieu of appealing the decision of the contracting officer under section 6 to an agency board, a contractor may bring an action directly on the claim in the United States Court of Claims, notwithstanding any contract provision, regulation, or rule of law to the contrary.

(2) In the case of an action against the Tennessee Valley Authority, the contractor may only bring an action directly on the claim in a United States district court pursuant to section 1337 of title 28, United States Code, notwithstanding any contract provision, regulation, or rule of law to the contrary.

(3) Any action under paragraph (1) or (2) shall be filed within twelve months from the date of the receipt by the contractor of the decision of the contracting officer concerning the claim, and shall proceed de novo in accordance with the rules of the appropriate court.

(b) In the event of an appeal by a contractor or the Government from a decision of any agency board pursuant to section 8, notwithstanding any contract provision, regulation, or rules of law to the contrary, the decision of the agency board on any question of law shall not be final or conclusive, but the decision on any question of fact shall be final and conclusive and shall not be set aside unless the decision is fraudulent, or arbitrary, or capricious, or so grossly erroneous as to necessarily imply bad faith, or if such decision is not supported by substantial evidence.

(c) In any appeal by a contractor or the Government from a decision of an agency board pursuant to section 8, the court may render an opinion and judgment and remand the case for further action by the agency board or by the executive agency as appropriate, with such direction as the court considers just the proper, or, in its discretion and in lieu of remand it may retain the case and take such additional evidence or action as may be necessary for final disposition of the case.

(d) If two or more suits arising from one contract are filed in the Court of Claims and one or more agency boards, for the convenience of parties or witnesses or in the interest of justice, the Court of Claims may order the consolidation of such suits in that court or transfer any suits to or among the agency boards involved.

(e) In any suit filed pursuant to this Act involving two or more claims, counterclaims, crossclaims, or third-party claims, and where a portion of one such claim can be divided for purposes of decision or judgment, and in any such suit where multiple parties are involved, the court, whenever such action is appropriate may enter a judgment as to one or more but fewer than all of the claims, portions thereof, or parties.

SUBPENA, DISCOVERY, AND DEPOSITION

SEC. 11. A member of an agency board of contract appeals may administer oaths to witnesses, authorize depositions and discovery proceedings, and require by subpena the attendance of witnesses, and production of books and papers, for the taking of testimony or evidence by deposition or in the hearing of an appeal by the agency board. In case of contumacy or refusal to obey a subpena by a person who resides, is found, or transacts business within the jurisdiction of a United States district court, the court, upon application of the agency board through the Attorney General; or upon application by the board of contract appeals of the Tennessee Valley Authority, shall have jurisdiction to issue the person an order requiring him to appear before the agency board or a member thereof, to produce evidence or to give testimony, or both. Any failure of any such person to obey the order of the court may be punished by the court as a contempt thereof.

INTEREST

SEC. 12. Interest on amounts found due contractors on claims shall be paid to the contractor from the date the contracting officer receives the claim pursuant to section 6 (a) from the contractor until payment thereof. The interest provided for in this section shall be paid at the rate established by the Secretary of the Treasury pursuant to Public Law 92-11 (85 Stat. 97) for the Renegotiation Board.

APPROPRIATIONS

SEC. 13. (a) Any judgment against the United States on a claim under this Act shall be paid promptly in accordance with the procedures provided by section 1302 of the Act of July 27, 1956, (70 Stat. 694, as amended; 31 U.S.C. 724a).

(b) Any monetary award to a contractor by an agency board of contract appeals shall be paid promptly in accordance with the procedures contained in subsection (a) above.

(c) Payments made pursuant to subsections (a) and (b) shall be reimbursed to the fund provided by section 1302 of the Act of July 27, 1956, (70 Stat. 694, as amended; 31 U.S.C. 724a) by the agency whose appropriations were used for the contract out of available funds or by obtaining additional appropriations for such purposes.

(d) (1) Notwithstanding the provisions of subsection (a) through (c), any judgment against the Tennessee Valley Authority on a claim under this Act shall be paid promptly in accordance with the provisions of section 9 (b) of the Tennessee Valley Authority Act of 1933 (16 U.S.C. 831 (h)).

(2) Notwithstanding the provisions of subsection (a) through (c), any monetary award to a contractor by the board of contract appeals for the Tennessee Valley Authority shall be paid in accordance with the provisions of section 9 (b) of the Tennessee Valley Authority Act of 1933 (16 U.S.C. 831 (h)).

AMENDMENTS AND REPEALS

SEC. 14. (a) The first sentence of section 1346 (a) (2) of title 28, Undited States Code, is amended by inserting before the period a comma and the following: "except that the district courts shall not have jurisdiction of any civil action or claim against the United States founded upon any express or implied contract with the United States or for liquidated or unliquidated damages in cases not sounding in tort which are subject to sections 8 (g) (1) and 10 (a) (1) of the Contract Disputes Act of 1978".

(b) Section 2401 (a) of title 28, United States Code, is amended by striking out "Every" at the beginning and inserting in lieu thereof "Except as provided by the Contract Disputes Act of 1978, every. . ."

(c) Section 1302 of the Act of July 27, 1956, as amended (70 Stat. 694, as amended; 31 U.S.C. 724 a), is amended by adding after "2677 of title 28" the words "and decisions of boards of contract appeals".

(d) Section 2414 of title 28, United States Code, is amended by striking out "Payment" at the beginning and inserting in lieu thereof "Except as provided by the Contract Disputes Act of 1978, payment. . ."

(e) Section 2517 (a) of title 28, Undited States Code, is amended by striking out "Every" at the beginning and inserting in lieu thereof "Except as provided by the Contract Disputes Act of 1978, every. . ."

(f) Section 2517 (b) of title 28, United States Code, is amended by inserting after "case or controversy" the following, "unless the judgment is designated at partial judgment, in which event only the matters described therein shall be discharged,".

(g) There shall be added to subsection (c) of section 5108 of title 5, United States Code, a paragraph (17) reading as follows:

"(17) the heads of executive departments or agencies in which boards of contract appeals are established pursuant to the Contract Disputes Act of 1978, and subject to the standards and procedures prescribed by this chapter, but without regard to subsection (d) of this section, may place additional positions, not to exceed seventy in number, in GS-16, GS-17, and GS-18 for the independent quasi-judicial determination of contract disputes, with the allocation of such positions among such executive departments and agencies determined by the Administrator for Federal Procurement Policy on the basis of relative case load."

(h) (1) Section 2510 of title 28, United States Code is amended by—

(A) inserting "(a)" immediately before such section; and

(B) adding the following new subsection at the end thereof:

"(b) (1) The head of any executive department or agency may, with the prior approval of the Attorney General, refer to the Court of Claims for judicial review any final decision rendered by a board of contract appeals pursuant to the terms of any contract with the United States awarded by that department or agency which such head of such department or agency has concluded is not entitled to finality pursuant to the review standards specified in section 10 (b) of the Contracts Disputes Act of 1978. The head of each executive department or agency shall make any referral under this section within one hundred twenty days of the receipt of a copy of the final appeal decision.

"(2) The Court of Claims shall review the matter referred in accordance with the standards specified in section 10 (b) of the Contracts Disputes Act of 1978. The Court shall proceed with judicial review on the administrative record made before the board of contract appeals on matters so referred as in other cases pending in such court, shall determine the issue of finality of the appeal decision, and shall, as appropriate, render judgment thereon, take additional evidence, or remand the matter pursuant to the authority specified in section 1491 of this title".

(2) (A) The section heading of such section is amended to read as follows:

"§ 2510. Referral of cases by the Comptroller General or the head of an executive department or agency.".

(B) The item relating to section 2510 in the table of sections for chapter 165 of title 28, United States Code, is amended to read as follows:

"2510. Referral of cases by the Comptroller General or the head of an executive department or agency.".

(i) Section 1491 of title 28, United States Code, is amended by adding the following sentence at the end of the first paragraph thereof: "The Court of Claims shall have jurisdiction to render judgment upon any claim by or against, or dispute with, a contractor arising under the Contract Disputes Act of 1978.".

SEVERABILITY CLAUSE

SEC. 15. If any provision of this Act, or the application of such provision to any persons or circumstances, is held invalid, the remainder of this Act, or the application of such provision to persons or circumstances other than those to which it is held invalid, shall not be affected thereby.

EFFECTIVE DATE OF ACT

SEC. 16. This Act shall apply to contracts entered into one hundred twenty days after the date of enactment. Notwithstanding any provision in a contract made before the effective date of this Act, the contractor may elect to proceed under this Act with respect to any claim pending then before the contracting officer or initiated thereafter.

Speaker of the House of Representatives.

Vice President of the United States and President of the Senate.

I certify that this Act originated in the House of Representatives.

Clerk

4a. Associated General Contractors of America, Contractor's Equipment Manual, (excerpts)

CONTRACTORS' EQUIPMENT MANUAL

THE ASSOCIATED GENERAL CONTRACTORS OF AMERICA

Seventh Edition 1974

FOREWORD

Construction equipment such as cranes, dredges, trucks, and other heavy equipment is expensive. The equipment also has a limited useful life, a limited period of time in which it can be used economically on commercial projects. When the useful life of a piece of equipment is at an end, the equipment may be replaced and it should have produced enough earnings to cover the cost of a replacement. It is essential, therefore, that a contractor be able to estimate what it costs to own and maintain the equipment during its useful life. These aspects of the cost of equipment are identified as the cost of ownership and the cost of repair and maintenance in order to isolate them from costs such as operating labor, fuel, lubrication and expendable equipment supplies.

In 1920 the Associated General Contractors of America, Inc. published its first study of the expenses a contractor would be expected to incur in owning equipment in his construction activities. The study was revised and enlarged in 1930 and again in 1938. A supplement was published in 1944. Third, fourth, fifth, and sixth revisions followed successively in 1949, 1956, 1962, and 1966. Changes since 1966 in equipment and in construction practices have made the seventh revision necessary.

The tables that constitute the manual are a composite of information obtained from interviews, written responses to questions, and relevant literature. A representative cross-section of contractors, selected according to size, work volume, and kind of construction work performed, was interviewed. A summary of responses to interview questions was sent to other contractors for validation and written responses were received from them. A representative number of contractors experienced in the use and ownership of equipment thus contributed information on which this edition of the manual is based. This data base was reviewed by a special committee of AGC members to assure that the manual adhered to all AGC objectives and principles.

Contributors to the manual and members of the special committee wished it emphasized that the manual is only a guide and that the figures which appear in it are weighted averages. The individual contractor in using the manual should adapt the figures to his circumstances and conditions of use. The number of hours of useful life to be assigned to identical pieces of equipment, for instance, will vary. Useful life is influenced by weather conditions, the length of the construction season in the geographic area in which a piece of equipment will be used, the severity of working conditions in the area, the maintenance and servicing programs of the contractor, and other factors. In estimating the cost of ownership for a particular piece of equipment, a contractor may start with the averages presented in the manual, but he should then modify them to reflect his own practices and experiences.

This seventh edition lists the equipment types and sizes in the categories generally in use as construction equipment. Equipment units designed specially to meet unique job requirements are not included in the listings.

The hours included in the equipment listings are averages developed from the records and experience of contractors owning and operating such units of equipment. The rates for the equipment ownership expense items - depreciation, replacement cost escalation, interest on capital invested, and taxes, insurance and storage costs - are expressed as average percentages of the original acquisition cost of new equipment as purchased from a manufacturer or dealer. This document does not identify equipment prices. Further, the percentage rates contain no element of profit or general and administrative overhead expense.

The AGC Contractors' Equipment Ownership Expense Manual has gained acceptance in industry as a guide. It has served to alert contractors to the elements included in equipment ownership expenses, and it has provided a source of data in evaluating such expenses for equipment not always used in their particular operations.

USE OF THE MANUAL

THIS DOCUMENT SHOULD BE USED WITH THE UNDER-
STANDING THAT:

1. IT IS NOT A SCHEDULE OF RENTAL RATES.
2. IT IS A COMPILATION OF DATA ON THE AVERAGE
    COSTS OF OWNING AND MAINTAINING CONSTRUC-
    TION EQUIPMENT.
3. IT IS INTENDED AS A GUIDE ONLY, AND THE HOURS
    ASSIGNED TO TYPES OF EQUIPMENT AND ALL PER-
    CENTAGE RATES ARE AVERAGES, SUBJECT TO
    ADJUSTMENT TO FIT THE EXPERIENCE OF INDIVI-
    DUAL EQUIPMENT OWNERS.
4. NO ALLOWANCE FOR EQUIPMENT RENTAL OR
    LEASE COSTS, JOB OVERHEAD, GENERAL AND
    ADMINISTRATION, OR PROFIT IS INCLUDED IN ANY
    OF THE FIGURES LISTED IN THE SEVERAL CATE-
    GORIES OF EQUIPMENT OWNERSHIP EXPENSE IN
    THIS MANUAL.

ANNUAL EQUIPMENT OWNERSHIP EXPENSE

Those items of equipment cost which cannot ordinarily be directly allocated to specific projects undertaken during the ownership period are considered ownership expenses. As identified in this manual, ownership expense represents only one element of the total use rate* normally charged for contractor owned equipment while assigned to a project.

The annual equipment ownership expense, as identified in this manual, includes depreciation, replacement cost escalation, interest on the investment, taxes, insurance and storage. These six elements are expressed as annual percentages of the original acquisition cost of each unit of equipment as purchased new from a manufacturer or dealer (hereafter referred to as acquisition cost). This acquisition cost includes sales tax, the charges for transportation from the point of origin (factory, distributor's sales yard, etc.), to the point of receipt (contractor's yard, job site, etc.), and the cost of erection and making ready for use at the point of receipt. Any similar expenses incurred after the initial set-up are considered operating costs.

DEPRECIATION

Depreciation is defined as a measure of the declining value of property due to age and use. In this manual depreciation for each unit of equipment is based on its total acquisition cost which includes: 1) the purchase price, 2) sales tax, 3) charges for transportation from the point of origin to the point of receipt, and 4) charges for erection of the unit at the point of receipt. The acquisition cost of the unit of equipment should include all accessories and expendable components required for a specific equipment utilization. As an example, the acquisition cost would include: 1) the ripper attachments purchased with a crawler tractor, and 2) the original tires on a wheeled vehicle. Alternate and supplemental attachments are listed in a separate category in the manual; i.e., under tractor attachments.

In this manual depreciation of the acquisition cost, less salvage value, if any, of a unit of equipment is scheduled on the straight-line method

---

* Use rates as designated in this manual are distinctive from the rent paid to organizations engaged in leasing or renting equipment whose fees include allowances for the cost of equipment cleanup after rental, business overhead and profits.

based on the average economic life of the unit expressed in years. The average economic life in years is determined by dividing the average economic life in hours by the average use hours per year.

An average salvage value of 10 percent of the new acquisition cost has been used in preparing this manual for all units of equipment except those which, through normal usage, deteriorate or wear out to the point where the cost of reconditioning them exceeds the value of the unit on the used equipment market. Those units of equipment identified in the tabulations by an asterisk have "no salvage."

REPLACEMENT COST ESCALATION

In the earlier editions of this manual, variations in the purchasing power of the dollar were not considered significant over the relatively short life span of most units of construction equipment. No additional costs, therefore, were assigned to this element of ownership expense.

The trend of the country's economy indicates that the purchasing power of the dollar can no longer be considered fixed, even over a short period of time. A factor should therefore be included under ownership expense which will allow a unit of equipment to generate sufficient capital during its economic life to insure its replacement at the end of the depreciation period by a unit equal in all respects to the original unit.

The stated replacement cost escalation factor of 7 percent of the acquisition cost of the unit of equipment is an estimate of the average future increase in the price of new equipment. The percentage may vary from year to year. When assigned annually to the ownership expense of the unit it should allow for "like kind" replacement of the unit at the end of the depreciation period. Funds generated by the use of the factor will not be sufficient to purchase a replacement unit of equipment which has been "updated" through innovations and changes. Therefore such cost increases beyond those resulting solely from escalation should be assigned to equipment units for "updates" incorporated into the equipment units.

INTEREST ON INVESTMENT

The investment referred to is that which a contractor has in a unit of equipment and the interest is his average cost of obtaining a loan and/or using his capital for the investment.

In this manual the interest rate listed for each unit of equipment is expressed on an annual basis as a percentage of the acquisition cost. It is calculated to equal the interest generated on the average invest- ment at an interest rate of 11 percent, based on a banking prime rate of 9 percent plus 2 percent added as a private lender markup. This rate does not, however, include the added borrowing cost of required compensating balances.

The following formula was used to develop the annual percentage of the new acquisition cost of a unit of equipment. When applied each year over the depreciation period, it should generate the total inter- est due.

$$\text{Annual } \% = r \left[n+1 + s(n-1) \right] \div 2n$$

where: r = interest rate charged (prime rate + markup) as a percent.
n = equipment life in years.
s = salvage value as a decimal.

The examples below illustrate the use of the formula in calculating annual interest rate percentages for 1) a unit of equipment having a depreciation period of three years and no salvage value, and 2) a unit of equipment having a depreciation period of five years, and a salvage value of 10 percent.

1) $\text{Annual } \% = 11 \left[3+1 + 0(3-1) \right] \div 2(3) = 7.33\%$

2) $\text{Annual } \% = 11 \left[5+1 + .1(5-1) \right] \div 2(5) = 7.04\%$

The following table identifies the annual interest rate percentages used in this manual as calculated from the formula and rounded off to the nearest 0.5 percent.

Equipment Life Years	Salvage Value Percent	Annual Interest Rate Percent
2	0	8.5
3	0	7.5
4	10	7.5
5 thru 9	10	7.0
10 thru 20	10	6.5

TAXES, INSURANCE AND STORAGE

The costs of taxes, insurance and storage are entered in the manual as an average annual expense of 4.5 percent of the acquisition cost for all units, except marine equipment.

The annual tax rate covering property taxes and use taxes for all units of equipment in this manual is taken at 1.5 percent of the acquisition cost.

Insurance expense is the annual cost of premiums covering the units of equipment included in this manual. The risks covered include such items as fire and theft, property damage and third party liability. The average annual rate for insurance for all units included in the manual, except marine equipment, is considered to be 1.0 percent of the acquisition cost.

Storage expense includes the costs associated with storing equipment between successive jobs or operations. It includes the occupancy and maintenance costs of storage warehouses and/or yards, the wages of watchmen, the direct overhead involved in providing storage facilities, and the costs of transporting equipment to and from storage sites and handling it in and out of storage. In this manual the average annual storage expense for all units, except marine equipment, is taken at 2 percent of the acquisition cost.

Marine equipment operating at inland locations was assigned an additional 3.5 percent in this expense category - 1.0 percent more for storage costs and 2.5 percent more for insurance premiums - for a total of 8.0 percent. Coastal based units of marine equipment were assigned an additional 1.0 percent on insurance premiums for a total of 9.0 percent.

Storage costs vary over wide ranges from one section of the country to another in all construction operations, including inland and coastal marine operations. Adjustment for this element of equipment ownership expense, as for other elements, should be made by the user of this manual to meet the conditions in the storage area.

TOTAL ANNUAL OWNERSHIP EXPENSE

The total annual ownership expense is the sum of the percentages of depreciation*, replacement cost escalation, the interest on investment, **and taxes, insurance and storage, expressed as a percentage of the acquisition cost of each unit of equipment.**

---

* The annual depreciation percent used in this manual is equal to 100 percent of the acquisition cost less 10 percent salvage value, where applicable, divided by the average economic life in years.

EQUIPMENT	Average Economic Life In Hours	Average Use Hours Per Year	Average Annual Ownership Expense in % of New Acquisition Cost					Average Hourly Ownership Expense in % of New Acquisition Cost	Average Hourly Repair & Maintenance Expense in % of New Acquisition Cost	Combined Average Hourly Ownership and Repair & Maintenance Expenses in % of New Acquisition Cost	Contractor's Application of A.G.C. Schedules
			Depreciation	Replacement Cost Escalation	Interest on Investment	Taxes, Insurance and Storage	Total Ownership Expense				
Air Compressors, Portable High Pressure-free air delivered at 100 psi two stage and single stage, water or air cooled.											
Gasoline											
20-185 cfm	4400	1100	*25.0	7.0	7.5	4.5	44.0	0.0400	0.0272	0.0672	
210-250 cfm	5500	1100	18.0	7.0	7.0	4.5	36.5	0.0331	0.0127	0.0458	
Diesel											
78-185 cfm	9600	1200	11.2	7.0	7.0	4.5	29.7	0.0247	0.0173	0.0420	
210-1200 cfm	11200	1600	12.8	7.0	7.0	4.5	31.3	0.0195	0.0148	0.0343	
1400-2000 cfm	12800	1600	11.2	7.0	7.0	4.5	29.7	0.0185	0.0103	0.0288	
Air Compressor, Self-Propelled Free air at 100 psi, wheel mounted, gasoline or diesel.											
125-250 cfm	4400	1100	22.5	7.0	7.5	4.5	41.5	0.0377	0.0208	0.0585	
Air Compressors, Stationary High Pressure, with gasoline or electric motor and belt or coupling.											
46-160 cfm piston displacement	6600	1100	15.0	7.0	7.0	4.5	33.5	0.0304	0.0065	0.0369	
215-600 cfm piston displacement	9600	1600	15.0	7.0	7.0	4.5	33.5	0.0209	0.0065	0.0274	
600-1800 cfm piston displacement	14000	2000	12.8	7.0	7.0	4.5	31.3	0.0156	0.0065	0.0221	

* No Salvage

Modular, High Pressure										
to 300 cfm	9600	1600	15.0	7.0	7.0	4.5	33.5	0.0209	0.0065	0.0274
300 to 1900 cfm	14000	2000	12.8	7.0	7.0	4.5	31.3	0.0156	0.0065	0.0221
Low Pressure, with electric motor and belt or coupling; 50 psi & under 900-2100 cfm piston displacement	14000	2000	12.8	7.0	7.0	4.5	31.3	0.0156	0.0065	0.0221
Modular, Low Pressure 1000-3900 cfm	15200	1900	11.2	7.0	7.0	4.5	29.7	0.0156	0.0065	0.0221
Air Tools and Accessories										
Drills, Rotating										
Close-quarter, 7/8-2 in. diam.	2200	1100	*50.0	7.0	8.5	4.5	70.0	0.0636	0.0271	0.0907
Drifter, all sizes (see "Tunnel Equip.")										
Metal, 1/2-3 in. diam.	2200	1100	*50.0	7.0	8.5	4.5	70.0	0.0636	0.0712	0.1348
Drills, Wagon										
Crawler mounted, self-propelled all sizes	8000	1600	*20.0	7.0	7.0	4.5	38.5	0.0240	0.0271	0.0511
Wheel mounted, towed, all sizes	5500	1100	*20.0	7.0	7.0	4.5	38.5	0.0350	0.0288	0.0638
Grinder (see also "Surface Grinders")										
Concrete surfacing	3300	1100	*33.3	7.0	7.5	4.5	52.3	0.0475	0.0756	0.1231
Hammers										
Pavement breaking, 20-106 lb.	3300	1100	*33.3	7.0	7.5	4.5	52.3	0.0475	0.0449	0.0924
Sheeting driver, to 120 lb.	3300	1100	*33.3	7.0	7.5	4.5	52.3	0.0475	0.0082	0.0557
Sheeting driver, over 120 lb.	4200	1400	*33.3	7.0	7.5	4.5	52.3	0.0373	0.0084	0.0457
Hoists (see also "Hoists, Power")										
500 lb., single drum	8400	1400	*16.7	7.0	7.0	4.5	35.2	0.0251	0.0201	0.0452
750-8000 lb., single drum	9600	1200	11.2	7.0	7.0	4.5	29.7	0.0247	0.0194	0.0441
1250-2400 lb., double drum	9600	1200	11.2	7.0	7.0	4.5	29.7	0.0247	0.0172	0.0419
2400-5000 lb., double drum	9600	1200	11.2	7.0	7.0	4.5	29.7	0.0247	0.0132	0.0379
Jackhammer										
Small, medium or large	3600	1200	*33.3	7.0	7.5	4.5	52.3	0.0435	0.0664	0.1099
Pump, Sump										
Small, medium or tandem	2200	1100	*50.0	7.0	8.5	4.5	70.0	0.0636	0.0340	0.0976

EQUIPMENT	Average Economic Life In Hours	Average Use Hours Per Year	Average Annual Ownership Expense in % of New Acquisition Cost					Average Hourly Ownership Expense in % of New Acquisition Cost	Average Hourly Repair & Maintenance Expense in % of New Acquisition Cost	Combined Average Hourly Ownership and Repair & Maintenance Expenses in % of New Acquisition Cost	Contractor's Application of A.G.C. Schedules
			Depreciation	Replacement Cost Escalation	Interest on Investment	Taxes, Insurance and Storage	Total Ownership Expense				
Receiver 50-1275 cu. ft	11200	1400	*12.5	7.0	7.0	4.5	31.0	0.0221	0.0016	0.0237	
Sharpening Equipment – Forge	12000	2000	15.0	7.0	7.0	4.5	33.5	0.0167	0.0158	0.0325	
Forging Machine	16000	2000	11.3	7.0	7.0	4.5	29.8	0.0149	0.0158	0.0307	
Tamper Backfill, all sizes, air and hydraulic	3300	1100	*33.3	7.0	7.5	4.5	52.3	0.0475	0.0616	0.1091	
Vibrators Standard or heavy duty, motor in head	2000	1000	*50.0	7.0	8.5	4.5	70.0	0.0700	0.1050	0.1750	
Flexible type, 20-115 lb.	2000	1000	*50.0	7.0	8.5	4.5	70.0	0.0700	0.1050	0.1750	
Rigid type, all sizes	2000	1000	*50.0	7.0	8.5	4.5	70.0	0.0700	0.1050	0.1750	
Wrenches, impact (without sockets) Standard type: 1-1/4 – 4 in. bolt size capacity	3000	1000	*33.3	7.0	7.5	4.5	52.3	0.0523	0.0546	0.1069	
Controlled torque, 3/8 – 2 in.	2000	1000	*50.0	7.0	8.5	4.5	70.0	0.0700	0.0527	0.1227	
Automobiles – (see also "Trucks") Light	4000	2000	45.0	7.0	8.5	4.5	65.0	0.0325	0.0207	0.0532	
Medium	5000	2000	36.0	7.0	8.5	4.5	56.0	0.0280	0.0201	0.0481	
Heavy	6000	2000	30.0	7.0	7.5	4.5	49.0	0.0245	0.0186	0.0431	

* No Salvage

Bituminous Equipment									
Base Paver, self-propelled	6000	1000	15.0	7.0	7.0	4.5	33.5	0.0335	0.0158	0.0493
Brooms										
For tractor mounting	3000	500	*16.7	7.0	7.0	4.5	35.2	0.0704	0.0272	0.0976
Towed, engine driven	3000	500	*16.7	7.0	7.0	4.5	35.2	0.0704	0.0863	0.1567
Towed, traction driven	3000	500	*16.7	7.0	7.0	4.5	35.2	0.0704	0.0313	0.1017
Self-propelled	4800	800	15.0	7.0	7.0	4.5	35.2	0.0440	0.0395	0.0835
Distributors										
Truck mounting, pump to 400 gpm, 800-5000 gal. tank	6600	1100	15.0	7.0	7.0	4.5	33.5	0.0304	0.0346	0.0650
Trailer mounted, pump to 400 gpm, 1250-5000 gal. tank	6600	1100	15.0	7.0	7.0	4.5	33.5	0.0304	0.0426	0.0730
Finishing Machines (Pavers)										
Crawler mounted, self-propelled, diesel or gasoline										
10,000-16,000 lb. wt. class	6000	1000	15.0	7.0	7.0	4.5	33.5	0.0335	0.0730	0.1065
17,000-42,000 lb. wt. class	7000	1000	12.9	7.0	7.0	4.5	31.4	0.0314	0.0683	0.0997
Pneumatic tired, self-propelled, diesel or gasoline										
10,000-16,000 lb. wt. class	6000	1000	15.0	7.0	7.0	4.5	33.5	0.0335	0.0530	0.0865
17,000-36,000 lb. wt. class	7000	1000	12.9	7.0	7.0	4.5	31.4	0.0314	0.0530	0.0844
Heater, tank car, 2 or 4 wheel, one to three car capacity	8000	1000	*12.5	7.0	7.0	4.5	31.0	0.0310	0.0218	0.0528
Heater, combination circulating and steam tank car heater, mounted on trailer or truck	8000	1000	*12.5	7.0	7.0	4.5	31.0	0.0310	0.0171	0.0481
Mixing Plants; gasoline, diesel or electric										
Batch Type Mill										
2,000 - 5,000 lb. pug mill	8000	1000	12.5	7.0	7.0	4.5	31.0	0.0310	0.0267	0.0577
5,000 - 9,700 lb. pug mill	10000	1000	9.0	7.0	6.5	4.5	27.0	0.0270	0.0267	0.0537
9,700 - 12,000 lb. pug mill	10000	1000	9.0	7.0	6.5	4.5	27.0	0.0270	0.0235	0.0505
15,000 lb. pug mill	10000	1000	9.0	7.0	6.5	4.5	27.0	0.0270	0.0146	0.0416
Continuous Mix Type										
Factory Rating										
30-65 tph	6000	1000	15.0	7.0	7.0	4.5	33.5	0.0335	0.0146	0.0481

4b. Rental Rate Blue Book, Equipment Guide-Book Co. (excerpts)

RENTAL RATE
BLUE BOOK

**The Standard Reference
for
Rental Rates on All Classes
of Construction Equipment**

**Researched and Published to
meet the needs of the
construction industry in**

**RENTAL AGREEMENTS — CONSTRUCTION CONTRACTS
FORCE ACCOUNTS — CLAIM WORK — LITIGATION
COST ACCOUNTING**

**Published
by**

**Nielsen/DATAQUEST, Inc.
2800 W. Bayshore Road, Palo Alto, California 94303
P.O. Box 10113   Phone (415) 856-9100**

The Rental Rate Blue Book is a continuous service of Machinery Information Div. of Nielsen/DATAQUEST, Inc. Subscribers are mailed current revisions of each handbook section on a regular basis throughout the term of their subscription, and are entitled to explanations and quick reference data by the research staff of Rental Rate Blue Book.

Extraordinary research of rental rate guidelines from telephone, written, or other requests must be charged on a time and expense basis. The right to consulting services is not included in the price of subscription.

Subscribers must notify DATAQUEST, Machinery Information Division immediately upon CHANGE OF ADDRESS in order to ensure prompt delivery of current revisions and the monthly Equipment Guide News, provided free of charge to the subscribers of Rental Rate Blue Book.

Nielsen/DATAQUEST, Inc.
2800 West Bayshore Road
Palo Alto, California 94303
P.O. Box 10113   Phone (415) 856-9100

RENTAL RATE BLUE BOOK
FOR
CONSTRUCTION EQUIPMENT

§1, INTRODUCTION

EAE replaces EAY

1981 Equipment Guide-Book Div. of Nielsen/DATAQUEST
Rental Rate Blue Book

INTRODUCTION

The Rental Rate Blue Book for Construction Equipment is a comprehensive, current guide to cost recovery for equipment manufactured during the past five years. The rates in this manual are intended as guidelines paralleling amounts an equipment owner should charge during rental or contractual periods to recover all equipment-related costs.

These rates are derived from cost formulae and factors developed from our own research and from analytic methods used in the construction industry. Generally, these methods consider purchase price, depreciation, maintenance costs, overhead costs, and average annual use hours. Specific market conditions, such as local supply and demand, are not considered in these calculations. These rates are not a tabulation of rates being charged nationally. They do not reflect rates being charged by rental companies, except by coincidence.

The publication of these rates is not intended to influence the construction equipment rental market as a whole. To enter into agreement, combination, understanding, or action with any person or party with intent to establish rental rates at specific levels in this or any other handbook may constitute a violation of Fair Trade Practices and be subject to prosecution.

This publication is designed to provide accurate and authoritative information in regard to the subject matter covered. It is sold with the understanding that the publisher is not engaged in rendering legal or accounting services. While all efforts have been made to assure total accuracy, the variable nature of the information and informational sources precludes any warranties of specific accuracy in any specific instance.

INTRODUCTION

RENTAL RATE STUCTURE: Definitions and Methodology

Rental rates are based on equipment ownership and operating costs. These costs include:

A) *Purchase price* (minus a salvage value of ten to twenty percent). The initial capital expenditure, including sales tax and freight, is the starting point and framework for developing rental rates. This cost is recovered over an established economic life. Depreciation, as applied in this context, is actually a capitalization of the purchase price over time; it is not to be confused with methods of depreciation used for accounting and/or taxation purposes. For equipment currently being manufactured, the Rental Rate Blue Book uses the manufacturer's latest list price. For discontinued equipment, the last published list price is used in conjunction with the current resale value as established by professional appraisers, dealer and auction sales transactions, and end users.

B) *Overhead.* Allowances are made for overhead costs that directly affect equipment ownership. These costs include interest on investment, insurance, property taxes, storage, administration, licenses, and support facilities. Since these costs vary among owners and locales, a precise breakdown of these separate expenses is unrealistic. Therefore, a single percentage of the purchase price is used to cover these costs.

C) *Overhaul.* An allowance for overhaul costs is necessary to keep equipment in good operating condition throughout its economic life. This includes the periodic rebuilding of engines, transmissions, undercarriages, etc. Premature rebuilding of major components to maximize uptime is not a part of these calculations.

This total investment in equipment is annualized and then adjusted for the annual working season to obtain a monthly rental rate. Weekly, daily, and hourly rates are then derived from monthly rates, with a minimal percentage added to account for increased costs during shorter rental periods.

INTRODUCTION

AREA ADJUSTMENT MAPS

The area adjustment maps at the beginning of most sections are designed to show regional variations of average equipment ownership costs. The percentage by which the rental rates should be increased or decreased is calculated from computer analysis of several factors that influence ownership costs. These factors include local mechanics' labor, sales tax, freight, and climate. The most significant factor in regional variation is climate and its effect on the average annual use hours (the working "season"). A shorter working season means rates will be higher in order to recover fixed costs.

Information concerning regional variables is obtained from direct surveys of contractors and equipment users, government indexes, industry periodicals, and climatological and topographical maps. Every effort has been made to process and review this data for statistical certainty, but the research staff of Machinery Information Division, Nielsen/DATAQUEST, Inc. does not present these area adjustments as exact percentages or as well-defined locations. Whenever two or more figures surround a given locality, the users of these maps should refer to their own judgment and knowledge of their working area to decide which figure is most applicable.

Area adjustment percentages are meant to apply only to the rental rates; they are not intended to be adjustments to the "Estimated Operating Cost/Hour."

INTRODUCTION

ESTIMATED OPERATING COST PER HOUR

The estimated operating cost per hour includes the following expenses:

A)   The cost for *labor* and *parts* needed for routine, daily servicing of the equipment. This includes repairing and/or replacing small components such as pumps, carburetors, injectors, motors, filters, gaskets, and worn lines.

B)   The cost of operating expendables. These include *fuel*, computed in accordance with horsepower, duty cycle, and the price of fuel; *lubrications*, including filters, oil, and grease, as well as the labor involved in lubrication; *ground engaging components*, including tires, pads, blades, bucket teeth, etc. Tire costs are calculated by average tire life factors and take into consideration typical discounts from list prices. Electrical costs (where applicable) are calculated according to generally accepted duty cycles for the total motor load at $.04 per kilowatt hour.

Operator's wages are not included in the Estimated Operating Cost/Hour. Whenever operating costs are shown as "$...," not enough information has been received to justify an estimate.

The operating costs shown in the Rental Rate Blue Book are comparable to those listed in the Cost Reference Guide for Construction Equipment, whenever the codes for the sections are the same.

INTRODUCTION

HOW TO USE YOUR
RENTAL RATE BLUE BOOK

1. *Read the entire Introduction.* It contains information you need to use this book effectively.

2. Turn to the *Index* to find the section which has the type of equipment you are interested in.

3. Use the *Table of Contents* at the beginning of each section to locate the pages which cover the specific kind of equipment you are looking for.

4. Within a section, each type of equipment is listed in one of two ways.

    a. By manufacturer, in alphabetical order:

Model	Vibratory Drum Size	HP	Monthly
FERGUSON			
SP75DT	84"	120	$4,155.00
SP230T	78"	148	5,030.00
HYSTER			
C612B	72"	82	3,170.00
INGERSOLL-RAND			
SPF-42	72"	88	3,400.00
SPF-54	85"	109	4,825.00
SPF-60	100"	210	8,670.00

INTRODUCTION

HOW TO USE YOUR
RENTAL RATE BLUE BOOK

b. By size and type of equipment:

Rated Capy. (Tons)	Boom Length/ Type	HP	Monthly
155	70' (No. 22) w/Hammerhead	287	$17,170.00
165	70' T-1 (775)	289	19,440.00
175	60' Tubular w/Hammerhead	300	19,270.00

There are separate listings for gasoline, diesel, and/or electrical powered units for some equipment. Other specifications, such as transmission or bucket size, are given in order to facilitate equipment identification.

5. When HP is shown, it is the HP used for calculation of estimated operating costs per hour, or for identification of variations in like models of the same manufacturer. It is an estimated maximum continuous HP based on torque curves, BHP, Gross HP, power output curves, or other data available in manufacturers' specifications for the standard drive train. For motors, it is 1.341 times the kW rating or as listed by the manufacturer for a given RPM.

6. As cubic yard capacities of equipment vary with material and swell factors, comparisons will be kept consistent by using "struck capacity at an average weight of 3000 lbs. per cu. yd."

INTRODUCTION

HOW TO USE YOUR
RENTAL RATE BLUE BOOK

7.   Rental rates are given by the month, week, day, and hour for each piece of equipment as shown below:

Monthly	Weekly	Daily	Hourly	Estimated Operating Cost/Hr.
$115.00	$36.25	$10.20	$1.50	$1.50
130.00	42.00	11.80	1.75	1.90
165.00	52.50	14.70	2.20	2.30

8.   Rental rates should be increased or decreased to account for regional differences in cost of labor, freight, taxes, etc. The *percentage* by which basic rates should be increased or decreased is shown on the maps at the beginning of most sections. *Geology, topography, and climate, as they affect the average working season, are incorporated in these map adjustments.*

9.   To figure the *total cost per hour for renting a piece of equipment*, add the following items:

    Hourly Rental Rate for Equipment
    Rate for Attachments (where applicable)
    Estimated Operating Cost/Hr.
    Operator's Wages (including fringe benefits)
    Any other costs for operating or maintenance personnel required.

Remember that this total cost is a guideline. It is not meant to define the actual rate a lessor may charge. Also keep in mind that the actual rental rate may be increased or decreased by factors not taken into account in this book, such as unusually tough job conditions.

1981 Equipment Guide-Book Div. of Nielsen/DATAQUEST
Rental Rate Blue Book
EAE

INTRODUCTION

STANDARD INDUSTRY PRACTICES

RENTAL TERMS

Rental terms should be agreed upon by all parties prior to delivery of the unit. These terms should be spelled out in a written agreement between the LESSOR and the LESSEE. Absolute understanding should be reached on responsibilities pertaining to rental period, operating hours, rate basis, terms of payment, freight charges, taxes, insurance, cost of repairs, and mechanical condition of equipment. The agreement should be signed by both the LESSOR and the LESSEE.

RENTAL PERIOD

Rental rates usually begin at the LESSOR's warehouse and continue in effect until the equipment is returned to the warehouse. For out-of-town use, rates usually start on the date of the Shipment Bill of Lading and stop on the date of the return to the LESSOR's yard, or the date on Return Bill of Lading, whichever is stipulated by the LESSOR.

RENT BASIS

Average working periods are considered to be a regular single shift of eight hours per day — forty hours per week — 176 hours per month — for a total of twenty-two working days per thirty-day period.

INTRODUCTION

STANDARD INDUSTRY PRACTICES

OVERTIME

Overtime may be charged in one of two ways, depending upon the agreement:

1.   At the rate of 1/8th of the daily rate for each hour in excess of eight hours—1/40th of the weekly rate for each hour in excess of forty hours—1/176th of the monthly rate for each hour in excess of 176 hours within a thirty-day period.

2.   At 50% of the base rate for each additional eight-hour shift period: Two shifts—1-1/2 times the base rate. Three shifts—2 times the base rate. Fractions of a shift adjusted proportionally.

     Method "2" is most often used where the return for overtime is to be kept as close to "cost" as possible.

MECHANICAL CONDITION

The LESSOR is responsible for furnishing the equipment in good mechanical condition. The equipment should be inspected by the LESSEE, prior to signing the rental agreement.

On most rental agreements, the LESSEE acknowledges by his signature that the equipment is received in good condition.

INTRODUCTION

STANDARD INDUSTRY PRACTICES

COST OF REPAIR

The responsibility for the cost of repairs should be clearly understood by both parties and spelled out in the terms of the contract.

The rental rates set forth in this handbook are based on the following:

1. The LESSOR will pay all cost of repairs due to "normal wear and tear." The LESSEE bears all other costs.

    "Normal wear and tear" is defined as use of the equipment under normal working conditions, with qualified personnel providing proper operation, maintenance, and service.

2. Where it is known or expected that the equipment will be subject to conditions other than those described under "normal wear and tear," these general rates *cannot* apply and prior agreement of responsibility should be reached by the contracting parties. Particular attention should be given to conditions affecting rubber-tired hauling or crawler tractor equipment.

FREIGHT

Rental rates are F.O.B. LESSOR's warehouse, with the LESSEE paying all costs of freight and handling. Rental rates include the costs of dismantling and erecting machines, when required for transportation. Any additional charges incurred through loading or demurrage are paid by the LESSEE.

INTRODUCTION

ADDITIONAL CONSTRUCTION EQUIPMENT
REFERENCE GUIDES

Other publications related to the Rental Rate Blue Book are:

VALUE GUIDES

Rental Rate Blue Book for Older Equipment
Cost Reference Guide
Green Guide, Vol. 1
Green Guide, Vol. 2
Green Guide for Off-Highway Trucks and Trailers
Green Guide for Lift Trucks (Gas & Diesel)

SPECIFICATIONS BOOKS

Wheel & Crawler Tractors
Wheel & Crawler Loaders
Motor Graders
Motor Scrapers
Hydraulic Excavators
Hydraulic Cranes
Truck Cranes (Mechanical)
Crawler Cranes, Vol. 1
Crawler Cranes, Vol. 2
Crawler Cranes, Vol. 3
Off-Highway Haul Units
Compaction Equipment
Trenching Equipment
Log Skidders & Stackers
Lift Trucks, Vol. 1 (Gas & Diesel)
Lift Trucks, Vol. 2 (Gas & Diesel)
Personnel & Maintenance Elevating Lifts

TRACTORS & EARTHMOVING

TRACTOR — LOADER — BACKHOE
Standard Bucket Included
Gasoline Powered

Model	Capacity (Cu. Yd.)	Digging Depth	HP	Monthly	Weekly	Daily	Hourly	Estimated Operating Cost/Hr.
THE GENERAL								
LB-210	5/8	10' 2"	32.6	$1,140.00	$385.00	$120.00	$18.00	$4.15
INTERNATIONAL								
* 2412	3/4	12' 3"	46	940.00	320.00	99.25	14.90	5.15
* 2514 B	3/4	14' 0"	59	1,230.00	420.00	130.00	19.50	6.60
* 3400 A	3/4	14' 2"	58	835.00	285.00	88.25	13.20	6.00
* 3500 A	1-1/8	15' 5"	80	1,180.00	400.00	125.00	18.60	8.45
MASSEY FERGUSON								
* MF 20C	5/8	12' 2"	42	935.00	320.00	98.75	14.80	4.80
* MF 30	3/4	14' 1"	61	965.00	330.00	100.00	15.30	6.45
* MF 30B	3/4	12' 6"	42	1,015.00	345.00	105.00	16.00	4.95
* MF 40	5/8	11' 8"	42	870.00	295.00	91.75	13.80	4.75

* DISCONTINUED MODEL

TRACTORS & EARTHMOVING

TRACTOR — LOADER — BACKHOE
Standard Bucket Included
Diesel Powered

Model	Capacity (Cu. Yd.)	Digging Depth	HP	Monthly	Weekly	Daily	Hourly	Estimated Operating Cost/Hr.
ALLIS-CHALMERS								
714B	1	14' 0"	65	$2,075.00	$ 705.00	$220.00	$32.75	$5.80
* 715	7/8	14' 8"	65	1,215.00	415.00	130.00	19.20	4.85
715B	1	14' 7"	65	2,120.00	720.00	225.00	33.50	5.85
CASE								
480C CK	7/8	12' 0"	43	1,725.00	585.00	180.00	27.25	4.15
480D CK	7/8	12' 0"	43	1,910.00	650.00	200.00	30.25	4.40
* 580B	20 Cu. Ft.	14' 6"	43	1,085.00	370.00	115.00	17.10	3.50
580C CK	7/8	14' 0"	55	1,970.00	670.00	205.00	31.00	5.00
580D CK	7/8	14' 0"	55	2,230.00	760.00	235.00	35.25	5.40
580 Super D CK	7/8	14' 0"	55	2,405.00	820.00	255.00	38.00	5.60
* 680E CK	1-1/4	16' 6"	80	2,110.00	715.00	220.00	33.25	6.70
680G CK	1-1/4	16' 0"	80	3,045.00	1,035.00	320.00	48.00	7.65
780 CK	1-3/4	18' 0"	108	3,735.00	1,270.00	395.00	59.00	9.70

* DISCONTINUED MODEL

TRACTORS & EARTHMOVING

TRACTOR — LOADER — BACKHOE
Standard Bucket Included
Diesel Powered

Model	Capacity (Cu. Yd.)	Digging Depth	H.P.	Monthly	Weekly	Daily	Hourly	Estimated Operating Cost/Hr
DEERE								
* JD-310	5/8	15' 1''	52	$1,140.00	$ 390.00	$120.00	$ 18.10	$ 4.15
JD-310A	3/4	14' 7''	58	1,990.00	675.00	210.00	31.50	5.30
JD-410	1	15' 10''	66	2,215.00	755.00	235.00	35.00	6.05
JD-500C	1	15' 10''	80	2,875.00	975.00	305.00	45.50	7.60
JD-510	1-1/8	17' 0''	80	3,280.00	1,115.00	345.00	51.75	8.10
DYNAHOE (HY-DYNAMIC)								
140 III/140	1-1/4	14' 0''	90	2,345.00	800.00	245.00	37.00	7.45
160 III/160	1-1/2	16' 0''	90	3,415.00	1,160.00	360.00	54.00	8.55
190 III/190	1-1/2	19' 0''	95	3,765.00	1,280.00	395.00	59.50	9.20
190-4 III	1-3/4	19' 0''	126	4,805.00	1,635.00	505.00	76.00	12.10
200-4 III/200-4	2-1/4	20' 0''	163	6,395.00	2,175.00	675.00	100.00	16.15

* DISCONTINUED MODEL

© 1981 Equipment Guide-Book Div. of Nielsen/DATAQUEST
Rental Rate Blue Book

CAE

§9-63

TRACTORS & EARTHMOVING

TRACTOR — LOADER — BACKHOE
Standard Bucket Included
Diesel Powered

Model	Capacity (Cu. Yd.)		HP	Monthly	Weekly	Daily	Hourly	Estimated Operating Cost/Hr.
FORD								
340	16 Cu. Ft.	12' 0''	44.5	$1,595.00	$ 545.00	$170.00	$25.25	$4.10
* 420	16 Cu. Ft.	12' 0''	44.5	1,140.00	390.00	120.00	18.00	3.65
445	3/4	12' 0''	44	1,695.00	575.00	180.00	26.75	4.20
* 515	16 Cu. Ft.	12' 0''	56	1,200.00	410.00	125.00	19.00	4.25
* 535	1	15' 0''	56	1,305.00	445.00	135.00	20.60	4.40
545	3/4	12' 0''	56	1,880.00	640.00	200.00	29.75	4.90
* 550	1	13' 0''	56	1,395.00	475.00	145.00	22.10	4.60
555	1	14' 0''	56	2,150.00	730.00	225.00	34.00	5.35
* 650	1-1/4	15' 0''	71	1,440.00	490.00	150.00	22.80	5.55
* 750	1-1/2	17' 8''	89	2,180.00	740.00	230.00	34.50	7.35
755	1-1/2	17' 0''	89	3,160.00	1,075.00	335.00	50.00	8.35
THE GENERAL								
LB-480	1	14' 0''	60	2,465.00	840.00	260.00	39.00	5.90

* DISCONTINUED MODEL

1981 Equipment Guide-Book Div. of Nielsen/DATAQUEST
Rental Rate Blue Book

§9-64

CAE

TRACTORS & EARTHMOVING

SCRAPERS
SELF-PROPELLED
Diesel Powered

Model	Capy. (Cu. Yd.)	HP	Monthly	Weekly	Daily	Hourly	Estimated Operating Cost/Hr.
CATERPILLAR							
* 613	11	150	$ 3,205.00	$1,090.00	$ 340.00	$ 50.75	$12.80
613 "B"	11	150	5,365.00	1,825.00	565.00	84.75	15.50
621 "B"	14 - 20	330	10,760.00	3,660.00	1,135.00	170.00	32.40
623 "B"	22	330	11,545.00	3,925.00	1,215.00	182.50	33.95
627 "B" (Non-Push-Pull)	14 - 20	225/225	12,690.00	4,315.00	1,340.00	200.00	41.15
627 "B" (Push-Pull)	14 - 20	225/225	13,495.00	4,590.00	1,425.00	212.50	42.15
631 "D" (Cushion Hitch)	21 - 31	450	15,845.00	5,385.00	1,670.00	250.00	45.45
637 "D" (Non-Push-Pull)	21 - 31	450/225	19,545.00	6,645.00	2,060.00	310.00	62.80
637 "D" (Non-Push-Pull)	21 - 31	450/225	19,545.00	6,645.00	2,060.00	310.00	62.80

* DISCONTINUED MODEL

TRACTORS & EARTHMOVING

SCRAPERS
SELF-PROPELLED
Diesel Powered

Model	Capy. (Cu. Yd.)	HP	Monthly	Weekly	Daily	Hourly	Estimated Operating Cost/Hr.
CATERPILLAR (Cont.)							
637 "D" (Push-Pull)	21 - 31	450/225	$20,405.00	$6,940.00	$2,150.00	$322.50	$63.95
639 "D"	34	450/225	22,325.00	7,590.00	2,355.00	352.50	67.20
641 "B" (Cushion Hitch)	28 - 38	550	19,535.00	6,640.00	2,060.00	310.00	55.15
651 "B" (Cushion Hitch)	32 - 44	550	20,360.00	6,925.00	2,145.00	322.50	56.15
657 "B" (Non-Push-Pull)	32 - 44	550/400	25,185.00	8,560.00	2,655.00	397.50	84.25
657 "B" (Push-Pull)	32 - 44	550/400	26,725.00	9,085.00	2,815.00	422.50	86.30
* 660 "B"	40 - 54	550	12,880.00	4,380.00	1,355.00	202.50	52.25
* 666 "B"	40 - 54	550/400	15,015.00	5,105.00	1,585.00	237.50	75.85

* DISCONTINUED MODEL

T R A C T O R S & E A R T H M O V I N G

SCRAPERS
SELF-PROPELLED
Diesel Powered

Model	Capy. (Cu. Yd.)	HP	Monthly	Weekly	Daily	Hourly	Estimated Operating Cost/Hr.
CLARK							
110-9	9.5	160	$ 4,900.00	$1,665.00	$ 515.00	$ 77.50	$17.30
110-11B	11.0	174	5,535.00	1,885.00	585.00	87.50	19.50
* 110-15	15.0	225	5,660.00	1,925.00	595.00	89.50	23.60
110-15B	15.0	232	7,615.00	2,590.00	805.00	120.00	25.70
* 110H-T	16.0	140/140	6,465.00	2,200.00	680.00	102.50	28.25
110H-TB	16.0	140/140	9,895.00	3,365.00	1,045.00	157.50	30.90
* 210-H	23.0	300	7,755.00	2,635.00	815.00	122.50	31.35
210H-B	23.0	324	11,640.00	3,955.00	1,225.00	185.00	38.35

* DISCONTINUED MODEL

: 1981 Equipment Guide-Book Div. of Nielsen/DATAQUEST
Rental Rate Blue Book

T R A C T O R S & E A R T H M O V I N G

SCRAPERS
SELF-PROPELLED
Diesel Powered

Model	Capy. (Cu. Yd.)	HP	Monthly	Weekly	Daily	Hourly	Estimated Operating Cost/Hr.
DEERE							
* JD-760 "A"	9.5	152	$ 2,715.00	$ 925.00	$ 285.00	$ 43.00	$12.60
JD-762	11.0	175	5,495.00	1,870.00	580.00	87.00	17.05
* JD-860 "A"	15.0	215	4,720.00	1,605.00	495.00	74.50	18.80
JD-860 "B"	15.0	225	6,205.00	2,110.00	655.00	98.00	20.65
JD-862	16.0	250	7,490.00	2,545.00	790.00	117.50	23.40
FIAT-ALLIS							
161	15.0	229	6,885.00	2,340.00	725.00	110.00	21.70
260 B	15 - 21	325	9,595.00	3,260.00	1,010.00	152.50	30.40
261 B	23.0	325	10,535.00	3,580.00	1,110.00	167.50	32.45
262 B	15 - 21	325/171	11,710.00	3,980.00	1,235.00	185.00	41.95
263 B	23.0	326/171	13,110.00	4,460.00	1,380.00	207.50	44.15
* 460 C	24 - 33	422	7,900.00	2,685.00	835.00	125.00	35.70

* DISCONTINUED MODEL

1981 Equipment Guide-Book Div. of Nielsen/DATAQUEST
Rental Rate Blue Book

5. Findings of Fact and Decision by the Contracting Officer on a Claim Under a Federal Contract

UNITED STATES
DEPARTMENT OF THE INTERIOR
WATER AND POWER RESOURCES SERVICE

Engineering and Research Center
Denver Federal Center
Denver, Colorado 80225

June 9, 1980

IN THE MATTER OF CLAIM FOR ADDI-)
TIONAL COMPENSATION UNDER CON-)
TRACT NO. 8-07-DC-07292, DATED)   FINDINGS OF FACT
NOVEMBER 23, 1977, BETWEEN THE)   AND
UNITED STATES AND)   DECISION
CONSTRUCTION COMPANY, INC., FOR)   BY THE
MODIFICATION OF)   CONTRACTING OFFICER
SPECIFICATIONS NO.)
DC-7292, COLUMBIA BASIN PROJECT)

1. This findings of fact and decision is issued pursuant to the provisions of clause No. 6 of the General Provisions, as modified by the Supplement and Additional Supplement to the General Provisions, of the contract identified above.

2. Notice to proceed with the work was received by the contractor on November 29, 1977. Subparagraph 1.2.3.a. of the specifications requires completion of all contract work within 1005 calendar days after the date of receipt of notice to proceed, thereby establishing the date by which all work is required to be completed as August 30, 1980. The time for completion of the work has been extended by Order for Changes No. 9 (Part 1 of a 2-part Order) dated August 10, 1979, to and including April 30, 1981. As of the date of this findings of fact and decision, the contract work has not been completed.

3. The contractor, by letters dated August 7, 1979, and March 4, 1980, requested adjustments for changes in the cost of labor for his subcontractor. Adjustments for changes in the cost of labor are provided for under the provisions of specifications paragraph 1.3.7. Following receipt of these requests, the subcontract agreement between the contractor and, dated November 16, 1977, was reviewed by the Government and it was determined that the subcontract agreement did not specifically provide for adjustments for changes in the cost of labor as required by specifications paragraph 1.3.7. When advised of this by the Government's letter dated April 1, 1980, the contractor requested a formal decision by the contracting officer by letter of April 17, 1980.

4. Specifications subparagraph 1.3.7.a. provides that, "No adjustment will be made by reason of increased wages paid by any subcontractor unless the subcontract specifically states that the contractor will reimburse the subcontractor for the payment of such increased wages, and the amount of such adjustment is passed on to the subcontractor." The subcontract agreement between the contractor and the subcontractor does not include a statement that the contractor will reimburse the subcontractor for payment of increased wages and that the amount of such adjustment will be passed on to the subcontractor, nor does it contain a specific reference to paragraph 1.3.7. In his letter dated August 7, 1979, the contractor states that he was aware of the requirements of specifications subparagraph 1.3.7.a. and maintains that section A

of the subcontract agreement with specifically incorporates the plans and specifications of the prime contract into the subcontract as if fully set forth therein. Section A of the subcontract agreement provides, in part, "The parties hereto agree that the Plans and Specifications referred to above and all other documents constituting, or by reference made part of the prime contract, the attached general conditions, numbered as pages 1 through 3, and the following listed special conditions, exhibits and attachments, are hereby specifically incorporated by reference into this subcontract as if fully set forth herein: * * *". Except for the general reference to the plans and specifications in Section A of the agreement, the agreement does not include a specific reference to specifications paragraph 1.3.7 although various other paragraphs and provisions of Specifications No. DC-7292 are listed thereunder and on the general conditions attached thereto.

5. The requirements of specifications paragraph 1.3.7 were discussed with representatives of the contractor at the preconstruction conference on December 14, 1977. Although subcontract agreements between the contractor and the contractor and various other firms were executed prior to or on the date of the conference, several of the other subcontract agreements specifically refer to the adjustment for changes in the cost of labor provided for by paragraph 1.3.7 of the specifications. Therefore, the inclusion of the labor wage adjustment in subcontract agreements by specific reference in some cases and by a general reference in others is inconsistent and appears to render the contractor's argument invalid.

6. After a careful review of all the facts and circumstances, it is found that the subcontract agreement between the contractor and does not specifically state that the contractor will reimburse the subcontractor for the payment of increased wages and that adjustments will be passed on to the subcontractor as required by specifications paragraph 1.3.7. Further, it is found that the language contained in section A of the General Conditions of the subcontract agreement does not specifically refer to paragraph 1.3.7 of the specifications nor does the subcontract agreement mention adjustment for increased wages. Accordingly, it is determined that no adjustment can be made by reason of increased wages under the subcontract and the contractor's claim is hereby denied.

7. This final decision is made in accordance with the Disputes clause and shall be final and conclusive as provided therein, unless within 30 days from the date of receipt of this decision a written notice of appeal (in triplicate) addressed to the Secretary of the Interior is mailed or otherwise furnished to the contracting officer. The notice of appeal, which is to be signed by you as the contractor or by an attorney acting on your behalf, and which may be in letter form, should indicate that an appeal is intended, should refer to this decision, and should identify the contract by number. The notice of appeal may include a statement of the reasons why the decision is considered to be erroneous. The Interior Board of Contract Appeals is the authorized representative of the Secretary of the Interior for hearing and determining such disputes. A copy of the regulations governing contract appeals is attached to the contractor's copy of this findings.

Deputy Assistant Commissioner
Engineering and Research
(Contracting Officer)

6. Decision by a Federal Board of Contract Appeals

United States Department of the Interior

OFFICE OF HEARINGS AND APPEALS
INTERIOR BOARD OF CONTRACT APPEALS
4015 WILSON BOULEVARD
ARLINGTON, VIRGINIA 22203

APPEAL OF CONSTRUCTION CO., INC.

IBCA-1380-8-80   Decided: February 19, 1981

Contract No. 8-07-DC-   :
Water & Power Resources Service   : Denied

APPEARANCE FOR APPELLANT: Vice President & General Counsel
                                     Construction Co., Inc.

APPEARANCE FOR GOVERNMENT   Department Counsel
                                     Denver, Colorado

1. Contracts: Construction and Operation: Contract Clauses—Contracts: Construction and Operation: Subcontractors and Suppliers

Where a prime contract requires a specific statement in subcontracts in order for wage escalations to apply and the subcontract contains only the referenced requirements by incorporation by reference of the specifications and a general statement passing on applicable rights and privileges of the prime contractor to the subcontractor, the Board finds no ambiguity in the prime contract and no obligation for the Government to pay for the wage escalations of the subcontractor.

OPINION BY ADMINISTRATIVE JUDGE

There is no disagreement over the facts in this case submitted on the record. Appellant has elected to follow the accelerated procedures of the Board Rules in this appeal, claiming an estimated $20,000 for increased wages on behalf of its subcontractor, Inc. (hereinafter). Appellant's contract with the Government for construction and completion of the modification of the is dated November 23, 1977. The contract contains a provision for adjustment for changes in the cost of labor in specification paragraph 1.3.7, and the provision allows the adjustment to be made applicable to subcontractors. The provision states in pertinent part: "a. No adjustment will be made by reason of increased wages paid by any subcontractor unless the subcontract specifically states that the contractor will reimburse the subcontractor for the payment of such increased wages, and the amount of such adjustment is passed on to the subcontractor." Appellant's subcontract to is dated November 16, 1977, and does not contain specific reference to paragraph 1.3.7, or to any express language regarding the reimbursement of Power City for adjustments by reason of increased wages. The subcontract does contain a provision stating: "The Contractor grants to the subcontractor all of the provisions affording remedies, redress, rights and privileges that the Owner grants to the Contractor under the prime contract, insofar as they are applicable to the work to be performed under this subcontract." In addition, the subcontract incorporates the plans and specifications of the prime contract by reference.

Appellant claims that the provisions of paragraph 1.3.7 are applicable to the subcontract by reason of the incorporation by reference of the specifications and the language quoted above from the subcontract. Appellant seeks to invoke the *contra preferentum* rule to resolve a claimed latent ambiguity in the terms of the contract. The Government contends that there is no ambiguity in the contract terms and that the express language of paragraph 1.3.7 makes the Government's obligation to pay for a subcontractor's escalated wage costs contingent on the appellant's obligation to the subcontractor for such costs. In its brief, the Government points out that three other subcontracts awarded by appellant (Exhs. 10, 11, and 12) do contain specific language obligating appellant to reimburse the subcontractors for wage escalations.

Discussion and Findings

Regarding the claim of an ambiguity in the terms of the contract, the appellant does not point out the specific provisions that are believed to be ambiguous. The language of paragraph 1.3.7a is clear in requiring that wage adjustments shall depend on whether the subcontract specifically states that the contractor will reimburse the subcontractor for the payment of such increased wages. Therefore, if a lack of clarity in the contract terms exists, it arises because the express statement required by paragraph 1.3.7a is not included in the contract, and appellant relies on the incorporation by reference of the specifications and the general statement passing on to subcontractor the rights and privileges of the prime contractor. Appellant's position is untenable because that express language required to be included in subcontracts subject to wage adjustments is lacking. Appellant is in the position of creating an ambiguity in the manner of writing the subcontract, and then seeking to have the ambiguity resolved in its favor. If appropriate, the rule of *contra preferentum* would necessarily be applied to favor the Government. The contract between appellant and the Government clearly expresses the intent that subcontracts must contain a specific provision in order for the wage escalation adjustments to apply. We find no contract ambiguity.

The other issue in this appeal is the question of whether appellant is obligated to pay under the subcontract terms for the increased costs resulting from wage escalations. Appellant has not alleged that it is so obligated to pay. After first sought the wage adjustments in the early part of 1979 and found that the Government did not agree that the subcontract required the wage adjustments, requested appellant by letter dated March 28, 1979, to amend its subcontract to include the statement required by paragraph 1.3.7a. Appellant responded by letter dated April 25, 1979, stating: "We have investigated the situation and found that to receive the adjustment for changes in the cost of labor you must have specifically stated this requirement in your proposal and a specific statement with regard to the above must appear in the subcontract." A later letter dated August 7, 1979, advises the Government of appellant's interpretation of the subcontract terms to mean that the appellant is obligated to pass on the amount of any adjustment to the subcontractor. A second letter dated August 7, 1979, from appellant to advises that the requested amendment to the subcontract was not an acceptable solution, and that it would not affect the Government's obligation to make the wage cost adjustment.

In these circumstances, appellant has apparently concurred in the Government's position as stated in the April 25, 1979, letter, and has not accepted a liability to the subcontractor, independent of the Government's liability to pay. Appellant is in the position of saying that if the Government is willing to allow the wage adjustment increases, we will pay you but if not, we are not obligated to you for such costs. This is the crucial argument that is made by Government counsel. If appellant is not obligated by the terms of the subcontract to pay then the Government has no obligation to pay appellant. Appellant has carefully avoided any statement of obligation to pay increased wage adjustments to under the terms of the contract between them, but rather is willing to pass along the increases if the Government allows the adjustments. In effect, this position taken by appellant admits the validity of the Government's main argument that its responsibility is only for the properly written subcontract agreements for increases in wages. We find that the subcontract with did not contain the required specific language entitling to adjustments due to changes in wages and that absent such specific language as required by paragraph 1.3.7a, there is no obligation on the Government to pay for increased wages incurred by

Conclusion

Having found that no relevant ambiguity in the contract terms exists and that the subcontract with did not provide for wage adjustments under paragraph 1.3.7a of the appellant's contract with the Government, the appeal is denied.

Administrative Judge

I concur:

Chief Administrative Judge

7. Summary of Preconstruction Conference Held by the Water and Power Resources Service Southern Nevada Construction Office Specifications No. DC-7372

A preconstruction conference was held in the Conference Room of the Southern Nevada Construction Office at 9:00 AM, November 15, 1979 with (Smith/Jones JV) contractor for construction of (XXXXXX) and No. 7B Pumping Plants, (XXXXXXX) Switchyard a Modifications to Pumping Plants No. 1, 4 and 5, and additions to Switchyards No. 1, 1A and 2 under specifications No. DC-7372, Southern Nevada Water Project, Second Stage. The meeting was held in Englewood, Nevada. In attendance were:

Water and Power Resources Service:
Project Construction Engineer
Office Engineer
Field Engineer
Safety Manager
Chief, Contract Administration
Chief, Mechanical Inspection
Chief, Electrical Inspection
Resident Engineer
Chief, Construction Surveys

(Smith/Jones JV):
Five individuals from this joint-venture were present, no titles listed.

Other agencies:
Other individuals are listed from the Division of Colorado River Resources, the Southern Nevada Water System, and another firm.

(Within the minutes, we have substituted XX for names of participants.)

Preconstruction Conference
November 15, 1979
Specifications No. DC-7372

Jones/Smith Inc.

AGENDA

A. Introductions and Organization

    1. SNCO
    2. Contractor
    3. Contracting Officer and authorized representative

B. General Provisions

    1. Specifications and drawings—differences
    2. Changes
    3. Differing site conditions
    4. Disputes
    5. Material and workmanship
    6. Inspection and acceptance
    7. Superintendence by contractor (G.P. 11 and 1.2.11)
    8. Permits
    9. Other contracts (G.P. 14 and 1.2.9)
    10. Equal opportunity
    11. Taxes
    12. Supplements to General Provisions

C. Contract Administration

1. Labor and wage provisions
2. Subcontracts
3. Commencement, prosecution and completion of work (1.2.3)
4. Liquidated damages (1.2.4)
5. Construction program (1.2.6)
6. Small Business and Minority Subcontracting (1.2.12 and 1.2.13)
7. Payments and adjustments
    a. Funds available for earning (1.3.1)
    b. Progress payments (1.3.2)
    c. Posting securities in lieu of retained percentages (1.3.3)
8. Cost reduction incentive (1.3.14)
9. Correspondence
10. Submittals

D. Safety and Health

1. General requirement (1.1.4)
2. Safety of the Public (1.5.10)
3. Rollover protective structures (1.5.11)
4. Aerial lifts (1.5.12)
5. Protection of existing installations (1.5.15)
6. Security and access to work sites (1.5.9)
7. Electrical power for construction purposes (1.5.18)
8. Water for construction purposes (1.5.19)
9. Construction operations at regulating tank 7 (1.5.7)
10. Safety precautions for energized facilities (1.5.13)

F. Environmental Quality Protection

1. Landscape preservation (1.6.1)
2. Prevention of water pollution (1.6.2)
3. Abatement of air pollution (1.6.3)
4. Dust abatement (1.6.4)
5. Noise abatement (1.6.5)
6. Light abatement (1.6.6)
7. Disturbance of bighorn sheep (1.6.7)
8. Pesticides (1.6.8) and (3.6.4)
9. Cleanup and disposal of waste material (1.6.9)

G. Construction

1. Layout of work and quantity surveys (1.2.10)
2. Explosives, drilling and blasting (1.5.14)
3. Removing culvert and fence, Pumping Plant No. 7 (2.3.1, 2.4.1)
4. Excavation
    a. General (3.2.1)
    b. Structure (3.2.4)
5. Disposal of excavated material (3.2.5)
6. Backfill (3.3.1, 3.3.2)
7. Constructing pumping plant site embankments (3.4.1)
8. Removing and relocating reinforced concrete pressure pipe (4.1.1)
9. Concrete
    a. Placement schedule (5.1.2)
    b. Placement drawings (5.1.3)
10. Concrete in switchyards (5.2.2)
11. Cast-in-place concrete (5.3.1)
12. Precast walls and panels (5.5.2)

13. Switchyard steel structures (8.4.1)
14. Mechanical (Section 13)
    a. Manifolds (13.2.1)
    b. Traveling cranes (13.3.1)
15. Painting, lining, and coating (Section 15)

A. INTRODUCTION AND ORGANIZATION

1. *Southern Nevada Construction Office:*

Mr. XX opened the conference with introductions of Water and Power Resources Service personnel in attendance, briefly explaining their individual responsibilities and functions on jobsites and in direct dealings with Jones/Smith. He also introduced representatives of the Division of Colorado River Resources and Southern Nevada Water System, State and operating agencies working with SNCO on this Project.

2. *Contractor:*

Mr. introduced members of his organization who will be working with SNCO on this Project. Mr. J. XX of T. C. Jones Inc., will monitor this Project for the contractor and will be the contact person in this joint venture.

3. *Contracting Officer and Authorized Representative:*

Mr. XX explained he is the Contracting Officer's authorized representative on this contract and has authority to act in details of administering the contract. XX is the Contract Specialist assigned the responsibility of general administration of the contract. Changes involving expenditures under $10,000 can be made at Project level provided they do not involve a time extension. Any changes of major consequence will be handled by the Contracting Officer, Mr. XX located in Denver. (Subsequent to this meeting, XX was appointed Acting Contracting Officer.)

B. GENERAL PROVISIONS

1. *Specifications and Drawings–Differences:*

The contractor was advised that they are obligated to notify SNCO as promptly as possible of any differences or errors they note in the drawings during the course of the work. It was stressed that prompt notification is of utmost importance in any matters of conflict or disagreement. If there is a conflict between the narrative portion of the specifications and drawings, the specifications narrative will govern. Should items appear on drawings that are not contained in the specifications, they are considered to be a part of both.

2. *Changes:*

It was again stressed that prompt notification to SNCO by the contractor is of utmost importance if there are contract changes or monetary adjustments of any kind.

3. *Differing Site Conditions:*

The emphasis again is on prompt notification to SNCO by the contractor should anything different be encountered than shown on the specifications, drawings, or subsurface data in specifications.

4. *Disputes:*

The contractor was advised of the procedure to be followed in resolving a difference in interpretation of specifications: the contractor is to notify SNCO of the difference, and SNCO will render an opinion. If the contractor disagrees, they may ask for findings of fact from the Contracting Officer. Should there still be a dispute, the contractor may appeal.

The contractor questioned how cost proposals should be handled. They were informed that an agreement should be reached prior to work being accomplished. It was pointed out that before initiating a change, it would be prudent for the contractor to discuss the matter with SNCO so they (the contractor) can be given insights to our requirements. The contractor inquired whether they would be notified of our decision by letter and was answered in the affirmative.

5. *Material and Workmanship:*

It was pointed out to the contractor that materials furnished are to be as specified, in good condition and operational. SNCO has the right to use defective materials until the contractor provides proper materials.

6. *Inspection and Acceptance:*

There will be SNCO inspectors at all sites of work. The contractor was advised of SNCO procedures to perform on-site inspections of all activities. Acceptance of any portion of the work will require that portion to be a completed unit of work.

7. *Superintendence by Contractor (G.P. 11 and 1.2.11):*

The contractor advised SNCO that they will have an office located at the jobsite in addition to offices in Denver and Novato, California. They require three copies of all correspondence, one copy to each office. Enclosures should be mailed only to the Project office. There is a new address for the Denver office (300 Vallejo Street).

XX, Resident Engineer, will be the SNCO contact in the field. XX, Field Engineer, will be the ultimate field contact. The contractor will have supervisors on the jobsites who can speak for the contractor and resolve issues when problems arise without the necessity of a conference.

The contractor was told that the Water and Power Resources Service does not provide general space for a contractor, but right-of-way is available for temporary facilities. Arrangements can be made to use the existing facilities of the Southern Nevada Water System, other contractors, etc.

8. *Permits:*

It is the responsibility of the contractor to obtain all permits and licenses necessary to operate under the contract in the State of Nevada. The contractor stated that the City of North Las Vegas and Clark County now require use or building permits, and no temporary power can be obtained without these permits. The Southern Nevada Construction Office, however, does not feel a building permit is necessary.

9. *Other Contracts (G.P. 14 and 1.2.9):*

The contractor was informed that other contractors will be working at the same locations at approximately the same time, especially at the switchyard sites. A coordinated effort is expected between Smith/Jones and other contractors working in the area to accomplish the job.

10. *Equal Opportunity:*

This subject was bypassed for the present time. A separate discussion on this topic will be held in the future after submission of the Affirmative Action Plan by the contractor.

11. *Taxes:*

The contractor was advised that all taxes are their responsibility. Necessary taxes should be included in the bid.

12. *Supplements to General Provisions:*

Mr. XX pointed out that there is a supplement to the General Provisions, and the contractor acknowledged receipt of same.

C. CONTRACT ADMINISTRATION

1. *Labor and Wage Provisions:*

The contractor was advised of our payroll requirements. Anyone performing on-site work must appear on the payroll registers for either the contractor or a subcontractor except those classified as owner/operator (truck, backhoe, etc.).

The contractor has received a book setting forth labor standards provisions and the requirement to display safety posters. The contractor stated they need additional safety and EEO posters to be displayed at jobsites.

2. *Subcontracts:*

The contractor is responsible for all work performed by the subcontractor. The Southern Nevada Construction Office deals only with the primary contractor. Subcontract agreements are needed before firms can appear on the jobsite. Bonding is required on all subcontracts over $5,000. There are provisions for payment bond forms in accordance with paragraph 1.1.2. of the specifications.

The contractor was advised that subcontracts are needed only for subcontractors performing on-site work. If the contractor is just purchasing materials or equipment, only a purchase order need be submitted. A letter was mailed to the contractor on November 14, 1979, stating those bid items requiring purchase orders.

3. *Commencement, Prosecution and Completion of Work (1.2.3):*

The contractor will receive a formal letter from the Contracting Officer extending all completion dates under paragraph 1.2.3. of the specifications with the exception of Tabulation No. 1. The date of notice to proceed is October 11, 1979. A time extension of 179 days will be added to all completion dates, establishing a contract completion date of April 12, 1982.

4. *Liquidated Damages (1.2.4):*

Maximum liquidated damages will not exceed $600 per day.

5. *Construction Program (1.2.6):*

The contractor has submitted a construction program for approval. There was a question regarding the late starting date for construction of the switchyards. The contractor stated that work on other Government projects has been delayed because it is difficult to obtain materials from suppliers.

There is a dire need to have the switchyards completed earlier than stated in the contractor's schedule, especially Switchyards 2, 1A and Hacienda, as they are the biggest problems. Work on Switchyard No. 1 can start on November 1, 1980.

A letter will be sent to the contractor outlining revisions to the construction schedule. The contractor will have 30 days after receipt of the letter to make any necessary changes.

6. *Small Business and Minority Subcontracting (1.2.12 and 1.2.13):*

The contractor agrees to establish and conduct a small business subcontracting program which will enable small businesses and minorities to be considered as subcontractors and suppliers. The contractor will submit quarterly reports of subcontracting to small business concerns on Optional Form 61.

7. *Payments and Adjustments:*

a. *Funds Available for Earning (1.3.1):*

An allocation of 3.7 million dollars has been made for this contract for FY 80. A letter has been sent reserving 3.7 million dollars. If additional funds are needed, they must be requested. Should any allocated funds not be used, they will be allocated elsewhere.

b. *Progress Payments (1.3.2):*

The cut-off date for progress payments will be the 25th of the month to enable the Government to prepare the necessary documents and get them to the Finance Office by the 1st of the month so that a check can be issued the contractor by the 10th of the month. A representative from the SNCO field office will meet with the field representative of the contractor to agree on work accomplished during the month. The contractor was informed that the amount of work between the 25th and the end of the month is not estimated. A breakdown of the lump sum items must be submitted for use in determining payment. For payment for materials on inventory, the contractor was advised they must submit either a paid invoice or a letter indicating that title is vested in the contractaor and that the material is free of all liens and encumbrances from both the contractor and supplier.

Two forms will be transmitted to the contractor for completion and return with each month's progress estimate: (1) contractor's monthly summary of manhours and lost-time injuries report, and (2) certification of contractor conformity to labor standards. These forms can be obtained through SNCO.

The contractor will provide SNCO a listing of persons authorized to sign progress payment documents.

The contractor was advised to document all adjustments as soon as possible to that an equitable adjustment can be ascertained.

   c. *Posting Securities in Lieu of Retained Percentages (1.3.3):*

The contractor has the option of depositing approved interest-bearing negotiable securities in escrow in lieu of retaining percentages. If the contractor elects to exercise this option, a request must be submitted to Denver in accordance with paragraph 1.3.3. of the specifications.

8. *Cost Reduction Incentive (1.3.14):*

This provision allows the contractor to share in any savings on a fifty-fifty basis. The contractor indicated his understanding of this provision.

9. *Correspondence:*

Mr. XX reviewed the procedure for forwarding correspondence to SNCO: all correspondence to SNCO should be directed to the Project Construction Engineer. The Project Construction Engineer should also receive an information copy of all correspondence directed to Denver for approval.

The contractor advised that correspondence should be directed to Smith/Jones Inc., XX XX Lane, XX, California, with information copies to Jones Construction, Inc., XX XX Street, Denver, Colorado. When the contractor has a local office, correspondence will be directed to that address with information copies to XX and Denver offices.

10. *Submittals:*

The contractor was advised that all submittals from their subcontractors or suppliers must be made through the prime contractor. The specifications state which submittals are to be transmitted to Denver and which are to be sent to this office. It was stressed by Mr. XX that care should be taken to ensure that submittals are made to the proper office, as at least five days will be lost if correspondence is directed to the wrong office. It was requested that SNCO receive copies of transmittal letters for any submittals to Denver.

D. SAFETY AND HEALTH

  1. *General Requirement (1.1.4):*

The contractor has submitted his safety and health program which will be reviewed by this office and forwarded to Denver for approval. The contractor had expressed the desire to schedule the monthly safety meeting for the first Tuesday of the month. SNCO has another meeting scheduled for that time, so another date must be chosen. This will not affect approval of the contractor's safety program, however. A mutually acceptable date will be decided upon.

The contractor advised that he is aware of the OSHA regulations. Within the State of Nevada, the Nevada Industrial Commission has a safety division which carries out the OSHA regulations under a State plan. In answer to the contractor's question regarding frequency of visits by State inspectors, Mr. XX stated that State Industrial or Federal people may come onto the job at any time for a safety inspection. These inspections usually occur as the result of a worker reporting an unsafe condition.

There is a possibility the contractor may be allowed to use their own workers' compensation insurance carrier at some time during this contract. The contractor will check with the Nevada Industrial Relations Committee to determine if and when this may be done.

The contractor was given two copies of the booklet entitled "Safety and Health Regulations for Construction" and was informed they may have as many as they require. The contractor stated they have one copy at their office and will inform us if they require additional copies. This is the safety manual and contractor must abide by during construction activities. Approximately 80 percent of the book is taken directly from OSHA construction regulations. The last portion of the book is the Government supplement in which there are regulations governing areas OSHA does not cover. If the contractor wants to perform work outside these regulations and feels they have a plan that is as effective, and it is under the Government supplement, the SNCO Safety Manager can work with the contractor possibly to obtain a waiver directly from this office. There will be a safety meeting at a later date to cover these items in depth if necessary.

SNCO is to be advised of all accidents occurring on the job. The inspector is to be notified immediately of injuries. It is desirable that the inspector be informed of any accidents occurring near work sites so that this office will be aware of occurrences should any inquiries be made. Lost-time accident report forms are to be completed.

All equipment is to have a safety inspection prior to being placed in service. The contractor is bringing in a new crane which should have all the latest safety features. All off-highway earth handling equipment will be brake-tested. The contractor asked if each piece of equipment would be tested and was informed if equipment comes to the contractor directly from another of their jobs without going elsewhere it would not need to be tested. Equipment hired to haul to and from sites normally will not require testing if they are licensed by the County, but will be observed to ascertain that they are performing safely. Testing will be performed by the contractor and observed by Government inspectors prior to the equipment actually being used on the job.

Precautionary measures must be taken to prevent heavy equipment, particularly cranes, from going into powerlines. Various warning devices were discussed, including posting signs stating "CAUTION—POWERLINE OVERHEAD" in large, bold, red lettering or stringing large, orange balls along powerlines. Mr. XX commented this sometimes seems an insoluble problem, but recommended extraordinary measures be taken to ensure that equipment does not move into powerlines.

The contractor asked if the Bureau requires physical examinations for crane operators and was informed this requirement is contained in the safety manual. It was pointed out that crane operators and operators of hoisting equipment should have physicals to determine if there is any impairment of hearing or vision, color blindness, history of epilepsy, heart condition, or other serious health conditions. It was noted by SNCO that there had been recent problems in this regard, and they were pleased that the contractor recognizes and is concerned about this problem.

Paragraph 1.1.4. of the specifications sets forth the requirement that a weekly tool box safety meeting be held. The Government inspector in that area will probably sit in on these meetings. It was explained that the inspector on the jobsite will be in charge of ensuring that on-site safety rules are enforced by the contractor. In doing this, he will confine his discussions to the foreman level or higher unless there is imminent danger to employees. When the Safety Manager is on the jobsite, he will also confine his conversations to the superintendent or the foreman.

2. *Safety of the Public (1.5.10):*

All measures necessary to protect the public must be taken; primarily, anytime access to roads must be blocked or work creates a hazard.

3. *Rollover Protective Structures (1.5.11):*

Included in the contractor's safety program.

4. *Aerial Lifts (1.5.12):*

It was explained to the contractor that aerial lifts are considered to be any device used to transport personnel from one level to another. Contractor has determined aerial lifts will not be used.

5. *Protection of Existing Installations (1.5.15):*

The contractor is responsible for ascertaining where buried equipment is located and take necessary precautions to ensure it is not damaged.

The contractor's employees will be allowed to use sanitary facilities already at sites. The contractor will be required to maintain these facilities while in use.

6. *Security and Access to Work Sites (1.5.9):*

Security will be a big problem due to the high rate of vandalism in this area, particularly in the Twin Lakes area. Other areas, such as around Lake Mead, do not present such a problem. The contractor inquired about Hacienda and was assured there should be no problem at that site as there will be another contractor in the area and security can be handled jointly. There have been minimum problems at fenced facilities. The contractor suggested using guard dogs; there was no objection to this measure by SNCO representatives. Mr. XX suggested equipment be watched closely, as other contractors have had huge pieces of equipment stolen from jobsites.

7. *Electrical Power for Construction Purposes (1.5.18):*

Electrical power is available at several sites.

8. *Water for Construction Purposes (1.5.19):*

Water is available at all sites with the exception of Hacienda and Twin Lakes. Arrangements are now being made for water at these sites.

9. *Construction Operations at Pumping Plant 7 (1.5.7):*

The contractor was advised of the requirement to interface with other work already in existence. Connections should be coordinated through Southern Nevada Water System. Removal and relocation of the wasteway at Regulating Tank 7 cannot block the access road to Pumping Plant 7.

10. *Safety Precautions for Energized Facilities (1.5.13):*

The specifications contain the Bureau's electrical procedures for working on hot equipment. The contractor should coordinate with the power company to develop procedures for power outages. Shutdown schedules are more convenient during the winter months (October through April). During the summer months shutdown is inconvenient and at least one day's notice will be required.

F. ENVIRONMENTAL QUALITY PROTECTION

The contractor's attention was directed to those paragraphs in the specifications concerning this particular environment.

1. *Landscape Preservation (1.7.1):*

The contractor was cautioned to confine all work to rights-of-way as much as possible, as the desert environment does not "heal" as rapidly as other environments when disturbed. The work performed by this Project seems to be under constant scrutiny by a number of interested groups, and the contractor was assured that they would hear from one of these groups should any of the work operations appear to be detrimental to the environment. Landowners will have to be contacted for trespass rights in the course of the work.

Mr. XX pointed out that a portion of the work is in the Lake Mead Recreational Area administered by the National Park Service. They have been very cooperative in the past, but there is a tremendous amount of visitor traffic in this area and many people who will complain if they see anything extraordinary going on. The contractor was encouraged to coordinate any matters that might require attention by the National Park Service with that organization.

2. *Prevention of Water Pollution (1.6.2):*

The contractor was advised that anytime dewatering is performed as part of the work, water that could pollute Lake Mead should not be discharged into waterways. In areas where there may be large amounts of dewatering wastes off sites, particularly cement, it must be controlled and not dumped into drainage or sewer systems. Mr. XX stressed that no waste is to be washed into Lake Mead. The contractor commented their estimator had assured them they would encounter no water at any of the sites.

3. & 4. *Abatement of Air Pollution and Dust Abatement (1.6.3, 1.6.4):*

The contractor was advised that emission of dust into the air is scrutinized quite closely by the County dust control office. They were informed that methods using water to control the dust should be sufficient. The contractor inquired if a permit was required to disturb the topsoil and was informed that a permit was required.

5. *Noise Abatement (1.6.5):*

The contractor was informed that the County has established daylight operation hours in residential areas; there can be no activity before 6:00 a.m. or after 10:00 p.m.

6. *Light Abatement (1.6.6):*

Night work is permitted, if it is performed quietly, but no floodlights can be used that might disturb residents.

7. *Disturbance of Bighorn Sheep (1.6.7):*

The contractor was informed that there is a large herd of bighorn sheep in the area of operation, particularly around Pumping Plant 2 because of a watering hole. All of the Lake Mead Recreational Area controlled by the National Park Service is range for the bighorn sheep. The Park Service has requested that none of the Project activities be detrimental to these animals and that precautions be taken to assure that their water sources near jobsites are not polluted. The Park Service has requested they be notified at least 24 hours prior to any blasting operations so they may observe the effects of blasting on the sheep. The Park Service is quite sensitive about the treatment of the bighorn sheep, and it was stressed to the contractor that these animals should not be harrassed in any manner by the workers.

8. *Pesticides (1.6.8, 3.6.4):*

Application of pesticides must be performed in accordance with the manufacturer's regulations. None of the waste and none of the unused portions of mixing tubs are to be cleaned and dumped into any waterway that may eventually pollute any system.

9. *Cleanup and Disposal of Waste Material (1.6.9):*

The contractor will be responsible for hauling debris and waste material off the jobsites to a suitable disposal site. The contractor inquired if there would be a problem with burning waste materials, and was informed they should contact the County and the Fire Marshall for permission for burning. The contractor stated if there was any problem obtaining burning permits, they would haul the waste materials to disposal areas.

G. CONSTRUCTION

1. *Layout of Work and Quantity Surveys (1.2.10):*

Mr. XX, Field Engineer for SNCO, read the general provisions of paragraph 1.2.10 of the specifications. All survey work performed by the contractor will be subject to field and office review. SNCO will supply the contractor with survey books, and requested a copy of the contractor's survey notes be sent to this office for review for accuracy. The contractor asked when notes should be submitted and was informed the notes should be sent to this office as soon as completed so that there would not be a quantity of notes received for review at one time. Mr. XX clarified that SNCO is just interested in receiving copies of the sheets, not the book. The contractor was informed that the area is being staked now and should be finalized so that the contractor will have the data needed to begin construction when they reach the site.

2. *Explosives, Drilling and Blasting (1.5.14):*

Prior to any blasting operations, a blasting plan is required stating where, when, how, etc., the blasting is to be performed and the safety precautions to be employed during blasting. If any blasting is performed near homes, quite stringent methods must be employed to eliminate vibration.

3. *Removing Culvert and Fence, Pumping Plant No. 7 (2.3.1, 2.4.1):*

The contractor was informed that they would be required to remove some chain link fencing that would become the property of the Government upon removal. When the fencing is removed, SNCO will advise the contractor where to dispose of it.

4. *Excavation:*

a. *General (3.2.1):*

It was pointed out to the contractor that any overexcavation as a result of work operations not directed by the Government will be backfilled, compacted, etc., at the contractor's expense. Government expense is specifically for line and grade excavation.

b. *Structure (3.2.4):*

Blasting and line drilling operations will require controlled blasting operations.

5. *Disposal of Excavated Material (3.2.5):*

SNCO field engineers will meet with the contractor's field personnel before beginning field operations in Hacienda, Twin Lakes and switchyard areas, as the present specifications point out where excess material can be placed. There are specific areas for excavated material.

6. *Backfill (3.3.1, 3.3.2):*

No backfill will be placed against concrete walls until 28 days of cure has been obtained. Concrete strength will not be tested prior to the 28-day cure period. There are certain requirements in the specifications for compacted backfill, and this office will be conducting tests as material is compacted.

7. *Constructing Pumping Plant Site Embankments (3.4.1):*

Construction of forebay tank and flow control structures, including connection of intake manifold to the portion of intake manifold installed under these specifications, will be performed under another contract during the contract period covered by these specifications. To avoid interference with work of other contractors at these locations, the service yard embankments will not be constructed beyond the limits designated by the Contracting Officer until receipt of written notification that the work may begin as specified in paragraph 1.2.3. SNCO engineers will be working with the contractor in the field, as there are other contractors on site, and there are certain time periods when work can be carried out.

8. *Removing and Relocating Reinforced Concrete Pressure Pipe (4.1.1):*

The existing wasteway at Pumping Plant 7B will be removed and relocated to another facility if possible. The contractor was cautioned to use care when removing the pipe. If damage occurs, replacement will be at the contractor's expense. Existing pipe will be reused where possible, but damaged pieces will not be used.

9. *Concrete:*

a. *Placement Schedule (5.1.2):*

The contractor is required to submit a placement schedule 60 days after receipt of notice to proceed.

b. *Placement Drawings (5.1.3):*

Current requirement is that placement drawings be submitted for review and approval. Lift drawings are also required. All inserts should be shown on drawings. It was stressed that drawings should be submitted in a timely fashion, as typically they are submitted so late that there is not sufficient time for review prior to commencement of work. The contractor asked if drawings were to be submitted for everything, including Rebar. They were told this is the case and that Rebar was detailed separately. Rebar may be included on detail drawings. The contractor stated the only problem area they foresee will be the conduits. Mr. XX commented that paragraph 5.1.3 spells out what should be included on lift drawings.

10. *Concrete in Switchyards (5.2.2):*

It was noted there are a number of items included in paragraph 5.2.2 of the specifications that require additional information from the Contractor before the Government can design foundations. The contractor was requested to provide this information as soon as possible so that foundations may be designed more quickly. This item will be discussed more thoroughly at additional meetings in the next few weeks.

11. *Cast-In-Place Concrete (5.3.1):*

The contractor will use Bureau-mix designs for concrete. Concrete aggregates will require rescreening. The contractor stated that concrete buckets will be used for placing. The contractor also stated they are bringing in a big crane to be used in the placing operation.

12. *Precast Walls and Panels (5.5.2):*

The contractor will precast everything on site except T beams. XXX will construct the forms using fiberglass. The contractor was asked what kind of cure will be used and they indicated this would be discussed at a meeting to be held the following day. The mix design will be Type II cement consisting of 7.5 sacks per cubic yard with low sand content of 35-40% and no more than 3-inch slump. The concrete will be covered immediately after placement with Visqueen or a tarp. The schedule for the panels will begin in March 1980 with a completion time of 16 weeks. Mr. XX pointed out that the type of curing used on panels will be critical as related to temperatures, and that in this area heat is more a problem than cold. It was stressed that inadequate curing will prevent panels meeting the 5,000 pound stress requirement. The contractor was encouraged to look at Peter Kiewit's operations. The contractor indicated they would do more research on this subject.

13. *Switchyard Steel Structures (8.4.1):*

The Government will design one 69-kilovolt interrupter support after receipt of information from the contractor for the 69-kilovolt nondisconnect interrupter. SNCO requested this information be submitted as soon as possible in order to gain needed lead time for design.

14. *Mechanical:*

a. *Manifolds (13.2.1):*

The contractor was informed that the manifold alignment should be line-on-line because another contractor is involved. SNCO will work closely with the contractor, providing as much assistance as possible in fitting manifolds prior to placement. The contractor stated they will be using dummy sections between manifolds. This fact was very encouraging to SNCO engineers.

b. *Traveling Cranes (13.3.1):*

The contractor was informed that after cranes are assembled, they are obligated to operate the cranes for other contractors, if so needed, or operate them for the Government on an hourly rate based on actual cost of operation plus 10%. The cranes will be tested to 125% of capacity. After passing testing, the contractor is free to use the crane as they see fit.

It was noted at this point that qualified welders, as stipulated by specifications, will be required for welding performed on switchyard steel structures and on manifolds. Welds will be subject to nondestructive testing. Three types of tests will be performed: visual inspection, radiographic or ultrasonic testing, and magnetic particle and dye penetrant testing.

There will be a number of tests required after completion of construction: water supply will be tested for 125 pounds per square inch for 8 hours with no leaks; heating and air conditioning system shall be adjusted to deliver the specified cubic feet per minute under full-load conditions with acutal air quantity within 5% of quantity shown on drawings, and simulated dirty filter conditions will be tested; sewage system will have to be lead tested.

The contractor was questioned regarding what type of coating is to be used on manifolds. The contractor was informed that 1040 tapecoat only is not satisfactory. The contractor is uncertain at this time what type coating will be used, and their proposal will be submitted to this office for approval.

15. *Painting, Lining, and Coating (Section 15):*

Purchase orders for paint must be submitted to Denver for approval 45 days in advance of purchase. It was stressed that unapproved paint cannot be used.

Mr. XX announced that this completed the agenda items and that there was still time to discuss pertinent items if anyone had additional information of importance.

The contractor was asked when they anticipate being on the jobsite. They replied they will begin work the first week in December. Their office will be located at Twin Lakes with another (a trailer) at Pumping Plant 7B. The precast site will be located at Twin Lakes.

Mr. XXXX, of the Division of Colorado River Resources, stated that completion of Switchyard XX is critical to their construction schedule. A meeting should be scheduled between SNCO, Div. of Colorado River Resources, Southern Nevada Water System and Smith/Jones as soon as possible to coordinate these efforts plus the expansion of the XXXXXXXX Water Treatment Facility.

The conference adjourned at 11:30 AM.

Noted:_____   Date:_____

Project Construction Engineer

Concurrence: Smith/Jones, Inc.

_____

Title: _____

Date: _____

8. Report on Construction Contract Risks, Los Angeles Department of Public Works

JUNE 4, 1980

DEPARTMENT OF PUBLIC WORKS
COMMISSIONER MAX W. STRAUSS
REPORT NO. 1

TO THE HONORABLE BOARD OF PUBLIC WORKS
OF THE CITY OF LOS ANGELES

SUBJECT: PROPER ALLOCATION OF CONSTRUCTION RISKS BETWEEN OWNERS AND CON-
TRACTORS AS A COST SAVINGS CONCEPT

RECOMMENDATION:

That the Board of Public Works re-evaluate the standard specifications and special conditions for construction projects and the administration of construction contracts for the purpose of identifying those risks and responsibilities that can more equitably be borne by the City in order to strengthen the competitive bidding process and reduce construction costs.

DISCUSSION:

Of the many responsibilities assigned to the Board of Public Works, one of the most important is the development of the best public projects, at the lowest cost, in the least time. In order to properly carry out this assignment, the Board, through its various Bureaus and Divisions, must coordinate such diverse, but related, activities as site acquisition, funding, engineering, and lastly, but more important, construction.

The construction element usually entails the selection and purchase of construction services by contract. Several options are available to owners for the procurement of such services but, for the public owner, such as the City of Los Angeles, the most viable has been the competitive bidding process which epitomizes the best features of the free enterprise economic system.

Success of the competitive bidding process is almost fully dependent on the degree of competition generated. Experience has demonstrated a direct relationship between the cost of procured construction services and the number of bidders. The greater the number of bidders, the lower the cost—a simple example of the Law of Supply and Demand.

Although, the factors which influence the number of bidders are many and varied and mostly beyond our control, including the conditions which affect the market place (inflation, unemployment, interest rates, political turmoil, energy, etc.), nevertheless, within the parameters set by the market place, we can either restrict or enhance the number of bidders by the risks we impose on prospective bidders, the risks we are willing to assume, and those we are willing to share.

Many public agencies operate on a "No-Risk" policy. They say to bidders "Here are the plans and specifications for a project. Tell us what you can build it for and we'll hold you to that price regardless of anything that occurs, whether it's your fault or ours. If you later find discrepancies in the plans, they will be your responsibility or if you find evasive language in the specifications, we'll interpret it for you".

A no-risk policy is the greatest risk of all and will almost certainly result in the fewest number of bidders and the highest possible cost.

A more productive policy for maximizing bidders and minimizing costs would be one that recognizes risks that the owner is best able to assume and which he can best control, leaving to the bidder those risks over which he has control, and sharing those risks which no one can control.

Some risks and responsibilities should obviously be borne by the owner—full disclosure of known information, site access, prompt checking of shop drawings and timely progress payments. The owner who thinks of evading such responsibilities is engaged in self-delusion and will certainly pay for such evasion in the form of higher costs. Other responsibilities are clearly those of the contractor, such as project scheduling, construction methods, procurement of material and equipment, job safety, timely completion, and selection of sub-contractors. Except for legally mandated requirements, such as affirmative action and Minority Business Enterprises, any interference by the owner will surely result in additional cost.

Sharing some risks, such as escalating costs, would also serve to generate more bids at lower prices by decreasing the uncertainty that such risks entail, thereby minimizing the contingencies that a prudent bidder must include in his tendered price.

The presentation to bidders of vague information is self-defeating and frequently causes the owner to pay twice for the same work—once as a contingency included in the bid and again in the form of a claim for extra or changed work.

The typical contract of adhesion is written on the assumption that the successful bidder and the owner will be antagonists during the period of construction. This assumption almost always becomes a self-fulfilling prophesy. Every self-serving "protection" and every ambiguous or evasive clause built into the contract by the owner is a risk that is imposed on the contractor which he must translate into an increase in his bid price if, indeed, he is willing to assume the risk at all.

Specific Areas of Consideration

Some of the following items are partly or fully included in present City policies and practices but should be re-evaluated for optimal utilization.

1. Subsurface conditions—The owner should conduct a complete subsurface exploration and disclose all known and available subsurface information *without* any exculpatory disclaimers and *with* full responsibility for "Differing Site Conditions."

2. Owner-Changes and Defects in Design—The owner should bear full responsibility for owner-initiated changes in the work and for defects in design. The contractor should be entitled to additional costs due to such changes including consequential contract costs resulting from impact of the change.

3. Disputes and Change Orders—Procedures for prompt resolution of contract disputes should be established including increased authority of the resident engineer and prompt referral of disputes to the Board of Public Works. These procedures should be tailored to the particular circumstances of the work such as dollar amount, duration, complexity, funding urgency, etc.

4. Payments—The owner should be responsible for making timely required payments and should pay an appropriate rate of interest on late payments.

5. Performance Bonds and Retainers—Performance Bond requirements and retainage should be reduced as work progresses to more adequately and fairly reflect the exposure to damage to the owner and provision should be made to pay a proper rate of interest on retainages or the contractor should be permitted to post securities in lieu of retainage.

6. Delays—The contractor should be entitled to a prompt and appropriate time extension for delays due to unusual conditions beyond his control with respect to availability of materials, labor or equipment, severe weather, or industry or area-wide labor strikes which impact the work schedule. Increased costs due to such delays should be shared by the owner and contractor.

7. Escalation of labor costs—On contracts of long duration, increased costs should be shared by the owner and contractor. No general method for such sharing is recommended but should be developed on a job-by-job basis.

8. Catch-all clauses—Requirements to the effect that "all work necessary, whether specified or not, must be performed" should be eliminated.

9. *Construction Scheduling*—The precise method of scheduling should be left entirely to the discretion of the contractor who should be held strictly accountable and responsible for meeting the completion date as well as other critical contract dates.

10. *Liquidated Damages* should be based on realistic completion time provisions and evaluation of actual damages suffered in case of failure to complete on time. A realistic evaluation of benefits to be derived from early completion should also be made and a premium provided as an incentive for such early completion where warranted. Provision should also be made for cessation of liquidated damages upon "substantial completion" and/or "beneficial use" of a project.

11. *Warranty Items*—For items specified by the owner, the contractor should not be held responsible for a warranty period greater than that of the manufacturer.

12. *Permits*—All permits necessary for performance of the work should be obtained by the owner and included with the contract documents.

13. *Design Criteria*—The contract documents should include all design criteria with which the contractor must comply when submitting his design of temporary facilities for owner approval.

14. *Site access*—The owner should assume full responsibility for timely delivery of the construction site. If the construction is not so delivered, the contractor should be entitled to appropriate time extension and reimbursement for direct and indirect costs arising from such delay.

15. *Value Engineering*—On large projects, a cost saving incentive should be made available to prospective bidders.

16. *Mobilization Costs and Payment for Materials and Equipment Delivered but not Installed* should be realistically evaluated as an incentive to obtaining balanced bids, recognizing the contractor's out-of-pocket costs.

17. *Contract Award* should be made within 15 days of receipt of bids.

CONCLUSION: Considerable savings are available to the City by increasing the degree of certainty in construction contracts, i.e., assuming responsibility for uncertainties beyond the control of the contractor, specifying clearly the responsibilities of the contractor, disclosing all known information and data, removing from the contract all ambiguous, evasive, catch-all and exculpatory clauses, making timely contract awards, and sharing the responsibility for increased costs.

By recognizing "up-front" those costs which are rightly ours and which will be passed on to us in one way or another, we could generate more and better bids and maximize certainty for a "team" rather than an "antagonist" relationship with the successful bidder leading to timely completion with a minimum of disputes and claims.

NOTE:

For the past several years, this writer has had the privilege of participating in the work of the Committee on Contract Administration of the American Society of Civil Engineers and is indebted to the Committee for the tremendous effort devoted to evaluating construction risks, liabilities and practices and to Mr. George Fox, President of Grow Tunnelling Co. in New York, Chairman of the Committee.

Respectfully submitted,

MAX W. STRAUSS, COMMISSIONER
BOARD OF PUBLIC WORKS

llg

9. Risk and Liability Survey

The following questionnaire on construction industry risk is reprinted courtesy of the American Society of Civil Engineers. The complete survey and questionnaire responses were published in Volume II of the Proceedings of the Construction Division's Conference on Construction Risks and Liability Sharing, held in Scottsdale, Arizona, January 24-26, 1979.

Questionnaires

A poll of the Construction Risk Conference attendees resulted in a remarkable degree of accord on the mechanics and philosophy of risk-sharing among some disparate industry members. Respondents, for example, were virtually unanimous in approving the idea of changed conditions and variations in quantity clauses in construction contracts. This is especially noteworthy in that owners were the single largest industry component represented at the Scottsdale Conference.

A summary of the entire questionnaire and the responses follows. Some other striking statistics: 70% of those responding favored escalation clauses for labor and for materials, and 87% were in favor of reimbursement for delay. In a number of other areas, the responses of a surprising number of attendees suggested that risks on items such as delayed disputes resolution should be shared 50-50 between owners and contractors.

This concurrence is not due to a similarity of backgrounds. Attendees and, subsequently, the questionnaire respondents constituted a cross-section of construction industry disciplines, led in both cases by owners. Attendance at the January meeting was as follows: owners (mostly public sector), 43; designers, 37; contractors, 33; lawyers, 22; insurance industry representatives, 9; research, 2; academic, 6. Over two-thirds of these individuals responded to the questionnaire and the proportions were virtually the same -- more owners replied than any other single industry element.

This questionnaire is significant, the replies encouraging. No attempt was made to measure whether this hopeful state of affairs was the result of the respondents having attended the Scottsdale conference; if this was the case, the conference was more than worthwhile.

Analysis of questionnaire responses

The specialty conference was divided into four broad areas: identification and nature of risks; allocation of risks; contractual arrangements; and minimizing risks, mitigating losses. Responses are tabulated by total in the first category as a total; data in the other three sections is broken down by profession of respondent as well. Complete questionnaire data appear in the Appendix.

Session I - Identification and Nature of Risks

Respondees listed these items under each heading in descending order of importance.

Construction Related

#1 - Changes in the work - 42% rated very important
#2 - Availability of labor, materials and equipment - 39%
#3 - Late completion - 38%
#4 - Delayed site access of right of way - 38%
#5 - Defective design - 35%
#6 - Actual quantities of work - far down the list at 9%

Physical

Subsurface Conditions

#1 - Geology - 67%
#2 - Groundwater - 44%
#3 - Acts of God - far down the list, 10%

Contractual and Legal

#1 - Delayed disputes resolution - 59%
#2 - Delayed Payment on contract and extras - 48%
#3 - Change order negotiations - 47%
#4 - Indemnification and hold harmless - 42%
#5 - Owner-contractor-subcontractor-supplier failure - 23%
#6 - Failure of precondition to payment - again, in a negative
     response - 22%

Performance

#1 - Productivity - 59%
#2 - Conduct hindering performance of the work - 36%
#3 - Labor disputes - 33%

The following were listed at relatively low importance:

#1 - Productivity of equipment
#2 - Suitability, availability, accessibility of materials
#3 - Mistakes - defective work
#4 - Accidents - safety

Economic

#1 - Inflation - 76%
#2 - Cost of labor, material & equipment - 57%
#3 - National and international impacts - 49%

Political & Public

#1 - Environmental - 56%
#2 - Government Rules & Regulations - 37%

The following grouping was overwhelmingly accorded low importance:

#1 - Tax rate changes
#2 - Public disorder
#3 - Traffic maintenance

Session II - Allocation of Risks

In this portion of the questionnaire, respondees were asked to allocate the risks between the owner and the contractor, at varying amounts between 100% to the owner or 100% to the contractor, or something in between.

Construction Related

Predominantly allocated to the owner were:

#1 - Delayed site access or right of way - 96%
#2 - Defective design - 92%
#3 - Changes in the work - 73%

Predominantly for allocation to the contractor:

#1 - Availability of labor, materials and equipment - 71%
#2 - Late completion - 45%

In this category, however, a notable 37% were for a 50-50 allocation.

Physical

All in this category were predominantly allocated to the owner:

#1 - Subsurface conditions - Geology
#2 - Acts of God
#3 - Subsurface conditions - Groundwater

Contractual and Legal

Two items were predominantly allocated to the owner:

#1 - Failure of precondition to payment (i.e., bank loan, government financing) - 82%
#2 - Delayed payment on contract and extras - 76%

None were predominantly allocated to the contractor, however three were predominantly to be shared about equally by the owner and the contractor:

#1 - Owner-contractor-subcontractor-supplier failure
#2 - Delayed disputes resolution
#3 - Change order negotiations

Performance

All risks in this category were predominantly allocated to the contractor, with the one exception being Conduct Hindering Performance of the Work, allocated equally. The following were in varying percentages from 57% to 95% allocated to the contractor:

Productivity of Labor
Productivity of Equipment
Suitability, availability and accessibility of materials
Mistakes - defective work
Accidents safety- safety
Labor disputes
Contractor competence

Economic

One item was predominantly allocated to the owner:

#1 - National and international impacts

Two were predominantly allocated to the contractor:

#1 - Cost of labor, material and equipment
#2 - Labor contracts

An item which was allocated about equally between owner and contractor was:

#1 - Inflation

Political & Public

All items in this category were predominantly allocated to the owner, with the exception of Traffic Maintenance, which was divided between allocation to the owner and a 50-50 allocation between owner and contractor. Those mainly allocated to the owner were:

#1 - Environmental
#2 - Public disorder
#3 - Government acts and regulation
#4 - Permits & ordinances
#5 - Tax rate changes

Responses by Discipline

As discussed earlier, there was a surprising consensus among the various groups concerning the parties to whom risks should be allocated. The most significant difference concerns delayed disputes resolutions, where as may be expected, contractors were in a larger proportion for allocation more to owners than on a 50-50 basis. However, even here, 12 contractors responded for 100% allocation to the owner, while 9 were for 50-50 allocation.

Session III - Contractual Arrangements

Price Structure

88% favored and only 7% were not in favor of "hard money" contracts. Responses were more evenly divided for reimbursable type contracts, with 47% in favor and 21% not in favor.

Bid or Negotiated Contract

Approximately the same percentages apply with more respondents in
favor of bid and less in favor of negotiated contracts.

Specific Contract Clauses

Change conditions unforeseen site conditions - unanimously in
  favor.
Variation in quantities - virtually unanimous
Labor Escalation - 69% in favor
Materials Escalation - 70% in favor
Liquidated damages - 63% in favor
Reimbursement for delay - 87% in favor
Exculpatory clauses - defective design, subsurface or site infor-
  mation, "No damage for delay," quantities not guaranteed -- 88%
  were opposed.
Clauses for Quantities not guaranteed and Indemnification and Hold
  Harmless - approximately 50% disfavor, 33% favored and 17% no
  opinion.

Disputes Procedure

AAA Arbitration - 54% disfavored; 21% favored; and 25% no opinion
Courts - slightly more than 61% disfavored; 25% favored, 18% no
  opinion
Impartial Board - 77% favored; 9% disfavored; 14% no opinion
Mediation/Arbitration - 49% favored; 10% disfavored; 41% no opin-
  ion

Again, the breakdown of responses by discipline shows a remarkable
concurrence among the disciplines responding.

Session IV - Minimizing Risks - Mitigating Losses

The respondees rated the proposals they were asked to comment on in
descending order of endorsement as:

#1 - Disclosure of subsurface information to contractor - 99%
#2 - Extensive prebid subsurface exploration by owner - 97%
#3 - Obtain all permits and site right of way in advance of con-
     struction - 95%
#4 - Disclosure of design criteria to contractor - 80%
#5 - Prequalification of bidders - 71%
#6 - Contractor participation in design and budget process - 57%
     with 25% rejecting, and 17% expressing no opinion.
#7 - Wrap Up Insurance - 40% expressed no opinion; 35% endorsed;
     25% rejected
#8 - Prepurchase of Materials and Equipment - this was the only
     proposal with a negative vote - 47% rejecting; 34% endorsing;
     19% no opinion

The pattern of consensus among the disciplines obtains here too.

SUMMARY

A broad and seemingly representative cross-section of the different disciplines involved in the construction industry provided responses to this questionnaire. It is especially noteworthy that in spite of the different interests and expected differences in viewpoints of the several disciplines represented, the views and opinions indicated in the totals of answers seem to be similar to responses within any of the discipline groups.

Index